A-LEVEL AND AS-LEVEL   ECONOMICS

LONGMAN
REVISE
GUIDES

LONGMAN A-LEVEL AND AS-LEVEL REVISE GUIDES

Series editors
Geoff Black and Stuart Wall

Titles available
Art and Design
Biology
Business Studies
Chemistry
Computer Studies
Economics
English
French
Geography
Mathematics
Modern History
Physics
Sociology

A-LEVEL
AND AS-LEVEL

ECONOMICS

Barry Harrison

Longman

Longman Group UK Limited,
Longman House, Burnt Mill, Harlow,
Essex CM20 2JE, England
and Associated Companies throughout the world.

First published 1990
Seventh Impression 1993

British Library Cataloguing in Publication Data

Harrison, Barry, 1951–
    Economics.
    1. Economics
    I. Title
    330
ISBN 0-582-05167-3

Set in 10/12pt Century Old Style

Produced by Longman Singapore Publishers Pte Ltd
Printed in Singapore

EDITORS' PREFACE

Longman A Level Revise Guides, written by experienced examiners and teachers, aim to give you the best possible foundation for success in your course. Each book in the series encourages thorough study and a full understanding of the concepts involved, and is designed as a subject companion and study aid to be used throughout the course.

Many candidates at A Level fail to achieve the grades which their ability deserves, owing to such problems as the lack of a structured revision strategy, or unsound examination technique. This series aims to remedy such deficiencies, by encouraging a realistic and disciplined approach in preparing for and taking exams.

The largely self-contained nature of the chapters gives the book a flexibility which you can use to your advantage. After starting with the background to the A, AS Level and Scottish Higher courses and details of the syllabus coverage, you can read all other chapters selectively, in any order appropriate to the stage you have reached in your course.

Geoff Black and Stuart Wall

ACKNOWLEDGEMENTS

The author is grateful to the following examination boards for permission to reproduce their questions.

Associated Examining Board
Northern Ireland Schools Examination and Assessment Council
Scottish Examination Board
University of Cambridge Local Examinations Syndicate
University of London Examinations and Assessment Council
University of Oxford Delegacy of Local Examinations
Welsh Joint Education Committee

These Boards accept no responsibility for the accuracy of the answers provided. They are the responsibility of the author alone.

I am also grateful to the Controller of Her Majesty's Stationery Office, and to Lloyds Bank PLC for permission to reproduce material from their Economic Bulletin.

AUTHOR'S NOTE

This book aims to promote thorough understanding of those topics most frequently examined at Advanced Level. To achieve this, careful attention is given to explaining points of detail so that a clear understanding of each topic is encouraged. All teachers know that a topic which is understood is easily remembered!

In a subject such as Economics where change is frequent, it is important to be up-to-date if success in the examination is to be achieved. Recent editions of conventional textbooks are very useful here, but they rarely give guidance on how material can be arranged to answer examination questions. Nor do they show how recent examination questions reflect the changing emphasis placed on the different aspects of each topic. This book includes Tutor's Answers, Student's Answers and Outline Answers to recent examination questions. In all cases the aim is to show how familiar principles can be used to answer different questions and to provide a guide to the standard required for success.

I am pleased to acknowledge the helpful advice and encouragement provided by George Stanlake throughout the writing of this book. His comments led to many improvements in the clarity of the text. I am also grateful to my wife Lea who typed most of the book and who, along with my children Paul, Matthew and Simon, provided much encouragement. The editors of the series also provided encouragement and I am grateful for this. Finally I would like to take this opportunity of thanking my former teachers for all the help they have given in the past.

CONTENTS

NAMES AND ADDRESSES OF THE EXAM BOARDS

Associated Examining Board (AEB)
Stag Hill House
Guildford
Surrey GU2 5XJ

University of Cambridge Local Examinations Syndicate (UCLES)
Syndicate Buildings
1 HillsRoad
Cambridge CB1 1YB

Northern Examinations and Assessment Board (NEAB)
Devas St
Manchester M15 6EX

University of London Examinations and Assessment Council (ULEAC)
Stewart House
32 Russell Square
London WC1B 5DN

Northern Ireland Schools Examination and Assessment Council (NISEAC)
Beechill House
42 Beechill Road
Belfast BT8 4RS

Oxford and Cambridge Schools Examination Board (OCSEB)
Purbeck House
Purbeck Road
Cambridge CB2 2PU

Oxford Delegacy of Local Examinations (ODLE)
Ewert Place
Summertown
Oxford OX2 7BZ

Scottish Examination Board (SEB)
Ironmills Road
Dalkeith
Midlothian EH22 1LE

Welsh Joint Education Committee (WJEC)
245 Western Avenue
Cardiff CF5 2YX

1

EXAMINATION TECHNIQUES

ESSAY WRITING TECHNIQUES

DATA RESPONSE TECHNIQUES

MULTIPLE-CHOICE TECHNIQUES

REVISION

IN THE EXAMINATION

TOPICS AND COURSES

GETTING STARTED

All of the examinations covered by this book include an essay or free response paper. Many also include a multiple-choice paper and a stimulus or data response paper. The aim of this chapter is to provide guidance on how to prepare for your own examination and how to approach different types of examination question.

All candidates are assessed on their performance in the examination room for what is a relatively short period of time. However, this does not mean that there is a short cut to success. Success will only come as the result of consistent effort, thorough preparation and careful revision. A surprising number of students pay only lip service to this simple statement of fact, but experienced teachers will know that preparation for the final examination cannot be left until the last few weeks before the examination. Instead, throughout your course, you should regularly check your understanding of the basic concepts that have been covered. As part of this process of regular revision you should set down *outline answers* to past examination questions. Chapters 2–17 of this book contain recent examination questions set by the various examining boards and outline answers to these questions are also included. You should attempt all the questions set on the topics relevant to your own course. Even though some of the questions will not have appeared in the particular examination for which you are entered, preparing an outline answer to *all* the questions will develop your understanding of each topic.

Having completed an answer, or the outline of an answer, check your own approach against that given in the text. The answers given in the text are not to be considered as definitive; indeed, in some cases, it is possible to approach questions in a fundamentally different way. Nevertheless, by comparing your own answer with the one given in the text it will usually be possible to assess whether your own approach is along the right lines as well as to identify any mistakes you may have made. This is extremely important, since it is essential to learn from your mistakes if you are to improve your understanding of the subject. If, after comparing your answer with the one suggested in the text, you are unsure about the validity of your approach, check with your course tutor.

You will also find an *actual student answer* to a past question in each chapter. Look at the *examiner comments* on the strengths and weaknesses of that answer. This will give you a good idea of what the examiner is looking for in an answer. The *tutor's answer* included in each chapter should also give you guidance on what the examiner is looking for.

ESSENTIAL PRINCIPLES

During your course you will probably be required to produce *essays* for marking by the course tutor. Sometimes the marks obtained will count towards the final grade awarded on completion of the course, but more often essays (and other assignments) are simply set as an aid to understanding and learning. In either case you should ensure that each essay is written to the highest standard you are capable of achieving at that time.

Remember that writing essays sometimes involves drawing on knowledge from several parts of the course. The only way to be sure that you are answering a question fully is to understand all the topics that have been covered. To do this you must regularly revise the topics covered in class; a good rule of thumb is to spend about half an hour each week revising and testing your understanding of topics already covered.

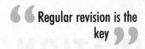 **Regular revision is the key**

Writing essays which are consistently of a high standard involves taking pride in your work as well as paying careful attention to many other points. These will be the subject of the remainder of this section.

PREPARING YOUR ESSAY

Obtain the essay title as early as possible and consider it carefully. Think what it means and what it is asking you to do. If you are unsure, a useful tip is to try and write in your own words on a sheet of rough paper what you think the essay title means. For example, if the essay title is: 'What are the reasons for government intervention in a market economy?' it is asking you 'Why do governments interefere with a market economy?' and to answer this you must state and explain these reasons.

PLANNING YOUR ESSAY

Once you have decided what the title means, you can plan what to put in your answer. Make a list of the following things:

What to put in your introduction

In general, this should be very brief and to the point. It is best to include a *definition* of the central topic of your essay where this is appropriate. For example, if an essay title asks you to 'Explain, what is meant by ...' or 'Define ...' then it is best to start with a definition. Therefore, in answer to the question 'Explain, with the use of relevant examples, what is meant by the term *opportunity cost*', you might begin by writing: 'Opportunity cost is usually defined as ...' Even where you are not specifically asked to define or describe something, it is good sense to do so; look out for this. For example, the title 'Economic goods are scarce goods – explain the meaning of this statement', doesn't *actually ask you* to define 'economic goods' but you must do so if you are to explain the meaning of the sentence. As well as a definition, it is usually helpful to outline, in the introduction, the stages that will appear in your argument.

Definitions are important

What to put in the body of your essay

Note down the major items you will be dealing with. Consider how to divide these up into separate paragraphs. Remember that each separate item should be dealt with in a separate paragraph. At this stage you should note down examples or facts that you intend to use, diagrams that you will draw, and additional definitions that you will state.

Whether to write a separate conclusion or not

In general, put one in. It will in any case serve as a useful summary of what you have said in your answer. For example, if you are asked 'Give the reasons for government intervention in a market economy', in your final paragraph you could write: 'We have outlined five reasons for government intervention in a market economy. These are; the instability that might arise in a market economy; the possibility of exploitation by monopolies; the extent to which inequalities occur; the hardship caused by economic change and the desire to alter the use of resources when social and private values are different'. Sometimes the essay title itself will be a question, so that in your conclusion you must actually state what your answer has been.

 **Review your findings**

WRITING YOUR ESSAY

Write neatly and legibly. Follow your plan. Take care to express your ideas correctly and in a way that is intelligible to others. Remember that all the sentences in one paragraph should be concerned with the same point and should follow logically from each other when you are outlining the argument. In general, do not use abbreviations. Do, however, make sure that you phrase things in a way that is appropriate to the title, so that it is clear that you are answering the question. Avoid making a numbered list of items; each point must be described in a complete sentence. For example, where you are describing the measures used in regional policy, one sentence could begin; 'One measure used in regional policy is …'. The second measure might be described in a sentence that starts; 'Another measure used is …' and so on.

Always try to write an essay to the best of your ability. If you do this, your essay technique will gradually improve. This is very important because if you do not learn to write clear, logical and well-reasoned essays in class or at home, success will be more difficult to achieve in the examination itself.

CHECKING YOUR ESSAY

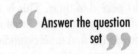
Answer the question set

Once you have finished writing, do not think the essay is ready to be handed in; first it must be checked by you. Look at your plan and check that you have included in your essay everything you intended to. It is amazing how easy it is to overlook something when you are busy writing. Check that you have really written a full and complete answer to the question. Have you dealt with all the parts to the question? Have you explained and described everything as fully as you could? It is a good idea to do this check some time after you have written the essay. Coming to it afresh will allow you to consider it more carefully.

LEARNING FROM YOUR MISTAKES

Learn from your mistakes

When the marked essay is returned to you, don't file it away and forget about it. You will find it difficult to improve your techniques unless you learn from your mistakes. This means reading over your essay after it has been marked, taking note of the comments that have been added and thinking about how it could be improved. This will dramatically reduce the likelihood of your making the same mistake twice and, coupled with regular revision, will markedly increase your chances of success in the examination.

DATA RESPONSE TECHNIQUES

Many of the major examining boards now include *data response* (i.e. stimulus-based) questions on their economic papers. Some boards set a *compulsory* data response paper, as in the GCE 'A' level papers set by the University of London School Examinations Board and the Associated Examining Board. However, others, such as the Oxford Delegacy of Local Examinations offer candidates the *option* of answering data response questions. Broadly there are three types of data response question:

- those based on hypothetical data

- those based on factual data

- those based on newspaper articles, or on extracts from official reports, etc.

Much of what has been written above about essays is still important, but because of the nature of data response questions it is impossible to give specific guidance on how to construct an answer. For example, in some cases it might be appropriate to include an introduction, but in others, where the question is highly structured and consists of several different parts, this might not be necessary.

What can be said is that in all types of data response question the purpose of giving data is to enable you to demonstrate an understanding of the principles contained in the data. In order to demonstrate understanding you must consider both the assumptions implicit in the data and the implications of any trends shown in the data.

This is very important because it enables examiners to distinguish between candidates who understand economic principles and can apply them, and candidates who have simply

Remember to use the data given

memorised them. When answering data response questions, examples should be taken from the data in order to illustrate your answer. This can sometimes be done by extracting the appropriate figures from the material given. At other times it is necessary to manipulate figures to obtain examples or to highlight trends in the data.

One point you should remember is that data response questions which involve arithmetic calculations are often easier than they at first appear. The best way to approach these is to use the information you are given to obtain, by calculation, as much *additional* information as will be helpful to you in tackling the question. Once you have obtained this it is often very easy to see the answer to particular parts of the question. However, do not neglect to mention the economic principles on which your answer is based. It is not your arithmetic ability which is being tested, but your ability to understand and apply economic principles.

MULTIPLE-CHOICE TECHNIQUES

Like data response questions, multiple-choice questions (sometimes called items) are becoming an increasingly common feature of examinations in economics. The most widely used type of multiple-choice question is the simple completion question. This consists of an opening statement (referred to as *the stem*) followed by a series of responses. Only one response (*the key*) correctly completes the statement in the stem, or answers the question it poses. The remaining responses are simply *distractors*. On the face of it, they appear as though they could be correct, but they are not. They are there simply to attract the unwary or the ill-prepared.

In the examination, the multiple-choice paper will consist of a relatively large number of questions (usually 30 or 50) to be answered in a relatively short period of time. This is the major advantage, as an examination method, of multiple-choice questions; they make it possible to test, in an examination, a wide range of subject knowledge and understanding. Such breadth of coverage is impossible to achieve by any other means under examination conditions.

Because multiple-choice questions can test both *descriptive knowledge* and *analytical ability*, they are not only a useful method of examining, but also an invaluable aid to learning. During your course you will find it very useful to assess your progress by using multiple-choice questions, whether you take a multiple-choice paper in the examination or not. Remember that each question has only one key, so a good check of your understanding would be your awareness of not only why the key is correct, but also why the other responses are incorrect.

REVISION

There are no hard and fast rules about when to begin final revision for the examination. This depends on the individual, the type of examination, the time available, and so on. All that can be said is that if you are to give yourself the maximum chance of success, thorough revision of all the syllabus is required. Nothing can be left out, otherwise you might find that there are compulsory questions you cannot answer, and that your choice of essay or data response questions is restricted. You should therefore begin revision at a fairly early stage and indeed final revision should simply build on an already solid foundation established by regular revision during your course.

A revision plan can help

It is probably best to begin revision by making a detailed plan of when each topic is to be covered. You should make every effort to stick to this plan. However, do remember that you are likely to find revision relatively easy at the start , but more difficult towards the end. Your plan should allow for this, and also for the fact that the more difficult topics will take longer to revise than others. You should take great care, therefore, to ensure that your plan sets realistic targets. Sticking to the plan will lead to growing confidence as you progress from one topic to the next and as your understanding of the subject as a whole grows.

How to revise is very much a personal matter, but you might find the following practical hints useful.

1 Rewrite your course notes on any topic in shortened form, using headings and making lists of points.

Some revision hints

2 Learn these lists; it is useful to remember how many points there are in each list, e.g. learn that there are three types of injection into the circular flow of income.

3 Make a separate list of clear and concise definitions.

4 Draw the main diagrams or charts used in any topic.

5 Write down some key facts and figures that you might learn.

6 Write down any examples or cases that illustrate important principles.
7 Learn these definitions, diagrams, facts and examples by rewriting them from memory and checking them against your notes.
8 Practise past examination questions and especially multiple-choice items and data response questions. For essays, remember there are two things to practise:

- planning your answer
- writing it in the time allowed

Before attempting any examination paper you must carefully read the instructions on the front of the examination paper. You must follow these instructions to the letter, noting in particular the total number of questions which must be attempted, and the number that should be attempted from each section. You should also note the total time allowed for completing the paper and bear this in mind when allocating time between questions. The remainder of this section provides guidance on how to approach the different types of examination question in the exam room.

ESSAYS

Choosing questions

Choose essay questions very carefully: read through all the questions, marking those that you think you might be able to answer. For these questions consider whether you can actually answer all the parts, as there is usually little point in attempting a question if you cannot answer all of it. Then choose the appropriate number of questions out of those that you can answer, selecting those that you feel you can answer best. Remember that your aim is to *show* the examiner that you know and understand economic; don't think that you can give a good answer to a question just because it is easy to answer *without* using economics.

Answer-plan

Plan what to put in your answer; write this down so that you can follow your plan. Think very carefully about actually answering the question. Note how many marks are allocated to each part of the answer. This is a guide as to how important each part is, so it also tells you how long to spend on each part.

Answer carefully

Write your answer carefully, expressing ideas precisely, using supporting evidence whenever available. Don't be vague and do give examples. Follow the rubric, i.e. set out your answer in the same way that the question has been set out; if the question is divided into two parts, (a) and (b), so your answer must be similarly divided. Make a note of the time you begin each question and spend only the appropriate amount of time on it. This is important because if you are to succeed to the best of your ability you must complete the paper.

Referring back

Keep referring back to the question and to your plan. It is easy, under examination conditions, to wander off the point and to include irrelevant material. Marks are not usually deducted for this, but economists know that the opportunity cost is very high. Time spent discussing irrelevant material is no longer available to discuss relevant material. The penalty for this kind of error might therefore be very serious. It only takes a short while to check that you are following your plan and that what you have written is relevant to the question that has been set.

Answer check

If you have any time left after completing your answers, check your work for errors and omissions. These can easily creep in under examination conditions.

DATA RESPONSE

Again, much of the suggested approach to the essay paper is still relevant here. However, in addition to thinking about the questions, it is necessary to consider how, in each case, the data can be *used* to answer the question. This almost certainly means recognising the economic principles illustrated by, or contained within, the data. On a first reading this is not an easy task and you should not abandon the idea of attempting a question merely because it is not immediately apparent how to answer it. A second or third reading will often provide you with insights that a first reading does not.

MULTIPLE CHOICE

All questions on the multiple-choice paper are compulsory, and you will have to work fairly rapidly through them to complete this paper. Despite this, don't try to do too much in your head. If you do, you are likely to become confused or to overlook some important point. Instead, draw diagrams, write down formulae to help you, and work fully through any calculations.

Because you must work quickly through this paper, it is particularly important to read the stem carefully. Under examination pressure it is easy to overlook a vital word. This is especially true where questions begin with a negative stem such as: 'Which one of the following is not an invisible export?' Before putting down your answer on the examination paper, therefore, you should quickly glance at the stem to ensure that you have not made an obvious error in your choice of response.

On this type of paper there will inevitably be some questions which are easier than others. Because of this you should not spend too much time on one question. If you are struggling with a particular question, it is best to miss it out and to go on to the next one. Remember to mark the question you have missed out, and be careful not to put the answer to succeeding questions in the wrong place. This is very easily done when you are using a computer marked card to record your answers. The only certain way to avoid doing this is to check the question number and answer number *before* recording your response. Do not forget to go back and answer any questions you have missed out. If you are still unable to answer them, eliminate any responses you know to be incorrect and make a guess from the remainder. You have at least a 20 per cent chance of being right where the question has five responses, and at least a 25 per cent chance where it has four! Eliminating incorrect responses increases the chance of being right still further.

> **You can eliminate incorrect responses**

TOPICS AND COURSES

Table 1.1 gives a broad indication of the topics and courses for which this book will be useful. Most AS syllabuses cover all seventeen topics, but in rather less breadth within each topic. Check your own syllabus.

CHAPTER AND TOPIC	A LEVEL								SCOTTISH HIGHER
	AEB	C	NEAB	L	NI	O	O&C	WJEC	SEB
2 The economic problem	√	√	√	√	√	√	√	√	√
3 Production, costs and returns	√	√	√	√	√	√	√	√	√
4 Demand, supply and price	√	√	√	√	√	√	√	√	√
5 Perfect competition and monopoly	√	√	√	√	√	√	√	√	√
6 Imperfect competition	√	√	√	√	√	√	√	√	√
7 The structure of industry	√	√	√	√	√	√	√	√	√
8 National income accounting	√	√	√	√	√	√	√	√	√
9 National income determination	√	√	√	√	√	√	√	√	√
10 Wages and trade unions	√	√	√	√	√	√	√	√	√
11 Interest, rent and profit	√	√	√	√	√	√	√	√	√
12 Money and banking	√	√	√	√	√	√	√	√	√
13 The value of money	√	√	√	√	√	√	√	√	√
14 International trade and protection	√	√	√	√	√	√	√	√	√
15 The balance of payments and exchange rates	√	√	√	√	√	√	√	√	√
16 Public finance	√	√	√	√	√	√	√	√	√
17 Management of the economy	√	√	√	√	√	√	√	√	√

Table 1.1 Topics and courses

A FINAL WORD

When you first start your course, set your sights on obtaining the highest grade. Stick to your aim throughout the course and gear the level of your effort accordingly. Pay particular attention to those topics which you do not fully understand and never assume that an individual topic is unimportant. In a subject like Economics, topics often interrelate and a full understanding of one topic is impossible without a full understanding of others. Remember that if you do find a topic difficult, other students will also find it difficult. This is why it is important to persevere. Not everyone succeeds in the examination, but those who persevere in seeking to overcome their problems have a clear advantage. At the end of the day, the highest grade is particularly important because few people achieve it. This book cannot guarantee success, but if used correctly, it should prove to be a valuable aid.

Further reading

Harrison, *Studying Economics at A Level*, Longman 1989
Stanlake and Harrison, *A Macroeconomics Workbook*, Longman 1984

CHAPTER

2

THE ECONOMIC PROBLEM: RESOURCE ALLOCATION

ECONOMIC TERMINOLOGY

SCARCITY AND CHOICE

OPPORTUNITY COST

THE MARKET ECONOMY

THE CENTRALLY PLANNED ECONOMY

THE MIXED ECONOMY

APPLIED MATERIALS

GETTING STARTED

Economics is the study of how society makes choices about *what* output is to be produced, *how* this output is to be produced and *for whom* it is to be produced. In other words it is the study of how society allocates its scarce resources amongst competing alternatives. The economic resources referred to in this definition are usually classified as: land, labour, capital and enterprise. This subject is covered extensively in Chapter 3 but the point to note here is that all societies must decide how to allocate their limited resources to given ends. The study of economics is largely concerned with this problem, and how society deals with it.

As well as being aware of the subject content, it is also important to be aware of the *methodology* used in the study of economics. In fact, economics is often termed a 'social science': 'science', because the approach used has much in common with that of the natural scientist, studying chemistry or physics for example; 'social', because the subject matter is the human being.

The basic approach is referred to as *scientific method*, but because we are concerned with analysing the behaviour of human beings, the controlled experiments of the 'natural sciences' (in which a single factor affecting the result can be excluded) are impossible in the study of economics. This makes it more difficult for economists to link cause and effect. Another problem for economists is that *individual* human beings react differently to external events, making predictions more difficult. Fortunately it is often easier to predict the reaction of *groups* of individuals to events because extreme reactions tend to cancel each other out.

As with any science, the main aim of economics is to develop *theories* (or hypotheses) which can help to explain the events we observe. There are two main ways of developing such theories. One is the *deductive approach*; here a theory is proposed, logical deduction is then applied to develop predictions, and a test is made of these predictions against the facts. For instance, one theory is that the amount of a commodity consumers wish to purchase will usually vary with its price. This prediction can then be tested against how consumers actually behave. If the facts do not support the theory it must be rejected in favour of other theories which better explain actual observations. An alternative way of developing a theory is to use the *inductive approach*. The facts themselves are the starting point for this approach, with any observed pattern or regularity in the facts giving the economist some guidance. He or she must then work backwards to induce a theory which, by logical deduction, actually predicts the pattern of facts observed. For example, we might observe that unemployment tends to rise in the winter and fall in the summer. Having observed this regular pattern we might produce a theory to explain it which could then be tested against the facts in the normal way.

ESSENTIAL PRINCIPLES

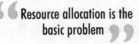

**ECONOMIC
TERMINOLOGY**

❝ Distinguish normative
from positive ❞

Normative and positive statements

One very important point arising out of the application of scientific method to economics is that care must be taken to avoid *normative statements*. These are matters of opinion which cannot be proved or disproved by reference to the facts, since they are based on *value judgements*. Normative statements can easily be recognised because they often contain verbs such as *should* or *ought*. For instance, to say that: 'The government's main aim should be the control of inflation', is a normative statement, since its validity cannot be checked against any facts. It is a statement with which we may either agree or disagree, but there is no way of *proving* that it is correct or incorrect. It is a matter of *opinion* rather than a matter of *fact*.

This contrasts markedly with *positive statements*. The accuracy of positive statements can be checked against the facts and they can be *proved* correct or incorrect. Therefore, to say that: 'The rate of inflation in the UK over the last twelve months has been 6 per cent', is a positive statement. By reference to the facts it can be proved to be correct or incorrect. Any statement which can be checked against the facts is a positive statement.

The distinction between positive and normative statements is particularly important in a subject like economics which embraces many controversial topic areas, since there is often a great temptation to express personal opinions which have little to do with any facts. It is irrelevant whether you personally approve or disapprove of trade unions, centrally planned economies, membership of the EEC or government policy in general. These are political matters and opinions can be expressed through the ballot box. As economists it is much more important to explain how institutions operate, the effect of their operation on the allocation of resources, the way in which they are likely to change in the future, and so on.

Micro and macro

Another very important distinction to be aware of is that between *micro* and *macro* economics. These terms come from the Greek words for 'small' and 'large'. **Microeconomics** is therefore concerned with the behaviour of small parts of the economy, such as an individual or a firm. It focuses on such topics as the wage rate in a particular occupation or the price of a particular product. **Macroeconomics** on the other hand deals with the economy as a whole and is concerned with such aggregates as unemployment, the rate of interest or the levels of exports and imports. The reason for the distinction is that small changes, such as a change in the price of a box of matches, have no effect on the economy as a whole. However, the distinction is not always as clear as this. A change in the price of oil might well have microeconomic *and* macroeconomic implications.

Note: Some of the topics covered in this chapter can be illustrated using supply and demand diagrams. A full explanation of these is not given until Chapter 4, so they are therefore omitted from this chapter. However, when you have read Chapter 4, refer back to this chapter and use supply and demand diagrams to explain how the price mechanism operates.

**SCARCITY AND
CHOICE**

THE ECONOMIC PROBLEM

The economic problem is summed up in two key words, **scarcity** and **choice**. To the economist scarcity has a very specific meaning and does not simply mean *rare* as many people often assume. To the economist something is *scarce* if society desires more of it than is currently available. By this definition most goods and services are scarce. After all, we can all think of things we desire which we do not currently possess; more records, more clothes, more cars and so on.

ECONOMIC CHOICES

❝ Resource allocation is the
basic problem ❞

The basic economic problem confronting all societies is how to allocate scarce resources between alternative uses. Resources are scarce because the collective desires of society for consumption at any moment in time exceed the ability to satisfy those desires. Because there are insufficient resources to produce all that is desired, society is forced to make choices. These choices are:

What, how and for whom?

- **What output will be produced ?** It is obvious that if society cannot produce all it desires, it must choose which goods and services to produce from the available resources. Any decision about *what* items to produce also implies a decision about *how much* of these items to produce. However, because resources are scarce, more of one thing implies less of something else.

- **How shall the output be produced?** Society must decide not only what output is to be produced, but also *how* the output is to be produced. There are various ways of producing any given output. In many of the world's poorer countries production is often *labour-intensive* (i.e. uses large amounts of labour *relative* to other factors of production) while production of the same goods in the richer countries is often *capital-intensive* (i.e. uses large amounts of capital *relative* to other factors of production). For example, this is true of most agricultural production.

- **For whom shall the output be produced?** Clearly if an output is produced there must be some means of allocating it to consumers and of deciding who receives what. In other words society must decide how its output is to be distributed.

The way in which society makes these choices gives rise to different economic systems and these are considered later in this chapter.

OPPORTUNITY COST

Because *all* output is created from scarce resources, it follows that these resources have alternative uses. How many uses can you think of for timber or labour for example? However, once resources have been used to produce a particular type of output they are no longer available to produce a different type of output. In choosing which goods and services will be produced from scarce resources, society also chooses which goods and services it will do without. If resources are used to produce one thing, society is forced to do without those other things that might have been produced from the same resources. This is very important to the economist and in choosing what to produce (or consume), the next most desired alternative sacrificed is referred to as the *opportunity cost* (or real cost) of what is produced (or consumed).

Be familiar with opportunity cost

In taking decisions about production and consumption, both policy-makers and private individuals are concerned with the concept of opportunity cost. For example, a local authority might be considering the construction of a new educational college. If land and capital are used to build houses, they cannot also be used to build the college. In this case we say that the opportunity cost of additional housing is the college which is sacrificed.

ECONOMIC GOODS AND FREE GOODS

It is clear that opportunity cost only arises when production or consumption involves foregoing an alternative. However, consumption of some goods involves no sacrifice and consequently has no opportunity cost. These goods are not created from scarce resources and are available in such abundance relative to the demand for them that it is possible for one person to consume them to complete satiety, that is, until no more are required, without depriving anyone else of consumption. Such goods are referred to as *free goods*. The most often quoted example of a free good is fresh air, but there are many other examples such as sand in the desert.

Economic goods have an opportunity cost

Economists distinguish free goods, which do not embody scarce resources, from those goods which do, by referring to the latter as *economic goods*. Because only economic goods have an opportunity cost (since free goods are not created from scarce resources) the three basic choices referred to earlier (What? How? and For Whom?) only refer to choices concerning economic goods.

Free goods have no opportunity cost

The term 'free goods' sometimes causes confusion. Not all goods and services for which no charge is made are free goods. Some 'goods', such as education or 'free' concerts, are made available without charge to consumers, but they are still created from scarce resources. Therefore, in providing them, the alternatives that those resources could have produced are foregone so they are *economic* goods and not free goods. Remember – if there is an opportunity cost, then the goods are *not* free goods even if no charge is made for them.

PRODUCTION POSSIBILITY CURVES

One way of representing the range of possible choices available to society is in the form of a production possibility curve. Such a curve is illustrated in Fig. 2.1 and for simplicity it is assumed that society can only produce two goods, X and Y.

Because society only has a limited amount of resources there is an upper limit on the amount of output that can be produced at any moment in time. A production possibility curve therefore shows the maximum output that society can produce given its existing resources. In other words all points *on* the curve represent points at which the economy is operating at full productive capacity, that is, full employment. Any point *inside* the curve must, therefore, indicate that there are unemployed resources in the economy. Thus, at point R in Fig. 2.1 there are unemployed resources in the economy, whereas at points S and T there is full employment.

A production possibility curve shows what society can produce with *existing resources* at any moment in time. However, over time, society's ability to produce output will increase because of improvements in the productivity of labour, greater technological progress, an increase in the size of the labour force and so on. Whatever the cause, if society's ability to produce output increases, this will be represented by an outward movement of the entire production possibility curve.

It might seem unrealistic to show the production possibilities available to society by considering only two goods. After all, a developed economy such as the UK produces a whole range of different goods and services. However, it is not necessarily unrealistic to concentrate on only two goods, as in Fig. 2.1. For example, good X could be *output provided through the public sector*, that is, state provided activities, whereas good Y could represent *output provided through the private or market sector*. Yet again, good X might represent the goods produced for immediate consumption (*consumer goods*) or goods such as machines (*capital goods*) which are used to produce other goods. Even more fundamentally we could consider the choice as being between *tangible goods* (X) and *services* (Y), and so on.

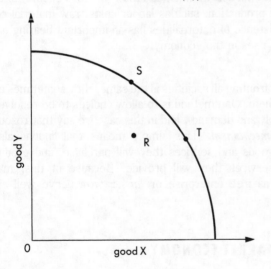

Fig. 2.1 A production possibility curve

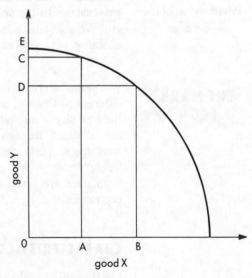

Fig. 2.2 Change in opportunity cost as the output of one good increases

Production possibility curves and opportunity cost

We can illustrate the principle of opportunity cost using a production possibility curve. The curve shows the maximum amount of one good that can be produced, given that a particular quantity of another good is required. For example, in terms of Fig. 2.2, if the economy is currently producing OC of good Y, the *maximum* amount of good X that can be produced is OA. However, if OB of good X is required, the maximum amount of good Y that can be produced is OD. In other words, the *opportunity cost* of an additional AB units of good X, is CD units of good Y, because this is the amount of good Y that must be *foregone* or sacrificed in order to have the additional units of good X.

It is also important to note that the shape of the production possibility curve indicates that the opportunity cost of any *given* increase in the output of one good will change as we move along the production possibility curve. For example, we have already seen that the opportunity cost of increasing the output of good X by AB units when we move from an output of OA of good X to an output of OB of good X, is CD of Y. However, if we increase the output of good X from zero to OA (roughly the same increase in the output of good X as AB) then the opportunity cost is much lower at only EC units of good Y. In other words, the opportunity cost increases as the output of any good increases.

There are several reasons for this, but the most obvious is that not all resources are equally well suited to the production of both goods. Some resources are better suited to the production of some goods than others and when resources *specialise* in producing the goods in which they are most efficient, higher levels of output will be produced. For example, at point E we are using some resources to produce good Y which are not well suited to the production of this good and therefore they are not very productive. Because of this, it is initially possible to produce good X at a relatively low opportunity cost by diverting those resources away from good Y which are better suited to the production of good X. Note, however, that as the production of good X increases, the opposite occurs, and the opportunity cost of producing extra units of X starts to increase.

EXTERNALITIES, SOCIAL COSTS AND PRIVATE COSTS

❝Be familiar with externalities❞

One important aspect of production and consumption in modern economies is that they frequently give rise to *externalities*. These are the spill-over effects of production and consumption which affect *society as a whole* rather than just the individual producers or consumers. Externalities might impose costs on society such as air pollution from the operation of motor vehicles or river pollution from the dumping of waste materials. On the other hand externalities might confer benefits (negative costs) such as the general increase in property values in a particular street that results from individual improvements to property. It is important to note that any costs and benefits resulting from externalities are not solely borne by the individuals or firms responsible for them. Instead they are borne by all the individuals or firms affected by them.

❝Private and social costs can differ❞

To derive the full *social costs* of production we must add the costs (or benefits) of these externalities to the *private costs* of production, such as labour costs, raw material costs, etc. We shall later see that the existence of externalities has an important bearing on the allocation of resources to different uses in the economy.

THE MARKET ECONOMY

Whilst the nature of the choices confronting all societies is the same, they sometimes adopt different methods of dealing with them. One method is to allow choices to be resolved by the free play of *market forces* (supply and demand), and in this case we say that resources are allocated through the *price mechanism*. This simply means that individuals, as consumers, freely choose which goods and services they will purchase, and producers freely decide which goods and services they will provide. Because of this, market economies are often referred to as free enterprise or *laissez faire* (leave well alone) economies.

CHARACTERISTICS OF THE MARKET ECONOMY

Limited role for the state

Market economies are characterised by an almost total lack of government intervention. Indeed in a strictly free enterprise economy, the only major role performed by the government would be that of creating a framework of rules or laws within which both private individuals and firms could conduct their affairs. Such rules would be necessary since, in their absence, there would be no protection from such activities as the addition of harmful substances to products, the false labelling of contents, fraudulent behaviour and so on.

The right to own and dispose of private property

One of the most important features of this kind of economic system is the right of individuals to own private property, and in particular to own and dispose of land and capital as factors of production. This is extremely important, and means that any individual possessing the necessary factors of production, or resources, is free to undertake production. Indeed in the absence of government intervention, they are free both to undertake production and to decide what they will produce.

Despite this, the decision to produce is not always undertaken by those individuals who own the necessary factors of production. Sometimes these are hired out to other individuals. Those individuals who do undertake production are known as *entrepreneurs*. Since the entrepreneur hires the factors of production or uses those currently in his/her ownership, he/she is a *risk-taker*, and since the entrepreneur also decides how resources will be organised and what they will produce, he/she is also a *decision-taker*. The entrepreneurial function is therefore that of risk-taker and decision-taker.

The existence of the profit motive

In making decisions about production, entrepreneurs are guided by the *profit motive*. In other words, the motivating force for the entrepreneur is assumed to be self-interest, with entrepreneurs producing whatever offers them greatest profit. Because of this, price changes provide *signals* to producers, and because of the effect of price changes on profit, producers react to these signals.

Reliance on the price mechanism to allocate resources

This is the most fundamental characteristic of market economies. Decisions about consumption are undertaken by millions of different people, each freely expressing their preferences for different goods and services. Decisions about production, on the other hand, are undertaken by tens of thousands of producers who freely decide which goods and services they are going to provide. There is little or no direct communication between each of these groups, and yet any change in the preferences of consumers is accurately and quickly transmitted to producers via its effect on the prices of goods and services which producers provide. These price changes ensure that the decisions of producers and consumers, although taken independently, are usually compatible with one another (see Chapter 4).

> Prices co-ordinate the decisions of producers and consumers

How do price changes achieve this? Consider, as an example, the case of a good which suddenly becomes more popular so that there is a market shortage at the *existing price*. In these circumstances the price of the good will rise so as to ration the available supply. However, the rise in price will make production of that commodity more profitable. Output will therefore increase as producers are now able to attract resources away from alternative uses by the offer of higher rewards. The process will operate in reverse when a product becomes less popular. It is particularly important to note that, because of their impact on price, changes in consumer demands lead to changes in the allocation of resources. Because of this, the consumer is said to be '*sovereign*' in market economies.

ADVANTAGES AND DISADVANTAGES OF MARKET ECONOMIES

The advantages and disadvantages of market economies are considered in detail in the 'Tutor's Answer' to Question 3 on pp. 20–22. Here is a list of the main points for reference purposes.

Advantages

- What is produced is dictated by the demands of consumers.

- Producers have an incentive (the profit motive) to respond quickly to changes in consumer demands.

- Competition encourages firms to use the least cost method of production.

- Resources are allocated to their 'optimum', or most efficient, use.

Disadvantages

- Prices reflect private costs rather than social costs. Therefore there might not be an optimum allocation of resources.

- Production is for profit, therefore there will be non-production of public goods and under-production of merit goods (see pp. 16–17).

- The economy is often unstable.

- There is inequality in the distribution of income and wealth. Yet it is only those with the ability to buy goods who are able to influence what is produced.

THE CENTRALLY PLANNED ECONOMY

An alternative method of allocating resources is for the government to issue directives or instructions to firms indicating what they should produce, the quantities that should be produced, and so on. In some cases this might be accompanied by complete physical rationing among consumers, but it is more usual to allow consumers a large degree of choice over the items they purchase.

The problems of planning

One obvious problem for this kind of system is to ensure that the demand of consumers matches the output of firms. We have seen that the price mechanism performs this function in free enterprise economies, but in centrally planned economies producers will only follow the instructions they are given. In this type of system the mechanism which 'signals' shortages of some commodities can often be the existence of long queues and empty shelves; whilst the signal for surpluses of other commodities is often the accumulation of stocks.

> Planners must consider all the linkages between outputs

Another problem faced by the planners is to ensure that the target levels of output assigned to various industries are compatible with each other. For example, in giving the steel industry a target level of output the planners must take into consideration the target levels of output assigned to other industries which use steel, such as car manufacturing and ship building. Similarly, when assigning a target to the steel industry the planners must ensure that a sufficient supply of coal is available to the steel industry. Hence the target given to the coal industry must take account of the target given to the steel industry and so on. These target levels of output should largely reflect the likely demands of society for consumption. The nature of planning is discussed more fully on pp. 18–19.

It is clear that the planners face an extremely difficult task, and although plans are normally expected to run for several years, in practice, they are often revised more frequently to take account of changes in consumer demands, technological change, the effects of the weather on agricultural production, and so on. Nevertheless, it is sometimes claimed that centrally planned economies have many advantages over market economies. The most commonly suggested advantages and disadvantages are summarised below.

Advantages of centrally planned economies

- Production is not undertaken for profit. It is argued therefore that there is greater likelihood of both public goods and merit goods being provided (see pp. 16–17); the government simply has to issue a directive to ensure production.

> Central planning does have some advantages, as well as disadvantages

- The production and consumption of demerit goods, which impose relatively large social costs on society, can be limited or prevented altogether; this might be done by using taxes (or subsidies) to bring prices more fully into line with social costs, or by direct restrictions on production and consumption.

- It is sometimes suggested that there is likely to be greater equality in the distribution of income and wealth in centrally planned economies. This is because the factors of production, with the exception of labour, are owned by the state, so that it is impossible for anyone to derive incomes from hiring out land and capital. Similarly, in a fully centrally planned economy, there are no private enterpreneurs who derive profits from combining the factors of production.

- It is claimed that centrally planned economies are likely to be far more stable than market economies. Economic management is entirely in the hands of the government, and consumers have far less power to influence production. Thus, if consumer demand for a particular good falls, it will not necessarily lead to unemployment in the industry. The planners might initially maintain production at existing levels and gradually reduce it over time by not replacing workers who leave the industry through retirement, etc. Any surplus output accumulated as a result of this might be sold abroad at reduced prices. It is clear that this could not happen where production is undertaken for profit, since such a policy would undoubtedly reduce the profitability of an industry.

Disadvantages of centrally planned economies

- There is general agreement among the critics of this system that an important disadvantage of centrally planned economies is the loss of consumer sovereignty. In other words, the state decides what is to be produced, and consumers have much less influence over production than in market economies. Because of this there are likely to be shortages of certain commodities and surpluses of others, with no automatic mechanism for their removal.

- There may be a tendency towards larger bureaucratic structures; government planning departments, rather than decentralised markets, govern resource allocation in such economies. The opportunity cost of employing people to gather information, process it and formulate plans, etc., is the alternative output these people could otherwise have produced.

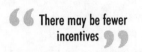

There may be fewer incentives

- Another important criticism of centrally planned economies is that because the profit motive is absent, there is less incentive to increase efficiency. In market economies any increase in the efficiency of firms will lower costs of production and increase profits. This provides a powerful incentive to increase efficency. For instance, it encourages the use of the latest advances in technology in the production process (i.e. **process innovation**) and the quest for new processes and products via research and development expenditure. However, production is not undertaken for profit in centrally planned economies, so there is less incentive to increase efficiency. Indeed, it is sometimes suggested that because any increase in efficiency will lead the planners to raise the target levels of output assigned to an industry, industries in such economies have an incentive *not* to increase efficiency. Whatever the truth of this, there is no doubt that a great deal of industry in centrally planned economies is considerably less efficient than industry in the West, where the profit motive guides producers.

- It is also suggested that the absence of competition in centrally planned economies is a disincentive to efficiency. There is less competition among firms in such economies, since each firm simply responds to the instructions it receives from the planners. So long as planners issue instructions for the continued production of any good or service this will be provided, even if firms make a loss (i.e., costs of production exceed sales revenue) in undertaking the production. Any loss that does arise will be underwritten by the state. The absence of competition might therefore discourage moves towards greater efficiency which, in a competitive market economy, would be necessary for the firm to survive. The ultimate sanction against inefficient firms in a market economy is that if they do not earn profits they will eventually be forced into liquidation.

- There is evidence that while high and stable levels of employment exist in certain Comecon countries, this is achieved by overmanning and inefficiency in the allocation of resources. Indeed the problem is made worse because factory managers tend to hoard labour, partly because targets are often raised suddenly and without warning.

- *Price controls* are frequently used in centrally planned economies in order to achieve greater equality. However, relatively low prices encourage over-consumption and this is one of the main reasons for shortages, for example of foodstuffs in many eastern-bloc countries. Here again the result is inefficiency in the allocation of resources.

There is another problem. Shortages create a demand for imports, but allowing the free import of goods and services is likely to be inconsistent with the plan for the economy. Hence, trade is likely to be restricted in centrally planned economies and, as we shall see in Chapter 14, international trade can have an important effect on the efficiency with which resources are used and therefore on the growth of living standards.

THE MIXED ECONOMY

Most economies are mixed

We have seen that both free enterprise and centrally planned economies have their respective advantages and disadvantages. For this reason neither is found in its extreme form in the economies of the world. It is often suggested that the economy of **Hong Kong** comes closest to being a **free enterprise economy**, and that of the **USSR** closest to being a **centrally planned economy**. However, both of these are more properly described as mixed economies because they each contain features of market economies and features of planned economies. The difference being that in Hong Kong there is *less* government intervention in the economy and *greater* reliance on the price mechanism to allocate resources than in the USSR. Both, therefore, are mixed economies, but the balance between the role of the market mechanism and the role of the government differs markedly. Of course with the developments in Perestroika in the USSR that difference, though still significant, is starting to narrow.

Because the role the government performs in the economy differs between countries, it is difficult to be precise about the exact nature of the mixed economy. Nevertheless we can identify certain functions performed by the government in most mixed economies, and these are examined below. We should remember, however, that the *extent* of the government's involvement in performing these functions will vary from economy to economy.

THE PROVISION OF PUBLIC GOODS

Characteristics of public goods

Know about public goods

This is a very important role for the government, because certain public goods are essential for the operation of developed economies. A *public good* has a number of characteristics. One is '**non-excludability**', which means that they cannot be provided for one citizen without simultaneously becoming available to others. In other words, once a public good is provided it is often difficult to actually stop a person consuming an extra unit if they wish to do so. This is true in the case of a lighthouse or street lighting for example. If a lighthouse is constructed, it is impossible to stop shipping in its vicinity from using it. Similarly if street lighting is provided, it is impossible to prevent any passer-by from taking advantage of it. Charges cannot therefore be levied on public goods because the benefits cannot be denied to those who refuse to pay.

Another characteristic of public goods is '**non-exhaustibility**' which means that consumption of an extra unit by one person does not diminish the amount available for consumption by others. In other words, once the public good is provided, the additional cost of making it available to an extra consumer is zero. Defence and law and order are often called public goods. An extra person can usually be defended by the armed forces, or be protected by the police and judiciary, at no extra cost! Since the opportunity cost is zero, resources will be allocated more efficiently if no charge is made for public goods.

THE PROVISION OF MERIT GOODS

Merit goods are different

As well as providing public goods, the government also undertakes to provide many other goods and services which add to the quality of life but which are not pure public goods. Merit goods do not possess the same characteristics as public goods; for instance people can be excluded from consuming them. They could therefore be provided through the market mechanism. However, many are deliberately provided free of charge through public bodies because their consumption confers relatively large social benefits on society which far outweigh their cost of provision. Examples of merit goods include state education, public health care, municipal housing, and so on.

Arguments for state provision of merit goods

- It encourages a greater consumption of goods which confer benefits on society as a whole. For example, providing education freely to children and health care freely to all, produces a more skilled and healthier workforce. The absence of these would seriously reduce labour productivity and adversely affect living standards. Similarly, economic efficiency, and hence living standards, would be reduced if the state did *not* provide an adequate road network, and so on.

- Inequality of income would limit their availability to lower income groups. In this sense the provision of merit goods redistributes income in favour of the poorer members of society. This is one of the main reasons for the provision of municipal housing.

Arguments against state provision

Despite these arguments it is important to remember that there is also a case *against* the provision of merit goods (and public goods) by the state.

- Such goods might be freely available to consumers, but they nevertheless must be paid for by the state. This involves higher levels of taxation or government borrowing than might otherwise be the case. The former might have disincentive effects (see Chapter 16) while the latter might be a cause of inflation (see Chapter 13).

- To provide merit goods freely to all makes no distinction between those who *can* afford to pay and those who *cannot*. It might also encourage over-consumption (in relation to the most efficient use of resources) and consequently divert resources away from other, more productive, activities. After all, if something is provided free of charge there is no opportunity cost to the consumer of additional consumption. Because of this, resources might be diverted into activities which, were the consumers asked to pay the *true* cost of provision, they might opt *not* to have, preferring instead some alternative which they feel offers better value for money. In other words, a decision by the state to provide merit goods limits consumer choice since it reduces the resources available to produce other goods and services. Providing merit goods through the state might, therefore, lead to a misallocation of resources away from those uses which confer greatest benefit on society. This might reduce the growth of living standards below their potential level.

CONTROL OF THE ECONOMY

One of the most important functions governments now perform is that of economic management. In other words, the government attempts to control the economy in order to achieve certain economic objectives. These may be summarised as a high and stable level of employment, stable prices, economic growth, an acceptable distribution of income and wealth and a sustainable balance of payments position with the rest of the world. Governments use a variety of techniques in their efforts to achieve these objectives, and we shall examine these more fully in Chapter 17. It is only important to note here that governments have made the pursuit of economic objectives one of their functions, and that they intervene in the economy to achieve these objectives.

Redistribution of income

Governments intervene in economies to create greater equality in the distribution of income and wealth than would otherwise exist. The most obvious way in which this is done is through a system of **taxation**, where the higher income earners are taxed more heavily than the lower income earners. Greater equality could also be achieved by the government providing certain goods **free of charge** or at a **subsidised rate**. Thus, for example, medical care is provided free of charge in the UK, whilst drugs issued on prescription are heavily subsidised. Finally, greater equality might be achieved through a **social security system** which provides payments from the state for the sick and aged, as well as to the unemployed and low income earners.

Modifying the system

Governments sometimes place taxes and subsidies on goods and services to influence their prices and hence the volumes produced and consumed. A tax on a product usually raises its price and so reduces consumption and therefore production, while a subsidy usually lowers price and stimulates consumption and therefore production.

Governments also attempt to modify the operation of the price mechanism by the use of *cost-benefit analysis*. This is a technique which attempts to assess the *net worth* of a particular project, after considering all the private and social costs and benefits arising out of the project. In other words, a money value is assigned to all of the externalities which stem from a project. The net value of externalities is added to the estimated value of private costs and private benefits from a project to give an estimate of its net worth. A positive result indicates that society will be 'better off' if the project goes ahead, whereas a negative result indicates that society will be 'worse off' if the project goes ahead (see 'Outline Answer' to Q.2 on p. 23).

> **"Cost-benefit analysis is widely used"**

Productive efficiency

Governments also intervene in the economy to try and achieve greater efficiency in production. This might mean bringing an entire industry into public ownership, that is, *nationalisation* or returning a nationalised industry to private hands, that is, *privatisation*. It might mean removing some of the legal regulations which prevent the emergence of competition in certain industries, that is *deregulation*. Greater efficiency in production might require subsidising expenditure on research and development or providing grants to encourage the purchase of new, high technology machinery by firms. It might involve the provision of grants to influence the location of firms, and so on. Of course, any assistance that is given for these purposes is highly selective, and firms do not always qualify for this kind of state aid. Nevertheless, the fact that it is given, implies government involvement in the economy.

THE FIVE YEAR PLAN

An article in the *Economic Review* of March 1986 (Vol 4, No 3) entitled *Industrial Planning in the Soviet Economy*, A. F. Freris, on which this section draws heavily, provides a discussion of the planning process in the Soviet Union. Even with Perestroika, many of these procedures are still used. The article concentrates on planning the industrial sector within a more general Five Year Plan covering all sectors. The plan for the industrial sector contains two main elements:

- deciding on the *gross output of industrial goods*
- deciding what proportion of this gross output is to be allocated as *inputs of other sectors* and what proportion is to be the *final output*

In fact the State Planning Committee (*Gosplan*), in association with the highest political authorities, decides on the overall composition of gross industrial output.

Flow of goods

The State Committee on Material – Technical Supply (*Gossnab*) then plans the flows of these goods (as inputs) between enterprises and between sectors, as it deems necessary in order to execute the output plan. Individual output plans are set for *each enterprise*, which then submit their estimates of the inputs required to execute the plan. Gosplan then has to ensure that the output plan as a whole, and broken down by the enterprise, is consistent with these various input requirements. Some idea of how difficult this is can be gained by remembering that the inputs of one firm are the outputs of other firms. So in planning total output, planners must ensure an appropriate level and composition of output. Otherwise there will be shortages in the shops, and so on.

Input-output tables

This enormously complex problem is solved by the use of *input-output* tables, and a simple example reproduced below is included to illustrate their use. Two industries are considered, coal and steel. The output of each has several possible uses. For example, the output of the coal industry could be used by the coal mines themselves in producing electricity, etc., or it could be sold to some other user. For simplicity only three possible uses are considered: coal is consumed internally (i.e. used by the coal industry itself), sold to the steel industry or consumed by households. Again we assume the output of the steel industry to have only three possible uses. Steel is either consumed internally (i.e. used by the steel industry itself), sold to the coal industry, or consumed by households. The *rows* of Fig. 2.3 show the amount of output consumed by each group and the *columns* show inputs into the production of that output. For instance, to produce 100 tonnes of coal we need an input of 10 tonnes of coal and 50 tonnes of steel.

purchases from \ sales to	coal	steel	consumers	gross output
coal	10	70	20	100
steel	50	30	40	120

Fig. 2.3

Source: The Economic Review, Vol. 3, No. 4, March 1986

The use of this is easily demonstrated. For example, if the planners decide to increase the output of coal destined for 'consumers' from 20 to 30 tonnes, the gross output of *coal* would have to increase from 100 to 110 tonnes. Since more coal is produced, more steel will be needed as input. If we assume a constant relationship between inputs and output then, since 50 tonnes of steel (and 10 tonnes of coal) are required to produce 100 tonnes of coal, an *extra* 5 tonnes of steel will be required to produce an *extra* 10 tonnes of coal. So the output of *steel* will have to rise to 125 tonnes. However, in order to produce more steel, more coal will be needed. To be precise, the output of *coal* will have to be increased by $5 \times 70/120$ tonnes. This will require a further increase in the output of *steel* and so on.

Key sector planning

It is a relatively simple task to obtain a *determinate solution* to this particular problem.

However, in the real world the problem is more complex, since there are many other industries to consider with each industry using a variety of inputs from other industries. Because of the increased complexity it is difficult to produce an input-output matrix for the output of the *entire economy*. Instead, the *authorities* concentrate on *planning* the output of a few *key sectors*, such as coal, steel, oil, electricity, and so on.

Annual plans

Once the output plan has been settled for each sector it is then allocated between enterprises (*firms*) within the sector. Gossnab then instructs each enterprise on when and where they are to deliver their output, and from whom they are to obtain their inputs. This process is repeated annually, because the Five Year Plan is broken down into five annual plans. The Five Year Plan provides the framework and general guidelines for planning. The annual plans provide more detail and, where necessary, amend the Five Year Plan to take account of changing circumstances.

Problems

Despite the fact that output is planned, there are several possible problems. For example, it is not sufficient to give an enterprise a monthly target of X tonnes of steel; rather it is necessary to specify the *precise* form output should take in terms of size, weight, quality, and so on. Another problem occurs because of the desire of Soviet managers to fulfil targets. Meeting targets entitles managers to a bonus and carries prestige in the community. This has led managers to exaggerate their input requirements and to understate their capacity (so that only a low target will be expected of them). Further, since overfulfilling the target results in the target being raised at the next planning stage, there is every incentive for managers to *only just* meet their required target. There is little doubt that Soviet industry operates at less than maximum efficiency.

GREEN ISSUES

'Green' issues are becoming increasingly important and the Lloyds Bank Economic Bulletin of September 1989 (No 129) is entitled *Being Economical with the Environment*. The point is made that most environmental problems arise from externalities. The focus of attention is air pollution and, as with all externalities, those responsible for air pollution often take no account of the effect of their actions on others. For example, one of the main causes of acid rain is the emission of sulphur dioxide into the environment from coal burning power stations. However, if a power station takes no account of this when pricing electricity the entire cost of any externality generated is borne by the community as a whole rather than by consumers of electricity.

Accountability for pollution

Because polluters typically take no (or at least little) account of their action on others this generally results in the output of polluting industries being greater than is optimal. If polluters were forced to *pay* for any externalities they impose on society, producers would almost certainly change their techniques of production so as to minimise pollution and consumers would almost certainly choose to consume less of those goods which cause pollution. One solution is therefore to levy a tax on polluters equal to the cost of removing the effect of the externality they generate. This will encourage firms to cut emissions and provides an incentive for them to research ways of permanently reducing pollution. Many economists believe this approach to be preferable to limiting the amount of pollution firms can impose on the environment by regulation. Such an approach provides no incentive to permanently reduce levels of emission.

Political impact

One possible problem with using taxation for this purpose is that to equal the cost of any externality imposed on the community, taxes would need to be set at relatively high levels and this would be politically unpopular. However, it is argued that a relatively small tax, by making consumers more aware of externalities, might bring about a reduction in consumption and therefore encourage producers to reduce pollution emissions. The reduction of taxation on lead free petrol is cited as an example of using taxation policy to bring about environmental benefits.

EXAMINATION QUESTIONS

1 Explain the concept of opportunity cost and discuss, with examples, its importance.

(London, Jan 1988)

2 What is cost benefit analysis?   (25)
   With reference to examples, discuss its application to public sector investment.   (75)
   (*Total 100 marks*)
   (London, Jan 1989)

3 Outline the main features of a free market economy and discuss its advantages and disadvantages.

(AEB, Nov 1987)

4 Suppose certain chemical firms discharge waste products into rivers and lakes.
   a) Explain why such discharges may constitute what is known as an 'externality'.   (5)
   b) Explain the argument which asserts that, from a social point of view, the level of chemical production in such circumstances may not be optimal.   (10)
   c) Consider whether government policy could lead to a socially more efficient level of chemical production.   (10)
   (*Total 25 marks*)
   (WJEC, 1987)

A TUTOR'S ANSWER TO QUESTION 3

A free market economy exists when there is little government intervention in the economy so that producers have almost complete freedom to decide what they are going to produce, and consumers have complete freedom to decide what they are going to purchase. In this type of economy, individuals who undertake production are guided by the profit motive, and consequently produce those goods and services which offer greatest profit.

In market economies the price mechanism ensures that consumer demands are compatible with the output of firms. Thus, for example, if a particular product suddenly becomes more popular so that there is a market shortage at the existing price, the price will rise so as to ration the available supply. However the rise in price will make production of that commodity more profitable. Because of this, output will increase as producers attract resources away from less profitable alternatives by offering higher rewards. The process operates in reverse when a product becomes less popular.

One of the main advantages of the market mechanism is that consumers, by their own actions, dictate the pattern of production. Because of this, the consumer is said to be 'sovereign' in market economies. By continuing to consume a commodity they are, in effect, voting for its continued production. By consuming more of a commodity they are voting more resources into the production of that commodity and, because resources have alternative uses, they are voting fewer resources into the production of other commodities.

However, this simple explanation does not fully convey the significance of the price mechanism's operation. Not only do producers have an incentive to respond to changes in consumer preferences, they also have an incentive to respond quickly and efficiently. Because there is freedom to own and hire the factors of production in free market economies, any producer who does not respond quickly to changes in consumer preferences will soon be driven out of business by those who do respond quickly. In other words the price mechanism answers both the 'What' and the 'How' questions.

Additionally, it is argued that the freedom to undertake production ensures a high degree of competition in the economy. This is extremely important and competition is the main regulator of economic efficiency in market economies. Any improvement in a firm's efficiency will lower its costs relative to its competitors and hence raise its profits from a given value of sales. It might also enable the more efficient firms to lower their prices relative to other firms, with the aim of attracting more consumers and further increasing profits.

Thus, the clear implication is that competition benefits the consumer. It encourages efficiency and lower prices, and might also encourage improvements in the nature of the products that firms produce. The incentive for firms to be efficient in market economies is, therefore, a powerful one. The more efficient firms make higher profits, while the least efficient firms are forced out of business because they are unable to compete with the lower prices offered by more efficient firms.

The price mechanism clearly encourages efficiency in production and distribution, but it is also claimed that its operation leads to an optimum, or ideal, allocation of resources. This is because the price consumers are willing to pay for a commodity represents their valuation of the resources used to produce that commodity. In other words, price is a measure of the value consumers place on a commodity. On the other hand, the cost of producing a commodity is the cost producers pay to attract resources away from other uses. In other words, financial costs of production are a measure of the opportunity cost of production. An optimum allocation of resources exists when the value society places on another unit of the commodity (shown by the price they are willing to pay for it) exactly equals the cost of attracting resources away from alternative uses (i.e. its opportunity cost). This must be so because if alternatives were more highly valued, resources would move into their production because entrepreneurs would offer them higher rewards. This is precisely what happens when demand for a good increases. Its price is bid up and production expands as resources are attracted away from alternatives. When price equals opportunity cost a 'Pareto optimum' allocation of resources is said to exist and this simply means that it is no longer possible to make one person better off without simultaneously making someone else worse off.

It seems, therefore, that the market mechanism operates with great efficiency in the allocation of resources. In practice, however, this is unlikely to be true. One reason for this is that an efficient or optimum allocation of resources can only exist when all prices in the economy fully reflect the *social* costs of production and consumption. However, prices in market economies are based entirely on *private* costs of production. Thus, if a product imposes relatively large social costs on society, then the free operation of the price mechanism will not lead to an optimum allocation of resources. This is simply because the social costs of production will be greater than the private costs, and hence market price will be *less* then the real (social) opportunity cost of production.

The fact that price is less than the full (social) costs of production leads to a higher level of consumption, and therefore production, than would happen if costs were based on the full social costs of production. In other words, society would over-produce this commodity, and under-produce others where social costs of production are less than private costs. In this case it is possible for society as a whole to increase its welfare by a reallocation of resources from those commodities which are over-produced in relation to the optimum level, to those which are under-produced. Thus, where social costs of production exist, the free operation of the price (or market) mechanism will *not* lead to the most efficient allocation of resources.

The price mechanism might also fail to allocate resources efficiently because it leads to the non-production of pure public goods. The problem is that these goods often confer benefits on society far in excess of their costs. However, they could not be provided through the market mechanism because they have characteristics of *non-exhaustibility* in production and *non-excludability* in consumption. Non-exhaustibility simply means that consumption by one person does not diminish the amount available to other consumers, so that the real opportunity cost of providing an extra unit of consumption is zero. Since a 'Pareto optimum' allocation implies price *equals* additional social cost, the appropriate price should be *zero*. Examples of such goods include street lighting, lighthouses, national defence, and so on. Non-excludability in consumption means that if these goods are provided for one person they are automatically available to others. However, no consumer would ever pay individually for the provision of these goods because it would be impossible to stop non-payers from consuming them. Hence pure public goods would never be provided through the market mechanism since they could never be profitable. By not providing public goods the market mechanism might again fail to allocate resources efficiently.

Another factor to consider is that free market economies are inherently unstable because of the ever-changing pattern of consumer demands. This has serious repercussions. A fall in demand for one industry's product is likely to lead to unemployment in that industry. This might adversely affect whole regions in which an industry is localised. More serious still is the unemployment which results from a general fall in consumer demand. In the absence of government intervention this might be heavy and persistent. Such unemployment represents inefficiency in the market mechanism, because an economy with unemployed resources is working below its productive potential. Hence, the output of goods and services is less than would be achieved if the economy operated at maximum efficiency. This provides justification for government intervention in the economy and the adoption of policies designed to improve the mobility of capital and labour. Free market economies are also criticised because they lead to considerable inequality in the *distribution of income and wealth.* Those who own land and capital derive incomes from hiring them out, but the vast majority of people have nothing but their labour to sell. In addition, when instability in the economy leads to unemployment the limited role for the government implies an absence of state aid in the form of supplementary benefit for example. Similarly those with relatively low incomes or with relatively large families receive no kind of state aid. This degree of inequality is unacceptable to most people.

In conclusion, it can be seen that in free market economies reliance on the price mechanism leads to an allocation of resources which is entirely dictated by consumer preferences. It provides an automatic mechanism for adjusting rapidly to changes in consumer preferences. However, there are many factors in the real world which prevent the market mechanism from allocating resources with maximum efficiency.

A STUDENT'S ANSWER TO QUESTION 1

Opportunity cost arises because society only has limited resources but appears to have an unlimited desire for the output which these resources are used to produce. Because society cannot have all that it desires it is forced to make choices. One important choice is what the available resources will be used to produce. In choosing what is produced society also chooses to forego the alternatives that might otherwise have been produced from its available resources.

Strictly defined opportunity cost is the next most desired alternative foregone. This is very important and opportunity cost is sometimes referred to as real cost since it expresses the cost of what we have in terms of what we do without. For example, if the government is considering additional expenditure on the armed forces, the real cost of this might be a reduction in expenditure on education. This is simply a reflection of the fact that if resources are committed to one use, they are not available for an alternative use.

The concept of opportunity cost has widespread application in economics. For individual consumers, the problem is deciding what to spend their limited incomes on. Most individuals have a scale of preferences and use their limited income to purchase those goods and services which give most satisfaction. However, in choosing to have more of one thing, they choose to have less of something else.

Another choice individuals must make is that between work and leisure. Since there is only a limited amount of time available each day, a decision to work longer hours implies a decision to have less time available for leisure activities. How much time individuals spend at work partly depends on how much value they place on leisure time. As the amount of time spent at work increases, the availability of leisure time decreases and this would tend to increase its value. It seems likely therefore that as the amount of work increases, the opportunity cost of leisure increases.

The principle of opportunity cost is also very important to firms. For example, it is often assumed that if firms decide to use their own funds for the purchase of new machinery rather than borrowing, this has no opportunity cost because no interest charges are incurred. However, this view is incorrect. Clearly the funds used to purchase the new machine have alternative uses and if invested elsewhere would earn interest for the firm. If the firm uses its own funds to purchase additional equipment, the opportunity cost might

❝ Good beginning but you might have gone on to illustrate the problem using a Production Possibility Curve ❞

❝ Give examples to illustrate ❞

❝ Good paragraph ❞

> be the interest that could be earned on the funds if they were invested elsewhere.
>
> Opportunity cost also has implications in the field of social economics. For example, the government provides education and health-care free of charge to citizens of the UK. The opportunity cost of this is not just the alternative output that the resources used to provide education and health-care could have produced. A healthy, well-educated labour force is much more productive than a labour force which is sick with disease and illiterate. The opportunity cost of providing education and health-care must therefore also be related to the output that would be lost if they were not provided.
>
> Clearly opportunity cost is an extremely important concept. It has relevance wherever a choice between at least two alternatives has to be made. In the subject of economics this means it has particular relevance to individuals, firms and governements.

❝ A good example of investment in human capital leading to external benefits ❞

❝ Some good points made but some applications of opportunity cost are not considered. It is very important in international trade theory; in decisions about saving/consumption by individuals, and in current/capital expenditure decisions by firms and government ❞

OUTLINE ANSWERS TO QUESTION 2 AND 4

2   **Definition:** Clearly you must begin your answer to this question with a definition of cost-benefit analysis. *Cost-benefit analysis* is a technique used to assess the full social costs and social benefits of a project and considers repercussions in the longer term as well as in the shorter term. The aim is to assign money values to all costs and benefits and then to discount these to present value (see p. 124), that is, to express their value in terms of the prices which prevail today. Only then is it possible to add costs and benefits together.

   Example: It would be useful to provide a simple example of the discounting process and to indicate its shortcomings, especially the difficulty in choosing an appropriate rate of discount. If social benefits outweigh social costs, this simply means that society's welfare will be improved if the project is carried out. However, this does not necessarily mean that the project should go ahead. Different projects might well result in an even greater gain to society. It simply means that society will benefit if this project is carried out.

   Specific Example – the Victoria Line: In considering whether to construct the Victoria Line, the government commissioned a cost-benefit study, which highlighted the importance of such factors as a possible reduction in road congestion due to commuters on the new line reducing use of the roads. In fact the main benefit of the Victoria Line was thought to be time-savings which, apart from convenience to commuters, also benefits society because it is likely to lead to increased punctuality at work and a consequent increase in output.

   Other Examples: A whole range of other projects could be considered, such as the construction of an additional motorway link, a rail-link between London and the Channel Tunnel, the construction of a nuclear power station, and so on. Whatever projects you consider the main point to stress is the diversity of costs and benefits that must be considered and the difficulties involved in valuing these.

4   a) An externality arises whenever the actions of one party (people or institutions) has some effect on another party which does not participate in the actions giving rise to the externality. Externalities can lead to costs being imposed or benefits being received and can arise from either consumption or production.

   In this case if chemical waste is discharged into rivers and lakes there will be a cost imposed on anyone using the polluted rivers or lakes. An obvious cost would be imposed on anglers since chemical pollution would kill fish and thus penalise anglers. However, if the pollution is severe enough, it might also prevent people swimming in lakes etc...

b) Dumping chemical discharges into rivers and lakes is a relatively cheap way of disposing of waste materials for firms. This is likely to lead to consumers being charged a *lower* price for the product than would happen if firms were prevented from dumping treated waste into rivers. Because of this there is likely to be over-consumption in relation to the optimum level.

c) It is possible that government intervention might lead to a socially more efficient level of chemical production. One way of achieving this would be to ban the production of chemicals which are associated with the discharges. However, this will impose other costs on society since particular chemicals will no longer be available.

A different approach would be to enforce legislation compelling producers to install equipment and to treat waste materials before discharging them into rivers and lakes so that they are rendered harmless to marine life. This is an appealing solution since the higher cost of production would undoubtedly result in higher prices. Therefore those involved in production and consumption of chemicals would pay a price closer to the true cost of production. In other words prices would be more closely related to opportunity cost.

A different approach would be to impose a tax on the product so that its price increases and consumers again pay the true opportunity cost of production. This would undoubtedly lead to a reduction in consumption and hence a lower level of pollution. However, some pollution would remain. On the other hand the government would have additional revenue.

You should consider these approaches in detail. The optimum solution depends on the effect of pollution on rivers and lakes and the rate at which the government is prepared to levy a tax on the polluters.

Further reading

Beardshaw, *Economics: A Student's Guide* (2nd edition) Pitman 1989: Ch 1, Introduction; What is economics about; Ch 6, The mixed economy.

Begg, Fischer and Dornbusch, *Economics* (2nd edition), McGraw-Hill 1987: Ch 1, An introduction to economics and the economy.

Stanlake, *Introductory Economics* (5th edition), Longman 1989: Ch 1, The nature, scope and methods of economics; Ch 2, Economic systems.

CHAPTER 3

PRODUCTION, COSTS AND RETURNS

GETTING STARTED

Production is defined as any economic activity which satisfies human wants. It therefore refers equally to the creation of goods or the supply of services. Indeed, to the economist the chain of production is only complete when a good or service is sold to the consumer.

For any community the volume of production depends on many factors, including the quantity and quality of the available resources, the extent to which they are utilised and the efficiency with which they are combined. The volume of production can therefore be increased when more resources or inputs become available, or when existing inputs yield a higher output. The latter is referred to as an increase in *productivity* and is usually measured as average product per worker. Thus productivity rises when average product rises.

When considering the causes of changes in output economists frequently distinguish between the *short run* and the *long run*. These are not fixed time periods, but instead are defined in terms of the time required to bring about changes in the input of various factors of production. Specifically, the *short run* exists when there is *at least one* fixed factor of production. In other words, the short run refers to a period of time when it is possible to vary the input of some factors of production but impossible to vary the input of at least one other factor. For example, sometimes it is impossible for firms to recruit skilled labour until more workers have been trained, but they usually have little difficulty in recruiting unskilled workers. It is important to note that any factor of production can be fixed in the short run. In contrast, the *long run* is the time period required to bring about a change in the input of *all* the factors of production. In other words, there are no fixed factors of production in the long run.

Marginal product is the *rate at which total product changes* as an additional unit of the variable factor is employed. For instance, the marginal product of labour is usually measured as the change in total output when one more, or one less, worker is employed. The concept of the margin is very important in economics and you must ensure you are familiar with it and fully understand it. You will see in this chapter that it is also applied to cost. *Marginal cost* is the rate at which total cost changes as output changes. However, at 'A'-level it is measured as the change in total cost of production when output is increased by one more unit.

Because costs of production vary as output varies, firms must decide what is their most efficient level of output. In fact, there are two kinds of efficiency: *economic efficiency* and *technical efficiency*. Firms are producing at their most economically efficient level when, given their current scale of operations, they are maximising profit, that is, earning as much profit as possible from the output they currently produce. On the other hand, firms are producing at their most technically efficient level when, given their current scale of production, average cost per unit is minimised. We shall see in Chapter 5 that only in certain circumstances will these levels of output coincide.

THE FACTORS OF PRODUCTION

DIVISION OF LABOUR

MOBILITY OF THE FACTORS OF PRODUCTION

COMBINING THE FACTORS OF PRODUCTION

THE LAWS OF RETURNS

THE FIRM'S REVENUE

APPLIED MATERIALS

THE FACTORS OF PRODUCTION

ESSENTIAL PRINCIPLES

LAND

Land was defined by early economists to include 'all the free gifts of nature'. It therefore includes the surface area of the planet as well as its mineral and ore deposits. As a factor of production land has special characteristics. It has no cost of production, is completely fixed in supply, that is, cannot be reproduced, and cannot be moved from one place to another.

LABOUR

As a factor of production, labour is defined as the physical and mental human effort used to create goods and services. The supply of labour to an economy is therefore very important in determining the level of output an economy is able to produce and depends on such factors as size of the population, length of the working week, number of hours worked per day and so on. However, the quality of labour is also important and this depends on general health and well-being as well as on education and training. More is said about the supply of labour to an economy in Chapter 4.

CAPITAL

Definition

Capital is defined by economists as any man-made asset which is used in the production of further goods and services. In general, it is the use to which a particular asset is put which determines whether it is capital. For example a motor car used by a salesman would be classed as capital, but a car used for social and domestic purposes would be classed as a consumer good.

Fixed and circulating capital

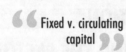

Fixed v. circulating capital

Economists distinguish between *fixed* capital and *circulating* capital. The former can be used time and again in the production process whereas the latter can only be used once. Fixed capital therefore includes such things as machinery and factory buildings, the road and rail networks, hospitals and educational buildings and so on, whereas circulating capital (also commonly known as working capital) consists of raw materials and work in progress.

Creation of capital

Capital is created from scarce resources and therefore has an opportunity cost. In order to create more capital it is necessary to consume less so that resources can be released for the production of capital. In other words, in order to accumulate capital a community must forego current consumption, that is, the community as a whole must save.

ENTERPRISE

This factor of production is more commonly referred to as the *entrepreneur*. The entrepreneur performs two important roles:

- hiring and combining the other factors of production
- risk taking by producing goods and services *in anticipation* of demand

DIVISION OF LABOUR

Division of labour refers to the way in which jobs are broken down into their various component parts so that each worker performs only a small part of the entire operation. Because of this, division of labour is often referred to as *specialisation*. In the production of many goods and services each worker specialises in a single task or small group of related tasks.

ADVANTAGES OF DIVISION OF LABOUR

Increased productivity

Division of labour leads to a far greater average product per worker being achieved than is possible in the absence of specialisation. But why is this increase in productivity possible?

Reasons for specialisation

- someone who performs the same task every day becomes very skilled at it and able to work much faster
- most of the worker's day is spent on production, no time is wasted moving from work area to work area, or changing one set of tools for another
- workers can be trained more quickly since there are fewer skills to learn
- breaking production down to a small number of repetitive tasks makes possible the use of specialist machinery which can be kept fully operational throughout the working day; machines are more efficient than humans so productivity is vastly increased
- workers can specialise in performing tasks in which they have a particular aptitude

Increased standard of living

The greater levels of productivity achieved through division of labour have led to an increase in living standards since higher productivity leads to lower costs of production and hence to lower prices (see pp. 50–53). The higher level of productivity has also led to a considerable reduction in the length of both the working week and the working year; even so a larger amount of goods and services are produced each year.

Increased range of goods available

The lower cost of production achieved by division of labour, and the consequently lower price of goods and services, has increased the *range* of goods and services available to most people.

DISADVANTAGES OF DIVISION OF LABOUR

Despite these advantages, division of labour has several disadvantages.

Increased boredom

Greater specialisation results in boredom as workers perform the same tasks throughout the working day. This can lead to low morale, which in turn leads to poor labour relations, higher absenteeism as well as carelessness and an increased number of accidents.

Lack of variety

Problems with specialisation

Output is standardised and large numbers of identical articles are produced. (Remember though, that a greater *range* of output is still being produced at a lower price. For most people, therefore, a greater variety of output is available.)

Worker interdependence

Specialisation leads to interdependence. Each worker in the production process depends on all other workers in the production process. A stoppage by a small group of workers can therefore cause considerable disruption.

SPECIALISATION

Specialisation is now widespread and can be observed in several ways:

- Specialisation of *workers* within an industry.
- Specialisation of *firms* within an industry. For example, in the car industry some firms specialise in supplying electrical components or tyres.
- Specialisation *by region*. Some industries are located in particular parts of the country. For example, the steel industry in Sheffield.
- Specialisation *by country*. For example, Brazil which produces coffee or Chile which supplies most of the world's nitrates.

DIVISION OF LABOUR AND THE SIZE OF THE MARKET

Division of labour is only possible if there is a large market. It is no use producing vast

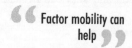

> The market can limit specialisation

quantities of output, even at relatively low prices, if there is only a small market for what is produced. Markets might be *limited* by several factors:

- consumers might demand variety, as with jewellery and haute couture clothes
- some areas are sparsely populated
- low incomes might restrict 'effective' demand (i.e. demand backed by purchasing power)
- personal services and repair work are not always easy to split into a number of stages

MOBILITY OF THE FACTORS OF PRODUCTION

Economists identify two types of mobility: *geographical mobility* and *occupational mobility*. The former refers to a physical movement of a factor of production from one geographical location to another, whereas the latter refers to a factor of production moving from one occupation to another.

IMPORTANCE OF FACTOR MOBILITY

A high degree of factor mobility is considered important to an economy for several reasons.

- The more mobile the factors of production, the easier it is to respond to changes in demand for different goods and services. This makes possible the production of a greater level of output and therefore a higher standard of living. It also reduces unemployment below levels that would otherwise exist.

> Factor mobility can help

- When demand for products increases, prices are pulled upwards and resources are reallocated via the price mechanism. However, when factors of production are mobile, prices are unlikely to rise so quickly, which results in a lower rate of inflation.
- In modern economies the rate of technological progress is rapid and in order to take full advantage of this it is necessary to have an adaptable and mobile labour force. Here again the use of new technologies makes possible an improvement in living standards.
- Changes in a country's rate of exchange can lead to sudden changes in the prices of, and demand for, exports and imports (see Chapter 15). Sales and purchases of these are recorded in the balance of payments. If a nation is to have a 'faavourable' balance of payments it will need to take advantage of sudden increases in demand for exports by rapidly producing more output. Extra output may also be needed rapidly to compete with imports. In both cases, mobile factors will help a more rapid output response.

COMBINING THE FACTORS OF PRODUCTION

All production requires the input of resources or factors of production. However, these can often be combined in a variety of ways, sometimes by using more of one factor relative to another, and vice versa. Profit-maximising firms, that is, firms which aim to make as large a profit as possible, will combine the factors of production so as to minimise the cost of producing *any given output*.

MEASURING CHANGES IN OUTPUT

Over time firms vary the level of output they produce within any given period, such as a week or a month. Sometimes they will increase output, sometimes they will reduce it. To do this they will change the input of factors of production. There are important laws which explain what happens to output as the input of factors of production changes. These are considered below. Here we define some important concepts which are used to explain the laws of returns:

Total product

This is simply the total output a firm produces within a given period of time. For example, the total product of a particular firm might be 1000 units per week.

Average product

This is usually measured in relation to a particular factor of production, such as labour or

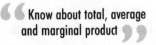

Know about total, average and marginal product

capital. Thus the average product of labour is measuured as Total product/Number of workers. For example, if the total product of the firm is 1000 units per week and 10 workers are employed, average product per worker is 1000/10, that is, 100 units per week. Changes in average product are referred to as changes in *productivity* and we shall see below that changes in productivity have an important impact on the firm's costs of production.

Marginal product

This is the *rate at which total product* changes as an additional unit of a *variable factor* is employed. For instance, the marginal product of labour is usually measured as the change in total product when *one more* worker is employed. If total product when the firm employs 10 workers is 1000 units per week, and this rises to 1080 units per week when the firm employs an additional worker, then the marginal product of the last worker is 80 units per week.

THE LAWS OF RETURNS

These are short run laws

Firms can change the level of production by changing the input of the factors of production. Remember though that changes in the input of all factors is not possible in the short run as there is at least one fixed factor of production. The *laws of returns* explain the relationship between changes in the input of *variable factors* and changes in the level of output. The general relationship is summarised in two laws which are sometimes combined into a single law known as the *law of variable proportions*.

The law of increasing returns

This law states that, in the early stages of production, as successive units of a variable factor are combined with a fixed factor, both marginal and average product will initially rise. In other words, total output will rise *more than in proportion* to the rise in inputs.

The law of diminishing returns

This law simply states that as successive units of a variable factor are combined with a fixed factor, after a certain point both marginal product and average product will fall. In other words, total output will rise *less than in proportion* to the rise in inputs. Eventually total output will even diminish as marginal product becomes negative.

AN ILLUSTRATION OF THE LAWS OF RETURNS

The changing nature of returns to a variable factor can be seen in Table 3.1. We assume

No of workers	Total product	Average product	Marginal product
1	4	4	4
2	10	5	6
3	20	6.7	10
4	35	8.8	15
5	50	10	15
6	60	10	10
7	65	9.3	5
8	65	8.1	0
9	55	6.1	−10

Table 3.1 Changing nature of returns to a variable factor

that an increasing amount of labour works on a fixed quantity of land, that each worker is homogeneous, that is, identical to all other workers and that the techniques of production are unchanged.

It can be seen that up to the employment of the fourth worker the firm experiences increasing marginal returns because the increase in total product is *proportionately greater* than the increase in input of the variable factor. This is clearly shown by the rising marginal product of each worker up to the employment of the fourth worker. When marginal product is rising, the *rate of increase* of total product must also be rising. The main reason why firms experience increasing returns is that there is greater scope for division of labour as the number of workers employed increases.

Diminishing marginal returns set in *after* the employment of the fifth worker when it is clear that the *rate of increase* of total product, that is, marginal product, *begins to fall*. Diminishing returns set in because the proportions in which the factors of production are employed have become progressively less favourable, reflecting the fact that there are limits to the gains from specialisation. It is useful to note that diminishing *marginal* returns may occur before diminishing *average* returns. Even if the marginal product is falling, as long as it is above average product, average product will still rise (see top half of Fig. 3.3). Here diminishing average product ony sets in after six workers are employed.

RETURNS TO SCALE

In the long run there are no fixed factors and firms can vary the input of *all* factors of production. When this happens there has been a change in the *scale of production*. If a change in the scale of production leads to a *more than proportional* change in output, firms are subject to *increasing returns to scale*. For example, if all factor inputs are increased by 10 per cent and output grows by more than this, firms experience increasing returns to scale. These are more generally referred to as *economies of scale*.

> **Returns to scale cover the long run**

It is sometimes suggested that firms might experience *constant returns to scale* as output grows so that a change in all factor inputs results in an *equi-proportional* change in output. This is certainly possible but there is no doubt that for the vast majority of firms, as the scale of production increases beyond a certain level, economies of scale quickly give way to *diseconomies of scale* or decreasing returns to scale. Here a change in the input of all factors of production leads to a *less than proportional* change in output.

Firms are interested in changes in returns because, as we shall see, a change in returns implies a change in a firm's costs. For this reason, economies of scale are sometimes defined as those aspects of increasing size which lead to falling average costs, that is, cost per unit produced. Diseconomies of scale are those aspects of increasing size which lead to rising average costs.

SOURCES OF ECONOMIES OF SCALE

The sources of economies of scale are many and varied, but they are usually grouped into certain categories. More information on economies and diseconomies of scale is given at the end of this chapter in the answers to questions 1 and 2 (pp. 39–43).

Technical economies

These are common in manufacturing, since they relate to the scale of the production unit. There are several reasons why costs might fall as the scale of production increases, including:

- **Greater scope for division of labour:** the larger the size of the production unit the more men and machines are able to specialise. In the manufacture of motor cars and household durable goods such as televisions and washing machines, the production process can be broken down, in some cases into hundreds of small operations. This facilitates the use of flow line assembly techniques which can have a profound effect on productivity. This gives larger firms a considerable advantage over smaller firms.

- **Indivisibilities:** certain items of capital expenditure are relatively expensive and cannot be purchased in smaller or cheaper units, yet they may help raise output substantially. The installation of automatic electronic control systems in industry, although expensive, yields substantial increases in efficiency. The fact that such equipment is indivisible gives larger firms a considerable advantage over smaller firms

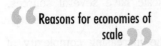

because the cost of such equipment is relatively high; but the *average cost* per unit of output falls dramatically as output expands. The use of computers in many large supermarkets to adjust stock levels as goods are sold yields considerable savings in labour time since up to the minute stock checks are now automatically available.

■ **Economies of linked processes**: most manufacturing output requires the use of more than one machine. Where machines work at different speeds, large firms are often able to operate more efficiently than small firms. In these circumstances it will require relatively high levels of output achieved by large firms to enable all the machines to be used to capacity. For instance, suppose two processes, A and B, are needed to produce an item; process A needs a machine which produces 20 units per hour, and process B needs a machine producing 50 units per hour. Only if output is as high as 100 units can both machines be fully used – with 5 machines in process A and 2 machines in process B. It is likely that, because of the cost involved, small firms will be unable to purchase machines in sufficient quantities to achieve the full utilisation of machinery. This will give the large firm an advantage over the small firm.

Marketing economies

Marketing embraces many activities, but the main economies of scale in marketing include:

■ **Economies from bulk purchases**: large-scale production requires the large scale input of raw materials. When firms place large orders for raw materials they are able to negotiate bulk discounts which substantially reduce the cost of each unit purchased. In other words the average cost of materials falls as the quantity purchased increases. The same reasoning explains why large retail chains can sell branded goods more cheaply than small independent retailers.

■ **Economies from bulk distribution**: where large quantities of output are to be transported, firms can often gain economies. For example, the average cost of transporting a given quantity of oil by sea is much lower when a single super tanker is used than when several smaller tankers are used. Similarly, the increasing use of articulated lorries is evidence that it is cheaper to transport in bulk when using the road network.

Financial economies

Large firms are frequently able to obtain finance more easily and on more favourable terms than smaller firms. Even a small reduction in the interest rates charged on borrowing, yields substantial savings where relatively large sums are involved.

Risk-bearing economies

A number of advantages can lead to large firms experiencing risk-bearing economies. However, the underlying factor is that large firms frequently engage in a range of *diverse* activities, so that a fall in the return from any one activity does not threaten the viability of the whole firm.

The law of large numbers involves a different kind of risk-bearing economy. Where demand for a firm's product is uncertain and subject to unpredictable changes, stocks of finished goods will be held to meet any unanticipated increase in demand. Large firms have a considerable advantage over smaller firms here since they are able to hold *proportionately* lower stocks of finished products, raw materials, spare parts for machinery and so on. For example, firms might well hold the same quantity of spare parts for a particular machine whether they have one machine or four or five, because not all machines will require the same spare part at the same time.

Managerial economies

This source of improved efficiency stems from the fact that large firms are able to offer the rewards necessary to attract the most capable staff whose ability and expertise may well lead to lower average costs.

SOURCES OF DISECONOMIES OF SCALE

While increases in scale frequently confer advantages on firms, in many cases there is a limit to the gains from growth. In other words, there is an optimum level of capacity and increases in scale beyond this level lead to *diseconomies of scale* which manifest themselves in rising average costs of production. Diseconomies of scale have several sources, including:

- **Managerial difficulties:** there is no doubt that the increasing complexity of managing large scale enterprises is a major source of inefficiency as firms grow beyond a certain size. Managerial expertise of the kind required to run larger and larger firms is relatively fixed in supply even in the long run and as firms grow beyond a certain size it becomes increasingly difficult to control and co-ordinate the various activities of planning, product design, sales promotion, and so on. This is especially true where a diverse range of products is produced and it is an important factor for explaining the emergence of diseconomies of scale.

- **Low morale:** organisations which employ large numbers of people sometimes suffer from low morale, perhaps because individuals feel they have little influence on decisions in large firms. Whatever the cause, low morale leads to high rates of absenteeism and a lack of punctuality. It may also lead to a lack of interest in the job which inhibits the growth of productivity and leads to a higher incidence of spoiled work which raises average costs of production and might lead to increased expenditure on quality control.

- **Higher input prices:** as the scale of production increases, firms require more inputs, and increasing demand for these might bid up factor prices. Additionally, when firms produce on a large scale and rely on full capacity utilisation of capital equipment to gain economies of scale, the power of trade unions is substantially increased. This might enable unions to negotiate wage awards in excess of the growth of productivity, thus increasing average labour costs.

- **Marketing diseconomies:** there may also be *diseconomies* associated with the efforts of firms to increase their market share beyond some particular level. It is often the case that firms which *already have* a significant market share, can only increase that market share by spending *proportionately* more on certain types of marketing expenditure. For example, if a firm has a market share of 75 per cent, an increase in *advertising expenditure* of even 100 per cent is unlikely to lead to a market share of 100 per cent. In other words the *advertising expenditure* per unit (that is, one percentage point) of additional market share rises as market share rises. Again, if a manufacturing firm with an 80 per cent market share attempted to supply the remaining retail outlets, including those with a small turnover in out of the way places, it would incur a more than proportionate increase in *distribution costs*. The point is clear. Beyond a certain market share, firms incur marketing diseconomies of scale and this would pull up long run marginal and average costs.

> " Greater size can bring problems "

COSTS OF PRODUCTION

THE SHORT RUN

In the short run it is possible to categorise the firm's costs as either fixed costs or variable costs. Clearly fixed costs are incurred on fixed factors of production and variable costs on variable factors.

Fixed costs

It is impossible to vary the input of fixed factors in the short run, therefore fixed costs do not change as output increases. Additionally, it is important to realise that fixed costs are incurred even when the firm's ouput is zero. Fixed costs include mortgage or rent on premises, hire purchase repayments, local authority rates, insurance charges, depreciation on assets, and so on. None of these costs is directly related to output and they are all costs which are still incurred in the short run, even if the firm produces no output. They are therefore sometimes referred to as *indirect costs* or *overheads*.

Because total fixed costs are constant with respect to output, *average fixed costs*, that is, total fixed costs divided by output, decline continuously as output expands (see Table 3.2). Diagrammatically, the behaviour of total fixed costs and average fixed costs as output expands are shown in Fig. 3.1.

Variable costs

Unlike fixed costs, variable costs are directly related to output. When firms produce no

OUTPUT	TOTAL FIXED	TOTAL VARIABLE	TOTAL	MARGINAL	AVERAGE VARIABLE	AVERAGE FIXED	AVERAGE TOTAL
0	100	0	100		0		
				50			
1	100	50	150		50	100	150
				45			
2	100	95	195		47.5	50	97.5
				40			
3	100	135	235		45	33.3	78.3
				30			
4	100	165	265		41.3	25	66.3
				15			
5	100	180	280		36	20	56
				10			
6	100	190	290		31.7	16.7	48.3
				5			
7	100	195	295		27.9	14.3	42.1
				10			
8	100	205	305		25.7	12.5	38.1
				20			
9	100	225	325		25	11.1	36.1
				40			
10	100	265	365		26.5	10	36.5
				60			
11	100	325	425		29.5	9.1	38.6
				85			
12	100	410	510		34.2	8.3	42.5

Table 3.2 Arithmetic example of short run change in costs as output expands

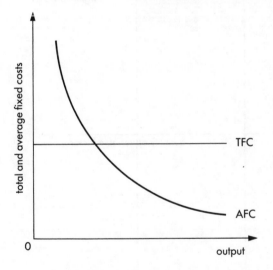

Fig. 3.1 The behaviour of fixed costs as output changes

Fig. 3.2 The behaviour of variable costs as output changes

Variable costs change with output

output they incur no variable costs, but as output is expanded variable costs are incurred. Because they vary directly with output these costs are sometimes referred to as *direct costs* or *supplementary costs*. Examples of these costs include costs of raw materials and power to drive machinery, wages of direct labour, and so on.

The relationship between marginal costs and variable costs

Marginal cost is the change in total cost when one more unit is produced, and is, therefore, entirely a variable cost. Because in the short run only the input of variable factors can be changed, it is clear that the sum of the marginal costs of producing each unit equals the total variable cost of production. Reference to Table 3.2 will confirm this.

Additionally, although variable costs vary directly with output, they are unlikely to vary proportionately because of the effect of increasing and diminishing returns. Fig. 3.2 shows the general shape of the total variable cost curve. It is clear that total variable costs at first rise less than proportionately as output expands and the firm experiences increasing returns. Subsequently, as the firm experiences diminishing returns, total variable costs rise more than proportionately as output expands.

The changes in total variable costs brought about by increasing and diminishing returns also imply changes in *average variable costs*. The relationship between average and marginal product and average variable and marginal cost is shown in Fig. 3.3. When the firm experiences increasing marginal returns, marginal product rises and marginal cost falls. Conversely, when the firm experiences diminishing marginal returns, marginal product falls and marginal cost rises. However, Fig. 3.3 also shows that when marginal cost is *below* average variable cost, the latter is falling, and when marginal cost is *above* average variable cost, the latter is rising. This is because in the short run marginal cost is the *addition* to total variable cost. When the last unit adds less to the total than the current average, then the average must fall; just as in any game, when your last score is less than your average, your average must fall. Average variable cost rises, however, when marginal cost lies above it. The implication is that the marginal cost curve cuts the *average variable cost* curve at its *minimum* point. (Similar reasoning explains why average product rises when marginal product is above it and falls when marginal product is below it, and why the marginal product curve cuts the average product curve at its maximum point.)

> ❝ Marginal product is related to marginal cost ❞

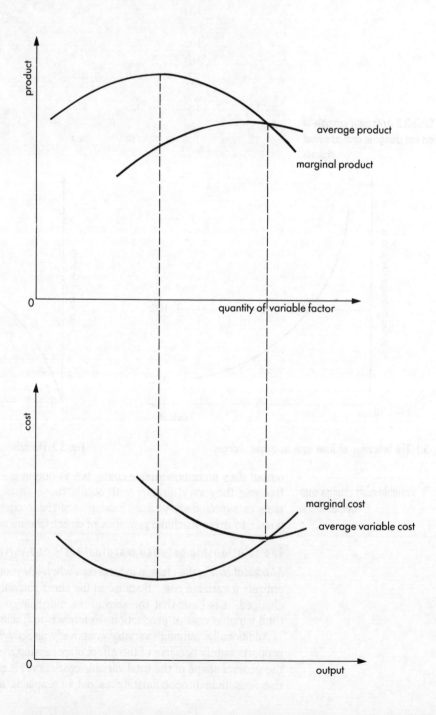

Fig. 3.3 The effect of changes in marginal and average product on marginal and average cost

Average total costs of production

These are more generally referred to simply as *average costs*, and for any given level of output they are obtained by dividing the total cost of producing that output by the level of the output itself. We know that *average fixed costs* fall continuously as output expands and that initially, because of increasing average returns, *average variable costs* fall. It follows that *average total costs* will initially fall. However, beyond a certain point average variable cost will begin to rise because of diminishing average returns, and once the rise in average variable costs more than offset the fall in average fixed costs, average total costs will rise. This is clearly shown in Fig. 3.4 which also shows that the marginal cost curve cuts the *average total cost curve* at the *minimum* point for exactly the same reason that it cuts the average variable cost curve at the minimum point. Table 3.2 (p. 33) provides an arithmetic example of how costs change in the short run as output expands.

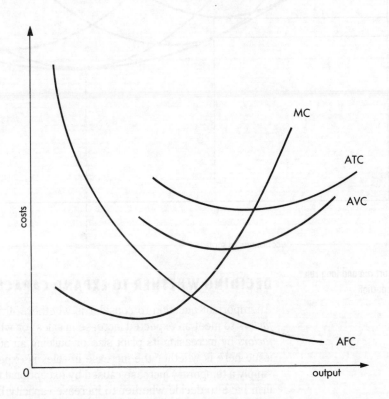

Fig. 3.4 The behaviour of different costs of production

THE LONG RUN

> *All factors can be varied in the long run*

In the *short run* the existence of fixed factors means that firms can only increase output by increasing the input of variable factors. In other words, firms have limited capacity. However, in the *long run* it is possible for firms to increase capacity. The most obvious reason for doing this is to make possible a greater level of output. However they might also increase capacity because this will lead to lower average costs of production (economies of scale). Fig. 3.5 shows the effect on costs of changes in capacity. Each SAC curve is a short-run average cost curve showing how average cost varies with output with some *given* level of capacity (i.e. the fixed factor capital).

If we consider an output OQ, it is clear that the firm can produce this with the level of capacity implied in SAC_1 at an average cost of OC_1 per unit. Alternatively, it could increase capacity to the level implied in SAC_2 giving an average cost of producing OQ units of OC_2. By increasing capacity the firm lowers its average cost of producing a *given* output.

More generally, by adjusting capacity in the long run, firms can minimise the cost of producing any *given* level of output. Indeed, the firm's long-run average cost curve (LAC) shows the minimum average cost of producing any given level of output after adjustments in capacity. It is therefore tangential to all the short-run average cost curves. For this reason the long-run average cost curve is sometimes referred to as an *'envelope curve'*, because it supports an infinite number of short-run average cost curves, each reflecting a different level of capacity.

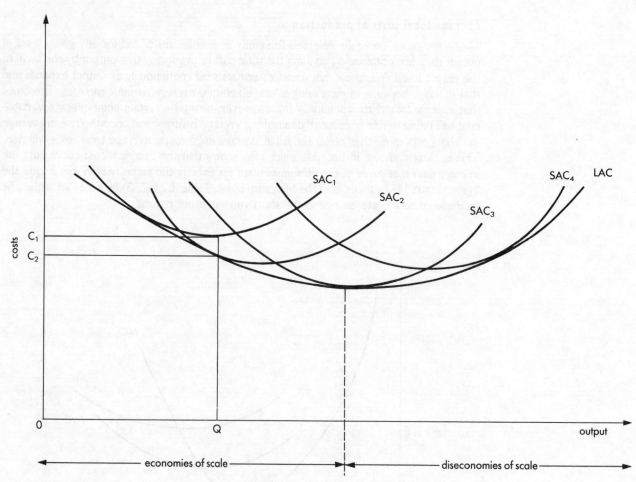

Fig. 3.5 Short run and long run costs of production

DECIDING WHETHER TO EXPAND CAPACITY

An important question to consider is whether a firm should increase the input of *variable factors* to meet an expected increase in sales, or whether it should increase the input of *all factors* by increasing its plant size or building an additional plant. Clearly the fundamental issue here is whether the increase in sales is expected to be permanent or whether it is simply a temporary increase caused by exceptional factors. Only in the former case will the firm have to decide whether to increase capacity by building an additional plant.

> ❝ Factors involved in planning decisions ❞

- If the firm's aim is to maximise profit, its decision about whether to expand capacity will depend on the behaviour of costs as output expands. In the *short run*, the crucial factor is whether it experiences increasing or diminishing returns as output expands. If the firm is experiencing increasing *average* returns, *average* cost will be falling, and in these circumstances there might be no cost advantage to the firm in changing the level of capacity. The firm is more likely to seek ways of raising output within the *current* level of capacity. This might involve using more labour, introducing overtime working, and so on, to raise output.

- If the firm is experiencing diminishing *average* returns, however, then *average* cost will be rising. Diminishing returns set in because it is impossible to increase the input of fixed factors in the short run. In the long run however, it is possible to vary the input of all factors of production and the option of increasing capacity by building an additional plant may well be considered by the firm. It may pursue this option if the increase in capacity leads to lower average costs of production because of economies of scale. In the long run, firms will adjust capacity to produce the required output for *economic* efficiency (maximum profits) in the most *technically* efficient (least cost) way.

THE LEAST-COST COMBINATION

So far, we have implicitly assumed that firms will aim to produce any given level of output in the cheapest possible way. This is a perfectly valid assumption when the ultimate aim of firms is to maximise profit. The combination of factor inputs which minimises the cost of producing any given level of output is referred to as the *least-cost combination*. It is achieved when firms have adjusted their inputs in such a way that for any factor of production, the ratio of its marginal product to price is exactly equal to the ratio of marginal product to price for all other factors of production. In other words, when:

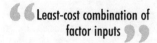
Least-cost combination of factor inputs

$$\frac{\text{marginal product of factor A}}{\text{Price of A}} = \frac{\text{marginal product of factor B}}{\text{Price of B}}$$

and so on, for all factor inputs.

When this condition is satisfied the last pound spent on each factor input yields exactly the same return in all cases. It follows that the cost of producing *any particular output* is at a minimum when this condition is satisfied. It would only be possible to reduce the total cost of producing that output if the last unit of one variable factor added more to total product than the last unit of any other variable factor, *per pound spent*. This is impossible when the marginal product/price ratios of all factor inputs are equal.

It follows from this that any change in the productivity or the price of a factor of production will lead to factor substitution. For example, if a firm uses two factors, labour and capital, and the price of labour rises while all other things remain equal, firms will cut back on their use of labour and increase their use of capital. This factor substitution will continue until equality between the marginal product/price ratios of both factors is restored.

THE FIRM'S REVENUE

Total revenue

The firm's total revenue (TR) is its total earnings from the sale of its product. Where firms produce a good which is sold to all consumers at the *same* price, total revenue is simply price (P) multiplied by quantity (Q) sold.

$$\text{Total Revenue} = \text{Price} \times \text{Quantity}$$
$$\text{TR} = \text{P} \times \text{Q}$$

Average revenue

This is simply total revenue divided by quantity sold. When firms sell their output to all consumers at the same price it is easy to show that price and average revenue (AR) are identical.

$$\text{Average Revenue} = \frac{\text{Total Revenue}}{\text{Total Output}}$$

$$\text{AR} = \frac{\text{TR}}{\text{Q}}$$

$$\text{AR} = \frac{\text{P} \times \text{Q}}{\text{Q}} = \text{P}$$

Marginal revenue

Strictly this is the *rate* at which total revenue changes as sales change. However, for practical purposes marginal revenue is usually defined as the change in total revenue from the sale of an additional unit.

APPLIED MATERIALS

Several studies confirm the existence of falling average costs as output expands up to a certain point. Most studies begin by identifying that level of output where average cost just reaches a minimum, often referred to as the *Minimum Efficient Size* (MES). The effect on cost of a given reduction in output can then be calculated.

GOVERNMENT GREEN PAPER

This approach was adopted by the government in their Green Paper entitled 'A Review of Monopolies and Mergers Policy' published in 1978. Annexe C of the Green Paper

PRODUCT	ESTIMATES OF MEPS*	UK – PRODUCED SALES OF PRODUCT	MEPS AS % OF UK PRODUCED SALES
Bread	30 sacks per hour 12–18 sacks per hour	2.2 million tonnes (17.3 million sacks)	about 1% about ½%
Beer	1 million bls p.a. 1–1.5 million bls p.a. 600,000 bls p.a.	35 million bls	about 3% 3–4% about 2%
Cigarettes	36 billion cigarettes p.a.	276 million lb (approx 170 billion cigarettes)	21%
Oil refining	10 million tonnes p.a. 5 million tonnes p.a.	114 million tonnes (crude input)	9% 4%
Detergent powder	70,000 tonnes p.a.	342,000 tonnes	20%
Steel	2–3 million tonnes p.a. 4–9 million tonnes p.a. 4 million tonnes p.a.	about 24 million tonnes (production)	8–12% 17–37% 17%
Electric cookers	300,000 units	1.04 million units	30%
Motor cars	½–1 million units p.a.	1.75 million units	29–57%
Commercial vehicles	20,000–30,000 units p.a.	416,000 units	5–7%
Bicycles	160,000 units p.a.	2 million units	8%
Aircraft	'Substantial economies of scale are available'		at least 100% (?)
Synthetic fibres	80,000 tonnes p.a. polymer manufacture	454,000 tonnes (production)	18%
Cotton and synthetic textiles	37.5 million sq. yd (288 Sulzer looms) 1,000 conventional looms	771 million sq. metres (production)	6%
Shoes	300,000 pairs p.a. 1 million pairs p.a. 1,200 pairs/day	189 million pairs	0.2% 0.5%
Building bricks	25 million p.a. 50–62.5 million p.a.	7,000 million bricks (5,580 million?)	0.4% 0.7%–0.9%
Cement	200,000 tpa (kiln capacity) 2 million tonnes p.a. 1.2 million tonnes p.a.	17.8 million tonnes	1% 11% 7%
Plasterboard	18–20 million sq. metres.	104 million sq. metres.	17–19%
Rubber tyres	5,000 tyres/day	30.3 million tyres (car & van)	about 6%

Table 3.3 Some engineering-type estimates of minimum efficient plant size (MEPS)*

*For several of the products listed more than one estimate is given.
Source: 1978 Green Paper. *A Review of Monopolies & Merger Policy. A Consultative Document,* HMSO 1978.

summarises the results of various studies into the extent of economies of scale in the UK. Table 3.3 presents a sample from the Review.

NEW SHARE ISSUE

Another illustration of how costs and size are related is given in Table 3.4 which shows how the cost of making a new issue of shares as a percentage of the amount raised *falls* as the *amount raised increases*. We shall see in Chapter 7 that shares are simply a stake in the ownership of a company, but here it is only important to note that the average cost of issuing shares falls as the size of the share issue increases. The data refers to the cost of making a fixed price offer for sale .

AMOUNT RAISED	NO OF FIRMS IN SAMPLE	AVERAGE COST %
Up to £3m	3	17.8
£3–5m	10	11.6
£5–10m	23	8.6
Over £10m	21	4.7

Table 3.4 Costs as a percentage of the amount raised

Source: Bank of England Quarterly Bulletin, Dec 1986.

EXAMINATION QUESTIONS

1 Define concisely total, average and marginal costs. Explain the relationship between the three types of cost. Should a firm cease production if it cannot cover its average costs?

(London, June 1987)

2 a) What are economies of scale? Illustrate your answer with examples. (7)
   b) Why are such economies only available in the long run? (8)
   c) Since economies of scale exists, why do long run marginal costs increase ultimately, as output increases? (10)

(Cambridge, November 1988)

3 a) Explain what is meant by the term 'production function' (7)
   b) Explain how a firm should choose its combination of factor inputs in order to minimise the cost of producing any given output. (8)
   c) Consider the effect on demand for capital by an industry if trade union activity succeeded in increasing real wages in the industry. (10)

(Welsh, June 1987)

4 a) Describe and explain the behaviour of a firm's average fixed cost and average variable cost as its output increases in the short run. (15)
   b) Explain how a firm may use knowledge of
      i) its marginal cost; and (5)
      ii) its average variable cost (5)
         in making decisions about its level of output in the short run.

(*Total 25 marks*)
(Scottish Higher, 1989)

A TUTOR'S ANSWER TO QUESTION 1

A firm's total cost of production is simply the total sum of all monetary costs incurred in producing a particular output. It is therefore the total fixed costs (such as rent on premises, insurance charges, interest payments, depreciation and so on) plus the total variable costs (such as raw material costs). This is sometimes written as:

$$TC = TFC + TVC$$

The average total cost of producing any given output is simply the total cost of producing that output divided by the level of output produced. This is sometimes written as:

$$ATC = \frac{TC}{Q} \qquad \text{(where } Q = \text{output)}.$$

We can also calculate the firm's average fixed cost and average variable cost. These are simply total fixed cost divided by output, and total variable cost divided by output, respectively. Again this is sometimes written as:

$$AFC = \frac{TFC}{Q}$$

$$and \ AVC = \frac{TVC}{Q}$$

and, by definition, $AFC + AVC = ATC$

Strictly, marginal cost is the rate at which total cost changes as output changes, but for practical purposes it is often measured as the change in total cost when the firm produces one more unit. It is sometimes written as $MC_n = TC_n - TC_{n-1}$. Because marginal cost is the cost of producing an additional unit, it is the additional variable costs the firm incurs as a result of the increase in output, and is unrelated to the firm's fixed costs of production.

Since marginal cost is the *rate* at which total cost changes as output changes it follows that when marginal cost is falling, total cost is rising at a *decreasing rate* because each additional unit produced adds less to total cost than the preceding unit. However, when marginal cost is rising, total cost is rising at an *increasing rate* because each additional unit produced adds more to total cost than the preceding unit. This relationship is illustrated diagrammatically below.

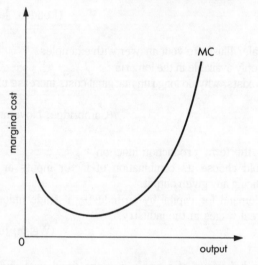
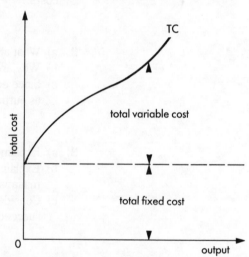

Fig. 3.6 Tutor's answer

At low levels of output, marginal cost falls as output expands because it is assumed that firms initially experience increasing returns to the variable factor. However, beyond a certain output the onset of diminishing returns results in rising marginal cost. The firm's marginal cost is therefore 'U' shaped and this accounts for the shape of the total cost curve.

The way marginal cost changes also affects the way average variable cost and average total cost change as output expands. When marginal cost is *falling*, total variable cost is rising. If marginal cost is *less* than average variable cost, then average variable cost must *fall* when marginal cost is rising it does not necessarily follow that average variable cost will be rising. If marginal cost is *less* than average cost, then average variable cost must *fall* because we are adding an amount to the total (when an additional unit is produced) which is *less than* the existing average (see Fig. 3.7). Conversely, when marginal cost is *above* average variable cost, average variable cost must *rise* because we are adding an amount to the total (when an additional unit is produced) that is *above* the existing average. It follows from this that the average variable cost is 'U' shaped and is cut from below at its minimum point by the marginal cost curve.

Similar reasoning explains why the average total cost curve is 'U' shaped and why it is cut at its minimum point by the marginal cost curve. Despite this the average total cost curve is different from the average variable cost curve because it also includes average fixed costs which fall continuously as output expands. This relationship between marginal cost, average variable cost and average total cost is illustrated diagrammatically in Fig. 3.7.

The distinction between fixed costs and variable costs is important in deciding whether firms should cease production. The firm is obliged to cover its fixed costs whether it undertakes production or not. For example, even when the firm produces no output it still incurs costs such as insurance charges, depreciation on assets, mortgage repayments,

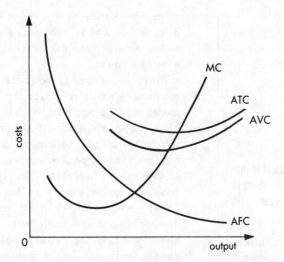

Fig. 3.7 Tutor's answer

rent on premises, and so on. However, variable costs are incurred only when the firm undertakes production. For example, when the firm produces no output it incurs no costs from purchasing raw materials or charges for power to drive the machinery, etc. Once a firm has incurred fixed costs its decision about whether to continue producing is therefore determined by whether its total revenue (the amount it earns from production) is sufficient to cover its total variable costs. Therefore, we must consider the circumstances in which the firm will be prepared to produce in the *short run* when fixed costs exist, and the circumstances in which it is prepared to produce in the *long run* when there are no fixed costs.

Economists treat fixed costs as bygones; that is, as something which has no influence on decisions taken by the firm in the short run. This is because fixed costs are the same whether or not the firm undertakes production or not. If total revenue *just covers* the total variable (running) costs incurred by producing, then the firm is neither better off nor worse off if it continues production. Clearly if total revenue is *greater than* total variable costs, then the firm makes at least *some* contribution towards covering the fixed costs already incurred by continuing in production. To cease production would leave the firm with a loss equal to its fixed costs, whereas if the firm undertakes production it will at least have a surplus over variable costs to set against its fixed costs, therefore incurring a smaller loss.

If the total revenue is *less than* total variable cost on the other hand, then the firm will be better off by ceasing production altogether. In this situation the firm's total loss is equal to its fixed cost by not producing, compared with a loss equal to the deficit of variable costs *added* to the fixed costs if it undertakes production.

If total revenue *exactly covers* total variable costs this implies that average revenue, that is, price, exactly covers average variable costs.

Firms will therefore undertake production in the short run if the *price* at which their product is sold is at least equal to the average variable cost of production. When *average revenue* and *average variable cost* are equal, *total revenue* is exactly equal to *total variable cost*. However, unless price at least covers the *average total cost*, firms experience a loss in the long run, where fixed costs count. By definition, when average revenue *exactly equals* average total cost, firms break even. While they will be prepared to accept losses in the *short run* as long as total variable costs are covered, they cannot accept losses in the *long run*. Therefore if firms are to continue in production in the long run, the price at which their product is sold must *at least equal* the average total cost of production.

A STUDENT'S ANSWER TO QUESTION 2

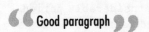

Good paragraph

a) Strictly, firms change the scale of production when there is an equi-proportionate increase in the input of all factors of production. When this leads to a more than proportionate increase in output, firms are said to experience economies of scale. However, it is the effect of this on average cost which is important and, assuming there is no change in the prices of the factors of production, when output rises by proportionately more than inputs, the firm's average costs of production must fall.

Because of this, economies of scale are more generally defined as those advantages of increasing size which lead to falling average cost.

There are several sources of economies of scale. *Technical economies* are particularly important in manufacturing. For example, the production line in a modern car plant provides the classic example of *division of labour*. In some cases the production line is almost a mile long and workers along its entire length perform a single or a small number of tasks. The production line also illustrates the principle of *indivisibilities*. It is impossible to have half a production line! Another example of this principle is the employment of specialist staff such as tax accountants in large firms where their specialised abilities can be fully utilised. This is not possible in smaller firms because an individual is not divisible into smaller parts.

Firms might also reap substantial *marketing economies*. Particularly important here are the discounts available on bulk purchases. The actual discounts granted to firms is a well kept secret, but its effect is readily observed in the lower prices charged for many goods by the larger retail outlets. There are also substantial economies available from *advertising*, especially for firms which produce a variety of products such as manufacturers of household electrical equipment. Here advertising costs per unit are *usually lower for larger firms* than for smaller firms. But there is another advantage. Advertising one product also advertises the firm's name, which is likely to have a positive effect on the sales of its other products at no extra cost.

Large firms have an undoubted advantage over smaller firms when raising finance. Quite apart from the fact that they have more assets to pledge as security, they are statistically less likely to default on a loan. Because of this, they are considered to be more credit-worthy borrowers and lower rates of interest are available to them.

Risk-bearing economies stem partly from firms diversifying. There are many examples of this. For example, the Imperial Group produces among other things, cigarettes, potato crisps, plasterboard, whisky, and so on. Another kind of risk-bearing economy is the *law of large numbers* which can be observed in the proportionately smaller number of idle vehicles a bus company maintains to cover unforeseen events such as a breakdown, as compared with a smaller bus company.

b) For purposes of analysis economists distinguish between the *short run* and the *long run*. This classification takes account of the fact that it is not always easy for firms to change the input of all factors of production and sometimes this can only be achieved after the elapse of a considerable period of time. When firms are unable to change the input of a particular factor of production this factor is described as a *fixed factor*, whereas an input which can readily be increased is described as a *variable factor*. In the long run all factors of production are variable and therefore the short run exists when the firm has at least one fixed factor of production.

Any factor of production can be fixed. Skilled labour is often difficult to recruit and certain items of capital equipment such as an oil-refinery or a dry dock can take a considerable period of time to construct. When firms have a fixed factor of production any increase in output is only possible by employing additional units of variable factors and working the fixed factor more intensively. However, the existence of the fixed

---

Margin annotations:

66 The main point is that efficient units only come in relatively large sizes 99

66 An individual is divisible as a unit of labour. It depends on the number of hours worked 99

66 Why? 99

66 Good paragraph 99

66 Why? 99

66 Make reference to the time period 99

66 Only in the short run 99

factor indicates that it is impossible for firms to change the scale of production because this requires a change in the input of *all* factors of production. Since it is impossible for firms to change the scale of production in the short run, economies of scale can only exist in the long run.

❝ Good paragraph ❞

c) While firms sometimes experience economies of scale as they grow, beyond a certain point they are likely to experience diseconomies of scale. In these circumstances long run average costs increase as firms grow. For average costs to be rising long run marginal costs must be rising and indeed must be above long run average costs.

There are many reasons why firms might experience diseconomies of scale. A very important source of such diseconomies is the inability of individuals to manage firms with the same degree of competence as they grow. In large organisations there are several departments, controlling and coordinating the activities of these becomes increasingly difficult and is often done less efficiently than in smaller firms. Falling levels of efficiency will put up long run marginal and average costs of production.

Another important factor is that as profit seeking organisations grow they will exploit the most profitable opportunities first. However, as they grow they might be forced to accept higher costs. For example, a farmer producing wheat will use the most productive land first but in order to produce more might be forced to draw into production land that is less and less productive. Similarly manufacturing firms might initially locate in the least cost site but as they grow they might have to located in higher cost sites. This will clearly raise long run marginal and average costs of production.

❝ Well illustrated ❞

It is also possible that larger firms will suffer a greater incidence of lost days through strikes and absenteeism. It is sometimes suggested that a possible reason for this is that workers in large firms feel they have less influence on the activities of the firm and are less committed to it. If this is true it would certainly explain why firms experience higher long run average costs beyond a certain size. Indeed, because of the widespread application of the principle of division of labour, the absence of a few key workers can cause severe disruption to production.

Firms might also experience marketing diseconomies as they attempt to increase their market share beyond a certain size. Beyond a certain level each additional pound spent on marketing activities such as advertising has decreasing impact on sales. As market share grows it becomes increasingly difficult to attract consumers away from alternative brands or to persuade additional customers to enter the market.

❝ This is an excellent answer. Many different examples are used to illustrate points and a very sound understanding is displayed throughout ❞

OUTLINE ANSWERS TO QUESTIONS 3 AND 4

3   a) A production function simply shows the relationship between the output of a good and the inputs, that is, factors of production, required to produce that output. Typically production functions are used when studying the behaviour of firms, such as the effect on output of an increase in costs or the effect on costs of an increase in output. In algebraic form production functions are often written as:

$$Q = f(L,K,T)$$

Where $Q =$ output, $L =$ labour, $K =$ capital and $T =$ technology.

The simplest type of production is that which shows increasing and diminishing returns as more labour is used in production, as on p 29.

b) This part of the question is analysed under the heading 'Least Cost Combination' on p 37.

c) An increase in real wage rates raises the cost of labour relative to capital. If there is perfect substitutability between capital and labour the rule is simply to equate the marginal productivity/price ratios as analysed on p 37 and this would imply an increase in the demand for capital. However, in practice there is unlikely to be perfect factor substitutability and where capital can only be purchased in large and expensive units there will not necessarily be any change in the demand for capital. Another point to consider is that the substitution of capital for labour implies redundancies. Where there is effective trade union resistance to this there will not necessarily be any change in the demand for capital. Firms' expectations of future demand are also important. If they expect demand for the product to fall in the future they might not be willing to purchase additional capital. The importance of each of these factors must be considered in some detail. However, while these factors might explain why there is not *perfect* substitutability between capital and labour, there is plenty of evidence that capital is substituted for labour.

4 a) In answering this part of the question it is necessary to define average fixed costs and average variable costs. Average fixed costs decline continuously in the short run as output expands but, as we have seen, the behaviour of average variable costs is dictated by the laws of returns. In answering this part of the question it is necessary to explain *why* costs behave as they do and in particular to stress the relationship between the behaviour of returns and the behaviour of short run variable costs.

b) The importance of marginal costs to firms has been explained earlier. In answering the second part of b), it is necessary to explain that if firms are to continue production in the short run, their total revenue must at least cover their total variable costs. This implies that price must be ⩾ average variable cost. Knowledge of variable costs could therefore influence decisions in the short run.

Further reading

Begg, Dornbusch and Fischer, *Economics* (2nd edn), McGraw-Hill 1987: Ch.6, Output, supply by firms: revenue and costs, Ch. 7, Developing the theory of supply: costs and production.
Stanlake, *Introductory Economics*, (5th edn) Longman 1989: Ch. 6, Costs of production, Ch. 7, The scale of production.

DEMAND, SUPPLY AND PRICE

GETTING STARTED

This chapter is about the determination of market prices. A market can be defined as any arrangement which brings buyers and sellers of particular products into contact. The collective actions of buyers for a particular product establishes the market demand for that product, and the collective actions of sellers establishes the market supply. The interaction of these forces of demand and supply, i.e. market forces, establishes the market price for any given product.

Care must be taken in using the terms demand and supply because they have very precise meanings. Demand does not simply mean the desire to possess. It also means the willingness and ability to purchase articles. Effective demand is therefore the desire to possess something, backed up by the ability to pay for it. However, it is not enough to know the quantity demanded and supplied at particular prices. The time period is also relevant. Producers, for example, are interested in the time period over which demand will materialise. To say that demand is 1,000 units at a price of £2 is an incomplete statement. We need to know whether this quantity will be demanded per day, per week, per month, etc.

At any moment in time, demand and supply are expressed as functions of price. In other words, any other factors which might affect demand or supply are assumed to be constant. The implication of this are discussed later, but because it is a common source of confusion it is emphasised here.

ESSENTIAL PRINCIPLES

THE LAW OF DIMINISHING MARGINAL UTILITY

❝ An important law ❞

Economists equate the term utility with satisfaction. Utility is important because economists assume that only goods and services which possess it, i.e. which confer satisfaction, will be demanded. Additionally, economists assume that consumers 'act rationally' and this implies that they aim to maximise their total utility, that is, to gain as much utility as possible, given the limited income they possess and the prices they face. *The law of diminishing marginal utility* simply states that as consumption of a product increases, each successive unit consumed confers less utility than the previous unit. In other words, as consumption increases, marginal utility falls.

CONSUMER EQUILIBRIUM

Equilibrium can be thought of as a state that exists when there is *no tendency to change*. In the present context equilibrium will exist when consumers achieve their aim, that is, maximise satisfaction given their limited income. When this is the case they will have no incentive to change the quantities of the different goods and services they currently purchase because to do so will result in a reduction in the amount of satisfaction they receive from their purchases. In other words consumer equilibrium exists when a consumer *cannot* increase his total utility by reallocating his expenditure. This occurs when the following condition is satisfied:

❝ The condition for maximum utility ❞

$$\frac{MU_A}{P_A} = \frac{MU_B}{P_B} = \frac{MU_n}{P_n}$$

Where MU = Marginal Utility
P = price
A, B, n = goods purchased

This condition simply implies that consumer equilibrium exists when the ratios of marginal utility and price are equal for all goods consumed. When this condition is satisfied, it is impossible for the consumer to increase his total utility by rearranging his purchases because the last pound spent on each good yields the same addition to total utility in all cases. This must maximise total utility because, for example, if the last pound spent on product B yielded *more* utility than the last pound spent on product A, then the consumer could increase his total utility by buying more of B and less of A. This is impossible when the ratios of marginal utility and price are equal, as is illustrated in Table 4.1. It is assumed

QUANTITY CONSUMED	GOOD A			GOOD B		
	PRICE (£)	TOTAL UTILITY	MARGINAL UTILITY	PRICE (£)	TOTAL UTILITY	MARGINAL UTILITY
1	2	15	15	4	25	25
2	2	27	12	4	48	23
3	2	37	10	4	68	20
4	2	46	9	4	86	18
5	2	53	7	4	102	16
6	2	56	3	4	116	14
7	2	57	1	4	128	12
8	2	55	-2	4	139	11

Table 4.1 Ratios of marginal utility and price

that only two goods, A which costs £2 per unit and B which costs £4 per unit, are available, and that the consumer has a total budget of £18. Given the consumer's budget, the existing prices, and the levels of utility available from consumption, equilibrium is achieved when 3 units of good A and 3 units of good B are purchased:

i.e. $\dfrac{MU_A}{P_A} = \dfrac{MU_B}{P_B}$ with $\dfrac{10}{2} = \dfrac{20}{4}$

With a budget of £18 it is impossible to achieve a higher level of utility by varying the combination of A and B consumed. For example, if we bought one *less* B and two *more* A with the income released, total utility would fall.

THE DEMAND CURVE

THE INDIVIDUAL'S DEMAND CURVE

Once achieved, equilibrium can only be disturbed if there is a change in some factor that influences the level of consumer satisfaction. This could be the result of a change in the consumer's income, a change in the prices of other goods and services available to consumers, a change in the range of quality of goods and services available, and so on. However, since at any moment in time all factors that affect demand, other than price, are assumed to be constant, it is changes in *price* which are important to us at present. More specifically, the question we have to answer is this; if all other things remain unchanged, how will a change in the price of one good affect the amount of the good a consumer purchases?

We can answer this question by looking again at Table 4.1. using the information given here let us consider what would happen to the amount of good B consumed if there was a reduction in its price from £3 per unit to £2 per unit, and all other things remained unchanged. Because the consumer's aim is to maximise utility, his reaction to the price reduction is predictable. He will simply rearrange his purchases so as to achieve equilibrium following the price reduction. Applying the equilibrium condition:

$$\frac{MU_A}{P_A} = \frac{MU_B}{P_B}$$

> **A lower price will mean greater consumption**

leads to the conclusion that (with income still £18) the consumer will increase his consumption of good B to 7 units, and cut consumption of A to 2 units. When this is done the equilibrium condition is satisfied because:

$$\frac{MU_A}{P_A} = \frac{MU_B}{P_B} \text{ with } \frac{12}{2} = \frac{12}{2}$$

This rearrangment of purchases occurs because as the price of one product falls, the price of obtaining a given level of satisfaction from consuming that product also falls. The price per unit of satisfaction (i.e. utility) obtained from a product therefore becomes cheaper after a price reduction, and a consumer will react by increasing consumption of the product whose price has fallen. The implication is that for the individual consumer, price and quantity demanded vary inversely. This general relationship is illustrated in Fig. 4.1.

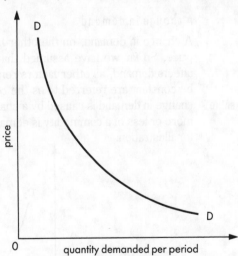

Fig. 4.1 A typical demand curve

So widely applicable is the inverse relationship between price and quantity demand that we refer to Fig.4.1 as a *normal* demand curve. Any other demand curve is referred to as *exceptional* since it is an exception to the general rule that price and quantity demanded vary inversely. Exceptional demand curves are considered later in the chapter.

MARKET DEMAND CURVES

The total market demand for a commodity at any given price is simply the total amount demanded by each consumer at that price. Market demand curves are therefore simply the horizontal summation of each individual's demand curve. Since, for each individual, quantity demanded varies inversely with price, this general relationship will be embodied in the market demand curve. A typical, or normal, market demand curve therefore has the same general shape as the individual's demand curve, illustrated in Fig. 4.1.

A CHANGE IN QUANTITY DEMANDED AND A CHANGE IN DEMAND

Great care must be taken in the use of these terms because, although they appear similar, they imply entirely different things.

A change in quantity demanded

For any product a change in quantity demanded is *always caused by a change in its price*. A change in quantity demanded therefore refers to a movement along an *existing* demand curve. Fig. 4.2 is used as a basis for illustration.

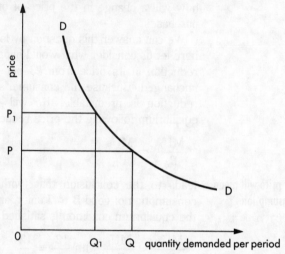

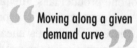

Fig. 4.2 A rise in price leads to a contraction of demand and a fall of price leads to an expansion or extension of demand

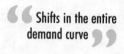
Moving along a given demand curve

If price rises from OP to OP₁ quantity demanded falls from OQ to OQ₁. This is referred to as a reduction in quantity demanded or a *contraction* of demand, that is, demand contracts from OQ to OQ₁. No other term can be used to describe this. Conversely, if price falls from OP₁ to OP, quantity demanded rises from OQ₁ to OQ. This rise in quantity demanded can also be referred to as an *extension* or *expansion* of demand, since demand extends (expands) from OQ₁ to OQ. Again, either of these terms is acceptable, but no other term can be used in this context.

A change in demand

A change in demand, on the other hand, is caused by a change in some factor other than price. So far we have assumed that at any moment in time price is the only factor that affects demand, all other factors remaining constant. These factors which are assumed to be constant are referred to as the *conditions of demand*, or the parameters of demand. A change in demand is caused by a change in the conditions of demand and means that either more or less of a commodity is demanded at *each and every price*. Fig. 4.3 is used as a basis for illustration.

Shifts in the entire demand curve

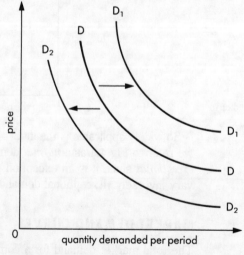

Fig. 4.3 A change in the conditions of demand

Demand for this commodity is initially represented by DD. A movement, or shift in demand to the right, to D₁ D₁ is referred to as an *increase in demand* because a greater amount is demanded at any given price than previously. Conversely, a movement, or a shift in demand to the left, from DD to D₂D₂, is referred to as a *decrease in demand* because a smaller amount is demanded at any given price than previously.

Causes of changes in demand

A change in demand is always caused by a change in at least one of the conditions of demand. These include:

Reasons why demand curves do shift

- **Changes in disposable income**: this is one of the most important determinants of demand. An increase in disposable income, that is, income available for spending will lead to an increase in demand for most goods and services. There are exceptions (see below and p.57) but rising income is undoubtedly the most important reason why demand for most goods and services increases (an outward shift of the demand curve) over time.

- **Changes in the price of substitutes**: many goods are substitutes for one another. For example, a glance round the shelves of any supermarket will show that for most foodstuffs there are many competing brands. In this situation a rise in the price of one good will lead to a *contraction* in the quantity of that good demanded and an *increase* in the demand for its substitutes. The relationship between substitute goods is referred to as *competitive demand*.

- **Changes in the price of complements**: certain goods are jointly demanded. Fish and chips, bread and butter, gin and tonic, are all examples of complements. In these cases a rise in the price of one good will lead to a *contraction* in the quantity of that good demanded and a *decrease* in the demand (inward shift of the demand curve) for the complement.

- **Changes in the weather**: some goods are demanded seasonally and at certain times of the year demand for these goods will increase. Christmas cards, fireworks and Easter eggs are obvious examples, but more generally there is greater demand for ice-cream in the summer than in winter, while there is greater demand for overcoats in winter than in summer. Changes in seasons thus cause *changes in demand* for certain goods and services.

- **Changes in tastes and fashions**: for certain products, such as clothes, changes in fashions can bring about marked changes in demand. The more fashionable a good becomes, the more demand for it will increase, and vice versa.

- **Changes in population**: changes in the *size* of a country's population bring about changes in the demand for most goods and services. However, changes in the *structure* of the population, such as the age and sex profiles, will also lead to quite substantial changes in demand for most goods and services.

- **Advertising**: an increase in a firm's effective advertising will cause an increase in demand for the product being advertised.

EXCEPTIONAL DEMAND CURVES

It is sometimes suggested that in some cases demand might vary directly with price. Some reasons suggested for this include:

Some unusual demand curves

- **Giffen's Paradox**: the English economist Giffen is credited with the idea of suggesting that in subsistence economies, if the price of basic foodstuffs such as bread and potatoes increases, quantity demanded will also increase. One possible reason for this is that as price rises the higher price makes it impossible for consumers to purchase better quality foodstuffs. They therefore substitute the poorer quality foodstuffs despite the fact that the price of these has increased! Despite its appealing logic, there is no empirical evidence to support this hypothesis and indeed it is uncertain why it is referred to as Giffen's paradox since there is no evidence that he even suggested the idea!

- **Veblen goods**: in this case it is argued that the attractiveness of some goods increases as their price increase. It is argued that some goods are purchased for ostentatious purposes and as their price rises so does their attractiveness because they provide a means of displaying superior wealth. Alternatively it is possible to argue that if consumers believe that the price of a good reflects its quality then quantity demanded might increase as price increases. In other words, consumer ignorance might provide an explanation for exceptional demand curves.

SUPPLY

The total market supply of any commodity at a particular price is equal to the total amount that all individual firms which produce that commodity will supply at that price. The market supply curve is therefore the horizontal summation of all individual firms' supply curves. In other words we simply add the amount that every firm supplies at each and every price. Like demand curves, supply curves are drawn on the assumption that all factors that affect supply, except price, are constant.

A CHANGE IN QUANTITY SUPPLIED

Economic theory indicates that market supply and price vary directly. In other words, that a greater amount is supplied at higher prices than at lower prices. There are two main reasons for this:

- It is assumed that firms produce for profit, and, other things being equal, at higher prices it becomes more profitable to expand output.
- At higher prices it becomes possible for *marginal firms*, that is, firms which cannot cover their costs at lower prices, to undertake production. As price rises, more firms enter the industry and market supply rises.

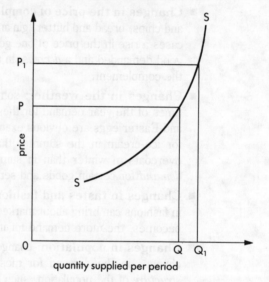

Fig. 4.4 A normal supply curve showing an extension or expansion of supply when price rises and a contraction of supply when price falls

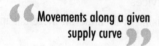

Movements along a given supply curve

A normal supply curve is illustrated in Fig. 4.4. It is important to stress that the same rules used when describing demand apply when describing both movements along a supply curve and movements of a supply curve. Thus when price rises in Fig. 4.4 from OP to OP$_1$, there is an *expansion* or *extension* in the quantity supplied from OQ to OQ$_1$. Conversely, a fall in price from OP$_1$ to OP leads to a *contraction* in quantity supplied from OQ$_1$ to OQ.

A CHANGE IN SUPPLY

Shifts in the entire supply curve

A change in supply implies a *complete shift of an existing supply curve*. When more is supplied at any given price than previously we refer to an *increase* in supply. This is illustrated in Fig. 4.5 by a movement of the supply curve to the right from SS to S$_1$S$_1$.

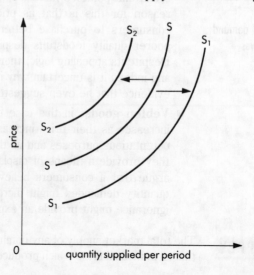

Fig. 4.5 A change in the conditions of supply

When less is supplied at any given price than previously, we refer to a *decrease* in supply. This is illustrated by a movement of the supply curve to the left, from SS to S_2S_2 in Fig. 4.5.

Causes of changes in supply

Changes in supply such as those illustrated in Fig. 4.5 can only be caused by a change in at least one of the conditions of supply. The most important causes of a change in supply are considered below.

■ **Changes in costs of production** If all other things remain equal, a change in costs will change the level of profit available from producing any particular commodity.

> **"Reasons why supply curves do shift"**

● Specifically, a rise in costs will reduce profits and lead some firms to cut back on output, while other firms will cease production altogether. So, if all other things remain equal, a rise in costs of production will lead to a *decrease* in supply.

● Conversely, a fall in costs will lead to higher profits at any given price and so will lead to an *increase* in supply.

● Despite this, it is possible to pay a higher reward to any factor of production and yet leave costs of production unchanged. For example, a 5 per cent increase in wages which is accompanied by a 5 per cent increase in productivity will leave average labour costs unchanged and therefore the supply curve will not move. However, when costs rise by *more than productivity*, this will lead to a decrease in supply, and when costs rise by *less than productivity* there will be an increase in supply.

■ **Changes in the prices of other commodities**. Some goods such as beef and hides are jointly supplied. This simply means that it is impossible to supply one good without also supplying the other good. In these circumstances, a rise in the price of one good will lead to an *increase* in the supply of the other.

For example, if the price of beef rises, there will be an *expansion* in the quantity of beef supplied. This in turn will lead to an *increase* in the supply of hides, since *at any given price* for hides more hides are now being supplied.

■ **Changes in the weather**. This can have important repercussions on the supply of certain agricultural commodities.

● Favourable weather conditions can produce a bumper harvest of certain commodities and a consequent increase in supply.

● Conversely, unfavourable weather conditions will lead to a poor harvest and a decrease in supply.

■ **Changes in indirect taxation and subsidies**.

● A rise in indirect taxation such as a higher rate of VAT, will have the same effect on producers as a rise in costs of production. It will reduce the profit available to producers at any given price, and will consequently lead to a *decrease* in supply. In fact, the effect will be to shift the entire supply curve vertically upwards by the full amount of the tax.

The following example illustrates this, and for simplicity we assume the imposition of a lump sum tax of £1 per unit.

PRICE (£)	QUANTITY SUPPLIED BEFORE TAX	QUANTITY SUPPLIED AFTER TAX
7	145	125
6	125	105
5	105	90
4	90	

After the tax is imposed, producers receive £1 less than previously at any given price. They will therefore supply at each price the amount they would have previously supplied at a price of £1 less. For example, when producers receive £4 per unit, they will supply 90 units. After the tax is imposed, producers actually receive £4 per unit when the market price is £5. They will therefore only supply, at a market price of £5, what would previously have been supplied at a market price of £4.

● A subsidy has exactly the opposite effect. It represents a payment to suppliers in addition to any revenue received from sales and therefore raises the amount of profit obtained from supplying any given level of output. In the case of a specific subsidy such as £1 per unit, the effect will be to shift the supply curve vertically downwards by the full amount of the subsidy.

THE DETERMINATION OF MARKET PRICE

In free markets, prices are determined by the interaction of demand and supply. With given demand and supply functions only one price is sustainable. This is the *equilibrium price*, and it is the only price at which demand and supply are equal. This is illustrated in Fig. 4.6.

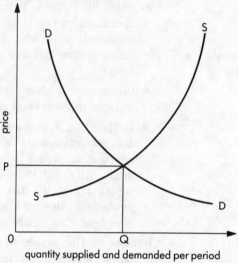

Fig. 4.6 Market equilibrium

quantity supplied and demanded per period

> Equilibrium means a state of rest

With demand and supply given by DD and SS respectively the equilibrium price is OP, because it is the only price at which supply and demand are equal. At prices above OP, supply exceeds demand and there is a market surplus of this commodity. The existence of this surplus will cause the price to fall. As the price falls producers will cut back production (supply contracts) and consumers will purchase more (demand expands) until supply and demand are equal at quantity OQ. Conversely, at prices below OP there is a market shortage and this shortage will cause the price to rise. The higher price will persuade producers to expand output. Only when the price is OP is there equilibrium in the market, with no tendency for producers or consumers to revise their decisions.

CHANGES IN MARKET PRICE

We have seen that prices are determined by demand and supply. It follows that once equilibrium has been established, prices can only change if there is a *change* in the conditions of demand and/or supply. This is fairly straightforward. However, it is essential to be clear about the *causes* of changes in price, otherwise it is impossible to predict the *effects*.

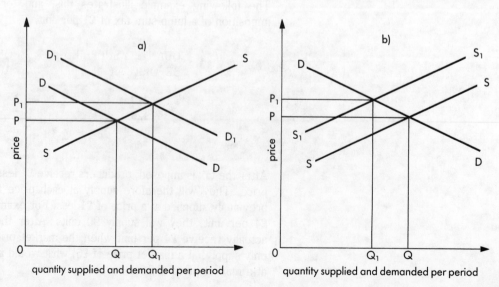

Fig. 4.7a) The effect of an increase in demand

Fig. 4.7b) The effect of a decrease in supply

quantity supplied and demanded per period

quantity supplied and demanded per period

Fig. 4.7 shows that it is possible for different causes of a rise in price to have different effects.

Fig. 4.7a) shows the effect of an *increase in demand* from DD to D_1D_1. Price rises from its original equilibrium of OP to OP_1 and there is a rise in the equilibrium quantity demanded and supplied from OQ to OQ_1.

Fig. 4.7b) on the other hand, shows the effect of a *decrease in supply* from SS to S_1S_1. Again, there is a rise in price from OP to OP_1 but this time there is a fall in the equilibrium quantity supplied and demanded from OQ to OQ_1. Clearly, the effect of a rise in price on equilibrium output depends on the cause.

PRICE ELASTICITY OF DEMAND (PED)

This is usually referred to simply as elasticity of demand. It measures the responsiveness of quantity demanded to changes in price. Elasticity of demand can be measured in several ways but it is most commonly measured as:

$$\text{Price E of D} = \frac{\text{percentage change in quantity demanded}}{\text{percentage change in price}} = \frac{\triangle Q/Q \,.\, 100}{\triangle P/P \,.\, 100}$$

or

$$\text{Price E of D} = \frac{\triangle Q}{Q} \div \frac{\triangle P}{P} = \frac{\triangle Q}{Q} \times \frac{P}{\triangle P}$$

$$= \frac{P}{Q} \times \frac{\triangle Q}{\triangle P}$$

Where the elasticity of demand is less than 1, demand is said to be *inelastic* and where it is more than 1, demand is said to be *elastic*. The larger the value of elasticity, the more responsive is quantity demanded to changes in price.

In most cases a given demand curve does not possess a constant elasticity. In fact, the value of elasticity associated with a *given price change* varies all the way along a given demand curve. This is illustrated in Fig.4.8.

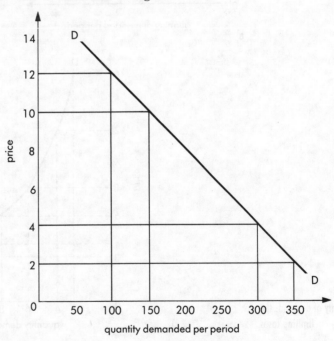

Fig. 4.8 The changing value of elasticity of demand

price

quantity demanded per period

For the straight line demand curve $\triangle Q/\triangle P$ is a constant $= {}^{50}\!/_2 = 25$

At price $= 2$, price E of D $= {}^2\!/_{350} \times 25 = {}^1\!/_7$

At price $= 4$, price E of D $= {}^4\!/_{300} \times 25 = {}^1\!/_3$

So even if the demand curve is a straight line, price elasticity of demand varies along its entire length, since the ratio P/Q varies; in fact P/Q rises as price rises, so that elasticity of demand rises as we move up the demand curve. If the demand curve is not a straight line, the ratio $\triangle Q/\triangle P$ will vary *as well*!

> **Elasticity can vary along the demand curve**

Note: strictly speaking price elasticity of demand is negative for all normal demand curves because a *rise* in price leads to a *fall* in quantity demanded and vice versa. However, the negative sign is usually omitted and this convention is followed here.

ELASTICITY: THE LIMITING CASES

There are three exceptions to the general rule that the value of elasticity varies along the length of a demand curve. The three exceptions are illustrated in Fig. 4.9.

- In Fig. 4.9a) a change in price has no effect on quantity demanded and, therefore, demand is totally inelastic.

- In Fig. 4.9b) any increase in price leads to an infinitely large change in quantity demanded and therefore, demand is said to infinitely elastic.

- In Fig. 4.9c) the proportionate change in quantity demanded is exactly equal to the proportionate change in price that brings it about along the entire length of the demand curve. Elasticity of demand is therefore equal to unity at all points along the entire length of the demand curve.

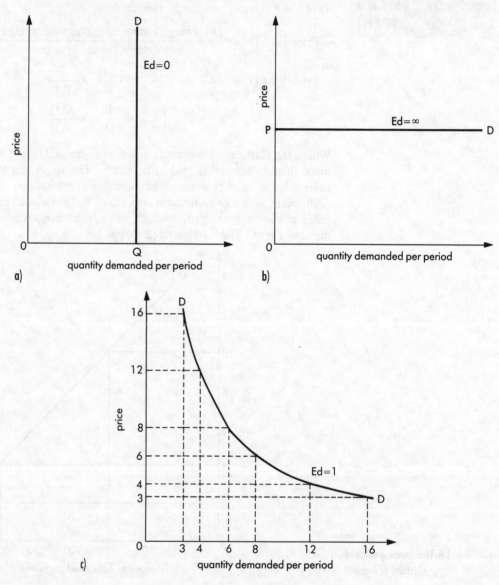

Fig. 4.9 Elasticity of demand: the limiting cases

ELASTICITY OF DEMAND AND TOTAL REVENUE

Elasticity of demand has a crucial bearing on the way total revenue is affected by a change in price. The following relationships exist:

> **"Price elasticity of demand will affect total revenue"**

- When demand is inelastic (PED<1), a rise in price leads to a rise in total revenue and a fall in price leads to a fall in total revenue.

- When demand is elastic (PED>1), a rise in price leads to a fall in total revenue and a fall in price leads to a rise in total revenue.

- When demand has unit elasticity (PED=1), a rise or fall in price has no effect on total revenue.

DETERMINANTS OF PRICE ELASTICITY OF DEMAND

There are several factors which influence the value of price elasticity of demand for any particular product. The most important of these are summarised below.

The availability of substitutes

This is probably the most important determinant of elasticity of demand for any particular product. When there are few close substitutes available for any particular product, demand will tend to be less elastic and therefore less responsive to changes in price. For example, demand for petrol in *total* is less elastic than demand for any *particular brand* of petrol.

The proportion of income spent on the commodity

"Factors affecting price elasticity of demand"

When the cost of a commodity is a relatively small proportion of total expenditure, demand will tend to be less elastic. For example, spending on pencils accounts for a very small part of total expenditure. Consequently a rise in the price of pencils would have little impact on total expenditure, and we would therefore expect demand for pencils to be little affected by a change in their price – i.e. demand to be relatively inelastic.

The number of uses the commodity has

When a commodity has several uses, demand will tend to be less elastic. For some of these uses a change in price is likely to have or no effect on quantity demanded. For example, electricity has many uses and this is one reason why demand for electricity tends to be inelastic.

Whether the commodity is a necessity or a luxury

It is difficult to define what is meant by the terms necessity and luxury. However, if a good is considered a necessity, demand for it will tend to be inelastic. Demand for luxuries will be more elastic.

Whether the commodity is habit-forming

Some goods, such as cigarettes, are habit-forming and in these cases demand will tend to be less elastic.

Time period

For most goods demand is less elastic in the short run than in the long run. For example, a rise in the price of domestic gas is likely to have only a minor effect on consumption in the short run. In the longer run, economies can be made by wearing warmer clothing around the house, by better insulation, by switching to electricity for cooking and heating, etc, so that demand may then become more responsive to changes in price.

PRICE ELASTICITY OF SUPPLY (PES)

Just as elasticity of demand measures the responsiveness of a change in quantity demanded to a change in price, so elasticity of supply measures the responsiveness of a change in quantity supplied to a change in price. Elasticity of supply is measured in the same basic way as elasticity of demand, except, of course, we measure changes in quantity supplied.

i.e.   Price E of S = $\dfrac{\text{\% change in quantity supplied}}{\text{\% change in price}}$

or   Price E of S = $\dfrac{P}{Q} \times \dfrac{\triangle Q}{\triangle P}$

Again, there are three exceptions to the general rule that elasticity of supply varies along the entire length of the supply curve. These are illustrated in Fig. 4.10.

- In Fig. 4.10a) elasticity of supply is zero because any change in price has no effect on the quantity supplied.
- In Fig. 4.10b) elasticity of supply is infinite because an increase in price leads to an infinitely large change in quantity supplied.
- In Fig. 4.10c) elasticity of supply is unity because any change in price leads to an equiproportionate change in quantity supplied. (This is true of any straight line supply curve passing through the origin.)

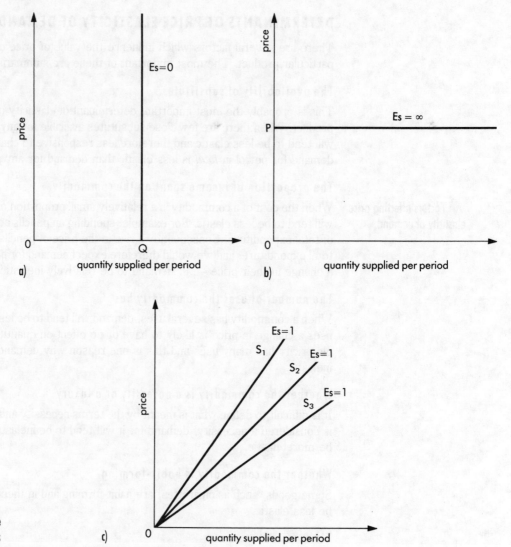

Fig. 4.10 Elasticity of supply: the limiting cases

DETERMINANTS OF ELASTICITY OF SUPPLY

The main determinants of elasticity of supply are briefly summarised below.

The time period

This is an important factor and in general supply is more elastic in the long run than in the short run. In fact, economists identify three time periods:

- *The momentary period* is so short that it is impossible to expand supply. Supply is completely inelastic in the momentary period as when a trawler lands its catch at the quay.

- *The short period* during which it is possible to expand supply by using more of the variable factors. For example, trawlers might stay at sea longer and take on additional crew members. However, the existence of fixed factors limits the scope for increased output. Supply is, therefore, relatively less elastic during the short run.

- *The long period* during which all factors are variable and supply is therefore more elastic than in either of the previous situations. Here it is possible to have more trawlers as well as additional crew members and so on.

66 **Factors affecting elasticity of supply** 99

Factor mobility

Although supply is more elastic in the long run, the degree of elasticity will still partly depend on factor mobility. The greater the mobility of the factors of production, the greater the elasticity of supply. For instance, a rise in the price of a good, due, say, to an increase in demand, raises the producer's profits. If he can easily attract land, labour and capital from other uses by offering higher rewards (i.e. factors are mobile) then he will be more able to expand supply in response to the higher price.

Availability of stocks

Where a product can be stored without loss of quality or undue expense, supply will tend to be elastic, at least while stocks last. This explains why the supply of processed food will tend to be more elastic then the supply of fresh food.

Behaviour of costs as output changes

When firms are subject to relatively small increases in average costs as output expands, supply will tend to be more elastic. However, if firms experience diminishing returns or diseconomies of scale which are severe enough, costs will rise steeply as output expands and in these circumstances supply will tend to be less elastic.

The existence of surplus capacity

Even if average costs do increase by small amounts as output increases, supply might be relatively inelastic if firms do not have surplus, or unused, capacity. If they are operating at full capacity it will be impossible to bring about significant changes in output in the short run.

Barriers to entry

In certain cases it might be difficult for additional firms to enter an industry and undertake production. These barriers might take a variety of forms (see pp. 72–3) but their existence will tend to make supply less elastic than otherwise.

INCOME ELASTICITY OF DEMAND

This measures the responsiveness of demand to changes in *income*.

i.e.

$$\text{Income E of D} = \frac{\text{\% change in quantity demanded}}{\text{\% change in income}}$$

> **Inferior goods have negative income elasticities**

For most goods income elasticity of demand will be positive, that is, a rise in income will lead to an increase in demand. However, there are exceptions to this rule, and for some goods a rise in income leads to a decrease in demand. Such goods are referred to as *inferior goods* or *Giffen goods* (see p. 49). By and large inferior goods consist of cheaper but poorer quality goods that lower income groups purchase. Bread is one of the most often quoted examples of an inferior good, being regarded in the UK as a poor quality substitute compared with other staple items such as meat, fish, etc. The consumption of bread has declined markedly in the western world as incomes have increased and this supports the view that bread is regarded as an inferior good in the western world.

> **Giffen goods and inferior goods are different**

Note: all Giffen goods have a negative *income elasticity of demand* so they are inferior goods. However, Giffen goods also have positive *price elasticity of demand*.

CROSS ELASTICITY OF DEMAND

This is a measure of the responsiveness of *demand for one good* to a change in the *price of another*.

i.e.

$$\text{Cross E of D} = \frac{\text{\% change in quantity demanded of good X}}{\text{\% change in price of good Y}}$$

> **The sign of cross elasticity of demand is important**

- If the cross elasticity of demand between two goods is positive, the goods are *substitutes*; a rise in the price of say, good Y, leads to an increase in the demand for good X. Moreover, the greater the positive value of cross elasticity between two goods, the greater the degree of substitutability between them.

- If the cross elasticity of demand between two goods is *negative*, the goods are *complements*; a rise in the price of, say, good Y leads to a decrease in demand for good X. Again, the higher the negative value of cross elasticity between two goods, the greater the degree of complementarity between them.

APPLIED MATERIALS

COMMON AGRICULTURAL POLICY (CAP)

A widely documented case study on the use of *minimum prices* is the Common Agricultural Policy (CAP) operated by the EC. Basically minimum prices are established for agricultural

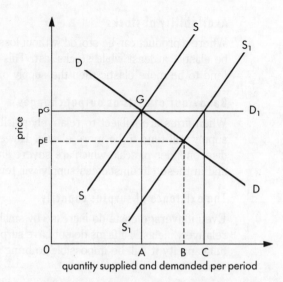

Fig. 4.11 The operation of a
guaranteed price support scheme

commodities. If prices fall below the minimum level, farmers sell to 'intervention agencies' which buy up the surplus at the guaranteed minimum price. In other words demand is perfectly elastic at the guaranteed minimum price! This is illustrated in Fig. 4.11

In Fig. 4.11 the free market supply and demand curves are represented by DD and SS resectively and the equilibrium price in a free market would be P^G. However, suppose P^G is also the minimum price guaranteed to producers by the authorities, and, in order to maintain this minimum price, the authorities are prepared to purchase any excess supply. The demand curve for this product therefore becomes DGD_1. For example, if a bumper harvest results in a shift in supply to S_1S_1, in a free market, price would fall to P^E. To *prevent* this the authorities purchase the excess supply AC at the guaranteed minimum price. In the real world, such purchases by the *intervention agencies* has led to the notorious beef, butter and grain mountains as well as the milk and wine lakes.

In practice it is difficult to distinguish between a *shift* in a demand curve and a *movement along* a demand curve, since the latter occurs when all factors which affect demand, other than price, are constant. In the real world this is an impossible condition to achieve. Consequently, when more of any commodity is sold this could imply an *increase* in demand, an *expansion* (*extension*) of demand, or, indeed, a combination of both. In the latter case it is extremely difficult to quantify the relative effect of each.

ANNUAL REPORT OF THE NATIONAL FOOD SURVEY COMMITTEE

Values for income and price elasticities of demand for foodstuffs are published in the *Annual Report of the National Food Survey Committee*. Table 4.2 shows estimates of the value of *income elasticity of demand* and *price elasticity of demand* for certain foodstuffs. Of the foodstuffs listed, fresh fruit has the highest income elasticity of demand at 0.66, which implies that for each one per cent rise in income, expenditure on fresh fruit rises by 0.66

ITEM	INCOME ELASTICITY OF DEMAND 1987	PRICE ELASTICITY OF DEMAND* 1982–87
Liquid milk	−0.13	0.13
Cheese	0.26	−1.53
Carcase meat	0.21	−1.17
Fresh fruit	0.66	−0.53
Bread	−0.18	−0.25
Cakes and pastrie	0.07	−0.86
Beverages	−0.05	−0.28
Fresh potatoes	−0.43	−0.14

* The negative elasticity coefficient arises because for all normal goods price and quantity vary inversely. A rise in price leads to a fall in quantity demanded, and vice versa. For convenience the negative coefficient is ignored in most texts.

Table 4.2 Income and price
elasticities of demand

Source: Household Food Consumption and Expenditure 1987, Annual Report of the Food Survey Committee, HMSO.

Elasticity with respect to the price of beef and veal, mutton and lamb, and pork.

	BEEF & VEAL	MUTTON & LAMB	PORK
Beef & Veal	1.24	−0.06	0.10
Mutton & Lamb	0.15	−1.75	0.03
Pork	0.25	0.03	−1.86

Table 4.3 Some cross elasticities of demand

Source: Household Food Consumption and Expenditure 1987, Annual Report of the Food Survey Committee, HMSO

per cent. The *negative* income elasticity of demand for fresh milk, bread and fresh potatoes implies that these are inferior goods, although *within* each category there might be exceptions. For example, the demand for *brown* bread is likely to have a positive income elasticity of demand.

Table 4.3 provides estimates of *cross price elasticities of demand* for beef and veal, mutton and lamb, and pork. In general these statistics are consistent with conventional economic theory. The *positive* cross price elasticity of demand for beef and veal with respect to pork implies that these foods are considered to be *substitutes*. A one per cent rise in the price of beef and veal causes a 0.1 per cent increase in the demand for pork. Notice however, the *negative* cross price elasticity of demand for beef and veal with respect to mutton and lamb. This implies that these foods are considered to be *complements*, with a one per cent rise in the price of beef and veal causing a 0.06 per cent fall in the consumption of mutton and lamb! No-one would seriously suggest that this was true. A more likely explanation is that the estimate is inaccurate. Gathering accurate *real world data* to illustrate some of the relationships known to exist can sometimes be very difficult indeed.

EXAMINATION QUESTIONS

1   Examine the factors which could be expected to determine the price of houses in a free market. (50)

   To what extent can government policies affect house prices? (50)

   (Total 100 marks)

   (London, June 1989)

2   The demand for potatoes tends to be inelastic in response to changes in both price and income.'

   a) What do you understand by the term 'elasticity of demand'? (5)

   b) Why is this concept important to the sellers of goods and services? (10)

   c) What factors can affect the price elasticity of demand for a good or service? (10)

   (Total 25 marks)

   (Scottish Higher, 1987)

3   What is meant by market disequilibrium?

   Describe and illustrate the circumstances in which such a disequilibrium might be

   a) temporary,

   b) persistent.

   (AEB, Nov 1987)

4   In 1977 a severe frost seriously depleted the coffee harvests in Brazil, the world's largest coffee producing country, and resulted in a decrease in world coffee production

of approximately 20%. The repercussions in the coffee market in the USA, the world's largest coffee consuming nation, are shown in the table below:

	1976	1977
Price ($/lb)	2.01	3.20
Quantity (lbs)	12.8	9.4

Prices are in 1976 dollars (i.e. adjusted for general inflation between 1976 and 1977). Quantities are in pounds of coffee per head per year consumed in the USA.

Source: Begg, Dornbusch and Fischer, *Economics*, British Edition (Mcgraw Hill).

a) Explain why the increase in the price of coffee in the USA in 1977 can plausibly be seen as a consequence of the frost damage to the Brazilian harvest. *(6)*

b) Assuming that changes in the incomes and tastes of consumers in the USA can be ignored, what do the data suggest about the price elasticity of demand for coffee in the USA? *(6)*

c) What effect on the incomes of world coffee producers, in 1977, is suggested in the data? *(6)*

d) What means of permanently raising the incomes of world coffee producers is suggested by the 1977 experience? Why would such means be difficult to implement in practice? *(7)*

(Total 25 marks)
(Welsh, 1989)

A TUTOR'S ANSWER TO QUESTION 1

In a free market prices are determined by the interaction of supply and demand. For normal goods, demand is inversely related to price whereas supply is directly related to price. Since a house is a normal good the diagram below can be used to illustrate the determination of price in a typical housing market. The supply of housing in this market is represented by SS and DD represents the demand for housing. The equilibrium price in this market is OP and no other price is sustainable. At prices greater than OP, supply of housing exceeds demand and this excess supply will pull price down. At prices below OP, demand for housing exceeds supply and the excess demand will pull prices upwards. In a free market the price of this type of housing will therefore be OP.

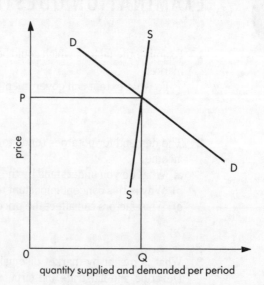

Fig. 4.12 Tutor's answer

However, in order to better understand the determination of house prices it is necessary to analyse the factors that determine supply and demand in both the short run and the long run. In the short run the supply of housing will be relatively inelastic, so that changes in the price of housing will have relatively little effect on the amount available. In the short run there is a fixed stock of housing since it takes a considerable period of time to purchase suitable land, obtain planning permission and construct additional housing. In other words, in the short run, supply is determined by the willingness of house owners to sell from *existing* housing stock. Any rise in property prices might encourage an *extension* of supply if it persuades property owners to renovate and sell housing not currently occupied because it is in a state of disrepair. It might also be possible to persuade house owners to sell property not currently occupied because it is kept as a second home or held with the intention of selling when prices rise. However, neither of these is likely to have a significant impact on market supply and, therefore, supply will tend to be relatively inelastic in the short run.

Demand on the other hand will tend to be relatively elastic, that is, responsive to changes in price, assuming sufficient funds are available for house purchase. However, there are two factors which are relevant when we consider the cost of house purchase. Clearly there is the *actual purchase price* of the house. But since most people borrow the funds to buy a house it is also necessary to consider the *rate of interest* charged on funds borrowed for this purpose. As recent experience demonstrates, the price of housing can change rapidly, even in the short term. As house prices rise, demand will tend to *contract* though if prospective buyers expect prices to *go on rising* in the future any increase in house prices might not discourage buying significantly.

Of far more significance in the short term are changes in the rate of interest. Again recent experience demonstrates that interest rates can change rapidly and that such changes can have a dramatic effect on the demand for housing. As interest rates rise the amount of funds that must be committed to meet interest payments each month increases and this discourages people from buying a house. The *availability* of mortgage finance is also an important factor influencing demand for housing. In the past shortages of funds have led to a lower demand for housing than otherwise might have been the case.

In the *long run* the supply of housing is much more elastic. The most important factor here is the amount of housing started in the *previous period*. The higher the price of housing, the greater the rewards to those who build them and therefore the greater the incentive to purchase land for development purposes and to construct additional housing. The increased supply in the longer period has an important impact on price. If all other things remain equal, the greater the number of housing starts in one period the lower the price of housing when these are completed, though whether prices actually fall depends on demand. These issues are considered later.

Another important factor in the long run is sales of council housing. Such sales take a considerable amount of time to organise and so are not relevant in the short run. However, in the long run such sales represent a considerable increase in the supply of housing available for purchase. This has been an important factor influencing supply in the last decade, with successive conservative governments placing much more emphasis on private ownership of housing than previous governments had.

In the long run the most important factor determining demand for housing is the level of *real disposable income*, because this determines the ability to borrow. Because real disposable income tends to rise over time, the demand for private housing rises over time, more than offsetting the effect on demand of increases in the cost of housing. The diagram overleaf (Fig. 4.13) is used to illustrate the possible effects of changes in supply and demand on the price of houses.

SS and DD show the initial supply and demand curves for housing in one period. S_1S_1 shows an increase in market supply in the future brought about by an increase in the number of housing starts in the previous period. If there is no change in demand, the effect is to pull down the price of housing from OP to OP_1. This might also reduce the number of housing starts (which will have an effect on house prices in the future). On the other hand, it is possible that as incomes increase the demand for house ownership will increase, and this is illustrated by a shift in demand to D_1D_1. In this case house prices rise to OP_2 – despite the increased supply!

As previously implied the government can have a powerful impact on the price of housing. Two ways in which they might exert influence on house prices have already been discussed, namely by encouraging sales of council houses and by changes in the rate of interest. However, there are many other ways in which the government might influence house prices. Since they do not directly control house prices their influence is exerted by policies which result in changes in the supply or demand for housing.

Within limits, certain tax concessions are given on interest charges on funds borrowed

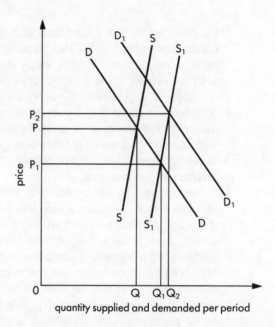

Fig. 4.13 Tutor's answer

for house purchase. Currently an owner-occupier is able to deduct the interest paid on a house mortgage loan up to a maximum of £30,000 from gross income before income tax is calculated. By *changing the limits for tax concessions* governments can change the cost of buying a house. For example, if the government increases the amount of tax relief available to those who borrow funds to purchase a house, this will reduce the cost of house purchase and might be expected to increase the demand for housing.

Another way in which the government might influence the demand for housing is by introducing (or removing) *rent controls* which will alter the relative price of renting accommodation compared with house ownership. If it becomes more attractive to rent rather than buy accommodation, there will be a reduction in the demand to purchase housing. However, the existence of rent controls by reducing the return to landlords might persuade them to sell property rather than offer it for rent and this would increase the supply of housing on the market. If all other things remain equal, the combined effect would be a reduction in the price of housing. Removing controls would have the opposite effect, and might persuade landlords to refurbish and rent out property previously left empty.

A different way in which governments might influence the price of housing is by *changing building regulations*, making it easier or more difficult to obtain planning permission for the construction of additional housing. Easier planning permission would most likely lead to an increase in the supply of housing, so influencing the price of housing. Similarly the introduction or raising of *grants to renovate derelict property* might be expected to increase the supply of housing.

Clearly the government has great power to influence the price of housing, especially through changes in the rate of interest. *However, in the long run the main determinant of demand for house ownership is real disposable income.* The government is unable to vary this simply to bring about changes in the demand for housing, even if it wished to. This, therefore, limits the ability of the government to control house prices in the long run.

A STUDENT'S ANSWER TO QUESTION 4

a) The world's supply of coffee fell by approximately 20 per cent from the level that existed in 1976. Such a substantial reduction in supply will lead to higher coffee prices in the world's largest consuming country, especially in the short run, because lack of available substitutes will tend to make demand for coffee relatively inelastic. This situation is illustrated diagrammatically.

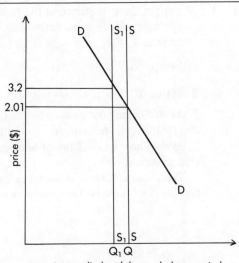

Fig. 4.14 Student's answer

> Explain why you have drawn the supply curve with zero elasticity

> Explain *why* demand is inelastic, i.e. why PED < 1

> Good point

> Good

> It might be possible for the government to set up a single buying agency which would then export coffee and exploit its monopoly position

Supply and demand for coffee are initally represented by SS and DD respectively. The reduction in supply subsequently shifts the supply curve to S_1S_1, and, given the relatively inelastic demand for coffee, price rises from $2.01 per pound to $3.2 per pound.

b) Elasticity of demand is a measure of the reponsiveness of demand to changes in price. It can be measured using the formula $\%\triangle Q/\%\triangle P$. Using the information we are given we can calculate elasticity of demand as 26.6%/59.2% = 0.45 approx. Demand for coffee in the USA is, therefore, inelastic.

c) Since we are only given data about the USA it is impossible to calculate the effect of the reduction in the supply of coffee on the incomes of the world's coffee producers. However, since the USA is the largest consumer of coffee, the data we are given is likely to be useful as a guide to the impact on the incomes of the world's coffee producers. Because demand for coffee in the USA is inelastic, a rise in price will result in a rise in expenditure on coffee and therefore will lead to a rise in the incomes of coffee producers. When demand is inelastic a rise in price will lead to a proportionately smaller fall in quantity demanded so that total expenditure increases following the price increase.

d) The answer to part c) suggests that one way of permanently increasing the incomes of world coffee producers would be to permanently raise the price of coffee. This would mean bringing about a permanent reduction in the supply of coffee. However, in practice, there are many small producers of coffee and this would make it virtually impossible to bring about a reduction in the total supply of coffee.

> A good answer – brief and to the point

OUTLINE ANSWERS TO QUESTIONS 2 AND 3

Question 2

a) You should begin by explaining that elasticity is a measure of responsiveness of changes in quantity demanded to changes in price (price elasticity of demand) and income (income elasticity of demand) and that the larger the coefficient of elasticity the greater the change in quantity consumed following a change in price or income. You should also show how elasticity can be calculated.

b) Elasticity of demand is important to producers for a variety of reasons (although they might not necessarily be aware of how to calculate elasticity). For example, you should explain the importance of the relationship between price elasticity of demand and total revenue and the importance of income elasticity of demand in estimating which products are most likely to benefit from future increases in real income.

c) See p. 55.

Question 3

You could begin your answer to this question by explaining that equilibrium is a state of rest and that there is no tendency to change once equilibrium is reached. You could then go on to explain how an equilibrium price is achieved in free markets starting with a situation of disequilibrium.

The *cobweb theorem* is useful in explaining the circumstances when disequilibrium in a free market might be temporary or permanent. Fig. 4.15 is used to illustrate this point. In

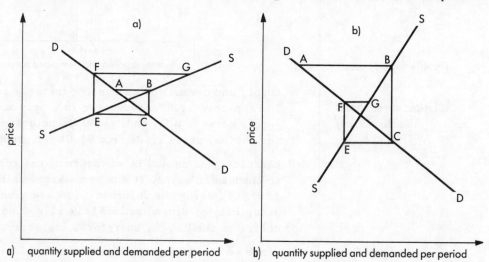

Fig. 4.15a) An explosive cobweb
b) A converging cobweb

Figs. 4.15a) and 4.15b) SS and DD represent the long run supply and demand conditions for a particular commodity. Let us consider the effect in both cases of an increase in price above the long run equilibrium price caused by a temporary reduction in supply, perhaps because of an usually poor harvest. We begin at point A. The higher price encourages increased production of size AB. However, since there is no change in demand the excess supply will force price down and we move to point C. This represents a lower price than anticipated and consequently producers will cut back on production and we move to point E. The reduction in the amount supplied implies a market shortage at the lower price and so price rises. We move to point F and so on. Note that Fig. 4.15a) shows a *converging* cobweb so that each change in production results in a move closer to long run equilibrium while Fig. 4.15b) shows an *explosive* cobweb where each change results in a move further away from equilibrium. You must explain the causes of this in terms of differences in the elasticities of demand and supply in each case.

You could also mention the conditions which would give rise to a cobweb process. In cases where there are many buyers and many sellers of a product and it is easy for producers to increase or reduce production (perfect competition, see Chapter 5) we might expect to find adjustment to long run equilibrium following this sort of pattern.

Another factor that might give rise to market disequilibrium is government intervention in the economy. For example, price controls in many eastern-bloc countries has led to disequilibrium in many markets for food. This is illustrated by the existence of shortages, long queues and even physical rationing in some cases! Such disequilibrium will continue until the price mechanism is allowed to function more freely.

Further reading

Begg, Fischer and Dornbusch, *Economics*, (2nd edn) McGraw-Hill 1987: Ch. 3, Demand, supply and the market; Ch. 4, The effect of price and income on demand quantities; Ch. 5, The theory of consumers choice.

Beardshaw *Economics: A student's Guide*. (2nd edn) Pitman 1989: Ch. 9, Demand and Utility; Ch. 10, Elasticities of demand and supply; Ch. 11, Markets in movement; Ch. 12, Agricultural prices: a case study.

Maunder et al, *Economics Explained*. Collins 1987, Ch. 5, Demand and supply; Ch. 7, Demand and supply elasticity.

CHAPTER 5

PERFECT COMPETITION AND MONOPOLY

PERFECT COMPETITION

COMPETITIVE EQUILIBRIUM

MONOPOLY

BARRIERS TO ENTRY

PRICE DISCRIMINATION

PERFECT COMPETITION AND MONOPOLY – A COMPARISON

APPLIED MATERIALS

GETTING STARTED

Before embarking on this chapter you should ensure that you fully understand the operation of market forces as explained in Chapter 4. You should also understand the behaviour of costs as output changes, the distinction between fixed and variable costs and the relationships between average, marginal and total values as explained in Chapter 3.

We have already seen in Chapter 4 that in free markets prices are determined by supply and demand. However, this generalisation does not imply that price determination is completely beyond the influence of all firms (or consumers). If firms are able to influence supply and/or demand conditions for their product, they can clearly influence the price at which that product is sold. In fact, we shall see that the influence of any particular firm on the price of its product depends largely on the number of competing firms in the industry and the type of product sold. Differences in these two factors give rise to different market forms and these are usually categorised as *perfect competition, monopoly, monopolistic competition* and *oligopoly*. The latter three are classed as *imperfect markets* because firms are able to exercise some degree of control over price. The former market is classed as *perfect* in the sense that any *individual* seller or buyer is powerless to influence the price of its product.

Perhaps the major reason why economists are interested in market structure is not so much to understand the behaviour of firms, important though this is, but rather the fact that different market structures lead to differences in the allocation of resources. The pattern of resource allocation in one market structure might be considered preferable in certain ways to the pattern in a different market structure. With this in mind we proceed to an analysis of perfect competition and monopoly. Other forms of imperfect competition are considered in the following chapter.

PERFECT COMPETITION

ESSENTIAL PRINCIPLES

CONDITIONS FOR A PERFECTLY COMPETITIVE MARKET

A market is said to be perfectly competitive when buyers and sellers believe that individually their own behaviour has no influence on market price. The conditions which give rise to this particular market structure may be summarised as:

■ There are large numbers of both buyers and sellers in the market, each buying or selling such a small amount of the product that individually they are powerless to influence market demand or market supply.

■ Consumers are indifferent from whom they make purchases because all units of the commodity are homogeneous. In other words, they regard the product that an individual firm supplies as a perfect substitute for the product that any other firm in the same market supplies.

■ There is perfect knowledge of market conditions among buyers and sellers so that each is fully informed about the prices producers in different parts of the market are charging for their product.

■ Buyers are able to act on the information available to them and will always purchase the commodity from the seller offering the lowest price.

■ There are no long run barriers to the entry of firms into the market, or their exit from the market.

> **The assumptions of perfect competition**

These conditions are never fully satisfied in the real world but some markets display many of the characteristic features of perfect competition. For example an individual farmer has little influence on the price of potatoes. (Buyers are well informed about prices, the product is homogeneous and the individual farmer produces only a small proportion of the total market supply.)

THE MARKET AND THE FIRM

These conditions ensure that in perfectly competitive markets all firms charge an identical price for their product. Any firm attempting to charge a price above that of its competitors will face a total loss of sales. This will occur because consumers are aware of the higher price the firm is attempting to charge and, since the product is homogeneous, they will have no particular preference for this firm's product.

On the other hand, perfectly competitive firms have no incentive to lower the price of their product since they can sell their entire output at the existing market price. The firm in perfect competition is therefore a *price taker*, that is, it accepts the market price as beyond its control. Because of this, all firms in perfectly competitive markets perceive their own demand curves, and the demand curves of their competitors, to be perfectly elastic at the ruling market price. Fig. 5.1 shows the determination of market price in a perfectly

> **The firm in perfect competition is a price-taker**

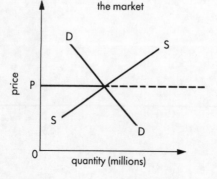
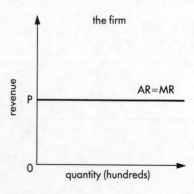

Fig. 5.1 The relationship between the market price and the firm's demand curve in perfect competition

competitive market and the individual firm's demand curve at this price. Market supply and market demand are represented by SS and DD respectively. Given these supply and demand conditions the ruling market price is OP, and the firm perceives its own demand curve to be perfectly elastic at this price.

AVERAGE AND MARGINAL REVENUE

Because the firm sells its entire output at the ruling market price, each additional unit of output sold adds exactly the same amount to total revenue as each preceding unit sold. Therefore, for the firm in perfect competition, marginal revenue is constant at all levels of output and equal to market price. We shall see later that this relationship between price and marginal revenue, which is usually expressed in the form Price (AR) = (MR), is peculiar to firms in perfectly competitive markets.

"Here AR = MR"

COMPETITIVE EQUILIBRIUM

SHORT RUN EQUILIBRIUM 1: SUPERNORMAL PROFIT

Profit maximisation

Since the firm is powerless to change the price of its product, it maximises profit by adjusting output to the point where marginal revenue equals marginal cost. Fig. 5.2 shows the market equilibrium, and the short run equilibrium position of the individual firm in perfect competition.

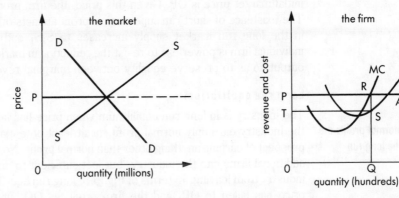

Fig. 5.2 Short-run equilibrium: supernormal profit

Given the price and costs shown in Fig. 5.2, the firm's equilibrium (i.e. profit maximising) output is OQ, because this is the output level which equates marginal revenue with marginal cost. At levels of output below OQ, marginal revenue > marginal cost, so that an expansion of output adds more to total revenue than it does to total cost. In these circumstances, total profit can be increased by expanding output. Conversely, at output levels greater than OQ, marginal revenue < marginal cost and a reduction in output will reduce total costs by more than it reduces total revenue so that total profit will rise. It follows that profit can only be maximised when marginal revenue = marginal cost, and this simple rule applies whatever market structure we are considering.

"MR = MC for maximum profit"

Details of *marginal revenue* and *marginal cost* enable us to determine the firm's *profit maximising output*, but it is *total revenue* and *total cost* which tell us the *actual level of profit* earned. With details as shown in Fig. 5.2, (price OP and output OQ) total revenue = OP × OQ = OPRQ while total cost = OT × OQ = OTSQ. Total revenue minus total cost gives total profit equal to PRST. Alternatively, we can say that average revenue (OP) minus average cost (OT) equals average profit (RS) and this multiplied by output (OQ) gives total profit of PRST. It is usual to include an element of *normal profit* in the firm's average cost of production because normal profit is the minimum level of profit required to keep the firm in the industry in the long run. It can therefore be regarded as a cost which must be met if the firm is to stay in production in the long run.

"Normal profit can be regarded as a 'cost' of producing"

Effects of supernormal profit

In this case it is clear that the firm is earning *supernormal profit* because AR > AC. The existence of supernormal profit will, in the long run, attract other firms into the industry. Perfect knowledge of market conditions will ensure that firms outside the industry are aware of the level of profits earned, and the absence of long run barriers to entry will ensure they are able to enter the industry and undertake production.

Transition

While changes in the output of an individual firm in perfect competition will have no perceptible effect on market supply, the influx of many new producers into the industry will clearly have a marked impact. If market demand for the industry's product is constant, the increased market supply will pull down price. Nevertheless, firms will still be attracted into

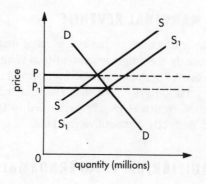
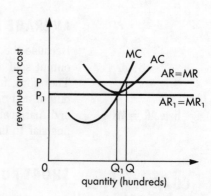

Fig. 5.3 The adjustment from supernormal profit to long-run equilibrium

the industry so long as supernormal profits exist. Only when these have been competed away, with all firms earning only normal profit, will the industry be in equilibrium. The adjustment from short run equilibrium to long run equilibrium is shown in Fig. 5.3.

Market supply and market demand are initially given by SS and DD respectively, and the initial market price is OP. Given this price, the firm produces its equilibrium output, OQ. The existence of short run supernormal profit attracts other firms into the industry so that in the long run market supply increases to S_1S_1 and market price falls to OP_1. The individual firm is powerless to resist the reduction in market price and is forced to adjust its output so as to preserve equality between marginal revenue and marginal cost.

Long run equilibrium

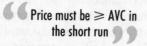

> **Only normal profits are made in the long run**

The industry is in long run equilibrium when price has fallen to the extent that all firms in the industry earn only normal profit, or at least potential entrants to the industry see no prospect of earning anything other than normal profit. Normal profit is insufficient to attract additional firms into the industry, but just sufficient to dissuade those firms already in the industry from leaving. In terms of Fig. 5.3, long run equilibrium is established when market price has fallen to OP_1 and the firm produces OQ_1 units. Given this price and output combination the firm's total revenue ($OP_1 \times OQ_1$) is exactly equal to its total cost ($OP_1 \times OQ_1$) including normal profit, and since the firm equates marginal revenue with marginal cost this is the maximum attainable profit given the ruling market price OP_1.

SHORT RUN EQUILIBRIUM 2: SUBNORMAL PROFIT

For all firms, irrespective of market structure, production can only continue in the long run if *at least* normal profit is earned. However, in the short run, firms may be prepared to accept a return below normal profit. For instance, a firm might be willing to continue producing in the short run as long as total revenue from production is at least equal to the firm's *total variable costs* of production, i.e. as long as AR ≥ AVC. The reason for this is simple. In the sort run firms are obliged to meet their fixed costs whether they undertake production or not. Therefore:

- If total revenue from production is only *just sufficient* to cover the *total variable costs*, it follows that the firm is making no contribution towards covering its fixed costs. It is therefore neither better off nor worse off, if it remains in the industry.

- If total revenue is *greater than total variable costs*, then by continuing in production, the firm makes at least some contribution towards covering the fixed costs already incurred. To cease production would leave the firm with a loss equal to its fixed costs, whereas if the firm undertakes production it will at least have a surplus over variable costs to set against its fixed costs.

- If total revenue is *less than total variable cost*, the firm will be better off by ceasing production altogether. If it produces nothing, the firm's total loss is equal to its fixed cost. This compares with a loss equal to the deficit on variable costs *added* to the fixed costs if it undertakes production.

> **Price must be ≥ AVC in the short run**

It is clear, because of this, that in the short run, the *minimum acceptable price* if the firm is to undertake production is that price which exactly equals the minimum short run average variable costs of production. It is for this reason that the minimum average variable cost is sometimes referred to as the '*shut down*' price.

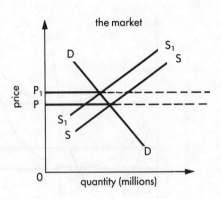

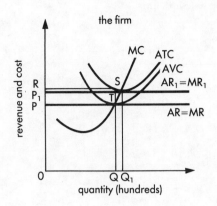

Fig. 5.4 The adjustment from
short-run loss to long-run
equilibrium

Loss situation

The loss situation is analysed diagrammatically in Fig. 5.4.

The minimum acceptable short run price is OP. This price is exactly equal to the *minimum average variable cost*, and the firm's loss is exactly equal to its fixed costs, whether it undertakes production or not. Thus, with price OP, the firm's equilibrium output is OQ and total revenue = total variable cost = OPTQ. Total cost = ORSQ. Total revenue – total cost = PRST. This is a *negative* value, representing the loss made by the firm, which in this case just equals the firm's fixed cost.

Effects of loss situation

However, such losses cannot be sustained indefinitely and in the long run some firms will be forced to leave the industry. This will shift market supply to S_1S_1 and raise market price to OP_1. Given this market price the firm's profit maximising output is OQ_1 and the firm just earns normal profit, since total revenue is $OP_1 \times OQ_1$, which exactly equals total cost. So, the *minimum acceptable long run price* is that price which just equals the *minimum average total cost* of production including normal profit.

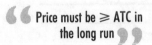
Price must be ⩾ ATC in the long run

LONG RUN EQUILIBRIUM

We have seen that in the long run neither supernormal profit nor subnormal profit can continue to exist. Whilst either is possible in the short run, their very existence will lead to changes in the number of firms in the industry, and hence, in market supply, causing changes in the market price of the product. The industry is in long run equilibrium when there is no longer any tendency for firms to enter or leave, and this occurs when all firms in the industry are making normal profit.

SHORT RUN AND LONG RUN SUPPLY IN PERFECT COMPETITION

We have seen that firms in perfectly competitive markets are powerless to resist price changes and can only preserve equality between marginal cost and marginal revenue by adjusting *output*. However, since price is equal to marginal revenue for the firm in perfect competition, it follows that the firm adjusts its output so as to equate marginal cost with price. Thus the *short run* supply curve of the firm in perfect competition is that part of its marginal cost curve which lies above its average variable cost curve. If price falls below minimum average variable cost the firm will cease production altogether, since total revenue will no longer cover the total variable costs of production. The firm would then be making no contribution to fixed costs; quite the reverse, it would be making still greater losses by continuing to produce. However, at all prices *above* the minimum average variable cost, the firm will undertake production in the short run, although it will only continue production in the *long run* if price is at least equal to average total cost. Fig. 5.5 illustrates the firm's short run supply curve.

OP is the minimum price at which the firm will undertake production in the short run. At this price the firm will supply OQ units. If market price rises to OP_1 the firm will increase output to OQ_1, and so on. The *short run supply curve* of the firm is therefore that part of its marginal cost curve which lies above the average variable cost curve. The short run supply curve of the *industry* is clearly the sum of each *individual* firm's short run supply curve. However, the *long run supply curve of the industry* is more complex because of the entry or

The MC curve is the supply curve under perfect competition, but distinguish short run supply from long run supply

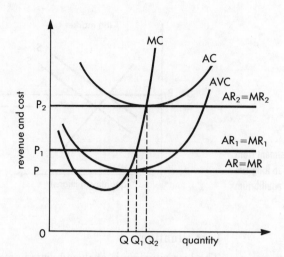

Fig. 5.5 The supply curve of the firm under perfect competition

exit of firms. In fact, the very absence of barriers to entry or exit of firms ensures that the long run supply curve of a perfectly competitive industry is perfectly elastic at the market price which just enables firms to earn normal profit, i.e. OP_2 in Fig. 5.5. The reasoning behind this assertion is illustrated in Fig. 5.6.

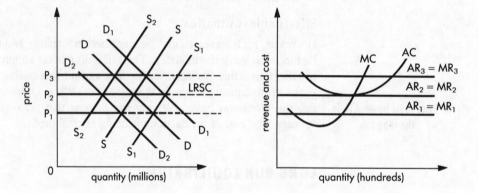

Fig. 5.6 The long-run supply curve of the industry in perfect competition

If market supply and market demand are initially represented by SS and DD respectively, then market price is OP_2 and the firm and industry are in long run equilibrium because only normal profits are earned. An increase in demand to D_1D_1 raises market price to OP_3 enabling existing firms to earn supernormal profit. In the long run this attracts other firms into the industry, market supply shifts to S_1S_1, market price falls to OP_2 and all firms in the industry are again in long run equilibrium, since normal profits are earned and there is no longer any tendency for firms to enter the industry.

The opposite would occur if market demand fell to D_2D_2. In the long run losses would force some firms out of the industry, market supply would fall to S_2S_2 and long run equilibrium would be restored. The industry's long run supply curve is therefore shown as LRSC, which is perfectly elastic at OP_2, the market price which just enables firms to earn normal profit.

PERFECT COMPETITION AND THE ALLOCATION OF RESOURCES

The most important feature of perfect competition is its impact on the allocation of resources. It is clear from the discussion above that under perfect competition, price exactly equals marginal cost. This is a fundamental feature of perfectly competitive markets, and it is suggested that it implies an optimum allocation of resources in perfect competition. If price measures the value consumers place on an extra unit of the commodity, and marginal cost measures the cost of attracting resources away from alternative uses, then it follows that the price of the last unit of the commodity produced is equal to its opportunity cost of production. This is an optimum allocation of resources because if price is greater than marginal cost, society desires more of this commodity in preference to alternatives since they are prepared to pay an amount greater than the cost of attracting resources away from alternatives. Conversely, if marginal cost is greater than price, society values alternatives more highly since they are not prepared to pay an amount

> 66 Price = MC is an optimum allocation of resources 99

equivalent to the cost of attracting resources away from these alternatives. Only under perfect competition is this optimum allocation of resources achieved.

It is also clear from our discussion that in the long run the firm in perfect competition is forced to the point of maximum technical efficiency. In other words, given the existing level of capacity the firm is forced to produce at the point of minimum average cost. Again, this is *not* true of any other market structure.

MONOPOLY

A *pure* monopoly exists when supply of a particular good or service is in the hands of a single supplier. For convenience we usually analyse monopoly in terms of a single firm but a monopoly can also exist when a small group of firms jointly co-ordinate their marketing policies and so act as a single supplier. The latter situation which is examined more fully later in this section is referred to as a *cartel*.

Because market supply is in the hands of a single supplier, a monopoly has great power to influence the price of its product. However, this does not imply that it has total power to fix price, since it cannot control consumer demand. In effect the monopolist has two choices:

" Choices of the monopolist "

- to fix price and allow demand to determine supply (output)
- to fix supply (output) and allow demand to determine price

The inability to control market demand makes it impossible for a monopolist to simultaneously fix both price and output.

Average and marginal revenues

Unlike the firm in perfect competition, the monopolist's average and marginal revenues will be different. This is because the monopolist faces a downward sloping demand curve and is forced to reduce price in order to expand sales. Table 5.1 is used as a basis for illustration.

OUTPUT/SALES	AVERAGE REVENUE (£)	TOTAL REVENUE (£)	MARGINAL REVENUE (£)
0	—	—	—
1	10	10	10
2	9	18	8
3	8	24	6

Table 5.1

In order to expand sales from 1 unit to 2 units, it is necessary to reduce the price of both units. Hence, price falls from £10 per unit to £9 per unit and the marginal revenue, i.e. the change in total revenue, is £8. Similarly, when price is reduced from £9 per unit to £8 per unit, marginal revenue falls to £6. Hence marginal revenue will always be less than price (average revenue) under monopoly.

The monopolist's equilibrium price and output

We have already seen that for all producers profits are maximised when marginal cost

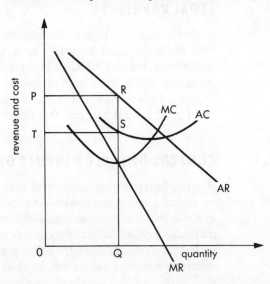

Fig. 5.7 Equilibrium under monopoly

equals marginal revenue. Based on this principle Fig. 5.7 illustrates the monopolist's equilibrium output.

The monopolist maximises profit when price is OP and output OQ because at this price and output combination marginal revenue equals marginal cost. Total revenue (OPRQ) minus total cost (OTSQ) gives a profit equal to PRST.

Note: the monopolist is earning supernormal profit, and one of the characteristic features of monopoly is that it is possible to earn this level of profit even in the long run. If supernormal profits continue in the long run this implies the existence of barriers which restrict the entry of additional firms into the industry. These barriers are therefore the very essence of monopoly power and their nature is examined in the following section.

> The monopolist can retain supernormal profits in the long run

BARRIERS TO ENTRY

Barriers to entry of firms into a market might take a variety of forms and indeed entry into any particular market might be restricted by the existence of several barriers. These might include any of the following.

TECHNICAL BARRIERS

In certain industries there is a natural tendency towards monopoly in so far as supply is most efficiently undertaken by a single firm. This is especially true of those industries where technical economies of scale make the minimum efficient scale of operation very large indeed. For example, because of indivisibilities, some organisations have relatively high fixed costs so that average total costs continue to fall as output expands over relatively large ranges. This is true in the production of industrial gases, where it has been repeatedly argued that the British Oxygen Corporation's almost total domination of the UK market is at least partly based on the existence of substantial economies of scale in production. It is also true of the public utilities supplying gas, water, electricity, and so on, through a grid system. Such industries are referred to as *'natural monopolies'* because distribution is most efficiently undertaken by a single supplier.

> Barriers to entry are vital to monopoly power

The existence of substantial economies of scale provides some justification for the existence of large firms but not necessarily for the existence of monopoly as such. Indeed, it is increasingly the case that a great deal of manufacturing industry is dominated by a few large scale producers (*oligopoly*) rather than by a single large scale producer. For example, in chemicals, petroleum, tyres and motor vehicle production, a small number of firms satisfy the entire market. Nevertheless, it is true that progressively falling average costs as output increases confers enormous advantages on large scale producers. These cost advantages might well prevent the emergence of competition and lead to monopoly, whether of the 'pure' or 'dominant firm' variety. Not only would a firm attempting entry into the industry have to match the capacity of existing producers, it would also need to consider the effect on market price of a substantial increase in market supply. Whilst it may be possible for a single large firm to earn supernormal profit, if two large firms were to supply the market they might both make losses!

LEGAL BARRIERS

In certain markets, legal regulations might prevent the emergence of competition. In the UK, the nationalised industries have been granted the sole rights to supply particular goods or services. Additionally, patent rights might ensure a monopoly position by preventing other firms from producing identical products. However, this barrier is only temporary and lasts only as long as the life of the patent (usually 16 years). In any case, it is often possible to circumvent this safeguard by producing similar products.

CONTROL OF FACTOR INPUTS OR RETAIL OUTLETS

Where a firm has complete control over the supply of a factor of production it may be able to exercise monopoly power over the products produced by that factor. An obvious example might be the ownership of land containing the only known deposits of a specific mineral. An equally effective monopoly might result from a single firm owning the key retail outlets for a product. Both the major petrol producers and the breweries have made active efforts to acquire retail outlets for their respective products.

AGREEMENTS BETWEEN SUPPLIERS

An effective monopoly can exist when firms in an industry agree to co-operate rather than compete. The most formal type of agreement between producers is known as a *cartel* and this exists when a single agency organises the marketing of a product supplied by several firms. The aim of the cartel is often to restrict market supply of the product, thereby forcing up price and increasing profits for the members of the cartel.

These are largely illegal in the UK, with just a few cartel type organisations operating within the law. The most obvious examples are the agricultural marketing boards. Where cartels do exist, both in the UK, and abroad, they present a formidable barrier to entry into the market. Any potential entrant must either join the cartel or compete with it. Existing members may not allow the newcomers to join the cartel and effective competition may be uneconomic because of the need to produce on a large scale, or uneconomic because of the effect on market price of a sizeable increase in industry output.

PRICE DISCRIMINATION

Price discrimination arises when a monopolist sells the same product in two or more markets at different prices. In other words, consumers pay different prices for the *same* product. This must not be confused with the situation that exists when a firm supplies *different* products that are sold at different prices; this is *not* price discrimination. Neither is it price discrimination if price differences are based on different transport costs or service charges. Instead, price discrimination implies that differences in price are the result of deliberate policy by the monopolist. Price discrimination and the conditions under which it might occur are discussed in the 'Tutor's Answer to Question 3 on pp. 76–8

PERFECT COMPETITION AND MONOPOLY – A COMPARISON

ALLOCATIVE EFFICIENCY

It is often argued that the allocation of resources under perfect competition is superior to that achieved under monopoly. This is because under perfect competition output is pushed to the point at which marginal cost equals marginal revenue. This, as explained on pp. 70–71, implies the value society places on the last unit of output consumed exactly equals the opportunity cost to society of producing that unit. The same is not true under monopoly since, in order to maximise profits, the monopolist always charges a price greater than marginal cost. Under monopoly there is, therefore, an efficiency loss in terms of the allocation of resources and the extent of this loss for a particular product is illustrated in Fig. 5.8.

" Price > MC in monopoly "

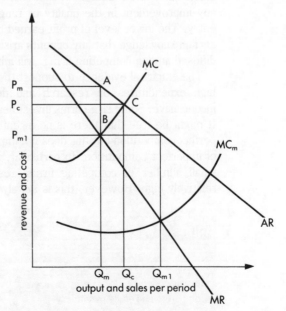

Fig. 5.8 Price and output under monopoly and perfect competition

AR is the *market demand curve*. It shows the quantity demanded at any given price. MR is the *monopolist's* marginal revenue curve but has no relevance for perfect competition since it is the MR curve for a single supplier supplying the whole market. In perfect competition, the market is supplied by many firms. MC is the marginal cost curve facing the monopolist and it is assumed that this is identical to the sum of all of the individual firms' marginal cost curves in perfect competition. In equilibrium the monopolist charges a price of OP_m and produces OQ_m. The perfectly competitive *industry*, on the other hand, is in equilibrium when MC = AR (since each firm in perfect competition equates MC with price [AR]). Under perfect competition price is therefore OP_c and output is OQ_c. The efficiency loss to society is therefore equal to the area ABC.

In addition it is sometimes suggested that price is greater and output lower under monopoly than under perfect competition. However, this is not necessarily true. If economies of scale exist, these will be exploited by the monopolist but will not be available to firms under perfect competition because of their relatively small scale of production. In this case the monopolist's marginal cost curve will be given by MC_m and price and output for the monopolist will now be OP_{m1} and OQ_{m1} respectively. Society's resources are not used to greatest possible efficiency because price does not equal MC, but price is still lower and output greater under monopoly than under perfect competition!

> Economies of scale are an important consideration

PRODUCTIVE EFFICIENCY

It was argued on p. 71 that under perfect competition output is pushed to the point of maximum *technical efficiency*, that is, minimum average cost. In fact, in the long run under perfect competition, technical efficiency and economic efficiency (price = MC) coincide. Under monopoly this is not the case as shown in Fig. 5.7. The monopolist restricts output to the profit maximising level and at this point average cost is still falling. The monopolist therefore operates with excess capacity and does not exploit all potential economies of scale. Here again, as Fig. 5.8 demonstrates, this might simply mean that monopoly is not as efficient as possible but society still gains in terms of lower prices and greater output than would exist under perfect competition.

RESEARCH AND DEVELOPMENT

It is sometimes suggested that monopoly might lead to more rapid technological progress which in turn could lead to more inventions, improved techniques and the introduction of new and improved products than would be achieved by perfectly competitive markets. The higher level of profit earned under monopoly facilitates the finance of costly research and development programs. Furthermore, a greater incentive to undertake such programs exists since any reduction in cost that results will increase the monopolist's profit, while any improvement in the quality or range of goods produced will strengthen barriers to entry. The lower level of profit earned by firms in perfect competition, together with the certain knowledge that any benefits arising from research and development will quickly be diffused among competing firms, will inhibit expenditures in such markets.

The empirical evidence to support the view that monopoly is associated with relatively high expenditures on research and development and rapid technological advance is inconclusive. Some large firms invest heavily in this type of expenditure but others do not. It might be true that there is no incentive to invest in research and development under perfect competition but this does not imply that there is no incentive under different forms of imperfect competition. In particular, as Table 5.2 below illustrates, when there are a small number of competing firms, research and development expenditure might be relatively high. However, this is *not* always the case!

INDUSTRY	CONCENTRATION %	R & D EXPENDITURE %
Aerospace	79	16
Computers and office machinery	67	11.9
Insulated wires and cables	83	1.5
Motor vehicles and parts	67	1.7
Pharmaceutical products	34	11.3
Shipbuilding and repairs	79	0.3

Table 5.2 Concentration and research and development in 1981

Source: Census of Production 1981, Business Monitor 1981

STABILITY AND RATIONALISATION

One way in which monopoly will almost certainly be preferable to perfect competition is when markets are unstable because of sudden changes in demand or supply. A single firm is able to respond to these changes in a more orderly way than a group of firms whose activities are uncoordinated.

APPLIED MATERIALS

Although no market is perfectly competitive in the textbook sense of the term, some markets are very much more competitive than others. Tables 5.2 and 5.3 give some idea of the extent of concentration in certain markets and on the correlation in certain markets between concentration and R and D expenditure (Table 5.2).

INDUSTRY	NET OUTPUT %	EMPLOYMENT %
Tobacco	99	99
Cement, lime and plaster	88	87
Sugar and sugar products	64	59
Glass and glassware	53	44
Brewing and malting	51	46
Footwear	37	31
Printing and publishing	22	19

Table 5.3 Concentration, output and employment in 1984 (shares of largest five firms)

Source: Business Monitor 1987

MONOPOLIES AND MERGERS COMMISSION

On the other hand there are many situations where a market is dominated by a single firm and several have been investigated by the Monopolies and Mergers Commission. A significant number of these investigations have revealed the existence of excessive profit in certain situations. A well known example is that of Hoffman la Roche, a manufacturer of drugs, which, through its subsidiary Roche Products, had a monopoly in the supply of chlorodiazepoxide and diazepam from which librium and valium are made. The Commission reported that Roche Products had used its monopoly position to charge excessive prices for its products and had consequently earned an excessive rate of return of 70 per cent on capital employed. This must be judged against the current government target of 21 per cent profit for pharmaceutical companies supplying the NHS.

Despite this the Commission has not always condemned firms which earn a relatively high rate of return on capital employed. For example, in its report on the 'Supply of Cat and Dog Foods in the United Kingdom' the Commission noted that although Pedigree Petfoods had earned an impressive rate of return of 44 per cent on capital employed, this was due to its relative efficiency. The Commission commented that: 'Pedigree Petfoods derives great advantage from its use of capital and financial control of a kind exceptional among large companies in this country'.

PRICE DISCRIMINATION AND AIRLINE TICKETS

An article entitled *Price Discrimination and Airline Tickets* in the *Economic Review* Vol 6 No 1 Sept 1988, provides an interesting case study on price discrimination. In this article it is alleged that on any transatlantic flight carrying up to 390 passengers there might be as many as 100 different prices for the same journey! Clearly this comes very close to achieving perfect price discrimination where every consumer pays a different price for the same good. The article highlights the importance of different elasticities of demand in the creation of different prices. Different elasticities of demand arise partly because of differences in the ability of individuals to finalise their travel plans. Those with greatest flexibility have a lower elasticity of demand for any given flight and might only be encouraged to make a booking by the offer of stand-by tickets with a relatively low price. The question of market segmentation is also addressed. After all, a seat on a flight is potentially transferable so why don't consumers buy at the lower price and resell at a higher price? In fact each ticket has the purchaser's name printed on it, and, since a passport needs to be produced at the time of departure, this prevents the resale of tickets.

EXAMINATION QUESTIONS

1   'It is average costs which tells a firm whether to produce at all, but marginal cost which tells it how much to produce.' Discuss the accuracy of this statement for a perfectly competitive firm;
    i) in the long run
    ii) in the short run

(Northern Ireland, 1988)

2   When, if ever, may the existence of monopoly be justified? Evaluate different ways in which the problems posed by monopoly may be reduced.

(AEB, June, 1989)

3   Is it a) profitable and b) desirable for a monopoly supplier to practise price discrimination?

(London, Jan, 1989)

4   a) Explain what is meant by monopoly profits?   (15)
    b) What reasons are there for believing that a monopoly agreement between a number of firms may be more harmful than a single firm monopoly, from society's point of view?   (5)
    c) Why does the state grant monopoly rights in the form of patents to particular firms?   (5)

(Welsh, 1989)

A TUTOR'S ANSWER TO QUESTION 3

Price discrimination occurs when a supplier charges different consumers different prices for the *same* product. Such price differences are not based on differences in the cost of supplying each consumer. Instead they are a means of increasing the supplier's profit, taking advantage of the fact that some consumers are more prepared to pay higher prices than others.

Price discrimination must not be confused with the situation that exists when a firm supplies different products. Thus, first and second class travel on trains or in the air are different products and although they are sold at different prices this is not price discrimination. Neither is it price discrimination if prices are based on different transport costs or service charges. Some examples of price discrimination are given later, but first it is necessary to consider the conditions that make price discrimination possible and profitable.

One condition necessary for price discrimination is that there must be at least two distinct markets for the good or service, and there must be no seepage between these markets. This means that it must be impossible or uneconomic for consumers to purchase in the lower priced market and re-sell in the higher priced market. For this to be the case there must be barriers which prevent resale. Sometimes these exist because the nature of the product makes storage and resale impossible. This is particularly true of services, and lower priced haircuts for senior citizens or half-priced travel for minors are examples of this. In some cases markets might be separated because of mutual advantage. For example, motor car manufacturers charge different prices for spares to their service agencies than to independent stockists. Similarly in food processing, large discounts are available to the supermarket chains compared with small independent grocers.

Another condition necessary for price discrimination is that supply must be in the hands of a monopolist so that competing firms are unable to undertake production and undercut the monopolist in the higher priced markets.

These conditions make price discrimination possible, but they do not make it profitable. For this to be the case elasticity of demand must be different in at least two of the markets. If it were not, there could be no additional profit to the monopolist from price discrimination, and, since the aim of the monopolist is to maximise profit, price discrimination would not occur. The importance of different elasticities of demand can be explained in terms of the diagram (Fig. 5.9).

Markets A and B are two distinct markets separated in some way so that seepage between them is impossible. Fig. 5.9 also shows the combined market, that is, the

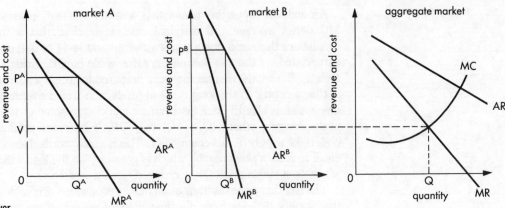

Fig. 5.9 Tutor's answer

summation of the AR and MR in the two separate markets. If we assume that in all three diagrams the scales on the axes are the same, it is clear that the elasticity of demand at any given price is different in markets A and B. This is crucial in deciding what price to charge in each market so as to maximise profit.

To do this the monopolist simply applies the profit maximising rule that marginal cost equals marginal revenue to the aggregate of the demand curves for markets A and B. This gives the profit maximising output OQ, but not the profit maximising price. To obtain this the monopolist must equate marginal cost with marginal revenue in *each individual market*. This gives a profit maximising price in market A of OP^A and of OP^B in market B, that is, a higher price in the market with the less elastic demand. The sum of the sales in each market is equal to the total amount produced. There is no other distribution of output OQ between the two markets (and therefore no other market prices) which could increase total profit. For instance, selling one unit less in market A and one more unit in market B would lead to a loss of revenue because it is clear that marginal revenue in market B would rise by less than it would fall in market A. Total revenue would therefore fall, and, with marginal costs unchanged, profit would fall. Profit is therefore maximised when $MR^A = MR^B = MC$.

There is no unambiguous answer as to the desirability of price discrimination, although consumers in the lower priced market clearly benefit compared with those in the higher priced market! However, the main way in which consumers might benefit is when price discrimination enables a monopolist to earn a profit from some activity that might not otherwise be possible. The diagram below is used as a basis for explanation.

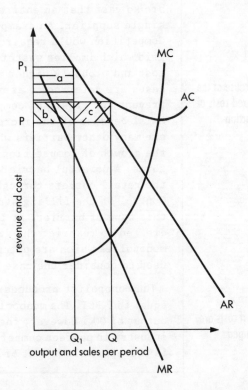

Fig. 5.10 Tutor's answer

AR and MR depict the monopolists' average and marginal revenue curves while AC and MC depict average and marginal cost. It is clear that if the monopolist charged all consumers the same uniform price there is no level of output at which a profit could be earned. Indeed the *loss minimising price* would be OP, giving a loss equal to area 'b' plus area 'c'. Even if the monopolist were prepared to accept a short run loss, such losses could not be accepted in the long run and production would eventually cease. However, if the monopolist is able to price discriminate and charge some consumers (OQ_1) a price of OP_1 while charging others ($Q_1 - Q$) only OP, it becomes profitable for the monopolist to undertake supply of this commodity. This is easily verified since the *increase* in revenue is equal to area 'a' plus area 'b'; which is greater than the loss which is made (area 'b' + area 'c') when a single price OP is charged (area a > area c).

The fact that price discrimination makes production profitable does not necessarily imply that society benefits from discrimination. However, if we consider the case of a doctor providing medical services to an isolated community it is possible to argue that society does benefit from discrimination. For example, in the terms of Fig. 5.10, by charging wealthier patients a higher price the whole community benefits because the alternative is no doctor at all!

Despite the fact that it is possible for the community to benefit from price discrimination, the general conclusion is that such discrimination serves only to increase monopoly profits at the expense of consumers. It is therefore usually condemned as an undesirable practice. Nevertheless, the increased profits might still benefit the community if they are used to finance research and development into the creation of new or improved products, or improvements in productive efficiency. There is no general rule and whether price discrimination benefits society can therefore only be judged by examining each individual case.

A STUDENT'S ANSWER TO QUESTION 2

Strictly a monopoly exists when there is a sole supplier of a good or service. In such cases there exists the possibility that consumers will face higher prices than might otherwise exist. Whether this happens or whether consumers benefit in other ways from the existence of monopoly depends on the behaviour of each individual monopolist.

One reason for the emergence of monopoly is that economies of scale are so vast that an entire market can most efficiently be served by a single supplier. An example of this is the supply of electricity. Competition would require the creation of more than one national grid which implies wasteful duplication of capital, higher average cost and probably higher prices for the consumer as a result. Such cases are referred to as natural monopoly because the barriers which prevent the growth of competition are natural in the sense that they exist because of the increased efficiency of size. However, there are many other barriers which are deliberately created to restrict the growth of competition. Such barriers might take a variety of forms. A powerful barrier would exist if a monopolist had control of the retail outlets through which his product was distributed. Control of the filling stations by the petrol majors is an example of this type of barrier. It is these barriers which are deliberately created to restrict the growth of competition that give rise to monopolies which are potentially undesirable. The diagram shown is used to consider the case against monopoly.

The monopolist produces where MC = MR and earns supernormal profit equal to P_MRST. The monopolist charges a price of OP_M and products an output of OQ_M. However, the equilibrium price and output of the industry in perfect competition would be OP_C and OQ_C respectively. It is therefore clear that price is higher and output greater under

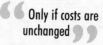
No. It is because of the relatively high fixed costs of production

Only if costs are unchanged

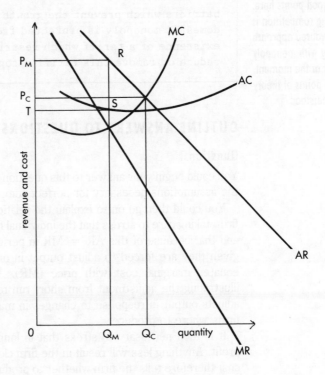

Fig. 5.11 Student answer

"Doubtful – greater efficiency means higher profit for the monopolist"

"No. They need not buy the product"

"No. The monopolist aims to maximise profit. The highest possible price exists when only one unit is sold!"

"Improved technology can often be copied"

"Good paragraph"

"Explain why not"

perfect competition than under monopoly and this is the main reason why monopoly is thought to be undesirable.

Another reason why monopoly might be considered undesirable is that the absence of competition means there is less incentive for the firm to produce efficiently. Consumers are forced to pay whatever price the monopolist charges and because monopolists aim to maximise profit they will always charge consumers the highest possible price. When there is competition there is a powerful incentive to invest in improved technology so as to reduce costs and so gain a competitive advantage over other firms in the industry. Monopolies are therefore likely to restrict technological advances and society will be worse off as a result.

Because of these disadvantages, the government takes action to deal with the problems posed by monopoly. Indeed the government has set up a Monopolies and Mergers Commission to investigate the behaviour of monopolistic firms referred to it as well as to investigate the likely effects on market domination of any proposed mergers which are referred to it. The Commission has the power to obtain any information it requires from firms under investigation which is relevant to its enquiry but it has no statutory power to enforce its recommendations. Instead it can only make recommendations in its report. It is for the secretary of state to decide whether these recommendations should be implemented. In the extreme, power exists to compel monopolies to divest themselves of some of their assets thus creating competition in the industry.

Sometimes monopolies are created by the state. The most complete barriers to entry are the sole rights of supply granted to the nationalised industries. One way of dealing with monopolies of this nature is to privatise the industry and remove any other legal barriers to entry. This is what happened when British Telecom was privatised and the competing firm, Mercury, was established.

A different approach available to the government is to tax the profits of a monopolist. This would not protect the public from the abuses of monopoly but it would mean that rather than there being a redistribution of income from consumers to the monopolist, there would be a redistribution from consumers to the state.

Another way of tackling the problems of monopoly is to remove the

> Some good points here. Encouraging competition is certainly the favoured approach to dealing with monopoly situations at the moment. However some points of theory are not well understood

barriers which prevent the growth of competition. For example, if a domestic monopoly is protected from foreign competition by the existence of a tariff which restricts imports, the government might reduce or remove this tariff altogether.

OUTLINE ANSWERS TO QUESTIONS 1 AND 4

Question 1

You could begin your answer to this question by defining perfect competition and explaining the assumptions necessary for perfect competition to exist (see p. 66).

You could then go on to explain the relationship between the market and the individual firm, taking care to stress that the individual firm is powerless to influence the market price and that because of this AR = MR in perfect competition. Because firms take price as given they are forced to adjust output in order to maximise profit. To do this the firm equates marginal cost with price (MR). You could illustrate this by explaining and illustrating the adjustment from short run to long run equilibrium showing how the firm adjusts output in response to changes in market price. Marginal cost therefore tells the firms where to produce.

It is then necessary to stress that in long run equilibrium the firm earns only normal profit. Anything less will result in the firm closing down and leaving the industry. Average cost therefore tells the firm whether to produce in the long run. However, in the short run firms will accept losses if they can at least cover their variable costs, that is, if AR ≥ AVC. In the short run AVC therefore tells the firm whether to produce.

Question 4

a) It is best to begin with a definition of monopoly and to follow this with a discussion of monopoly equilibrium. You should explain the difference between normal and supernormal profit and show the level of supernormal profit earned by a monopolist. The important point to stress about monopoly profit is that it is sustainable even in the long run as long as there are barriers which prevent the emergence of competition. Indeed the essence of monopoly power is the ability to restrict the growth of competition and you should discuss with examples some of the barriers which might exist.

b) This question asks about the welfare loss from monopoly and you must explain what this is. One reason why agreements between producers might be harmful to society is that they are less easy to identify than pure monopoly situations. However, the main reason is that single firm monopolies confer benefits on society which are unavailable to cartels because they consist of many smaller firms. In particular many of the economies of scale which a monopolist might reap will not be available to members of a cartel. Another factor is that cartels inevitably fix prices at levels high enough to protect the less efficient firms. Hence average cost for the group will be higher than it would be for the single firm monopoly.

c) You could begin your answer to this part of the question by explaining that a patent prevents one firm from copying the product or process that has been patented by another firm. The state grants patent rights to particular firms in order to encourage research and development. In the absence of this protection it is unlikely that firms would be so willing to invest in research and development since any advances would quickly be copied by rival firms. This would reduce the gains to society from improved efficiency in production, from improvements in the range of goods produced and from the development of new products.

Further reading

Begg, Dornbusch and Fischer, *Economics* (2nd edn), McGraw-Hill 1987: Ch 8, Perfect competition and pure monopoly: The limiting cases of market structure.
Galt, *Competition. Monopoly and Public Policy*, Longman 1989: Ch 1, Competition and monopoly, Ch 5, Monopoly and restrictive trade practice's policy in operation.
Harrison, *Pricing and Competition in the Private Sector*, Longman 1983: Ch 2, Pricing. Competition and Market Structure

CHAPTER

6

IMPERFECT COMPETITION

MONOPOLISTIC COMPETITION

OLIGOPOLY

ALTERNATIVES TO PROFIT MAXIMISATION

APPLIED MATERIALS

GETTING STARTED

In Chapter 5 we looked at two market structures, perfect competition and monopoly. These are extremes and while some markets might possess some of the characteristics of perfect competition and monopoly, neither is particularly common in the real world. Indeed most market structures in the real world contain many imperfections but fall short of pure monopoly. It is these markets which we will consider in this chapter.

**MONOPOLISTIC
COMPETITION**

" *The products are
different* "

ESSENTIAL PRINCIPLES

This market structure has features of both perfect competition and monopoly. In particular, there are no barriers to entry into the industry, but each firm produces a product which is differentiated in some way from the products of its rivals. Such product differentiation is often achieved or reinforced by branding and advertising. Because each product is differentiated, each firm has a monopoly over the supply of its own product. It therefore faces a downward sloping demand curve for its product with respect to price. This, in turn, implies that its marginal revenue curve lies beneath its average revenue curve.

EQUILIBRIUM: THE SHORT RUN AND THE LONG RUN

The short run

As with other market structures we assume that the firm aims to maximise profit. It therefore produces that level of output at which MC = MR. The firm's short run equilibrium position is shown in Fig. 6.1a).

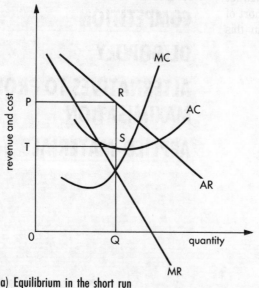

Fig. 6.1a) Equilibrium in the short run

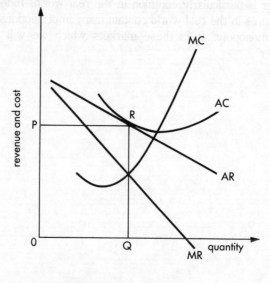

Fig. 6.1b) Equilibrium in the long run

" *There is freedom of entry
in monopolistic
competition* "

The firm is in equilibrium when it produces OQ units and charges a price of OP per unit. At this price and output combination, it earns supernormal profit of PRST. However, this cannot represent a long run equilibrium position because the existence of supernormal profit will attract more firms into the industry. Indeed, firms will continue to enter the industry until supernormal profits have been competed away and each firm earns only normal profit. The firm's long run equilibrium position is shown in Fig. 6.1b). The extra firms attract some, but not all, of the firm's customers. This can be shown as a leftward shift of the firm's demand (AR) curve, until it just touches its AC curve.

The long run

In the long run, total revenue = total cost = OPRQ. Each firm, although maximising profit (MC = MR) earns only normal profit since, at output OQ, price = average cost. Consequently there is no tendency for firms to enter or leave the industry. However, this does not imply that monopolistic competition confers the same benefits on society as perfect competition. In particular, we can identify two important ways in which society is worse off:

■ In the long run, equilibrium output is not pushed to the point of maximum technical efficiency, i.e. minimum average cost. The firm in monopolistic competition therefore operates with excess capacity in the long run. This under-utilisation of capacity leads both to higher average costs than would exist if output were expanded and consequently to higher consumer prices.

■ In the long run, equilibrium output is not pushed to the point at which resources are allocated in the most efficient manner, i.e. a 'Pareto optimal' resource allocation. This requires price to equal marginal cost, yet here, price is greater than marginal cost. This means that if output were expanded until price = marginal cost, resource allocation could be improved, but this will not happen because the firm will make a loss.

OLIGOPOLY

> **Here a few large producers dominate**

> **Firms need to take into account the actions and reactions of each other**

A market is oligopolistic when a few large scale producers dominate the industry. For this reason oligopoly is sometimes referred to as 'competition among the few'. Firms supply competing brands of a product and any 'action' in terms of price and non-price strategies by one firm would almost certainly be matched by the firm's rivals. Because of this, the distinguishing feature of oligopolistic markets is that there is a high degree of interdependence between each firm in the industry. This implies that individual firms will be obliged to consider the effect of their actions on rival producers, and the possible course of action they in turn might pursue.

THE KINKED DEMAND CURVE

The existence of interdependence provides a possible explanation for the relative price stability that sometimes characterises oligopolistic markets. The suggestion is that an individual firm in oligopoly fears that if it raises price, other firms will not follow suit. Instead, they will be content to hold their own price constant and attract consumers away from the firm which has raised the price. Because of this, the individual firm perceives demand for its product to be relatively elastic if it raises price. On the other hand, if an individual firm lowers price its competitors in the market will be compelled to match the price cut, otherwise they will lose a disproportionate amount of sales. The individual firm therefore perceives demand for its product to be relatively inelastic if it lowers price. The implications of this are illustrated in Fig. 6.2.

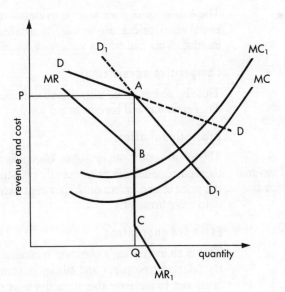

Fig. 6.2

> **Reasons for the kinked demand curve**

Because the firm perceives demand to be relatively elastic if it raises price and relatively inelastic if it reduces price, it perceives its demand curve (DAD₁) to be kinked at the ruling market price (OP). It therefore has little incentive to alter price from OP. This can be seen from Fig. 6.2 which shows that because the firm perceives its demand curve to be kinked, it has a discontinuous marginal revenue curve. In fact, when price is OP marginal revenue is indeterminate because the firm is currently operating at a common point (A) on what is effectively two separate demand curves (DD and D₁D₁), with associated marginal revenue curves. The region BC is therfore referred to as the region of indeterminacy. It implies that even when costs are changing, so long as marginal cost remains within the region of indeterminacy, changes in costs will have no effect on the profit maximising price and output combination, because the firm will still be producing where MC = MR. For example, in Fig. 6.2 when marginal cost rises from MC to MC₁ this has no effect on the price the firm charges or on the output it produces.

PRICE LEADERSHIP

Another possible reason for relative price stability in oligopolistic markets is that there might be an accepted *price leader*. Price changes are initiated by the leader and other firms in the industry simply follow suit. The role of price leader might be acquired because a firm is the largest producer in the industry, in which case we refer to '*dominant firm leadership*'. Alternatively, the price leader might be the firm which most accurately perceives changes in market demand for the product. In this case we refer to '*barometric price leadership*'. Whatever the basis of leadership, its existence would explain price stability because price changes will only be initiated by a single firm. This firm would not be confronted with price cutting by other firms and therefore price would tend to be relatively stable.

PRICE WARFARE

Whilst prices in oligopolistic markets sometimes appear relatively stable, at other times they can be highly unstable. This is particularly common when demand for the industry's product is falling, because, as sales fall, average fixed costs will rise. Individual firms are prevented from raising price because they would lose sales to competitors, and this would simply exacerbate their problems. Because of this, falling sales imply falling profits, and in these circumstances the temptation for a firm to cut its price in an attempt to prevent further loss of sales is sometimes overwhelming. However, when demand for the product is falling, an individual firm can only increase sales by attracting consumers away from rival firms. To prevent this, rival firms may well retaliate if faced with a price cut, so that profits fall still further. This may then lead to a further round of price cutting, i.e. a price war will be under way.

NON-PRICE COMPETITION

The existence of price wars is evidence of competition in oligopolostic markets. However, even when prices are stable, non-price competition between rival producers is often intense. This can take a variety of forms, including:

Competitive advertising

This is common in oligopolostic markets. Advertising is used to reinforce product differentiation and harden brand loyalty.

Promotional offers

These are common in some oligopolistic markets such as household detergents and toothpaste. Such offers frequently take the form of veiled price reductions such as 'two for the price of one' offers or '25 per cent extra free'. In the case of petrol a common technique is to offer 'free gifts'.

" Types of non-price competition "

Extended guarantees

This is an increasingly common technique in many of the markets for consumer durables. By offering free parts and labour guarantees for longer periods than their competitors, firms aim to increase the attractiveness of their product.

ALTERNATIVES TO PROFIT MAXIMISATION

" Firms may have various objectives "

This chapter has stressed profit maximisation as the goal of firms. However, in practice, it is doubtful whether firms pursue this goal to the exclusion of all other goals. This is especially true in modern corporations where ownership is in the hands of shareholders, but day-to-day control is exercised by salaried managers. Profit maximisation is likely to appeal to shareholders, because it will lead to higher dividends, but salaried managers might be more interested in pursuing other goals. Two alternatives are considered below.

THE SALES-MAXIMISATION MODEL

Rather than maximising profit, it has been suggested that salaried managers might attempt to maximise sales revenue, subject to achieving a target rate of profit. Managers have good reason for maximising sales revenue, since it often affects their salaries and their

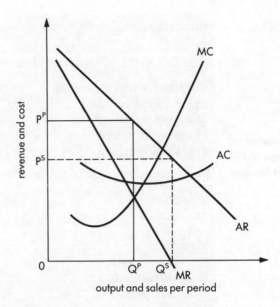

Fig. 6.3

security of tenure. In general, a higher level of sales revenue is rewarded with a higher salary. In addition, as Fig. 6.3 shows, maximising sales revenue implies a greater level of output, and therefore a greater market share, than is achieved when profit is maximised. The profit maximising price and output are OP^P and OQ^P respectively, whereas the sales revenue maximising price and output are OP^s and OQ^s respectively.

Note: price is lower and output greater when sales revenue is maximised than when profit is maximised. When $MR = O$, total (i.e. sales) revenue is a maximum.

The lower price and greater market share might offer greater protection against the emergence of competitors and in this sense might offer better prospects of long term survival. Profit maximisation, on the other hand, by showing the level of profit that can be achieved, might encourage competitors to enter the industry and threaten the long term survival of those firms already in the industry. Because of this it is sometimes argued that maximising sales is, in effect, maximising *long run* profits.

Another reason firms might prefer sales maximisation as the major goal is that for many firms fixed costs are relatively high. The larger the output, the smaller the average fixed cost. Here again this might give greater protection against the emergence of competition and might maximise long run profits.

BEHAVIOURAL MODELS

Behavioural theories stress that firms might pursue several goals simultaneously. Each goal is set as a result of bargaining between the various groups involved, such as managers, shareholders, trade unions, and so on. Where goals are in conflict with one another they must be ranked in order of importance and priority given to one rather than the other. For example, the level of output which maximises sales revenue is likely to be greater than the level of output which maximises profit. If, as a result of bargaining, profit maximisation is given priority, output will be cut back. Bargaining within the firm can clearly lead to different priorities at different times, so that behavioural models stress that no single goal can be assumed to be consistently followed by the firm.

An extension of the behavioural model is that of *satisficing*. This approach stresses that firms seek a satisfactory minimum level of achievement for various goals rather than a maximum level for any single goal. This means that many possible outcomes of price and quantity could then be regarded as situations of equilibrium for the firm.

APPLIED MATERIALS

Table 6.1 gives some idea of the extent of concentration in certain markets. It shows the combined market share of the five largest producers in certain industries, that is, the five firm concentration ratio. It also shows expenditure on research and development by these firms as a percentage of sales revenue for the industry. Table 6.2 again shows the five firm concentration ratio in certain industries along with output and employment in these firms as a percentage of total output and employment in the industry.

INDUSTRY	CONCENTRATION %	R & D EXPENDITURE %
Aerospace	79	16
Computers and office machinery	67	11.9
Insulated wires and cables	83	1.5
Motor vehicles and parts	67	1.7
Pharmaceutical products	34	11.3
Shipbuilding and repairs	79	0.3

Table 6.1 Concentration and research and development in 1981 (largest five firms)

Source: Census of Production 1981, Business Monitor 1981

INDUSTRY	NET OUTPUT %	EMPLOYMENT %
Tobacco	99	99
Cement, lime and plaster	88	87
Sugar and sugar products	64	59
Glass and glassware	53	44
Brewing and malting	51	46
Footwear	37	31
Printing and publishing	22	19

Table 6.2 Concentration and employment in 1984 (largest five firms)

Source: Business Monitor 1987

Note: neither table shows the extent to which an industry is dominated by a *single* firm. The top firms could be of widely differing size.

THE WORLD OIL MARKET

An article entitled *The World Oil Market: An Example of Oligopoly* is published in The Economic Review, Vol 5, No 2, Nov 1987. This article focuses on the way price is set in this industry which consists of a few large scale suppliers of an homogeneous product. It is pointed out that in the early days of OPEC no formal mechanism existed for setting price and dominant firm price leadership provides the best explanation of the way prices were set. Saudi Arabia, by far the largest producer of oil, functioned as the dominant firm and adjusted its output so as to maintain the market price that met its objectives. In more recent years however, OPEC has operated more as a cartel and has aimed to reduce uncertainty over the way rivals might react to price changes and to increase the total profit of cartel members by assigning quotas to each member. The problem with all cartels is that once quotas have been agreed the temptation for an individual is to secretly increase the amount it sells thereby raising its own profit. This is the main reason why cartels tend to be unstable and in the article Nigeria and the United Arab Emirates are cited as two countries who exceeded their quotas. This prompted Saudi Arabia and its ally Kuwait to increase production and thus depress the price of oil in order to punish those countries who exceeded their quotas and by so doing threatened the stability of the OPEC cartel. The result of their actions was the dramatic reduction in the price of oil in 1986. This undoubtedly provided a measure of discipline in respect of quotas and thus stabilised the cartel, but another motive for Saudi Arabia's actions seems to have been to safeguard its market share. The success of the OPEC cartel in raising oil prices has led to a sustained reduction in the amount of oil demanded. By effectively committing OPEC to smaller price rises Saudi Arabia hoped to slow down the reduction in demand for oil and thus safeguard its revenue from oil.

THE MONOPOLIES AND MERGERS COMMISSION

The investigations of the Monopolies and Mergers Commission are again relevant because many of the markets investigated by the Commission more closely resemble the model of oligopoly rather than monopoly. There is no doubt that in these markets the rival producers recognise the high degree of interdependence which exists between them. Evidence of this interdependence is clear in the following extract from the Commission's report into the supply of ceramic sanitaryware. There are four major producers in the industry and on two occasions, in 1975 and 1976, individual companies increased their list prices in the expectation that their competitors would do so to the same extent, but were quickly forced to rescind or reduce their increases when they found that their competitors did not raise their prices as expected.

EXAMINATION QUESTIONS

1   How is the pricing policy of a firm producing apples likely to differ from that of one producing petrol? Discuss why, when crude oil prices fall, petrol prices tend not to fall.

(JMB, 1989)

2   If demand for the product of an imperfectly competitive industry increases, what happens to the price of the product, the output of the industry and the profits of the firms within the industry? How may the existence of barriers to entry affect the outcome?

(CLES, Nov. 1988)

3   Do you agree that successful advertising benefits both the advertiser and society? Explain you answer.

(CLES, Nov. 1988)

4   The following passage is adapted from an article by Anthony Thorncroft entitled *How Companies Fix Prices*

Pricing in practice is exceptionally far removed from the view of traditional economic theory on how companies fix their prices. According to traditional economic theory, price is determined at the level of output at which marginal revenue equals marginal cost. But a recent survey by Industrial Market Research, into how 220 manufacturing companies fix their prices, suggests otherwise. Many prices are 'cost-plus' prices, arrived at by taking a view on the average costs of producing a particular output and then adding a profit margin. Only a third of companies investigate the acceptability of their prices before fixing them. Few companies make use of price in their advertising; they see price as important rather than as vital in overall marketing strategy. As the report says: 'Price is seen as a handicap that has to be carried on the competition stakes while the race itself is won or lost on the basis of quality, applicational engineering or reputation'. Companies increase prices when costs go up, but rarely reduce them if costs ever fall. Price changes are not seen as a means of expanding market share and seldom are scientific methods used to assess the impact of pricing decisions. Hardly any of the firms investigated tested prices.

a) i)   Explain the statement: 'According to traditional economic theory, price is determined at the level of output at which marginal revenue equals marginal cost' (lines 2–4).   (4)

   ii) Suggest reasons why firms may adopt 'cost-plus' pricing (line 5).   (5)

   iii) If prices are usually determined on a cost-plus basis, has the traditional theory of the firm any relevance?   (6)

b)   Why may firms use methods of competition other than price changes in order to expand their market share?   (5)

(*Total 20 marks*)

(AEB, June 1987)

A TUTOR'S ANSWER TO QUESTION 2

Imperfect competition exists when there are many firms producing a slightly differentiated product. In other words each firm's product is considered to be a very close substitute for the product of all other firms in the industry. All firms aim to maximise profit and there is assumed to be perfect information so that consumers are aware of the prices charged by different firms in the industry, and entrepreneurs are aware of the level of profit that producers earn. This information is important to entrepreneurs because there are no barriers to entry and the potential level or actual level of profits will determine whether firms are encouraged to enter or leave the industry.

In some cases product differention exists only because of branding and the use of trade marks. In others there are very slight differences in the additives put into different products. Other techniques involve differences in design, styling, colouring, packaging etc. Whatever the basis on which differentiation is achieved, it has the effect of giving each producer a monopoly over his particular brand of the product. For example, there are many producers of wrist watches, but only one firm produces Gucci watches!

Because there are only slight differences between the different products in imperfectly competitive markets, demand for the product of an individual firm is relatively elastic. Nevertheless, because of perceived differences on the part of consumers, any firm raising its price will retain some brand loyalty. Firms in imperfect competition therefore face a downward sloping demand curve. Because of this the firm's marginal revenue curve will lie below its average revenue curve.

It is assumed that the firm aims to maximise profit and therefore equilibrium is achieved when marginal revenue equals marginal cost. The firm in the diagram below is in equilibrium when it charges a price of OP and produces OQ units of output. Given the cost

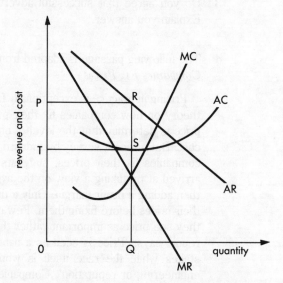

Fig. 6.4 Tutor's answer

and revenue conditions in the diagram it is clear that the firm is earning supernormal profits equal to PRST. Because there is perfect information and no barriers to entry, the existence of these supernormal profits will attract other firms into the industry. Demand for any given firm's product will therefore fall and will probably become more elastic because of the increased number of substitutes available. It is also likely that increased competition for the resources used to produce this commodity will drive up factor prices. The combined effect of these commodity will drive up factor prices. The combined effect of these developments will be to erode the profits of firms in the industry, and indeed firms will continue to enter the industry until all firms are earning only normal profit. This is just sufficient to encourage those firms already in the industry to remain, but insufficient to persuade other firms to enter the industry. The diagram (Fig. 6.5) shows the long run equilibrium price and output of a firm in imperfect competition. The firm is in equilibrium because the price and output combination OP, OQ is achieved by equating marginal cost with marginal revenue. However, at this price and output combination, average revenue exactly equals average cost and therefore the firm is in long run equilibrium and, if it is typical of other firms in the industry, the industry is also in long run equilibrium.

If there is now an increase in demand for the industry's product this will pull up price and result in firms achieving supernormal profit. This increase in demand leads to a higher price and an increase in output. However, it also leads to the firm earning supernormal profit. Therefore, although the *firm* is in equilibrium, the *industry* is not because the existence of supernormal profit will encourage other firms to undertake production.

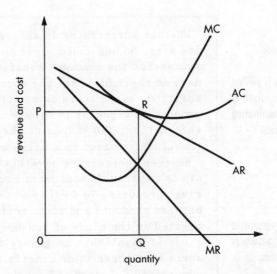

Fig. 6.5 Tutor's answer

In the long run, as more firms enter the industry, total market supply will increase, as will the number of competing brands. As explained above, the individual firm will now face a reduction in demand for its product and its demand curve is likely to become more elastic at any given price. This implies that in equilibrium the price of the firm's product will fall compared to the level that existed shortly after the increase in demand. Equilibrium will be restored when all firms in the industry earn only normal profit, as illustrated in Fig. 6.5 above. In the long run therefore it is clear that the increase in demand for the industry's product has no effect on the profit of the individual firm, although in the short run it does lead to an increase in profit.

We can be equally certain that in both the short run and the long run the *output* of the industry will increase. It will increase initially because each individual firm raises output in response to the increase in demand and in the long run because there will be influx of additional firms to more than compensate for any reduction in the output of original firms.

Again in the short run it is easy to predict that the *price* for the firm's product will rise following the increase in demand for the industry's product. However, it is impossible to predict the *long run* effect of the increase in demand on the price of the firm's product since this depends on several factors, and the specific effect of each is unknown. For example, it depends on the final effect on demand for the product of each individual firm, that is, the effect after additional firms have been attracted into the industry. It also depends on the extent to which increased competition drives up the prices of factor inputs and hence of costs of production. Because of this it is possible for the firm to be in long run equilibrium earning only normal profit at a price greater than, or lower than, that which existed before the increase in demand.

The possible effects on price, output and profits explored here are all based on the assumption that there is freedom of entry into the industry. However, if there are *barriers* which prevent firms from entering the industry, any increase in demand which pulls price upwards will lead to an increase in profits that will continue as long as barriers prevent the emergence of competition. In this case the increase in demand will lead to an increase in price, profit and output that will continue into the long run, and the firm's long run equilibrium position will be as shown in Fig. 6.4 above.

At price OP in Fig. 6.4, the firm's equilibrium output is OQ and the firm earns supernormal profit equal to PRST. As long as barriers to entry exist and there are no further changes in demand or costs, the firm will continue to earn these supernormal profits indefinitely.

A STUDENT'S ANSWER TO QUESTION 3

"Very clear definitions"

There are two types of advertising *informative* and *persuasive*. Informative advertising, as its name suggests, simply aims to provide consumers with information on which to make decisions about their purchases. Persuasive advertising, on the other hand, aims to persuade consumers that one product is in some way superior to competing products.

Good

But there is still an opportunity cost involved in gathering and disseminating information

Even persuasive advertising gives consumers information

An excellent paragraph

Very good

Whether advertising is successful or not must be judged in terms of its aims. No one would argue that if informative advertising is successful the consumer benefits. The more information consumers have at their disposal the more rational their choices will be. In addition, since there is no attempt to persuade consumers that one product is superior to others consumers are not provided with false information. The judgement they exercise when making choices will therefore be based on a full understanding of the facts.

However, persuasive advertising is a different matter,. Here the aim is to persuade consumers to purchase one product in preference to rival products. To do this it is necessary to highlight differences between products and if no real differences exist they must be created in the minds of consumers. This is done by advertising and since it highlights imaginary differences between products, it seems that there is no benefit to society from this type of advertising. Indeed, if consumers are provided with misleading information they will make decisions which do not maximise their welfare because they are based on an incorrect interpretation of information. In the case of imaginary differences consumers believe they are buying something that in reality does not actually exist!

However, the advertiser might derive great benefits from advertising. One possible benefit is that successful advertising will have a favourable effect on demand for the firm's product. This might imply that the firm experiences an increase in demand for the product it has advertised. It might also reduce the elasticity of demand for its product. These are the aims of persuasive advertising and both possibilities might enable the firm to charge a higher price for its product and increase its profits. However, if profits increase because a firm is able to charge higher prices for its product this might be considered a disadvantage from society's point of view. On the other hand, there are possible gains which might partly offset this disadvantage. Increased profits will lead to higher tax payments and this money might be spent in ways which benefit society. Higher profits might also finance research and development and lead to cost reductions in the future as well as the development of new and improved products. Again society benefits from this.

Despite these advantages there are other factors to consider. In particular, advertising can be used as a means of restricting the entry of new firms into an industry. Where existing producers spend relatively large sums of money advertising their products, a potential new entrant to the industry must at least match the advertising expenditures of existing producers if it is to effect entry into the market. This represents a considerable barrier to entry because existing producers finance current advertising from current sales receipts. However, a potential new entrant cannot do this and must finance advertising expenditures in *anticipation* of sales receipts. This not only involves heavy expenditure which firms must have the ability to finance, it also involves considerable risk because there is no guarantee that, having financed advertising expenditures, firms will be successful in breaking into a new market. Because of this, persuasive advertising might discourage the growth of competition and although this might work to the advantage of the advertiser, it is doubtful that it will work to the advantage of society as a whole.

Another important factor to consider is the effect of advertising expenditure on a firm's costs and the way in which this affects the price paid by consumers. Any expenditure on advertising adds directly to a firm's costs of production and might therefore lead to higher prices. As previously argued these higher prices might not

benefit society. However, it is often argued that advertising
actually lowers the price which consumers pay. If advertising is
successful in increasing demand for a firm's product and the firm
gains economies of scale as it expands production, then average
costs of production will fall. If these cost reductions are passed
on to consumers in the form of lower prices then both the firm and
society gain from advertising. This is usually suggested as the main
way in which society gains from advertising. However, whether there
is any gain in practice depends on whether firms gain economies of
scale and whether the benefits of these are passed on to society.

Successful advertising might benefit society and the advertiser
but it does not *necessarily* do so. Clearly if advertising is
successful the advertiser must benefit otherwise advertising would
be unsuccessful. Whether society also benefits depends on whether
the gains of successful advertising are passed on to society or
whether they are simply used to increase the advertiser's profit.

> 66 Advertising revenues also make independent television and radio, along with the production of provincial newspapers, possible. An important point is that if one believes in competition one must believe in persuasive advertising – it is the main instrument of competition! An encouraging answer which is perceptive and clear 99

OUTLINE ANSWERS TO QUESTIONS 1 AND 4

Question 1

A firm producing apples is unlikely to have a pricing policy as such since the market for apples has many of the features of a perfectly competitive market. The firm is therefore likely to be a *price taker*. In answering this question it is necessary to explain the features of perfect competition and to stress their applicability to the market for apples. For example, the good is homogeneous (one Cox's Pippin is regarded as being the same as any other Cox's Pippin), firms supply only a small proportion of the total market, consumers are likely to be well informed about prices and indifferent from whom they buy, and so on.

The market for petrol, on the other hand, is *ologopolistic*. Again you must explain what this means and why it describes the market for petrol. The characteristic feature of such markets is *interdependence* between producers. In such markets no individual firm is free to adopt a pricing policy without considering the reaction of its rivals. In fact price changes in the petrol industry seem to be intiated by the *barometric* price leader. Furthermore, it is often suggested that cost-plus pricing is used by oligopolists to determine prices. You must clearly explain both of these using real world examples if possible. You could use the kinked demand curve to show the importance of interdependence between producers and to explain why, when costs of production change, this does not necessarily result in a change in prices. However, as well as the petrol price stability policies of the petrol majors there is another factor to consider; petrol prices now are determined by the price paid earlier for crude oil! Because of this, a fall in the price of crude oil does not bring about an immediate reduction in the price of petrol.

Question 4

a) i) You could begin your answer to this question by stating that traditional theory assumes that firms aim to maximise profit and then go on to explain why profit is maximised when MC = MR. You must then go on to relate price to profit maximisation showing how monopolists set price by producing where MC = MR, and how firms in perfect competition accept the market price as given and simply adjust output to ensure that MC = MR.

    ii) In the real world firms might not be profit maximisers and different aims will lead them to adopt different pricing strategies. Even if they do aim at profit maximisation they do not possess accurate enough information to allow them to adjust price and output until MC = MR. In any case, strict profit maximisation implies changing prices in response to each short run change in demand so firms might lose the goodwill of consumers if there are frequent changes to price lists. Less frequent adjustments might be administratively more convenient. Nevertheless, firms must make a profit to survive. Covering costs plus a mark-up ensures they do this in a less risky manner than attempting to maximise profit.

Several points could be made here. For example, the usefulness of any theory depends on its predictive powers. If the traditional theory of the firm predicts the behaviour of some firms it has relevance. More generally the theory might be relevant where firms are price takers and profit maximisation is necessary for survival. It is not necessary for firms to calculate MC and MR to maximise profit. Cost plus pricing can also achieve this objective especially if firms aim at long run profit maximisation (see pp. 84–5). It is often suggested that the traditional theory of the firm provides a bench mark against which to compare the actual behaviour of firms.

b)   If firms believe they face a kinked demand curve then non-price competition might be a preferable strategy. To answer this part ot the question you must discuss the implications of the kinked demand curve and the different forms of non-price competition (see pp. 83–4).

Further reading

Begg, Fischer and Dornbusch, *Economics* (2nd edn) McGraw-Hill 1987: Ch. 9, Market structure and imperfect competition.

Maunder et al, *Economics Explained*, Collins Educational 1987: Pricing and output decisions in monopolistic competition and oligopoly.

Stanlake, *Introductory Economics*, (5th edn) Longman, 1989: Ch. 15, Competition in theory and practice.

CHAPTER 7

THE STRUCTURE OF INDUSTRY

SMALL FIRMS

THE GROWTH OF FIRMS

APPLIED MATERIALS

GETTING STARTED

In this chapter we examine the reasons for the continued existence of small firms and the different methods by which firms grow. The motives for growth are also examined in some detail.

We have already seen in Chapter 3 that large firms sometimes gain *economies of scale* and so have cost advantages over small firms. Despite this, small firms continue to survive and are very common in some sectors such as retailing. This is very important since the government has repeatedly stressed its aim of encouraging an expansion of the small firm sector as an integral part of its economic strategy.

Before you proceed with this chapter, an important point to bear in mind is that although it is brief in comparison with some other chapters, this does not imply that it is comparatively unimportant. Examination questions on this topic are still fairly frequent!

SMALL FIRMS

ESSENTIAL PRINCIPLES

There is no uniform measure of size and, therefore, no single criterion against which a firm can be judged small or large. Statistically the most wisely used measures are in terms of employment or turnover (i.e total revenue) per year. However, capital employed is also sometimes used as a measure of size.

REASONS FOR SURVIVAL

Despite the advantages of economies of scale which are experienced by large firms, small firms continue to survive. There may be many reasons for this including:

66 **Why the small firm survives** 99

- Many people prefer to be self-employed and so set up their own business. However, not all people classed as self-employed would also be classed as owning a firm, for example window cleaners. Those that do own a firm often remain 'small' out of choice.

- Small firms have limited access to finance. Many rely on their own savings and that of other family members. This severely restricts growth.

- Small firms often supply small markets. This is true of small independent retailers which often serve neighbourhood communities. Some firms produce specialist goods which cannot be mass produced. In other words small firms flourish where consumers demand variety.

- Sometimes the nature of production is such that size gives no advantage. This is true of repair and window cleaning for example.

- Firms supplying personal services are often small because the nature of the product means that growth does not confer the same advantages on producers as growth of a manufacturing firm does. This is true of hairdressing, for example.

- Small firms often supply a small part of a much larger market that is of no interest to larger firms. For example, Wimpey and Barrett build housing estates but have no interest in barn conversions or house extensions. These are carried out by small jobbing builders. The two groups survive alongside each other but neither competes directly.

- Large firms often sub-contract work to smaller firms. It is often cheaper for larger firms to do so because they can accept a greater volume of work without incurring an increase in overheads. In this sense they act as agents, providing work for smaller firms and charge a fee for their services. (It is doubtful that the clients know the work is sub-contracted or they would contact the firms doing the work direct!)

- In recent years the government has actively encouraged the growth of smaller firms. In particular, measures have been introduced to encourage the unemployed to set up their own businesses and VAT regulations have been changed to ease the cash flow situation of small firms. There is also an Enterprise Allowance Scheme which pays unemployed people £40 per week for a year while they set up their own business. As a result the numbers of self-employed have increased by over 40 per cent to about 1.88 m. Furthermore, the Business Expansion Scheme (BES) provides tax relief on investment by individuals in unquoted public companies, that is, those companies without a Stock Exchange quotation. There is no doubt that these measures have had a powerful impact on the growth of small firms.

THE ROLE OF SMALL FIRMS IN THE ECONOMY

Since the government has done so much to help the growth of the small firm sector it is reasonable to ask why they are considered important. One reason is that if individuals can be encouraged to set up in business rather than remain unemployed this reduces the unemployment figures and might also improve the allocation of resources. After all if workers are unemployed the opportunity cost of this is the output they might otherwise have produced. It is also possible that as unemployment falls and therefore social security payments fall, the government will be able to reduce taxation. This is important because it is frequently alleged that a lower burden of taxation will increase incentives (see pp.

236–8). Small firms might also promote employment because they tend to be more labour intensive than larger firms, so having a proportionately larger effect on employment as they grow.

However, there are other ways in which the growth of the small firm sector might be important to the economy. In particular they are important in providing training and it is generally argued that they can respond more flexibly to changes in market conditions because of their ability to vary output more quickly than larger firms.

THE GROWTH OF FIRMS

There are many reasons why any individual firm might grow but the major factors are probably a desire to achieve increased profits and/or a desire to achieve greater security. Of course, larger firms are not always the most profitable or the most secure, but because they often experience economies of scale they have clear advantages in both of these areas over smaller firms.

The methods by which firms grow can be classified as *internal* or *external*.

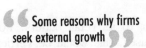
Internal and external growth

- Internal growth occurs when firms plough back profits into additional fixed assets and so expand their productive capacity.
- External growth occurs when one firm combines its existing assets with the assets of at least one other firm.

ACQUISITIONS AND MERGERS

An *acquisition* occurs when one firm purchases another firm from its shareholders. This is often referred to as a *take-over* of one firm by another firm. A *merger* on the other hand is a voluntary agreement between two or more firms to combine their assets into a single firm. While the techniques used to achieve external growth might differ, the motives are often the same.

Reasons for amalgamation

Firms might prefer external growth for a variety of reasons. There might be specific reasons depending on the type of amalgamation or integration which takes place. These are discussed in the following section. Here we focus on some of the more general factors that might explain why firms amalgamate.

Some reasons why firms seek external growth

- External growth can mean the immediate transfer of existing brand loyalty and goodwill which takes time to build up and is not immediately available when a firm grows internally. In other words, when one firm acquires another firm it also acquires whatever consumer loyalty exists for the acquired firm's brands. The advantage of this is that if a firm grows internally it has to *persuade additional customers* to consume its products.

- External growth is sometimes used as a means of *diversifying*. Diversification is important because it increases security for a firm. A firm that produces only a single product, or a small number of related products is vulnerable to changes in demand for its product. Diversification increases the chances of long run survival. Here again it might be considered more expedient to acquire an existing firm already in the market than to attempt entry into the market as an outsider. In such cases the costs of entry can sometimes be high and when an additional producer undertakes supply it usually means an increased number of firms competing for the same fixed market. This can be a dangerous strategy!

- Sometimes external growth offers the prospect of better locations. This is particularly important in retailing.

- Amalgamation might be a means of pooling expertise and sharing the costs of R & D expenditure as in the case of electronics where the R & D expenditures are high. This is particularly appealing when an industry is dominated by an existing producer or where there is a threat of increased competition from abroad.

- A possible motive for an acquisition is *asset stripping*. This occurs when one firm takes over another firm with the intention of breaking the firm up into smaller units which are then resold. This is likely to happen when the price of a firm's equity on the stock market does not reflect the real values of its assets. One reason for this is that management of the firm is incompetent so that profits and dividends have been relatively low. If this were the only reason for asset stripping it might seem that it performed a useful role and the threat of being taken over would most likely encourage efficient management. However, the threat of being taken over might actually encourage inefficiency rather than a long run perspective. They might therefore prefer to recommend higher dividends to shareholders rather than ploughing back profits into long run growth and projects likely to increase long run efficiency. This is a very real possibility. Corporate raiders are always on the look out for possible gains from asset stripping regardless of why these possible gains exist. For example a firm might find the value of its equity is reduced if it has embarked on an expansion program using ploughed-back profits. It therefore could be vulnerable to the threat of a take-over before the benefits of its policies materialise.

HORIZONTAL AND VERTICAL INTEGRATION

Horizontal integration

Horizontal integration occurs when firms in the same industry and at the same stage of the production process amalgamate. There are many motives for horizontal integration:

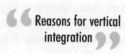
Reasons for horizontal integration

■ Sometimes firms integrate in order to rationalise production, that is, concentrate production in the most profitable units. Such a policy, by reducing capacity in the industry, might reduce fixed costs and also result in higher prices. The combined effect might be to raise the overall profitability of firms in the industry.

■ Another motive might be to take advantage of economies of scale, especially technical economies in the case of manufacturing firms. Since firms are at the same stage of production the desire to reap economies of scale is a particularly important motive for horizontal integration.

■ It is possible that horizontal integration might be motivated by the desire to create a monopoly in the industry. Whatever the motive, since firms are at the same stage of production, it is easy to see that horizontal integration could lead to the formation of a monopoly. For example, if a firm is able to gain control of the retail outlets or of the supply of a particular input, it could effectively restrict the growth of competition and exercise monopoly power.

Vertical integration

Vertical integration occurs when firms in the same industry but at different stages of the production process amalgamate. We can identify:

● *vertical integration backwards*: this occurs when firms amalgamate with other firms in a way which brings them closer to their raw material suppliers. For example, if a newspaper publisher took over a paper mill this would be vertical integration backwards.

● *vertical integration forwards*: this brings a firm closer to its retail outlets. For example, if a brewery took over a chain of public houses, this would be vertical integration forwards.

There are several possible reasons for vertical integration:

Reasons for vertical integration

■ Firms might integrate vertically for strategic reasons. In the case of backward integration the aim might be to safeguard the delivery or quality of raw material. The aim of forward integration might be to ensure that the firm has a chain of retail outlets through which its products can be distributed.

■ Firms might improve and control the image of the retail outlets through which the product is distributed with the aim of increasing sales.

■ Firms might gain economies of scale from either forwards or backwards integration. The increased size of the firm might make financial or managerial economies possible for example. There might also be economies from linked processes (see p. 31).

■ Integration might lead to a reduction in costs. For example, when a firm acquires control of raw material supplies, inspection costs and reject rates might fall. In addition, having a reliable source of raw materials might enable firms to operate with lower stocks. Similarly if firms acquire retail outlets they might be better able to predict market demand or respond more quickly to any increase in market demand. Here again firms will be able to operate with lower stocks than previously.

APPLIED MATERIALS

LLOYDS BANK ECONOMIC BULLETIN

The Lloyds Bank Economic Bulletin No 117, September 1988 looks at the *Benefits of the Mergers Boom*. Fig. 7.1 shows how the value of mergers and acquisitions has changed over the years.

£bn

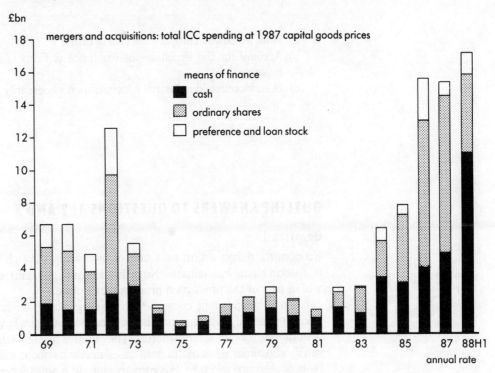

Fig. 7.1 *Source*: Lloyds Bank Economic Bulletin No.117, September 1988

Despite this, the increase in the number of amalgamations does not imply a trend towards monopoly power. Instead, a more important motive at present appears to be the opportunity to diversify, particularly by acquiring companies which are undervalued on the stock market because of inefficient management.

One important point that is stressed is that a merger which reduces competition and increases the profits of the firms which merge, does not necessarily act against the public interest and this is important in establishing any policy aimed at regulating mergers. For example if, after a merger, the firm raises its prices and earns higher profits partly because of this and partly because economies of scale lead to lower average costs, consumers are clearly worse off. However, if the gain to shareholders is greater than the loss to consumers, society as a whole is better off as a result of the merger. In fact, it is alleged that even with a relatively high elasticity of demand of 2, a reduction in average costs of only 5 per cent is sufficient to offset a price increase of 20 per cent in terms of providing a net gain to society!

The implication is that a mergers policy which emphasises competition may be second best from the point of view of society, since it is size which brings net gains. Policy might be better directed to ensuring the redistribution of income from a merger is desirable from society's point of view.

It is suggested that one way in which society might benefit from the increasing threat of a merger is that it might encourage greater efficiency from management. However, it might also encourage short term policies to appease shareholders (see p. 95) or the deliberate pursuit of policies aimed at reducing the attractiveness of a company as a possible target for a take-over.

EXAMINATION QUESTIONS

1   Explain what the economist means by a 'firm' and why organisations as diverse as ICI and a corner shop can be said to possess the same essential characteristics from the economic viewpoint. Consider the possible reason why approximately 90 per cent of firms in the UK are 'small'.

(JMB, 1987)

2 a) Explain the trend towards increasing size of firms selling in national and international markets. *(13)*

b) Discuss the costs and benefits for consumers and employees resulting from the trend described in a). *(12)*

(Total 25 marks)

(Scottish Higher, 1989)

3 a) How would you compare the size of firms? *(5)*

b) Account for the simultaneous existence of firms of different size within the same industry *(7)*

c) Is an increase in industrial concentration necessarily undesirable for the economy? *(8)*

(Total 20 marks)

(Cambridge, June 1988)

OUTLINE ANSWERS TO QUESTIONS 1, 2 AND 3

Question 1

Economists define a firm as a unit of ownership through which decisions are taken to transform inputs into outputs. Note that a firm might control any number of *establishments* where part of the production process takes place.

ICI and independent corner shops possess some similar characteristics and you are asked to identify and discuss these. One obvious similarity is that they both exist to generate a profit for their owner(s). They do this by combining the factors of production to satisfy consumer demand. In both cases decisions about what to produce and how it is to be produced are taken by the *entrepreneur*. In a small independent corner shop this role might be performed by one person; it is shared between salaried managers and shareholders in joint stock companies such as ICI. In answering this part of the question you should therefore consider the functions of the entrepreneur (see p. 26).

The latter part of the question asks about the reasons for the survival of small firms. The relevant points are discussed on p. 94 but you should also try to include examples to illustrate these points. The retail trade, the professions, repair work, photography, bespoke tailoring and building are examples where small firms are common.

Question 2

The main reason for the trend towards large firms is undoubtedly the availability of significant economies of scale particularly in manufacturing but also in the provision of certain services such as financial services. Economies of scale are discussed on pp. 30–31.

However, another factor is that governments now adopt a more lenient attitude towards the growth of large firms and even when a merger threatens to create a monopoly situation there is no automatic referral to the Monopolies and Mergers Commission for investigation. Even when an investigation by the MMC produces an unfavourable report on the desirability of a merger, the government sometimes allows the merger to proceed.

The most likely reason for this is that economies of scale lead to larger firms abroad as well as in the UK. These firms seek further expansion by increasing international sales and have been encouraged by a reduction in certain barriers to trade. For example membership of the EC has encouraged the growth of large European firms.

Question 3

a) Firm size can be measured in various ways, such as numbers employed, value of capital employed, value of turnover, etc. Remember that the same criterion must be used when comparing the size of firms in the same industry.

b) Industries can consist of firms of differing size for many reasons. The main reason for the existence of larger firms is of course economies of scale. However, larger firms might not compete as aggressively against smaller firms as they could, so as to avoid their own emergence as a monopoly. Smaller firms can offer more personal attention which is important when consumers demand variety, as in clothing for example. In addition they can often respond more quickly to changes in demand by consumers than larger firms. In some cases smaller firms supply part of the market which is of no interest to larger firms. In building for example, there are large firms such as Wimpey and Barrett who have no interest in tendering for house extensions because they have expensive pieces of capital equipment which can only be used economically on large projects. Jobbing builders on the other hand have no such overheads. In retailing large firms offer lower prices but smaller corner shops offer convenience and personal service since they are often prepared to deliver groceries and in some cases to extend credit to regular customers. Sometimes they might also offer competitive prices because they organise themselves into a large buying chain for example, Mace VG.

c) Increasing size and concentration of production in fewer hands is traditionally thought to reduce competition within an industry. However, an oligopolistic market is highly concentrated and yet competition in such market is often fierce! You could discuss the different types of competition that might exist in oligopolistic markets (see p. 84). However, increasing concentration often implies a reduction in competition. When there are many firms and a low degree of concentration there is greater consumer choice and therefore a high degree of competition.

It is also possible that increasing concentration will result in barriers to entry and it is possible that firms in a protected market will slow down the process of innovation because they have less incentive to invest in R&D. There might also be *diseconomies of scale* from increasing concentration especially the lack of managerial expertise required to control and co-ordinate more larger firms.

Further reading

Griffiths and Wall (eds) *Applied Economics: An Introductory Course* (3rd edn) Longman 1989, Ch. 4, The small firm; Ch. 5, Mergers and acquisitions in the growth of the firm. Stanlake *Introductory Economics* (5th edn) Longman 1989, Ch. 7, The scale of production; Ch. 8, British industry – size and structure.

GETTING STARTED

National income is a measure of the value of the output of the goods and services produced by an economy over a period of time. Since national income measures production per period of time it is referred to as a *flow concept*. There is often considerable confusion between stocks and flows. A *stock* is the total accumulated quantity of any item existing at a particular time. A *flow*, on the other hand, measures the rate at which that stock is changing. When we are running a bath, for example, the quantity of water in the bath itself is the total stock of water, whereas the rate at which we are adding to that stock of water is the flow of water. Similarly, when we measure national income we are measuring the flow of output over a period of time, and this period is invariably one year.

National income is defined as a flow of output; however, it is the money value of that flow of output which is usually measured. It is not really practical to measure it as so many houses, so many cars, so many washing machines, and so on, produced annually because we have no way of adding these together except in terms of their money value. Nevertheless, one reason for computing national income figures is to provide an accurate estimate of changes in the volume of output produced during one year, which can then be compared with other years. It would be misleading to simply compare the money value of output produced in two separate years because inflation will lead to a higher money value in later years irrespective of whether the volume of output has increased. In order to see what has happened to real national income when two years are compared, we must remove the effect of inflation on prices from data. In order words, we must measure national income at constant prices. An example will illustrate how this is done.

	National income (£m)	Index of prices
Year 1	50,000	100
Year 2	55,000	105

Between Year 1 and Year 2 the money value of national income has increased by 10 per cent. However, prices have increased by 5 per cent over the same period, so that the value of national income in Year 2 in terms of Year 1 prices is:

$$£55,000 \times \frac{100}{105} = £52,381\text{m (approx)}$$

Because we have measured national income at constant prices we can say that the *volume* of output or *real national income*, has increased by approximately 4.8 per cent compared with a rise in money national income of 10 per cent.

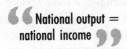

THE CIRCULAR FLOW OF INCOME

ESSENTIAL PRINCIPLES

IN THEORY

We have seen that national income is the *value of output* produced by a country over a period of time. However, the factors of production which create this output will receive rewards in the form of wages, interest, rent and profit. For the economy *as a whole* the value of output produced must be exactly equal to the gross income paid to the factors of production. This is unlikely to be true for any *individual firm* in the economy because, in addition to paying factor rewards, firms will use part of the revenue from selling their output to cover other costs of production in respect of raw material purchases, power to drive machinery, and so on. Nevertheless, for all firms in the economy, the aggregate value of final output produced must be identically equal to the value of gross factor incomes. Hence national output equals national income.

66 National output = national income 99

IN PRACTICE

In practice, indirect taxes and subsidies may distort this identity. Indirect taxes are collected by the Customs and Excise Department; they are placed on goods and services and are paid by firms during the process of production. The most widely known indirect tax is *VAT*. Indirect taxes will raise the market prices of the goods or services above those which are necessary to cover all factor rewards We must therefore *subtract* indirect taxes from the value of output if we are to arrive at our identity. Subsidies will have the opposite effect, reducing market prices below factor cost, so that these must be *added* to the value of output, if the identity is to be maintained.

ADDITIONS TO STOCK AND WORK IN PROGRESS

It is possible to look at national income in yet another way. Incomes received by the factors of production over any given period of time must be equal to the total expenditure on national output over the same period of time. However, at any moment in time this will not necessarily be true. Some output will only be partially complete, while some will be complete but not yet sold. In both cases labour will have been paid, with the result that gross factor incomes will exceed aggregate expenditure. The official statistics refer to incomplete or unsold output as 'additions to stock and work in progress'. Over time, as additions to stock and work in progress are sold, the flow of expenditures will exactly equal the flow of gross incomes paid to the factors of production. However, statistics are compiled at the end of some accounting period when there will always be unsold output and work in progress. For accounting purposes it is therefore convenient to treat the item 'additions to stock and work in progress' as output which has been purchased by firms. In other words, it is regarded as investment by firms and as such is counted as expenditure.

BASIS OF THE CIRCULAR FLOW OF INCOME

66 We can use income, output and expenditure as methods of measurement 99

By adopting the procedures outlined above we are left with the basic accounting identity:

National Income ≡ National Output ≡ National Expenditure

This accounting identity is the basis of the circular flow of income illustrated in fig. 8.1.

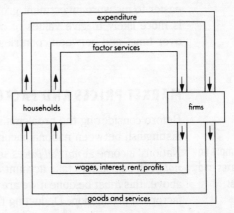

Fig. 8.1 The circular flow of income

As it stands this diagram is highly unrealistic. It neglects the fact that saving and investment take place in the economy; it neglects the role of government in the economy and also the fact that in the real world international trade takes place. However, the diagram does illustrate the very important principle of the circular flow of income, and we shall see in Chapter 9 that it forms the basis of an understanding of the actual flows of income in the economy.

Gross Domestic Product (GDP) is the value of output produced by factors of production located *within* the UK. In other words, it is the sum total of all incomes earned by UK residents when producing goods and services with resources located inside the UK. However, the main official measure of total output is *Gross National Product* (GNP). This measures the total value of output produced, and incomes received, by UK residents from the ownership of resources, *wherever these happen to be located*. GNP therefore takes account of the fact that some UK residents earn incomes such as rent and profit from owning resources located abroad.

FLOW OF INCOME FROM ABROAD

The flow of income from abroad mainly arises because foreign subsidiaries remit payments to the UK parent company. These are referred to as *property income received from abroad*. Similarly, foreign subsidiaries located in the UK remit payments abroad and these are referred to as *property income paid abroad*. The difference between these two flows of property income is referred to as *net property income from abroad*. It may be positive or negative, depending on whether there is a net inflow or net outflow of funds:

i.e. GDP + net property income from abroad = GNP.

Gross National Product is the total value of incomes received by UK residents in the course of a year. It therefore includes the full value of plant and equipment produced during the course of the year (i.e. gross domestic fixed capital formation). However, over this period existing plant and equipment will have *depreciated*, that is, declined in value due to wear and tear and obsolescence. In order to obtain a true measure of national income an appropriate deduction for capital depreciation must be made:

i.e. GNP – depreciation = Net National Product (NNP).

NNP is the aggregate that is most usually taken to mean national income.

WHY IS GNP THE OFFICIAL MEASURE?

This raises the very interesting question that if net national product is national income, then why is GNP the main official measure of the value of incomes received? The answer is simple. Net national product is *conceptually* the better measure, but in practice it is impossible to accurately estimate the value of depreciation. How can we accurately measure the value of wear and tear over the course of a year, or assess the rate of obsolescence? In fact, estimates of depreciation are extremely imprecise and tend to be influenced more by the technicalities of income tax than by other considerations. It is far easier to measure investment gross than net. It is therefore GNP rather than NNP which is more likely to give values of output and income which can be meaningfully compared over time, and between countries.

MARKET PRICES AND FACTOR COST

Before considering the problems involved in actually measuring national income, we must distinguish between national income at market prices and National income at factor cost. National income at *market prices* simply means that the value of output and expenditure has *not* been adjusted to take account of the effect of indirect taxes and subsidies. As we noted above, this must be done if we are to obtain an accurate estimate of the incomes paid to the factors of production. Deducting that part of expenditure paid in taxes, and adding on any

OUTPUT[1]	£m	INCOME	£m	EXPENDITURE	£m
Agriculture, forestry, fishing	5901	Income from employment	226343	Consumers' expenditure	258431
Energy & Water supply	24184	Income from self-employment	32959	General government final	
Manufacturing	85552	Gross trading profits of companies	65596	consumption of which:	
Construction	21524	Gross trading surpluses of general		Central government	51689
Distribution, hotels & catering,		government enterprises	−177	Local authorities	34083
repairs	48963	Rent	24798	Gross domestic fixed capital	
Banking, finance, insurance,		Imputed charge for consumption		formation	70767
business services & leasing	63903	of non-trading capital	3235	Value of physical increase in	
Transport	16227	Less stock appreciation	−4858	stocks & work in progress	627
Communications	9688	Statistical discrepancy	−2282		
Public administration, defence &		Gross Domestic Product at		Total Domestic Expenditure at	
compulsory social security	24895	factor cost	352237	market prices	415597
Ownership of dwellings	20180	Net property income from abroad	5523	Exports	107506
Education & health services	31681			Imports	−112030
Other services	22366	Gross National Product	357760	Gross Domestic Product	411073
Adjustment for financial		Less capital consumption	−48238	Statistical discrepancy	3382
services[2]	−20545			Net property incomes from abroad	5523
Statistical discrepancy[3]	−2282	National Income	309522	Taxes on expenditure	−67980
				Subsidies	5762
Gross Domestic Product at					
factor cost	352237			Gross National Product	357760
Net property income from abroad	5523			Capital consumption	−48238
Gross National Product	357760			National income	309522
Less capital consumption	−48238				
National Income	309522				

1 The contribution of each industry to GDP after providing for stock appreciation
2 To avoid some double counting of interest paid on loans and interest received by financial institutions
3 The statistical discrepancy includes all errors and omissions. It has a different value in the expenditure estimates than in the estimates for output and income because estimates of GDP are built up from independent data on incomes expenditure. The statistical discrepancy is the difference between these estimates, but there is no implication that expenditure estimates are superior in accuracy.

Source: National Income and Expenditure, HMSO 1988.

Table 8.1 United Kingdom national income in 1987 (£ million)

subsidies received by firms, leaves us with national income at *factor cost*; i.e. NNP at market prices – indirect taxes + subsidies = NNP at factor cost. (See Table 8.1)

MEASURING THE NATIONAL INCOME

National income can be measured in any one of the three ways. In theory because they all purport to measure the same aggregate, they should all give exactly the same total. However, in practice this is unlikely to be the case. We are dealing with extremely large aggregates arising out of tens of millions of transactions of varying amounts paid over varying time periods. In these circumstances it would be miraculous indeed if all three measures gave exactly the same result. Additionally, we shall see below that some transactions are recorded in one measure of national income (namely expenditure), but because of illegal dealings there is no counterpart in other measures. The existence of this so-called 'Black Economy' also makes it unlikely that all three aggregates will balance.

In discussing the three methods of measuring national income we shall frequently illustrate our points with reference to Table 8.1.

THE OUTPUT METHOD

A country's national income can be calculated from the output figures of all firms in the economy. However, this does not mean that we simply add together the value of each firm's output. To do so would give us an aggregate many times greater than the national income because of *double counting*. The point is that the outputs of some firms are the inputs of other firms. For example, the output of the steel industry is partly the factor input for the automobile industry, and so on. Clearly, to include the total value of each industry's output in national income calculations would mean counting the value of the steel used in automobile production twice. Double counting can be avoided by summing the *value added* at each stage of production, **or** by adding together the *final value* of output produced.

Whichever method is used to obtain the value of output produced, we must ensure that both additions to stock and work in progress are included in the output figures for each sector. These output figures are shown in the first column of Table 8.1. Given this, certain adjustments to the output figures are needed in order to obtain the value of the national income.

Summing value added avoids double counting

Public goods and merit goods

We have already seen in Chapter 2 that the government provides many goods and services through the non-market sector, such as education, medical care, defence, and so on. Such goods and services are clearly part ot the nation's output, but since they are not sold through the market sector, strictly they do not have a market price. In such cases the value of the output is measured at *resource cost* or *factor cost*. In other words, the value of the service is assumed to be equivalent to the cost of the resources used to provide it. For instance, the education and health services output were together valued at £31,681m in 1987, but most of this was the cost of purchasing equipment and the cost of hiring teachers, doctors, nurses and administrators in providing that output, and only a small proportion of these services were sold on the market.

Self-provided commodities

A similar problem arises in the case of self-provided commodities, such as vegetables grown in the domestic garden, car repairs and home improvements done on a do-it-yourself basis, etc. Again, these represent output produced, but there is no market value of such output. The vast majority of self-provided commodities are omitted from the national income statistics, although an estimate of the rental value of owner-occupied dwellings is included (£20,180m in Table 8.1).

Exports and imports

Not all of the nation's output is consumed domestically. Part is sold abroad as exports. Nevertheless, GDP is the value of domestically produced output and so export earnings must be included in this figure. If exports were omitted, the value of output produced would be less than the value of incomes received from producing that output. Table 8.1 shows that in 1987 export earnings accounted for over 30 per cent of GDP.

On the other hand, a great deal of domestically produced output incorporates imported raw materials and there is a considerable amount of consumer expenditure on imported goods and services. Expenditure on imports results in a flow of factor incomes *abroad*. Hence the value of the import content of the final output must be *deducted* from the output figures if GDP is to be accurately measured. Failure to do this would result in the value of total output exceeding the value of incomes received from producing that output. Table 8.1 shows that import expenditure was equivalent to almost 32 per cent of GDP in 1987.

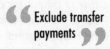
Remember to deduct imports

Net property income from abroad

This source of income to domestic residents will not be included in the output figures of firms. We have already noted that the net inflow $(+)$ or outflow $(-)$ of funds must be added to GDP when calculating the value of domestically *owned* output, i.e. GNP. This gives a figure of £357,760m for GNP in 1987. When we subtract depreciation of capital (capital consumption) we are left with a national income (NNP) of £309,522m.

THE INCOME METHOD

When calculating national product as a flow of incomes it is important to ensure that only *factor rewards* are included. In other words, only those incomes paid in return for some productive activity and for which there is a corresponding output, are included in national income. Of course, it is the *gross value* of these factor rewards which must be aggregated, since this represents the value of output produced. Levying taxes on factor incomes reduces the amount factors receive, but it does not reduce the value of output produced! Income from employment (£226,343m) and from self-employment (£32,959m) together make up over 72 per cent of GNP in 1987. When calculating the aggregate value of factor incomes, adjustments might also be necessary for other reasons.

Gross values of income are summed

Transfer payments

The sum of all factor incomes is not the same as the sum of all *personal* incomes, since the latter includes transfer payments. These are simply transfers of income within the community, and they are not made in respect of any productive activity. Indeed, the bulk of all transfer payments within the UK are made by the government for social reasons. Examples include social security payments, pensions, child allowances, and so on. Since no output is produced in respect of these payments they must not be included in the aggregate of factor incomes.

Exclude transfer payments

Undistributed surpluses

Another problem in aggregating factor incomes arises because not all factor incomes are distributed to the factors of production. Firms might retain part or all of their profits to finance future investment. Similarly, the profits of public bodies, such as nationalised industries, accrue to the government rather than to private individuals. Care must be taken to include these *undistributed surpluses* as factor incomes. It is therefore necessary to add the *gross value* of profits of companies (£65,596m), of public corporations (£6,623m) and of other public enterprises (−£177m), to income from employment and self-employment.

Stock appreciation

Care must be taken to deduct changes in the money value of stock caused by inflation. These are windfall gains, and do not represent a real increase in the value of output.

Net property income from abroad

When measuring either gross national product or net national product we have seen that it is necessary to add net property income from abroad to the aggregate of domestic incomes.

THE EXPENDITURE METHOD

> **Only expenditure on final output is added**

The final method of calculating national income is as a flow of expenditure on domestic output. However, it is only expenditure on *final output* which must be aggregated, otherwise there is again a danger of double counting, with intermediate expenditure such as raw materials being counted twice. Additionally, it is only expenditure on *current* output which is relevant. Second hand goods are not part of the current flow of output, and factors of production have already received payment for these goods at the time they were produced. We should note, however, that any income earned by a salesman employed in the secondhand trade, or the profits of secondhand dealers, *are* included in the national income statistics. The *service* these occupations render is part of current production!

Like the output and income totals, the value of expenditure in the economy must be adjusted if it is to measure national income accurately.

Consumers' expenditure

At £258,431m this is the major element in expenditure in 1987, accounting for over 62 per cent of total domestic expenditure.

General government final consumption

Since only domestic expenditure on goods and services is relevant, care must be taken to deduct any expenditure on transfer payments by the government or other public authorities. Such expenditures do not contribute directly to the current flow of output and, therefore, we must only include that part of public authorities' current expenditure which is spent directly on goods and services. In 1987 public authorities'expenditure on goods and services was £85,772m, that is, just over 20 per cent of total domestic expenditure.

Gross investment

Expenditure on fixed capital, such as plant and machinery, must obviously be included in calculations of total expenditure. Gross Domestic Fixed Capital Formation incorporates this item and, at £70,767m, was 17 per cent of total domestic expenditure. What is not so obvious is that *additions to stock and work in progress* also represent investment. The factors of production which have produced this, as yet, unsold output, will still have received factor payments. To ignore additions to stock and work in progress would therefore create an imbalance between the three aggregates of output, income and expenditure. Additions to stock and work in progress are therefore treated as though they have been purchased by firms. Care must be taken to include them in the aggregate of total expenditure. In 1987 the figure for this item came to £627m.

Exports and imports

We have already seen that it is important to include exports and exclude imports from our calculation of national income. Care must again be taken to ensure this when aggregating total expenditures.

Net property income from abroad

As before, when moving from *domestic* to *national* income, it is important to include net property income from abroad when aggregating total expenditures.

Taxes and subsidies

In measuring the value of expenditure we are attempting to measure the value of payments made to the factors of production which have produced that output. Indirect taxes raise total expenditure on goods and services relative to the amount received by the factors of production. Subsidies have the opposite effect. In order to avoid a discrepancy between the income and expenditure totals it is necessary to remove the effects of taxes and subsidies from the latter. The expenditure total is adjusted to *factor cost* by deducting indirect taxes and adding on subsidies.

NATIONAL INCOME AND THE STANDARD OF LIVING

" An important measure of standard of living "

The most widely used statistic for measuring changes in a country's standard of living is *per capita income*. This is GNP divided by total population and provides a measure of the average amount of output available per head per year. For comparisons to be accurate it is necessary to ensure that GNP is measured at constant prices from one year to the next, otherwise per capita income would probably rise because of inflation but this would not necessarily imply that living standards had increased. Even measuring per capita income at constant prices does not provide an unambiguous measure of changes in living standards. The reasons for this are considered in the Tutor's Answer on pp. 109–10.

INTERNATIONAL COMPARISONS OF THE STANDARD OF LIVING

Despite its shortcomings as a measure of living standards, per capita income is also used to compare the standard of living in different countries. However, there are several problems involved in such comparisons. These are briefly summarised:

- Countries sometimes differ in the way they compute GNP. For example, unlike the UK, the Soviet Union does not include bus journeys made to or from work. The reason is that such journeys do not represent output that becomes available for consumption. They simply enable people to undertake production of goods and services for consumption by others. When GNP is computed differently, per capita income will be an unreliable guide to international living standards.

- There may be substantial differences in the composition of GNP. For example, some countries spend very large amounts on defence compared with other countries. It could be argued that devoting resources to defence preserves liberty and in this way adds to the standard of living. However, it is equally true that the opportunity cost of defence expenditure is a lower output of goods for domestic consumption. Again some countries might devote considerably more resources to the accumulation of capital than others. This might make possible a higher level of output in the future, but only because consumption is foregone in the present. In such cases international comparisons of GNP per head might give a misleading indication of *current* living standards.

- There are other natural or climatic factors that might give rise to differences in the composition of output. Therefore some countries will devote fewer resources to the production of heat and light than is the case in countries where these are provided freely by nature. In the latter countries, resources that are not needed to provide heat and light are available for the production of other goods and services. Again, per capita income might not be very different in two countries, yet there might be marked differences in actual living standards when one country benefits relative to the other from goods provided freely by nature.

" Problems with international comparisons "

- In some countries per capita income might be relatively high in relation to domestic consumption. This is another important factor that might reduce the credibility of per capita income as a measure of living standards. Many OPEC countries, for example, have relatively high per capita incomes, but these are derived mainly from *export* earnings from the sale of oil unmatched by equivalent expenditure on imports. The true standard of living for most people in these countries is therefore relatively low, since domestic income per capita is well above domestic consumption per capita. The converse is also true. It is possible for countries to raise their standard of living in the short term by importing more than they export, that is, by running a *balance of payments* deficit. In this case domestic consumption is raised above its usual proportion of domestic income by increasing imports relative to exports.

Clearly variations between countries in the ratio of per capita income to per capita consumption can complicate the use of national income statistics in assessing standards of living.

■ Even if countries do have similar per capita incomes and similar per capita levels of consumption, they may still have different standards of living for the majority of their respective populations. This would happen where the distribution of income was more equal in one country than in the other. It might also happen where taxation was significantly higher for the majority of the population in one country than in the other.

■ Another factor to consider is the role of the 'black', or informal economy, i.e. those transactions which add to GNP but which are not recorded in the official statistics in different countries. If the black economy were equally significant in all countries, then per capita income would still be useful in comparing relative living standards. However, IMF estimates of the black economy put it as low as 2 per cent of GNP in some countries, and as high as 40 per cent in others. Additionally, living standards are influenced by the availability of leisure time, and the extent to which social costs are imposed on the population as a result of production and consumption. These factors clearly affect overall economic welfare and may vary considerably between countries, but they are not recorded in GNP. Because of this, differences in the standard of living between countries are quite consistent with similar per capita incomes.

■ For purposes of international comparisons there is the problem of converting per capita incomes into a *common unit* of account. In practice this involves converting all per capita incomes into a single currency ($ USA) by using *purchasing power parities* (see p. 108). Any inaccuracies in converting domestic currencies to dollars using purchasing power parities will impair the reliability of comparative per capita statistics.

USES OF NATIONAL INCOME STATISTICS

❝ Reasons for calculating national income ❞

Governments collect national income statistics for a variety of reasons. These can be briefly summarised as:

■ National income statistics are important in the formulation and assessment of macro economic policy. It is clearly important to know current levels of output and patterns of expenditure when formulating policies to combat unemployment, inflation, balance of payments deficits, and so on.

■ National income statistics are used to monitor changes in real income. This is important because changes in real income have an important bearing on changes in living standards.

■ National income statistics are used to make international comparisons between the home country's economic performance and that of other countries. A *relatively* slow growth of real income is a strong indication that the economy is doing less well than it might, and often leads to a detailed scrutiny of the reasons for this 'shortfall'.

■ Per capita income statistics provide a guide to the standard of living in different countries and are used as a basis for allocating aid to third world countries.

APPLIED MATERIALS

INITIAL RESIDUAL DIFFERENCE

Table 8.1 shows how the national income accounts for 1987 were built up at current prices to give gross domestic product, gross national product and national income. Despite efforts to ensure accuracy in the compilation of these statistics, there is a great deal of economic activity which is unrecorded. Such activity is usually referred to as the black economy. It is alleged that in the UK the size of the black economy casts serious doubts on the credibility of official statistics and deprives the government of substantial income tax revenue.

One way in which the size of the black economy can be estimated is by taking the difference between total expenditure and total factor income. This assumes that individuals and organisations have less incentive and opportunity to conceal expenditures than receipts of income. The difference between these two aggregates (known as the Initial Residual Difference) is estimated by the Central Statistical Office at 3½ per cent of GDP for the UK.

GDP in 1985 £	
COUNTRY	GDP PER HEAD
USA	9400
Canada	8500
Norway	8000
Luxembourg	7800
Sweden	7200
Denmark	7000
West Germany	6900
Japan	6600
Finland	6500
France	6500
Netherlands	6500
UK	6200
Belgium	6100
Austria	6000
Italy	5400
Spain	4400
Ireland	4000
Greece	3400
Portugal	3000

Source: Economic Progress Report No 189, March–April 1987

Table 8.2 International living standards in 1985

COMPARISON OF INTERNATIONAL LIVING STANDARDS

Despite the problems of measurement, GNP per capita is still the most widely used estimate of comparative living standards. Table 8.2 shows a recent comparison of international living standards in certain countries. Canada is the closest to the US in terms of real income per head, and Greece and Portugal the most distant, with the UK living standard on this measure about two-thirds of the US.

Purchasing Power Parities measure how many units of one country's currency are needed to buy exactly the same basket of goods as can be bought with a *given amount* of another country's currency. For example, how many pounds are required to buy what can be bought in the USA with a given amount of dollars. This is used as the basis for converting one currency into another currency for purposes of comparing certain aggregates such as GNP and GDP per head.

EXAMINATION QUESTIONS

1   Why might an increase in Gross National Product measured at constant prices be a misleading indicator of economic welfare?

(ODLE, June 1988)

2   'Gross National Product rose last year'
'Gross Domestic Product fell last year'
'Net National Product fell last year'
'Living standards rose last year'
Could all these statements be true simultaneously?

(ODLE, June 1987)

3   a) Distinguish between a country's Gross Domestic Product and its Gross National Product
    b) To what extent will these two measures differ for:
        i)   a developed economy;
        ii) a developing economy?

(CLES, June 1989)

4   The following information is taken from the CSO Blue Book (1987) edition.
National Product by Category of Expenditure – 1987

	£ million
Consumer's expenditure	234, 167
General government final consumption	79, 423
*Gross domestic fixed capital formation	64, 227
*Value of physical increase in stocks and work in progress	551
Exports of goods and services	97, 835
Imports of goods and services	101, 308
Taxes on expenditure	62, 273
Subsidies	55, 806
*Net property income from abroad	4, 686
*Capital consumption	46, 004

    a) Explain the meaning of each of the four terms marked with an asterisk(*)   (8)
    b) Showing your workings, calculate the values of each of the following:
        i)   Gross Domestic Product at market prices
        ii) Gross Domestic Product at factor cost
        iii) Gross National Product at factor cost
        iv) National Income   (8)
    c) Explain what is meant by the term 'National Income'. Why does the Blue Book provide estimates of the National Income in each of the years 1981 to 1986

measured at constant 1980 prices as well as providing estimates based on prices actually prevailing each year? *(4)*

(Total 20 marks)

(Northern Ireland, 1988)

A TUTOR'S ANSWER TO QUESTION 1

Economic welfare is usually measured in terms of the amount of goods and services that become available for consumption by society over any given period of time. Gross National Product (GNP) is important in determining this because it is a measure of the money value of all goods and services becoming available to the nation from economic activity. Dividing this by total population gives a measure of economic welfare which is usually referred to as per capita income. However, there are other components of economic welfare which are not included in any measure of GNP and this limits the use of GNP as a measure of economic welfare.

It is important at the outset to distinguish between gross domestic product (GDP) and GNP. The former is a measure of the money value of all goods and services produced within a nation's borders. However, it takes no account of the *ownership* of the resources used to produce these goods and services. Some resources, although they are located within the borders of one country, are actually owned by residents of another country. This happens when companies establish subsidiaries in different countries. This is important because although output is produced within one country, any part of the income so generated is transferred abroad. These incomes give the recipient country a claim on the output of the country from which they emanate and therefore have an important effect on economic welfare. The *net* value of all such cross border incomes is referred to as net property income from abroad and when the value of this aggregate is added to GDP this yields GNP. It is for this reason that GNP is a better indicator of economic welfare than GDP.

By measuring GNP at constant prices the effect of inflation on the value of output produced between one period and another period can be excluded. This enables us to compare changes in the *volume* of output between different periods. However, even if GNP at constant prices increases between two periods, this does not necessarily imply that economic welfare has increased. If population increases faster than GNP at constant prices, per capita income will fall and this implies a reduction in economic welfare.

Despite this it does not necessarily follow that an increase in per capita income always implies an increase in economic welfare. For example, between two periods, changes in GNP might be influenced by changes in the number of hours worked. A reduction in the size of the working week or an increase in the number of annual days' holiday will have a positive effect on economic welfare even though GNP might be adversely affected. Comparisons of economic welfare should therefore include a measure of the increased value of leisure.

Another factor to consider is that over time there will be qualitative changes in the goods society consumes. Accurate comparisons of economic welfare must make some allowance for the additional satisfaction this confers on consumers.

The government's privatisation programme might also reduce the reliability of GNP as an indicator of economic welfare. Public services such as education are valued at resource cost, but since the consumer has no choice about whether or not to purchase these commodities this estimate of their 'worth' is arbitrary. Indeed, if it *over-estimates* their worth for a particular commodity it is possible that a shift from public sector provision of services to private sector provision would raise the level of economic welfare without markedly affecting the size of GNP.

Problems also arise because many services are performed neither by the government nor the market and therefore do not appear in the national income figures. The services of housewives are the biggest omission here though gardening and home repairs are often done by members of the family. It is difficult to estimate the value of these but there is no doubt that their omission reduces the reliability of GNP as a measure of economic welfare. Despite this, their value is unlikely to change significantly from year to year and it is not thought that their exclusion seriously impairs the reliability of using GNP as a basis for comparing changes in economic welfare in the short term.

Military expenditure is another important factor to consider. A great deal of such expenditure is undertaken simply to avoid giving a military advantage to potential aggressors. However, economic welfare only grows to the extent that higher military expenditure confers a greater sense of security on society. Where society values the additional security at an amount less than total military expenditure, GNP will over-estimate the real value of output by that excess.

Environmental considerations are an increasingly important factor in assessing economic welfare. One consequence of modern production is the pollution of air, soil and water, as well as the degradation of the environment. Such environmental 'costs' are unrecorded but reduce the real value of GNP below the official figures. As a consequence, the reliability of measured GNP is reduced.

Another reason why GNP might not be entirely accurate as a measure of economic welfare is that no allowance is made for capital depreciation. Over time, part of the nation's capital stock comes to the end of its working life and is scrapped. In calculating GNP that part of output which simply replaces obsolete equipment is included and to this extent GNP inaccurately indicates the true value of economic welfare. Similarly, part of the nation's expenditure on education is necessary to maintain the stock of 'human capital' intact. It simply ensures continued availability of skills as people leave the labour force through retirement, and so on. Part of expenditure on education therefore simply covers 'depreciation' and its inclusion over-estimates the real value of GNP.

It seems that GNP does not accurately measure economic welfare because it omits several important factors and inaccurately records the value of others. However, it does measure the total value of output that becomes available for consumption and this is probably the most important factor in determining economic welfare.

A STUDENT'S ANSWER TO QUESTION 3

a) Gross domestic product is the value of output produced within a nation's borders during the course of a year. However, not all of the resources used to produce this output will be owned by the country within which that output is produced. Some will be owned by residents of others countries. These resources will receive payment and will generate a flow of income overseas. This flow of income is referred to as property income paid abroad. Any corresponding flow from overseas is referred to as property income received from abroad. The difference between these flows of income is referred to as net property income paid abroad. Adding net property income from abroad to gross domestic product gives gross national product.

> **Good – clear definitions**

b) A developed economy is likely to have invested funds abroad. To do this it will be necessary to save. If all funds are spent on consumer goods none will be available for investment and only in a developed economy are residents likely to be able to save. In a developing economy the people are very poor and need to spend all their income on the basic necessities of life such as food. In such countries there is very little saving and therefore *very little opportunity for investment overseas.* For developing countries property income received from abroad is therefore likely to be relatively small. On the other hand, because developed countries invest in developing countries, property income paid abroad is likely to be relatively high. For developing countries net property income from abroad is likely to be negative. For a developed country it might be positive or negative depending on how much that country has invested abroad and how much investment it has attracted from abroad. Similarly an important part of output produced in a developed country will be capital goods. However, a developing country will produce fewer capital goods as a proportion of both GNP and GDP. As previously explained, the bulk of its output will be consumer

> **Not necessarily. There will be overseas investment if there is a current account surplus in the balance of payments (see pp. 209–11)**

> **Unclear**

> Some have very large tertiary sectors

> Sometimes the fraction of GNP devoted to these activities is very high

> What kind of differences?

goods and there will be little opportunity to release resources for the production of capital goods.

Typically a developing country will have a large primary sector. In many cases agriculture is the largest industry but in some cases commodities, such as copper in Zambia, are particularly important. Developing countries tend to have small manufacturing sectors and even smaller tertiary sectors. This contrasts markedly with developed countries which have large manufacturing and tertiary sectors but a relatively small primary sector. Even in the UK where we often read of deindustrialisation, the manufacturing sector is large compared with developing countries. It is not surprising that developing countries have small manufacturing and tertiary sectors. Lack of investment restricts the growth of manufacturing and the tertiary sector produces an output that largely consists of 'luxury' goods. It might make us feel better to have our hair trimmed properly by a hairdresser but it is hardly a necessity. In a developing country few people could afford such a luxury.

In developed countries governments typically devote a great deal of expenditure to education and health care. In the UK, for example, about 9 per cent of GNP is devoted to education and health care. This is not true of developing countries which only devote a tiny fraction of GNP to these activities.

There is far more equality in the distribution of income in developed than less developed economies. Indeed in many less developed countries there are extremes of poverty while at the other end of the scale a few individuals are fabulously rich. This creates differences in the composition of GDP and GNP between developed and less developed countries.

These are the main reasons for differences in GNP and GDP in developed and less developed countries. The poverty of less developed countries makes it impossible for them to produce the same type of output as developed countries and in particular there is little scope for diverting resources away from the production of goods for current consumption to the production of capital goods which would increase production in the future.

> A good understanding of the basic points is shown here. However, there will also be considerable differences in the state of the balance of payments – many developing countries are heavily in debt. The accuracy with which statistics are compiled might also explain differences. Developing country statistics are usually less accurate and these countries may well have a larger 'black economy'.

OUTLINE ANSWERS TO QUESTIONS 2 AND 4

Question 2

It is probably best to begin your answer to this question by defining the terms GNP and GDP taking care to explain the difference between them (see p. 102). It is then easy to explain why GDP fell but GDP increased. You must then define Net National Product and explain that if GNP increased then NNP can only fall if depreciation increased by a still greater amount. Unless the increase in GNP was relatively small this would require a very substantial increase in depreciation. For example, in the UK a one per cent rise in GNP would require about an 8 per cent rise in depreciation before NNP could fall! Such an increase is unlikely and in practice there seems some inconsistency between a rise in GNP and a fall in NNP, although it is a possibility.

You must then define living standards, stressing that the most common measure is per capita income or GNP divided by total population. For living standards to have risen last year it is not sufficient that GNP should have increased. To raise living standards, GNP at *constant prices* should increase by more than population increases. The importance of this must be fully explained. It is also necessary to consider other factors that might affect living standards. For example an increase in GNP might be the result of an increase in the length of the working week, more women going out to work, etc. This may not necessarily mean an increase in the quality of life.

Question 4

a) These terms are explained in the text on pp. 102–6.

b) In answering this part of the question you must take care to explain what each aggregate you are calculating consists of and why each sub-total is added or subtracted. The numerical values are i) £374,895m, ii) £368,428m, iii) £373,114m and iv) £327,110m.

c) National income is defined in the text. It is initially measured at current prices for convenience. Current prices provide a common denominator enabling us to measure the money value of *total* output. It is measured at constant prices to give an indication of how the volume of output has changed over the period considered.

Further reading

Begg, Dornbusch and Fischer, *Economics* (2nd edn), McGraw-Hill 1987: Ch.19, Introduction to macro-economics and national income accounting.

Stanlake, *Macroeconomics* (4th edn), Longman 1989, Ch 2, The meaning and measurement of national income.

NATIONAL INCOME DETERMINATION

AGGREGATE DEMAND AND AGGREGATE SUPPLY

THE CONSUMPTION FUNCTION

PLANNED AND REALISED VALUES

THE EQUILIBRIUM LEVEL OF INCOME

LEAKAGES AND INJECTIONS

THE MULTIPLIER

THE PARADOX OF THRIFT

EQUILIBRIUM WITH UNEMPLOYMENT

INVESTMENT

APPLIED MATERIALS

GETTING STARTED

We have seen in Chapter 8 how national income is measured. In this chapter we analyse the forces which determine the size of national income. This is of major importance to an economy, since national income affects both living standards and the level of employment.

In the *short term*, the relationship between real national income and employment is simple: a higher level of output requires the input of more workers, and vice versa. This must be so, because in the short term all factors are constant. There is therefore no possibility of substituting capital for labour. Neither is there any possibility of technological advance leading to the substitution of more efficient capital for less efficient capital. Thus, an increase in real national income leads to more employment, and a fall in real national income leads to less employment.

The model of income determination analysed here is a simple version of the model developed by Keynes, who wrote in his *General Theory of Employment, Interest and Money*, 'The economic system in which we live ... seems capable of remaining in a chronic condition of sub-normal activity for a considerable period without any marked tendency towards recovery or towards complete collapse. Moreover ... full or even approximately full employment is of rare and short-lived occurrence.' Keynes therefore advocated direct manipulation of the forces which determine national income so as to achieve full employment. In the discussion which follows, it is assumed that prices are constant, so that any change in the money value of national income implies an equivalent change in real national income.

Throughout this chapter the following conventional notation is widely used. Where appropriate, definitions of these terms are given in the text.

Y	=	national income
Yd	=	disposable income
C	=	consumption
S	=	saving
I	=	investment
G	=	government current expenditure on goods and services
T	=	taxation (direct and indirect)
X	=	exports
M	=	imports
AD	=	aggregate demand
AS	=	aggregate supply
MRT	=	marginal rate of taxation
MPM	=	marginal propensity to import
APC	=	average propensity to consume
APS	=	average propensity to save
MPS	=	marginal propensity to save
$\triangle$	=	'a change in', e.g. $\triangle S$ = a change in savings
k	=	the multiplier

AGGREGATE DEMAND AND AGGREGATE SUPPLY

ESSENTIAL PRINCIPLES

The term *aggregate demand* refers to the total of planned expenditure for the economy as a whole. *Aggregate supply*, on the other hand, refers to the total output of all firms in the economy. Aggregate supply is therefore the same as *real* national income, which has already been defined as the total value of output produced at constant prices.

THE COMPONENTS OF AGGREGATE DEMAND

For purposes of analysis the components of aggregate demand can be grouped into planned expenditures by the various sectors of the economy. There are four sectors:

- the household sector
- the firm sector
- the government sector
- the international sector

Corresponding to this classification there are four types of expenditure in the economy:

- consumption spending by households
- investment by firms
- government expenditure
- sales of exports abroad

Each type of expenditure is examined in turn. It should be noted that aggregate demand refers to expenditures on the output produced by domestic firms, and does not therefore include expenditures on imports.

Consumption (C)

In the macro sense, consumption refers to the total spending of households on goods and services for their own private use. It is termed 'consumer's expenditure' in the national income accounts. Table 8.1 (p. 103) shows that consumer's expenditure is by far the largest component of aggregate expenditure, comprising 60 per cent of the total. However, care must be taken when analysing the contribution expenditure adds to national income. Part of consumer expenditure is on imports, and this represents spending by domestic residents on goods and services produced abroad. Only that part of consumption expenditure which is spent on domestically produced output adds to national income.

Investment (I)

Investment is the creation of any output that is *not* for immediate consumption. It consists of capital goods, such as factory buildings and machinery, as well as additions to the stock of raw materials, semi-finished goods or finished goods. Total investment is shown in Table 8.1 (p. 103) as gross domestic fixed capital formation, plus the value of the physical increase in stocks and work in progress. Although fixed investment is only about 20 per cent of GNP, it is highly variable. This gives investment an important role in the determination of national income. Again, we should note that imports of capital are excluded from total investment since they do not add directly to national income.

Clearly, in practice, investment will not only help determine the level of national income, but will in part be determined by the level of national income. A higher level of national income, and therefore output, will induce a higher level of investment. However, for simplicity, investment is usually assumed to be an *autonomous* or *exogenous* variable, that is one which does not vary with national income. Put another way, investment is assumed constant at all levels of national income.

Government expenditure (G)

The government is an extremely large spender in the economy, for example, in 1984 total (central + local) government expenditure on goods and services was equal to 25 per cent of GNP. However, not all government expenditure adds directly to aggregate demand. For example, in 1985–86 some 38 per cent of government spending is expected to consist of *transfer payments*, such as social security payments, family income supplement, and so on (see Table 16.4). These are not payments to the factors of production in return for services rendered, they are simply transfers of income within the community. Similarly, government spending on imports adds nothing to national income. However, the remainder of government expenditure represents spending on real domestic output and contributes directly to national income.

Sales of exports (X)

The sale of exports represents expenditure by foreigners on domestically produced output. Exports therefore make a direct contribution to national income, although this is only true of exports *net of import content*.

Summary of aggregate demand

In summary, using the notation established earlier, we can say that:

$$AD = C + I + G + X - M$$

<table>
<tr><td rowspan="4" style="vertical-align:top">THE CONSUMPTION FUNCTION

❝ Know how to calculate these propensities ❞</td></tr>
</table>

The main determinant of consumer spending in the short run is the *level of disposable income*, that is, gross factor income plus transfer payments minus direct taxation. Of course other variables, such as the distribution of income, the cost and availability of credit, and expectations of future income will also affect consumer spending, but these are only likely to change in the longer term.

The relationship between consumption and disposable income is known as the propensity to consume.

- The *marginal propensity to consume* is the rate of change of consumption with respect to disposable income, that is $MPC = \triangle C / \triangle Yd$.

- The *average propensity to consume* is the proportion of total disposable income spent on consumption, that is $APC = C/Yd$.

A *consumption function* shows the different levels of consumption at different levels of income, and is usually presented in the form $C = a + bY$, where a and b are constants. A consumption function of this type is called a *linear* or *straight-line* consumption function, and is illustrated in Table 9.1 and Fig. 9.1 which also includes the corresponding savings function. Initially we assume that any income not consumed is saved; in other words that we have a closed economy with no government so that there is no import spending and no taxation, with saving the only withdrawal.

For simplicity we assume that there is no direct taxation, and that a = £1.000m and b = 0.75. A certain amount of consumption expenditure will always be undertaken, no matter what the level of income. Thus, a is *exogenous* at £1,000m, since it does not vary with income. However, as income rises this will induce a higher level of consumption spending, the extent of which will depend on the size of b, the marginal propensity to consume. In Table 9.1 we note that each time national income rises by £1,000m, consumption rises by £750m, since b = 0.75.

It might seem puzzling that when income is less than £4,000m, consumption is greater than income. The reason for this is that consumption is partly financed by drawing on savings accumulated in previous periods. Since we are running down our previous savings to finance current consumption, the net change in savings is negative. We call this dis-saving by the community.

INCOME (£m)	CONSUMPTION (£m)	SAVINGS (£m)
0	1,000	−1,000
1,000	1,750	−750
2,000	2,500	−500
3,000	3,250	−250
4,000	4,000	0
5,000	4,750	250
6,000	5,500	500
7,000	6,250	750
8,000	7,000	1,000

Table 9.1

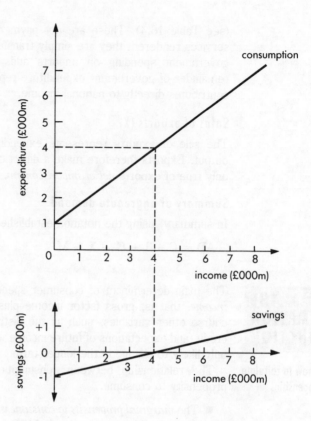

Fig. 9.1 The consumption function and the savings function

PLANNED AND REALISED VALUES

Distinguish planned from realised values

It is important to distinguish between planned and realised values (some textbooks refer to these as *ex-ante* and *ex-post* values, respectively). For example, planned expenditure in the economy is simply the aggregate spending each sector plans to undertake in the next accounting period. Realised expenditure, on the other hand, is the actual level of spending achieved by each sector over that accounting period.

Planned and realised values have most significance in relation to investment because any excess of spending over output (or of output over spending) manifests itself in *unplanned changes in stock*. Since additions to stock are recorded as investment in the official statistics, it follows that any unplanned increase in stocks is referred to as *unplanned investment*. The importance of unplanned investment and unplanned disinvestment is that since they are unanticipated, they lead producers to revise their planned levels of output in the following period. In this way unplanned investment or unplanned disinvestment will initiate *changes in national income*.

THE EQUILIBRIUM LEVEL OF INCOME

Equilibrium exists when there is no tendency to change. It follows that the national income can only be in equilibrium when there is no tendency for it to rise or fall. This can only occur when planned expenditure in one period exactly equals the planned output for that period. When this is the case, producers are receiving back in expenditure on their output an amount which exactly equals the amount they have paid out to the factors of production for producing that output.

We can easily establish that planned expenditure must equal planned output for equilibrium to be achieved. For example, if planned expenditure *exceeds* planned output, then firms will experience unplanned disinvestment as their stocks are depleted. Their response to this will be to raise output in the following period, so that national income will rise. On the other hand, if planned expenditure is *less than* planned output, then firms experience unplanned investment as their stock levels increase. Their response to this will be to reduce output in the following period, so that national income will fall.

It is clear that in equilibrium, planned expenditure in the form of aggregate demand (AD) must equal planned output in the form of aggregate supply (AS). This can be explained in terms of the notation established earlier.

Finding the equilibrium condition

$$AD = C + I + G + X - M$$
$$AS = Y$$
$$AD = AS \text{ in equilibrium}$$
$$C + I + G + X - M = Y \text{ in equilibrium}$$

NATIONAL INCOME (£m)	AGGREGATE DEMAND (£m)	UNPLANNED CHANGE IN STOCKS (£m)	TENDENCY OF CHANGE IN NATIONAL INCOME
1,000	3,500	−2,500	Increase
2,000	4,000	−2,000	Increase
3,000	4,500	−1,500	Increase
4,000	5,000	−1,000	Increase
5,000	5,500	−500	Increase
6,000	6,000	0	No change
7,000	6,500	500	Decrease
8,000	7,000	1,000	Decrease

Table 9.2

Table 9.2 provides a numerical example for the determination of equilibrium national income. It is derived from the following planned values (in £m).

$$C = £1,000m + 0.75YD$$
$$I = £600m$$
$$G = £900m$$
$$X = £500m$$
$$T = 0.2Y$$
$$Yd = Y - T$$
$$M = 0.125Yd$$

$$C + I + G + X - M = Y \text{ in equilibrium}$$

$$1,000 + 0.75Yd + 600 + 900 + 500 - 0.125Yd = Y$$
i.e. $$1,000 + 0.75(Y - 0.2Y) + 2,000 - 0.125(Y - 0.2Y) = Y$$
$$3,000 + 0.6Y - 0.1Y = Y$$
$$3,000 + 0.5Y = Y$$
$$3,000 = 0.5Y$$
$$6,000 = Y$$

> **Equilibrium means at rest**

- If aggregate demand were *greater than* £6,000m, then the value of output, Y, must rise.

- If aggregate demand were *less than* £6,000m, then the value of output, Y, must fall.

It is more usual to illustrate equilibrium diagrammatically and this is done in Fig. 9.2. Since both axes have the same scale, the 45° line which bisects them gives the path of all points of equality between planned expenditure and planned output (national income). It therefore shows all the possible equilibrium levels of national income within the range illustrated. It is clear that given the aggregate demand schedule shown, £6,000m is the equilibrium level of output (income). At levels of output below this, aggregate demand exceeds the value of national output and the tendency will be for the value of national output to rise. At levels of

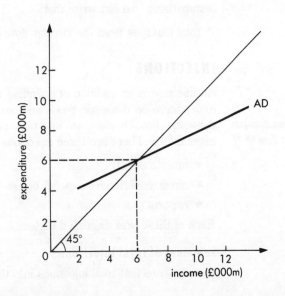

Fig. 9.2 The equilibrium level of national income

output (income) above this, aggregate demand is less than national output (i.e. aggregate demand is insufficient to purchase the existing level of output) and the tendency will be for the value of national output to fall. Only when Y = £6,000m is there no tendency for national output (income) to change, because aggregate demand is just sufficient to purchase the existing level of output.

LEAKAGES AND INJECTIONS

National income equilibrium can be looked at in another way, in terms of leakages and injections.

LEAKAGES

A leakage is a withdrawal of potential spending from the circular flow of income. A leakage occurs when any part of the income which results from the production of domestic goods and services is not used to purchase other domestic goods and services. We can identify three leakages from the circular flow of income:

- savings
- taxation
- import expenditure

Savings (S)

Savings is any part of income received by domestic households which is not spent. By definition, therefore, savings is a leakage from the circular flow of income, and we can write S = Yd − C

Taxation (T)

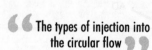
The types of leakage from the circular flow

There are two types of taxation, direct and indirect. Both are leakages from the circular flow of income. *Direct taxes*, such as income tax, reduce potential spending, since they reduce disposable income in relation to gross factor income. Part of the value of output produced is therefore not received by the factors of production, but is withdrawn from the circular flow by the government. On the other hand, *indirect taxes* such as VAT, reduce the receipts of producers in relation to total expenditure. In this case, part of the total spending undertaken by the community is not received by the factors of production since it is paid to the government in indirect taxes. The total tax leak from the circular flow of income is therefore the amount paid in direct taxes plus the amount paid in indirect taxes.

Imports (M)

Import expenditure represents the purchase by domestic residents of output produced abroad. Imports are therefore a leakage, since part of the income received by domestic residents is not returned to the circular flow as expenditures on domestic goods and services.

Summary of total leakages

Summarising, we can write that:

total leakages from the circular flow of income = S + T + M.

INJECTIONS

An injection is an addition of spending to the circular flow of income. It consists of any expenditure on domestic goods and services which does not arise from the spending of domestic households. An injection is therefore spending other than consumption expenditure. There are three injections into the circular flow of income. They are:

The types of injection into the circular flow

- investment (I)
- direct government expenditure on goods and services (G)
- exports (X)

Each of these was discussed earlier.

Summary of total injections

We can write that total injections into the circular flow of income = I + G + X.

AN ALTERNATIVE VIEW OF EQUILIBRIUM

Realised injections must always equal *realised* leakages, but the economy can only be in equilibrium when *planned* injections equal planned *leakages*.

- If planned injections into the circular flow of income are greater than planned leakages from it, then national income will tend to rise. This is because planned spending will exceed national output (income) so producers will experience unplanned disinvestment in stocks and will expand output in the following period.

- Conversely, if planned injections are less than planned leakages, then national income will tend to fall. Planned spending will now be less than national output (income) so there will be insufficient demand to purchase existing output. Producers will experience unplanned investment in stock and will reduce output in the following period.

It follows that national income can only be in equilibrium when *planned injections* equal *planned leakages*. The equilibrium condition may therefore be stated as:

$$I + G + X = S + T + M$$

This is clearly shown in Table 9.3 which extends Table 9.2 to include the various injections and leakages discussed above.

Note: planned injections are assumed to be exogenous and do not vary with income.

The appropriate values (in £m) are:

$$C = £1,000m + 0.75Yd$$
$$I = £600m$$
$$G = £900m$$
$$X = £500m$$
$$S = - £1,000m + 0.25Yd$$
$$Yd = Y - T$$
$$T = 0.2Y$$
$$M = 0.125Yd$$

National Income Y	Aggregate demand AD	Planned savings S	Planned taxation T	Planned expenditure on imports M	Planned government expenditure G	Planned export sales X	Planned investment I	Realised investment	Tendency to change in National Income
0	3,000	−1,000	0	0	900	500	600	−2,400	Increase
1,000	3,500	−800	200	100	900	500	600	−1,900	Increase
2,000	4,000	−600	400	200	900	500	600	−1,400	Increase
3,000	4,500	−400	600	300	900	500	600	−900	Increase
4,000	5,000	−200	800	400	900	500	600	−400	Increase
5,000	5,500	0	1,000	500	900	500	600	100	Increase
6,000	6,000	200	1,200	600	900	500	600	600	No Change
7,000	6,500	400	1,400	700	900	500	600	1,100	Decrease
8,000	7,000	600	1,600	800	900	500	600	1,600	Decrease

Table 9.3

The equilibrium level of income is £6,000m, because this is the only level of income at which planned injections equal planned leakages. (See also the solution on p. 120) Since planned spending exactly equals national output (income), producers will experience no unplanned investment in stock, i.e. planned investment = realised investment. There will be no incentive for producers to change output in the following period. If income is at any other level it will have a tendency to increase or decrease.

Again, equilibrium can be represented diagrammatically, this time using the injections and leakages approach. This can be seen in the lower part of Fig. 9.3 which uses the values of Table 9.3. The upper part of the diagram reproduces Fig. 9.2 in order to help us compare the two approaches. Planned injections (I + G + X) are constant at £2,000m. Planned leakages (S + T + M) vary with national income. To plot the leakages curve we can add together the various values of S, T and M in Table 9.3 at each level of national income. Alternatively, we can derive the leakages function by adding together the separate functions for S, T and M.

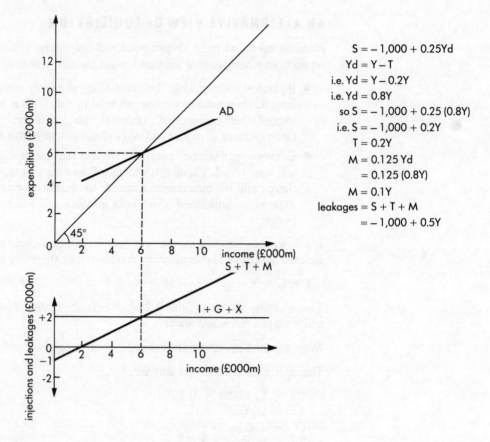

$$S = -1,000 + 0.25Yd$$
$$Yd = Y - T$$
i.e. $Yd = Y - 0.2Y$
i.e. $Yd = 0.8Y$
so $S = -1,000 + 0.25\,(0.8Y)$
i.e. $S = -1,000 + 0.2Y$
$$T = 0.2Y$$
$$M = 0.125\,Yd$$
$$= 0.125\,(0.8Y)$$
$$M = 0.1Y$$
leakages $= S + T + M$
$$= -1,000 + 0.5Y$$

Fig. 9.3 The equilibrium level of income

THE MULTIPLIER

> Be familiar with the multiplier

One of the most important features of the Keynesian model is that it shows how any change in injections or leakages can lead to a more than proportional change in national income. This is known as the *multiplier effect*. It arises because an initial change in injections or leakages leads to a series of changes in national income, the cumulative effect of which exceeds the initial change which brought it about. For example, if firms increase their investment in plant and equipment, and all other things remain equal, national income will initially rise by the same amount as the increase in investment. If we assume an absence of taxation, the increased expenditure on plant and equipment will in turn be received as rewards by the factors which have produced this output. Part of this (depending on the size of the MPC) will be spent, generating a further increase in income, part of which will also be spent, and so on. However, this process does not go on indefinitely. With each rise in income, a smaller amount will be passed on, and this will generate successively smaller changes in income.

A NUMERICAL EXAMPLE

A numerical example will help to clarify this. For simplicity we assume there is only one injection, i.e. investment, and one leakage, i.e. savings. Assume further that nine-tenths of any increase in income is spent on consumption and that investment in plant and equipment rises by £100m. The letter k is used to denote the multiplier. The increase in investment initially raised income by £100m, £90m of which is subsequently spent on consumption, so that output and income rise by a further £90m. Nine-tenths of this £90m is also spent on consumption, so that output and income rises by a further £81m, and so on. We can see that income goes on rising as a geometric progression diminishing to infinity. The first few terms of this series, together with the final value (in £m) are set out below.

$$\triangle I = £100m$$
$$\triangle Y = £100m + £90m + £81m + £72.9m + \ldots$$
i.e. $\triangle Y = £1000m$
$$k = \triangle Y / \triangle I = £1,000m/£100m = 10$$

This implies that an increase in injections causes an eventual increase in income which is ten times greater than the initial increase in injections.

Effect on savings

It is equally interesting to look at what happens to savings following the increase in investment. We have seen that for each increase in income there is an increase in consumption. But since not all of the increase in income is passed on, there must also be an increase in savings. In fact, since in this discussion savings is the only leakage from the circular flow, it follows that $\triangle Y = \triangle C + \triangle S$. In other words, savings also rises as a geometric progression diminishing to infinity, and the first few terms of this series, together with the final value (in £m), are:

$$\triangle S = £10m + £9m + £8.1m + ...$$
$$\text{i.e.} \quad \triangle S = £100m$$

The significant point is that, following an increase in investment of £100m, income goes on rising until households wish to save a further £100m. This is because equilibrium can only exist when planned injections equal planned leakages. Following an increase in planned investment, these two items are brought into equality by an increase in income which encourages the households to revise their savings plans upwards.

THE VALUE OF THE MULTIPLIER

The value of the multiplier can be obtained by using the formula:

$$K = \frac{1}{(1 - \text{common ratio})}$$

This can be applied to the example above. Thus

$$K = \frac{1}{1 - \text{MPC}} = \frac{1}{1 - 0.9} = 10$$

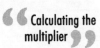
Calculating the multiplier

However, when there are other leakages from the circular flow of income, it is more usual to express the multiplier as:

$$K = \frac{1}{\text{marginal rate of leakage from gross income}}$$

In the four sector economy this can be written as:

$$K = \frac{1}{\text{MPS} + \text{MRT} + \text{MPM}}$$

For example, using the values from which Table 9.3 was derived (i.e. MPS = 0.25Yd, MRT = 0.2Y, and MPM = 0.125Yd) we can calculate:

$$K = \frac{1}{0.25(0.8) + 0.2 + 0.125(0.8)}$$
$$= \frac{1}{0.5}$$
$$= 2$$

THE BALANCED BUDGET MULTIPLIER

The balanced budget multiplier shows the effect on income of *equal* changes in government expenditure and taxation. It might be expected that the net effect would be zero and that income would remain unchanged. In fact, the following example illustrates that this is not the case.

Suppose there is an increase in government current expenditure of £100m, financed entirely by an increase in taxation of £100m, with MPC = 0.8Y and MPS = 0.2Y

■ The increase in government spending will lead to a diminishing series of *increases in income*. The first few terms and the eventual sum of this series (in £m) are:
$$\triangle Y = £100m + £80m + £64m + ... = £500m$$

■ The increase in taxation will lead to a similar series of *reductions in income*.

■ The change in tax, however, is not so straightforward as the change in government expenditure; part of any increase in taxation will be financed by a reduction in the amount saved. To the extent that this is the case, the increase in one leakage from the circular flow of income (tax) is in part compensated for by the reduction of another. In other words, the net change in leakages is less than the change in taxation. Thus, only that part of any increase in taxation which is financed by a *reduction in consumption*, rather than by a reduction in savings, has any effect on income.

In our example, the net increase in leakages is equal to 0.8T, because one-fifth of the increase in taxation is financed by a cut in savings. Only that part of any increase in taxation which leads to a reduction in consumption has any effect on national income. It follows that the increase in taxation of £100m will lead to a diminishing series of reductions in income. In this case the first few terms (in £m) and the eventual sum of the series are:

$$\triangle Y = -\frac{0.8\triangle T}{1 - 0.8}$$

$$\triangle Y = -(80 + 64 + 51.2 + \ldots) = -£400m$$

Thus, the *net* result of an equivalent increase in G and T is that income rises by £100m, i.e. by the increase in government expenditure. The *balanced budget multiplier* therefore has a value of one.

THE PARADOX OF THRIFT

❝ Attempts to save more can be self defeating ❞

We have already seen that in a two sector economy *realised savings* must always equal *realised investment*. However this does not imply that an increase in planned savings will always lead to an equivalent increase in investment. Indeed the *paradox of thrift* indicates that in some circumstances an attempt by the community to increase aggregate savings actually leads to a fall in aggregate savings and investment.

TWO SECTOR MODELS

In two sector models of the economy, the equality between savings and investment is often illustrated using symbols:

$$Y = C + I$$
$$Y = C + S$$
$$\therefore I \equiv S$$

It seems that on the basis of this identity, that an increase in savings must indeed lead to an increase in investment. However, the identity refers to *realised* savings and *realised* investment. If *planned* savings and *planned* investment are not equal, then INCOME will be changing so as to ensure that planned and realised savings equals planned and realised investment. Now, if the economy is initially in equilibrium and the community attempts to increase its savings when there is no simultaneous increase in planned investment by firms, firms will experience an *unplanned increase in stocks*. This is because they will be receiving back from the community an amount which is less than the value of output produced. This increase in stocks will ensure that realised investment equals the higher value of realised savings, but the change in investment was unplanned and will not therefore continue.

In fact, firms will react to an unplanned increase in stocks by cutting back on the amount of output they produce. As output falls, incomes will fall, and this will reduce the ability of the community to save. In other words, an attempt by the community to save more, actually leads to a reduction in savings. This is referred to as the 'the paradox of thrift' and it is illustrated in Fig. 9.4.

The economy is initially in equilibrium at OY with planned investment = planned savings = OX. An increase in the propensity to save at all levels of income shifts the savings function from SS to S_1S_1. This causes the equilibrium level of income to fall from OY to OY_1. The equilibrium level of savings and investment is now OX_1. In other words, the community's attempt to save more has actually resulted in a reduction in the amount saved (and a reduction in the level of investment).

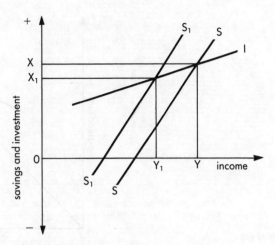

Fig. 9.4 The paradox of thrift

EQUILIBRIUM WITH UNEMPLOYMENT

THE DEFLATIONARY GAP

We have seen that with a given level of aggregate demand (i.e. given values for planned leakages and planned injections) there is only one possible equilibrium level of national income. Any other level will be unstable and the economy will be tending to move towards the equilibrium level. The main problem with which Keynes was concerned was unemployment, and he pointed out that it will only be by pure chance that the equilibrium level of national income and the full employment level of national income coincide. In fact, the economy can be in equilibrium with large numbers of the workforce unemployed. Keynes regarded the great depression of the 1920s and 1930s as just such a case.

In terms of the Keynesian model we can say that unemployment exists when aggregate demand falls short of the level necessary to achieve full employment at the current price level. Keynes argued that in cases such as this the government should pursue expansionary policies to raise aggregate demand and so reduce unemployment. This is analysed in Fig. 9.5.

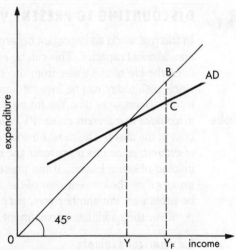

Fig. 9.5 The deflationary gap

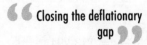

Closing the deflationary gap

With aggregate demand given by AD, the equilibrium level of income is OY. However, if OY_F is the full employment level of income, we can say that BC is the deficiency of aggregate demand compared with the level necessary to generate full employment. In fact, BC is referred to as the *deflationary gap*, and a government wishing to achieve full employment must pursue policies to close the deflationary gap, such as raising the level of G or reducing the level of T. Policies aimed at managing the level of aggregate demand so as to achieve various economic aims are discussed more fully in Chapter 17. Reducing the level of T would raise disposable income, and therefore increase C at any given level of gross income. This would be shown as an upward shift of the aggregate demand function (AD = C + I + G + X − M).

THE INFLATIONARY GAP: OVERFULL EMPLOYMENT

It is possible for the level of aggregate demand to exceed the level necessary to achieve full employment at the current price level. This case is analysed in Fig. 9.6.

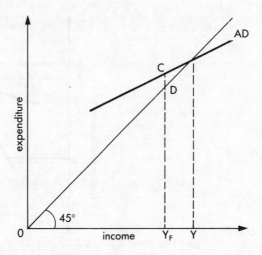

Fig. 9.6 The inflationary gap

In terms of Fig. 9.6 OY_F represents the full employment level of income. With aggregate demand equal to AD, the equilibrium level of income is OY. However, it is impossible to achieve an equilibrium level of real income which is greater than the level achieved at full employment, because physical output cannot be increased beyond that achieved at full employment.

In this case OY is an unattainable level of real income. Once the economy reaches the full employment level of output, OY_F, any excess of aggregate demand over the level necessary to achieve full employment, i.e. CD in Fig. 9.6, is therefore referred to as the *inflationary gap*. The government must pursue contractionary policies in order to close the inflationary gap and so stop prices rising. This implies the pursuit of policies to reduce aggregate demand by CD, such as reducing the level of G or raising the level of T.

> Closing the inflationary gap

INVESTMENT

DISCOUNTING TO PRESENT VALUE

In the real world an important determinant of investment is the expected net rate of return on additional capacity. This can be estimated by subtracting the estimated operating costs over the life of the asset from the expected revenue through additional sales. However, since cash today can be invested and so earn interest, it is worth more than cash in the future. Because of this, the future stream of net returns expected from the asset must be *discounted to a present value* (PV) *equivalent* which can then be compared with the current cost of the asset. The most obvious discount rate of use for this purpose is the *current rate of interest*, since this represents the return foregone if cash is used to purchase fixed assets instead of being loaned. If the present value (PV) of this future stream of net returns is *greater than* the current cost of the asset (its *supply price*), then additional investment will be profitable. Put another way, *net present value* (NPV) = PV – supply price; if NPV is positive, then additional investment will be profitable.

> Finding the present value of a flow of income

A numerical example

The problem can be set out numerically. For example, assume a firm is contemplating the purchase of an additional machine with an expected life of five years and a current cost (supply price) of £10,000. Assume further that expected annual net returns (i.e. expected revenue minus expected operating costs) are £5,000, £5,000, £3,500, £2,000 and £1,000 respectively. If the machine has no scrap value after 5 years and the current rate of interest is 10 per cent, then the present value of the future stream of earnings from buying the machine can be set out as follows:

$$PV = \frac{£5,000}{(1.1)} + \frac{£5,000}{(1.1)^2} + \frac{£3,500}{(1.1)^3} + \frac{£2,000}{(1.1)^4} + \frac{£1,000}{(1.1)^5} = £13,294$$

Thus, purchasing the machine is expected to yield a profit of approximately £13,294 at current prices. Subtracting the current cost of the machine, i.e. £10,000, still yields a positive net return of £3,294.

In other words the Net Present Value (NPV) = PV – supply price = +£3,294. Since NPV is positive, additional investment will be profitable.

THE MARGINAL EFFICIENCY OF CAPITAL

The preceding calculation is more important in explaining investment by individual firms than in explaining aggregate investment. Nevertheless, it forms the basis of the Keynesian approach to investment. The only difference is that instead of discounting to present value, we obtain *the rate at which future earnings must be discounted* in order to bring their present value into equality with the current cost of the capital asset (*the supply price*). Keynes referred to the *rate of discount* which brings a stream of future earnings into equality with current capital costs as the *marginal efficiency of capital*.

> **MEC is a rate of discount** "

- If the marginal efficiency of capital (MEC) is greater than the current cost of borrowing funds to finance the investment, that is the rate of interest (R), then additional investment will be expected to yield a profit.
- If MEC = R then there is neither gain nor loss from the investment.
- If MEC < R, then the investment will be unprofitable.

MEC schedule

At any moment in time different investment projects will have a different marginal efficiency of capital, but if these are aggregated then we can obtain a marginal efficiency of capital schedule. Assuming that firms aim to maximise profit, the marginal efficiency of capital schedule will show the demand for capital at various rates of interest. This is shown in Fig. 9.7. When the rate of interest is OR the aggregate demand for capital is OM.

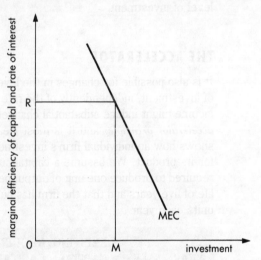

Fig. 9.7 The determination of investment

One important feature illustrated by the diagram is that the demand for capital varies inversely with the rate of interest. There are two main reasons for this:

- As investment increases, the return on additional investment, that is the marginal revenue productivity of capital (see p. 138), is likely to fall because:
  - greater investment will increase the amount of goods or services available; this will tend to depress their prices, reducing the expected revenue from extra investment projects, and therefore reducing MEC

> **Investment varies inversely with the rate of interest** "

  - as investment increases beyond some point, firms will experience diminishing returns to capital; a fall in the productivity of capital will also reduce the expected revenue from extra investment projects, and therefore reduce MEC
- Greater investment demand might pull up the cost of the capital asset, (i.e. the supply price of capital), and therefore reduce MEC.

The combined effect of these factors will be to reduce the return on additional investment, giving a downward sloping MEC schedule. Thus a reduction in the rate of interest will raise the demand for capital because it will make it profitable to undertake investment projects that were unprofitable at a higher rate.

Investment decision-making

Although there is no doubt that changes in the rate of interest influence investment decisions, the relationship is unlikely to be as precise as Fig. 9.7 implies. There are many reasons for this, including:

- A great deal of investment in the public sector is undertaken for social reasons. Economic considerations have far less influence on such investment.
- In practice it is extremely difficult to estimate the marginal efficiency of capital.
- The investment plans of large firms often stretch over several years and changes in the rate of interest are unlikely to persuade them to revise their plans once they have embarked upon them. Unplanned investment in stocks is unlikely to be affected by changes in the rate of interest.
- In times when the government is exercising tight control over the availability of credit, it might not be possible to obtain funds for investment, even when such funds can be used profitably.
- The volatility of expectations which will cause the MEC schedule to shift wildly to left or right.

Let us consider this last reason more fully. The current rate of interest is only one factor influencing the decision to invest. The *expectations* of people in the business world is another important consideration. Expectations often change rapidly, so the whole MEC schedule will be highly unstable. If expectations about future economic conditions decline, the expected revenues from investment projects will fall and the whole MEC schedule will shift to the left. The opposite will happen if expectations about the future improve. The fact that investment may therefore change substantially even when the interest rate is unchanged, means that there will be a poor statistical fit between the interest rate and the level of investment.

THE ACCELERATOR

It is also possible for changes in the level of income to exert a powerful effect on the level of investment, independently of the rate of interest. In other words, changes in the level of income might induce substantial changes in investment. This is usually referred to as the *accelerator principle*, and it is most clearly understood by reference to Table 9.4 which shows how an individual firm's investment decisions are influenced by changes in demand for its product. We assume a capital/output ratio of 2:1 (that is, two units of capital are required to produce one unit of output per period), that each unit of capital has an economic life of five years and that the firm has built up its capital stock by regular additions of 2,000 units each year.

YEAR	SALES	EXISTING CAPITAL	REQUIRED CAPITAL	REPLACEMENT INVESTMENT	NET INVESTMENT	GROSS INVESTMENT
1	5,000	10,000	10,000	2,000	0	2,000
2	6,000	10,000	12,000	2,000	2,000	4,000
3	7,500	12,000	15,000	2,000	3,000	5,000
4	8,000	15,000	16,000	2,000	1,000	3,000
5	7,750	16,000	15,500	2,000	−500	1,500

Table 9.4

Table 9.4 clearly shows the impact of changes in demand on investment. During Year 2 sales rise by 20 per cent, but this induces a rise in gross investment (i.e. net investment + replacement investment) of 100 per cent! The proportionate change in investment is not so spectacular in Year 3, with gross investment rising by only 25 per cent despite the greater (25 per cent) increase in sales. However, during year 4 there is a smaller proportionate increase in sales than in previous years, and this causes a decline in the *absolute* level of investment. A simple increase in sales is not therefore sufficient to induce an increase in investment. The level of investment will only go on rising when sales are rising at an *increasing rate*. The table also shows the effect of a reduction in sales on investment.

Effect of sales on investment

From the table we can see that $In = a\triangle Y$, where In is net investment, 'a' is the capital/output ratio (2), and $\triangle Y$ is the absolute change in sales. In practice it is unlikely that investment will vary with sales as precisely as implied in the table because:

- firms might meet increased demand out of stocks or might choose to lengthen waiting lists rather than increase investment

- firms might consider the increase in demand is only temporary, and will not therefore raise their investment
- rather than increasing investment to meet the extra demand it is more likely that firms will, initially at least, introduce overtime working, etc.
- there are likely to be technological advances which will raise the productivity of capital and so reduce the need for additional investment to meet increased demand for output
- firms might currently have excess capacity from which they can meet any increase in demand

Despite these qualifications there is no doubt that changes in income can exert a powerful influence on investment decisions. While the accelerator is not a precise model, it may, nevertheless, help to explain the instability of investment demand.

APPLIED MATERIALS

THE UK ECONOMY

One of the important concepts used in the Keynesian theory of income determination is the multiplier. However, in practice it is difficult to estimate the value of the multiplier. Nevertheless, it is unlikely that the marginal rate of leakage from changes in income will equal one. We can therefore be fairly certain that any change in injections will lead to a change in income that is larger than the change in injections. One estimate of the multiplier in the UK by M. Kennedy puts its value at 1.35. Other studies quoted by Kennedy (in Prest and Coppock (eds) *The UK Economy*) produce a different value for the multiplier (mainly because they are based on different assumptions), but they are not vastly different from the estimate given here and it seems there is general agreement that the multiplier has a relatively low value in the UK.

There may be several reasons for the relatively low value of the multiplier. There is no doubt that the UK has a relatively high propensity to *import*. Kennedy estimates its value at 0.24 of GDP at factor cost. Additionally, the rise in the savings ratio in the UK to relatively high levels in recent years implies a relatively high marginal propensity to save. However, there is general agreement that tax levels in the UK are not disproportionately high compared with other countries. It follows that the value of the multiplier in the UK is likely to be *relatively low*, largely because of the relatively high marginal propensities to import and save.

THE CONSUMPTION FUNCTION

An article in the Economic Review Vol 5, No 2 Nov 1987 entitled *The Consumption Function: theory and evidence* sets out to answer two basic questions. In summary these are:

a) Is there a stable relationship between consumption expenditure and disposable income?
b) Do changes in the rate of interest influence consumption expenditure?

The period studied runs from 1971 Quarter 1 (Jan – March) to 1987 Quarter 2 (April – June).

The typical Keynesian consumption function is usually expressed in the form C = a + bY where C is consumption spending, Y is the level of income and a and b are constants. It is suggested in the article that there was indeed an apparently stable relationship between changes in real consumption expenditure and real disposable income observed during the period under review, with the MPC equal to about 0.8. Furthermore it is shown that changes in income and changes in consumption follow the same basic pattern. A rise in income is followed, after about a year, by a rise in real consumption expenditure; and a fall income is followed, after about a year, by a fall in real consumption expenditure. The relationship between income and consumption is not therefore due to some statistical chance as might happen, say, if both had a natural, though unconnected, tendency to rise over time.

It is sometimes suggested that changes in the rate of interest, by changing the opportunity cost of current consumption, have an impact on consumer spending. This argument is examined by comparing changes in the real rate of interest with changes in consumer expenditure. It is shown that at best there is only a very weak relationship between these two variables during the period studied. Indeed it is pointed out that the

APC in 1975 when the real rate of interest was − 13.6% was almost indentical to the APC in 1982 when the real rate of interest was +5.88%.

Despite this conclusion the government has relied on rising interest rates during 1988 and 1989 to curtail consumer spending, that is, to deal with the 'consumer boom'. There is some evidence that after a time lag this policy did in fact lead to a reduction in consumer spending.

MANUFACTURING INVESTMENT IN THE UK

An article, again in the Economic Review Vol 6, No 3 Jan 1989, entitled *Investment Theory and Evidence* examines the behaviour of manufacturing investment in the UK over the last 18 years. The definition of investment used is gross fixed investment in plant and machinery for the manufacturing sector. The period of the investigation is 1971 (Q1) to 1987 (Q2).

After comparing changes in the rate of investment with changes in the real rate of interest it is argued that only a weak relationship exists between these two variables. It is suggested therefore that changes in the rate of investment are also caused by other factors.

Similarly the article tests the validity of the accelerator hypothesis. It is suggested that there are definite peaks in investment which are preceded by peaks in the output of the manufacturing sector. Indeed it is argued that a 1 per cent rise in output will be followed, three quarters later, by a 1.6 per cent increased in investment for the period considered. This suggests a type of accelerator relationship, though it is admitted that in practice the relationship will not be as stable as this.

EXAMINATION QUESTIONS

1 'Jobs boost as US firm announces new investment in west of Scotland factory.'
   a) Describe how a change in investment has a multiplier effect on national output and employment in the economy. (15)
   b) Explain the factors which determine the size of the multiplier effect. (10)
   (Total 25 marks)
   (Scottish Higher, 1988)

2 'Investment is a function of aggregate demand.' Discuss.

   (AEB, Nov 1987)

3 What factors influence the value of aggregate savings in the economy? Show how a fall in the level of planned savings will affect the equilibrium level of income.

   (Northern Ireland, 1987)

4 Study the data below, then answer the questions which follow.
   The following data is for a hypothetical closed economy which initially is in short run macroeconomic equilibrium.

   i)   The consumption function is given by the equation $C = 100 + 0.8Y_D$ where C denotes consumption in £ billion and Y_D denotes disposable after tax income in £ billion.
   ii)   All government revenue is raised by a 25% proportional income tax. Hence $Y_D = 0.75Y$ where Y denotes national income in £ billion.
   iii) Private investment spending = £1,400 billion.
   iv)   Government spending on goods and services = £2,500 billion.
   v)   National income (Y) = £10,000 billion.

   a) What are the initial values of consumption, savings and government tax revenue? (5)

   b) What is the relationship between the average propensity to consume and the marginal propensity to consume in this economy? How does the average propensity to consume vary as disposable income increases? (5)

   c) Suppose that private investment spending subsequently decreases to £1,000 billion.

What, other things being equal, is the change in national income that is predicted by the Keynesian income-expenditure model?

(5)

d) If government expenditure and the tax rate remain unchanged, what is the government budget deficit or surplus at the equilibrium level of national income following the decrease in private investment?

(5)

e) Suppose the government wishes to achieve a return to the original national income of £10,000 billion via increasing after-tax disposable incomes by means of non-taxable cash benefits paid to households. If the consumption function is unchanged, by how much must government expenditure on cash benefits increase?

(5)

(Total 25 marks)

(WJEC, 1988)

A TUTOR'S ANSWER TO QUESTION 1

a) According to conventional Keynesian theory the economy will always tend towards an equilibrium level of national income. This equilibrium exists when the amount of planned spending in one period exactly equals the amount of planned output by firms in the same period. In other words, equilibrium exists when planned aggregate demand equals planned aggregate supply. Any discrepancy between these in one period will result in changes in plans, and therefore changes in output, in the following period.

If we consider an economy which is initially in equilibrium, it is possible to show how an increase in investment has a multiplier effect on national output and employment. An increase in investment will create a situation where planned spending exceeds planned output at the existing level of national income.

Assuming there are unemployed resources in the economy, firms will respond to the increase in demand by increasing output. In order to increase output, additional workers will be drawn into employment and will receive incomes, along with the other factors of production. These workers will spend at least part of their incomes, and this implies that planned spending will again exceed planned output, even though national income has already increased above its original level. The proces will repeat itself. Firms will increase their planned output still further for the following period and will take on additional workers who will receive incomes, part of which they will also spend, and so on. It is this process which is referred to as the *multiplier*.

However, the multiplier does not imply that national income goes on rising indefinitely. The final increase in income following the initial change in investment depends on the magnitude of the increase in investment and on the size of the multiplier. In fact it can be shown that $\triangle Y = K \triangle I$ where $\triangle Y$ is the change in national income, K is the value of the multiplier and $\triangle I$ is the change in investment.

The multiplier has a finite value because *not all* of the income which is received in one period is passed on in the next period. In other words, there are *leakages* from the circular flow of income. These leakages take three forms: a tax leak, a savings leak and an import leak. The proportion of any increase in gross income paid in taxation is referred to as the *marginal rate of taxation* (MRT); the proportion of any increase in income which is saved is referred to as the *marginal propensity to save* (MPS); and the proportion of any increase in income which is spent on imports is referred to as the *marginal propensity to import* (MPM).

The *combined value* of these is referred to as the *marginal rate of leakage* (MRL) and it is this which determines the value of the multiplier because it determines what proportion of income is spent on domestic output at each stage. For example, if the marginal rate of leakage (MRL) is 0.5, this implies that 50 per cent of any additional income received will be spent on domestic output. Thus, if investment initially rises by £1,000m, the effect on national income will be:

$$£1,000m + £500m + £250m + £125m \ldots\ldots = \triangle Y = £2,000m$$

£1,000m is the *initial* change in investment. This leads to a further spending on domestic output of £500m in the next round. Then 50 per cent of this, that is, £250m, is again spent on domestic output. The final change in income is £2,000m, which implies that the multiplier has a value of 2.

The precise value of the multiplier is usually expressed in the form:

$$K = \frac{1}{\text{marginal rate of leakage}} = \frac{1}{\text{MRT} + \text{MPS} + \text{MPM}}$$

and multiplying this by the change in investment gives the final change in income.

The multiplier effect of a change in investment can also be illustrated diagrammatically using the conventional 45° or 'Keynesian Cross' diagram, as shown in the diagram below.

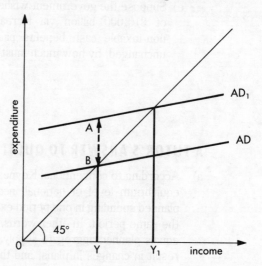

Fig. 9.8 Tutor's answer

AD is the initial level of aggregate demand and AD$_1$ shows aggregate demand after an increase in investment equal to AB. The initial equilibrium level of income is OY and the new equilibrium level is OY$_1$. Because the same scales are used on both axes it is clear that the increase in income (OY – OY$_1$) is greater than the increase in investment (AB), which implies that the increase in investment leads to a change in income which is equal to some multiple of the initial change in investment. In this case the value of the multiplier is equal to YY$_1$/AB.

b) The size of the multiplier is determined by the marginal rate of leakage (MRL). One important factor which affects the MRL is the distribution of income. Since higher income groups have a higher MPS than low income groups, a less equal distribution of income implies a lower value for the multiplier. The tax system can have an important effect here. Where taxation bears more heavily on lower income groups this will also reduce the value of the multiplier because these groups tend to have a higher MPC (i.e. lower MPS). For the same reason a general increase in taxation will reduce the value of the multiplier.

Some countries are heavily dependent on imports and have a relatively high MPM. In such cases the size of the multiplier will be lower than otherwise. A related factor is the overall level of economic activity in the economy. When the economy is close to full employment there will be *supply inelasticities* or *supply bottlenecks*. Firms will therefore find it difficult to recruit additional workers, to obtain additional supplies of raw materials, etc., in response to an increase in investment. This will limit any increase in output, and, if the increase in investment is large enough, might generate inflation because the higher level of demand for resources would pull up their prices. Such bottlenecks will also encourage the consumption of imports. An economy which is experiencing supply inelasticities will therefore tend to have a lower value for the multiplier.

Another factor that will affect the size of the multiplier is the response of firms to an increase in demand. Where firms currently have high stock levels they might choose to run down stocks rather than increase output in response to an increase in demand. Moreover, when an increase in demand is not considered to be permanent, firms might simply lengthen their waiting lists, or allow the higher level of demand to bid up the price of their products. In all these cases the value of the multiplier will be lower than otherwise.

The size of the multiplier will also be lower if 'crowding out' takes place. 'Crowding out' is the term used to describe the effect of an increase in public sector investment on private sector investment. In particular it is argued that an increase in public sector investment 'crowds out', that is, reduces, private sector investment. Where crowding out does take place an increase in public sector investment will have a smaller multiplier effect than an increase in private sector investment.

A STUDENT'S ANSWER TO QUESTION 4

a) $C = 100 + 0.8Y_D$ and $Y_D = Y - T = £7,500bn$
$= 100 + (0.8) 7,500$
$= £6,100bn$

66 Method well
displayed 99

$S = Y_D - C$
$= 7,500 - 6,100$
$= £1,400bn$

$T = 0.25Y$
$= £2,500bn$

66 No. MPC is constant but
APC declines as income
rises! 99

b) Average propensity to consume is total consumption/total income and marginal propensity to consume is $\triangle C/\triangle Y$. In this economy because MPC is constant, APC = MPC = 0. Because APC is constant, a change in disposable income has no effect on APC.

c) In this economy the multiplier (K) is equal to $1/1-MPC$, that is,

$$\frac{1}{1 - 0.6} = 2.5$$

Given the value of the multiplier, the change in income following a change in investment is equal to $K\triangle I$. From the figures we are given this works out to be $2.5(£1,000bn) = - £2,500bn$.

66 Investment only falls by
£400bn, to £1.000 bn 99

d) In equilibrium
$Y = C + I + G$
$= 100 + 0.8Y_D + I + G$
$= 100 + 0.8(0.75Y) + 400 + 2,500$
$= 3,000 + 0.6Y$
$\Rightarrow Y = £7,500bn$

66 Good analysis 99

In equilibrium $T = 0.25Y = £1,875bn$
The government, therefore, has a budget deficit $(G - T)$ of £625bn.

e) Since the original consumption function is unchanged, the value of the multiplier is unchanged at 2.5. In order to return to the original equilibrium level of income the government must therefore bring about an increase in income of £2,500bn. This implies an increase in cash benefits of £1,000bn because $\triangle Y = \triangle J$ where $K\triangle J$ represents any change in injections.

66 No. An increase in government spending on goods and services of £1000 bn will raise income by £2500bn, but part of any expenditure on transfer payments will be saved. To give the required level of income, $\triangle J = £1000$ bn and with MPC = 0.8 *transfer payments* must rise by £1250 bn. Calculation questions are often very easy but watch out for pitfalls 99

OUTLINE ANSWERS TO QUESTIONS 2 AND 3

Question 2

One way to begin your answer is to define and explain the accelerator showing how an *increase* in income has an accelerator effect on investment (see pp. 126–7). In this sense investment is a function of income. However, the rate of interest is also thought to be an important determinant of demand and you must explain the relationship between the marginal efficiency of investment and the rate of interest (see pp. 125–6). You should stress that investment is influenced by the rate of interest and is not simply a function of income.

In fact there are many factors which determine income. Expectations about future changes in income, future changes in the exchange rate, future changes in interest rates etc. are particularly important. The role of expectations is crucial in determining investment and you must use this role in examining the validity of the accelerator and MEI approaches to investment.

Question 3

There are many factors that determine the aggregate value of savings but the most important is undoubtedly income. In less developed countries there is little scope for saving whereas in developed countries a great deal of saving takes place for a variety of reasons. Another important factor is the availability of financial institutions in which people have confidence. Where such institutions are lacking, saving will be lower. At times when it has a budget surplus the government can be major saver. The customs of society can have a profound effect. In Victorian Britain, saving was considered a virtue and in modern Britain more and more people have taken out private pension schemes, have an occupational pension scheme or have insurance endowment policies to provide for their retirement. Changes in the rate of interest might also effect the level of savings although its influence is not thought to be strong in the UK. A fall in the level of planned savings implies a fall in the marginal rate of leakage and an increase in planned consumption expenditure. The equilibrium level of income will therefore rise by an amount equal to the additional consumption spending × the multiplier. In explaining this take care to stress the importance of planned expenditure and planned output in determining equilibrium. These points could be most effectively illustrated by means of a numerical example, but be careful not to get too bogged down in detail!

Further reading

Begg, Dornbusch and Fischer, *Economics* (2nd edn), McGraw-Hill 1987: Ch. 20, The determination of national income; Ch. 21, Aggregate demand, fiscal policy and foreign trade.

Stanlake, *Macroeconomics: An introduction* (4th edn), Longman 1989: Chs. 3–10.

CHAPTER 10

WAGES

THE MARGINAL PRODUCTIVITY THEORY

INDUSTRY'S DEMAND FOR LABOUR

DETERMINATION OF WAGES

THE EFFECT OF A TRADE UNION

COLLECTIVE BARGAINING

APPLIED MATERIALS

GETTING STARTED

We have seen in Chapter 8 that the value of all factor incomes received in a particular year is equal to a country's gross national product. In this chapter we are concerned with the share of national income that goes to labour in the form of wages. Reference to Table 8.1 (p. 103) shows that approximately 70 per cent of all incomes earned are wages.

With the exception of profit, the reward that any factor of production receives is clearly equal to the price which is paid to hire it. As with all prices in competitive markets, the price of any factor of production is determined by supply and demand. However, the factors of production are not demanded in order to obtain ownership, as is the case with consumer goods, but rather because of the stream of services they offer. For example, the demand for labour implies a demand for the mental and physical effort of workers involved in production. Because of this, the demand for labour (and indeed for any factor of production) is referred to as a *derived demand* rather than a direct demand. It is derived from the product which labour (and all other factors) produces.

The classical theory of income distribution is the *marginal productivity theory*. According to this theory firms will continue to employ factors of production until the employment of the marginal unit of each factor adds as much to revenue as it does to costs. For simplicity it is sometimes assumed that there is perfect competition in the market in which the product is sold so that firms sell their entire output at the *ruling market price*. In these circumstances the contribution of the marginal unit of any factor of production, that is its *marginal revenue product*, is equal to the factor's *marginal physical product* multiplied by the price at which the product is sold.

In markets which are not perfect, firms will be compelled to reduce price in order to sell more units. Because of this, marginal revenue product can only be measured as the change in total revenue when the additional output of the marginal factor is sold.

THE MARGINAL PRODUCTIVITY THEORY

ESSENTIAL PRINCIPLES

> MRP is the employers' concern

We have seen in Chapter 3 that the marginal physical product of labour is the addition to total output from the employment of the marginal worker. The *law of variable proportions* predicts that marginal physical product at first rises but subsequently falls as the employment of workers increases. However, employers are not so concerned with marginal physical product as with marginal revenue product (MRP) and profit maximising firms will continue to employ workers until the last person employed adds exactly the same to revenue as to costs, i.e. until MRP = MC.

This is the basic prediction of the marginal productivity theory, and it is possible to consider the implications of this in different market structures.

PERFECT COMPETITION IN THE FACTOR AND PRODUCT MARKETS

If we assume perfect competition in the product market, so that the firm sells its entire output at the ruling market price, and perfect competition in the labour market, so that the firm recruits workers at a constant wage rate, the profit-maximising condition is easily demonstrated.

NO. OF WORKERS	TOTAL PRODUCT	MARGINAL PHYSICAL PRODUCT	MARGINAL REVENUE PRODUCT	MARGINAL COST	TOTAL REVENUE PRODUCT	TOTAL COST	PROFIT
1	12	12	60	100	60	100	−40
2	26	14	70	100	130	200	−70
3	50	24	120	100	250	300	−50
4	90	40	200	100	450	400	50
5	140	50	250	100	700	500	200
6	200	60	300	100	1,000	600	400
7	254	54	270	100	1,270	700	570
8	304	50	250	100	1,520	800	720
9	340	36	180	100	1,700	900	800
10	358	18	90	100	1,790	1,000	790
11	374	16	80	100	1,870	1,100	770
12	378	4	20	100	1,890	1,200	690

Table 10.1

Table 10.1 assumes a constant market price for the product of £5 per unit and a constant wage rate of £100 per worker per week. It is clear that after the employment of the second person and up to the employment of the ninth person, each worker adds more to revenue than to cost. After the employment of the ninth worker the situation is reversed and each additional employee adds more to costs than to revenue. It follows that profit is maximised when nine people are employed.

The individual firm's demand for labour

The general relationship between MRP, ARP and the number of workers employed at a constant wage rate is set out diagrammatically in Fig. 10.1. At a constant wage (= MC = AC) of OW the profit maximising firm will employ OM workers, where MRP = MC. If the market wage rate increases to OW_1, the number of workers employed will fall to OM_1. It follows that when there is perfect competition in the factor and product markets, the firm's demand for labour curve is that part of its MRP curve which lies below its ARP curve. At wage rates above ARP the firm is making a loss and will not undertake production.

> The firm's demand curve for labour, under perfect competition

IMPERFECT COMPETITION IN THE PRODUCT MARKET

The fundamentals of the analysis are unchanged if we relax the assumption of perfect competition in the *product market*. There will still be a tendency for marginal revenue product at first to rise and to pull up average revenue product because of increasing returns. Subsequently, the onset of diminishing returns will mean that MRP will fall as

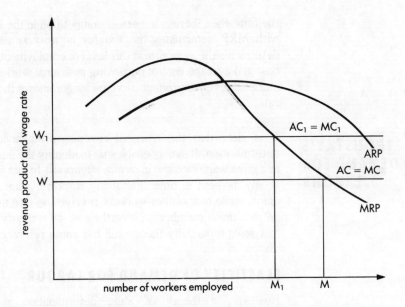

Fig. 10.1 Wage rates and
employment in perfect competition

successive workers are employed, and this will eventually pull down the ARP. However, with *imperfect product markets* there are now two reasons why marginal revenue product declines as employment expands beyond a certain point:

- the onset of diminishing returns
- firms with imperfect product markets must now reduce the price of all units in order to increase sales (see Chapters 5 and 6).

In imperfect markets then, marginal revenue product is determined both by marginal physical product and by the effect on market price of an increase in output. Because price will always fall in imperfect markets as output increases, the effect is to make the MRP curve fall more steeply then for firms in perfect competition. Nevertheless, where the firm recruits additional workers at a constant wage rate, its demand for labour is still given by its (now steeper) marginal revenue product curve.

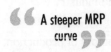

A steeper MRP curve

IMPERFECT COMPETITION IN THE FACTOR MARKET

When there is imperfect competition in the *factor market* the firm will be unable to recruit as many workers as it wishes at the ruling wage rate. Instead it will be compelled to increase wage rates in order to attract more workers. The marginal cost of employing additional workers will therefore rise as employment increases, so that the marginal cost curve will now lie above the average cost curve. Fig. 10.2 shows the equilibrium position of

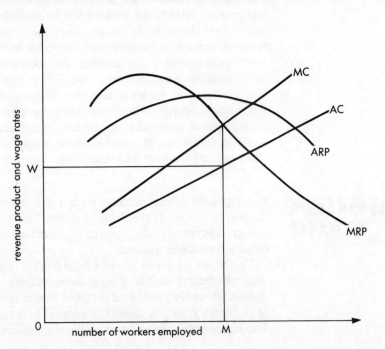

Fig. 10.2 Wage rates and
employment in imperfect
competition

the firm when there is imperfect competition in the factor market. The intersection of MC with MRP determines the *number of workers employed* and the average cost curve determines the *wage rate* at this level of employment. In other words because the marginal cost and average cost of employing additional workers are no longer the same, the firm's marginal revenue product curve no longer shows the demand for labour at any given wage rate.

INDUSTRY'S DEMAND FOR LABOUR

It is clear that the marginal revenue productivity theory is not a theory of wage determination. It simply enables us to identify the number of workers that will be employed at a *given* wage rate and in *certain situations*. In fact for most workers, wage rates *are* fixed at any moment in time. For many workers, wages are negotiated collectively by their union, while many other workers receive the rate negotiated by unions even though they are not union members. Nevertheless, as a theory of the firm's *demand for labour*, the marginal productivity theory still has some relevance.

ELASTICITY OF DEMAND FOR LABOUR

However, a theory of wage determination in competitive markets involves an understanding of the *market demand* and *market supply* conditions which relate to any particular occupation. If we know the number of workers each firm demands at any given wage rate, then we can derive the *industry's* demand for labour by adding together the *individual firm's* demand curves. Because each individual firm's demand for labour will also vary inversely with the wage rate, the industry's demand for labour will also vary inversely with the wage rate. In other words, market demand for labour will expand as the wage rate falls. The *elasticity* of an industry's demand for labour will, as with any factor of production, vary *directly* with:

> **Factors affecting elasticity of demand for labour**

- the elasticity of demand for the product produced by the industry
- the proportion of total costs of production accounted for by labour
- the elasticity of substitution between labour and other factors of production, in other words, the ease with which labour can be substituted by other factors.

The demand for labour will therefore be less elastic;

- the less elastic is the demand for the product it produces,
- the smaller the proportion of total costs accounted for by labour input,
- the less easy it is to substitute labour by capital or by other factors.

SUPPLY OF LABOUR AND THE WAGE RATE

The supply of labour to any particular occupation will vary directly with the wage rate. At higher wage rates more workers will be available for employment in the occupation and vice versa. However, in certain cases the supply of labour to an occupation might be relatively inelastic in the short run. For example, where the nature of work is highly skilled and requires considerable training, the supply of labour to the occupation will *not* rise substantially as wage rates increase. This is true of doctors and barristers, for example. Nevertheless, the supply of labour to *all* occupations will be more elastic in the long run than in the short run. Where wages increase in particular occupations, more people will be encouraged to undertake the necessary training, so increasing the amount of labour available. In the case of unskilled labour, supply will tend to be relatively elastic in both the short run *and* the long run, since little, if any, training is required.

DETERMINATION OF WAGES

In competitive labour markets wage rates are determined by the forces of supply and demand for labour. In these circumstances, different wage rates between occupations will reflect differences in the respective conditions of supply and demand conditions in two hypothetical labour markets.

The higher wage rate in one labour market is due entirely to the fact that *at any given wage rate* demand for labour is *greater* and supply of labour is *lower* than in the other labour market. However you should also note that in this labour market, demand for, and supply of labour are relatively inelastic compared to the labour market with the lower wage rate. The higher wage rate is therefore likely to reflect conditions in a market for skilled labour

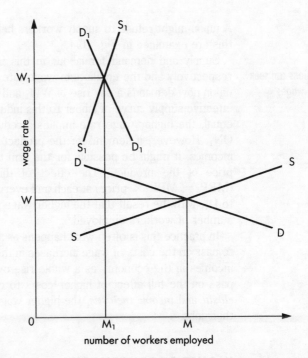

Fig. 10.3 Wage rates in different labour markets

and the lower wage rate is likely to reflect conditions in a market for unskilled labour. The different elasticity conditions will be an important factor in preserving the wage differential between these labour markets.

Given a free market and a particular set of supply and demand conditions for labour, only one wage rate is sustainable: that which equates supply of labour with demand for labour. It follows that wages in a particular occupation can only change if there is a prior change in the conditions of supply, or in the conditions of demand, or in both. Furthermore, differences in wage rates between occupations will reflect differences in the conditions of supply and demand for different types of workers.

THE EFFECT OF A TRADE UNION

A trade union is usually defined as a group of workers who band together to purse certain common aims, especially the achievement of wage increases for their members. A trade union can therefore influence the supply of labour to an industry depending on the extent to which the workforce are members of the union. Their ability to obtain such increases depends on several factors and in particular on the elasticity of demand for labour as discussed on p. 136. If all other things are equal, a union's ability to obtain higher wages is greater, the *less elastic* the demand for labour.

There are several areas to consider.

RESTRICTING SUPPLY

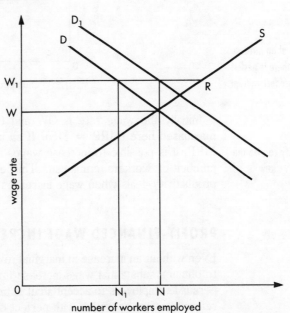

Fig. 10.4 The effect of a trade union on wage rates and employment in an industry

A union might refuse to supply workers below a particular wage rate. The implications of this are examined in Fig. 10.4.

Supply and demand for labour in this industry are initially represented by S and D respectively and the equilibrium wage rate is OW with ON workers employed. If a trade union now demands a pay rise of WW_1 and refuses to supply labour below OW_1, then the effective supply curve of labour to this industry becomes W_1RS. If all other things remain equal, the higher wage rate implies a reduction in the number of workers employed to ON_1. However, if demand for the product is rising, perhaps because of a general rise in incomes, it might be possible for the firm to finance the increase in wages by raising the price of the product. The effect of this will be to raise the demand for labour ($MRP = MPP \times$ price) at each and every wage rate. In this case the demand increases to D_1, with the result that the higher wage rate OW_1 does *not* lead to any reduction in the number of workers employed.

In practice this is often what happens as a result of an increase in wages. Firms are able to pass on the costs of wage increases in the form of higher prices, helped by the fact that incomes in the economy as a whole rise over time. However, when firms are *unable* to pass on the full effect of higher costs to consumers because demand is relatively *price elastic* and *income inelastic*, the higher wage increase might lead to some workers losing their jobs.

HIGHER PRODUCTIVITY

Another way in which a trade union might obtain a higher wage rate for its members is by increasing productivity. If all other things remain equal, it is possible to increase wage rates by the same percentage as an increase in productivity *without* increasing average costs of production. Of course, because of increased productivity the firm will have a larger output to sell. Provided price remains constant this again implies an increase in the demand for labour as each worker's marginal revenue product increases. Fig. 10.5 illustrates that in these circumstances it is possible for a firm to pay higher wages without necessarily reducing the number of workers employed.

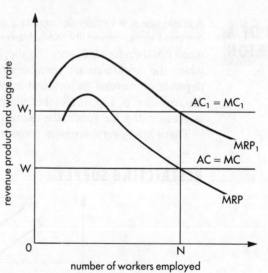

Fig. 10.5 The effect of an increase in productivity where there is perfect competition in the product market

Initially the wage rate is OW and ON workers are employed, because profits are maximised here (MRP = MC). If an increase in productivity shifts the MRP curve to MRP_1 it is possible to increase wages to OW_1 without there being any reduction in the number of workers employed. This explains why so much emphasis is attached to productivity deals when wage increases are negotiated.

PROFIT-FINANCED WAGE INCREASES

Even without an increase in marginal revenue productivity it might be possible for a union to obtain a substantial wage increase for its members. This would be possible if it could persuade employers to accept a cut in profits. Fig. 10.6 is used to illustrate this point and refers to a firm operating with perfect competition in the factor and product markets.

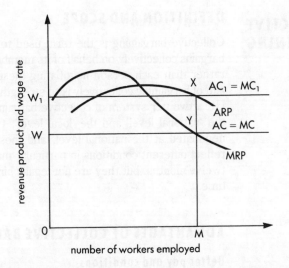

Fig. 10.6 The net contribution of labour to profit

If ARP and MRP represent the *net* returns to labour it follows that at the profit maximising level of employment (OM), employers earn a surplus of XY per worker. If unions can persuade employers to accept a smaller surplus it is possible to negotiate a higher wage rate above the existing level OW, without reducing the number of workers employed. For example, employers might be willing to offer a wage of OW_1 rather than risk the union taking industrial action with a consequent loss of output. If the union took this course profits might be seriously affected, and in these circumstances offering the higher wage rate might leave the firm earning the highest *attainable* profit.

REDUCING SUPPLY

In the long run unions might be able to reduce the supply of labour to the industry without any of its members becoming unemployed. The most obvious way in which this can be achieved is to reduce the number of workers taken on annually. A trade union can do this by restricting the number of trainees or apprentices taken on annually or by insisting on a reduction in the number of part-time workers. Over time, as workers leave the industry through retirement and job-changing, this will bring about a reduction in the supply of workers to the industry. The effect of this is illustrated in Fig. 10.7. In the long run a

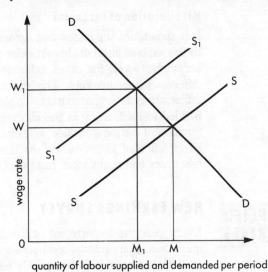

Fig. 10.7 The effect on wage rates of a reduction in the supply of labour to a particular occupation

reduction in the number of employees taken on annually shifts the supply curve of labour from SS to S_1S_1. As a result wages rise from OW to OW_1 and although *employment* in the industry falls from OM to OM_1, higher wages have not led to union members becoming unemployed. In this sense wage increases might be self-financing, because although the wage rate has increased, the total wage bill might actually fall. In recent years wage bargaining has often been accompanied by moves to increase the early retirement of workers and here again the aim is to offer a wage increase without proportionately increasing the total wage bill. Reducing the supply of labour might be particularly effective when productivity can be increased or when capital is easily substituted for labour.

COLLECTIVE BARGAINING

DEFINITION AND SCOPE

Collective bargaining is the term used to describe arrangements whereby a trade union bargains collectively on behalf of its membership about such matters as pay and conditions, rather than each person negotiating these matters individually with their employer. The aim of bargaining collectively is to strengthen the bargaining power of the workforce. In the UK a two tier system of collective bargaining is said to exist with bargains being struck at the 'national level' and the 'local level'. Often *minimum* level of pay and conditions are negotiated at the national level, and these are supplemented at the local level so as to reflect different conditions in particular markets. Agreements in the UK normally run for twelve months, but they are not legally binding and either party can terminate them at any time.

ADVANTAGES OF COLLECTIVE BARGAINING

Better pay and conditions

There seems little doubt that on average those workers who are members of a trade union have benefitted in terms of obtaining better pay and working conditions than could have been negotiated by individual employees.

Grievance procedure

Agreements reached through collective bargaining cover more than just the pay and conditions of employees. A very important area frequently covered is the establishment of procedures to be followed in the event of a dispute. It is widely agreed that the existence of this has reduced the incidence of industrial action.

DISADVANTAGES OF COLLECTIVE BARGAINING

Labour market imperfections

It has been argued that when unions negotiate the pay of their members they introduce a monopoly element into the labour market which might raise the price of labour but lead to a reduction in the numbers employed. It might also adversely affect the allocation of resources.

Misallocation of resources

It is sometimes suggested that agreements reached nationally have often had little regard to the national interest. In particular wage awards in certain industries establish minimum acceptable levels for other industries irrespective of supply and demand conditions in different labour markets. This process prevents the price mechanism from functioning efficiently in the labour market. To the extent that this has happened, collective bargaining has led to inefficiency in the allocation of resources and might be a source of inflation. Similarly if bargains include agreements to maintain employment levels even after the introduction of labour-saving machinery this will create inefficiency in the allocation of resources and might again raise costs and prices.

APPLIED MATERIALS

NEW EARNINGS SURVEY

Every year the Department of Employment publishes the New Earnings Survey which gives details on earnings and hours worked by all the different occupational groups. Table 10.2 shows average gross weekly earnings of full-time males in selected occupations in April 1988. There are clearly substantial differences in earnings between occupations.

A great deal of research has focused on the *union mark-up*, i.e. on the differential in rates of pay between union workers and non-union workers. Estimates of this vary widely. Earlier research in this area put the differential at 30 per cent or so, but more recent estimates put the differential much lower than this at around 10 per cent. No-one doubts that a differential exists, the problem lies in accurately measuring it. Realistically the differential is unlikely to be great. After all, if it was there would be a powerful incentive to join a union, but union membership is falling in the UK! In the peak year of 1979 trade union membership reached 13.289 million. It is currently less than 10 million and accounts for just over 50 per cent of the civilian labour force.

OCCUPATIONAL GROUP	AVERAGE GROSS WEEKLY EARNING (£)
Medical practitioners	511.5
Journalists	394.6
Accountants	324.3
Production and works managers	315.3
Policemen (below sergeant)	288.5
Secondary teachers	286.9
Coal miners (face trained)	281.6
Firemen	238.0
Ambulancemen	205.8
Motor vehicle mechanics	192.0
Nurses and midwives	191.3
Bricklayers	179.9
Refuse collectors	170.4
Caretakers	150.5
General farm workers	145.5
Hospital porters	145.1

Table 10.2 Average gross weekly earnings of full-time males in selected occupations in April 1988

Source: New Earnings Survey, Department of Employment 1989

WAGE DIFFERENTIALS AND TRADE UNIONS

A recent article in the *British Journal of Industrial Relations* by D. Blanchflower, ('Union relative wage effects: a cross-section analysis using establishment data'. Vol. 22, 1984) looks at the effects of trade unions on wage differentials. This is quite a difficult article but it has some interesting conclusions.

In general it provides statistical support for the view that the greater the extent of *unionisation* in an industry, the higher the level of wages. However, it also provides support for the view that other factors, such as *plant size*, might have a still more powerful effect on wage rates, with large plants having higher wage rates.

Another conclusion it proposes is that the result of union negotiations is to *narrow* the wage differential between skilled and semi-skilled workers. This is contrary to what might be expected, because there is no doubt that the demand for skilled workers is less elastic than the demand for unskilled workers. One possible reason for this is that trade unions often concentrate on advancing the cause of the lower paid; this factor may be particularly important when skilled and semi-skilled workers are in the same union (or bargain together), as typically occurs in most of British industry. The differential between skilled and unskilled may also narrow when union membership consists mainly of unskilled and semi-skilled workers.

EMPLOYERS AND PAY AWARDS

A different study by Blanchflower and Oswald in the *British Journal of Industrial Relations* Vol XXVI, No 3, 1988, attempts to identify the factors which employers thought important in determining the most recent pay award. The technique used was simply to send a questionnaire to different establishments. The results of these are reproduced in Table 10.3.

CITED INFLUENCES	PER CENT RESPONSES			
	UNION SECTOR* (Manuals)	NON-UNION SECTOR* (Manuals)	UNION SECTOR** (Non-manuals)	NON-UNION SECTOR** (Non-manuals)
All establishment could afford	11	5	9	7
Increasing cost of living	34	29	37	32
Going rate in industry	15	23	13	19
Merit/individual performance	4	20	5	33
Published norms	3	2	3	4
Internal pay structure	2	3	6	15
External pay structure	15	15	9	11
Government regulation	6	3	10	2
Strikes	1	0	0	0
Profitability/productivity	34	35	37	38
Economic climate	9	2	13	3
Other	13	7	15	6
Not answered	8	3	11	1
Number of establishments	488	613	356	904

Base *establishments with manual workers
 **establishments with non-manual workers

Notes: 1 Because managers could cite more than one influence, the columns sum to more than 100 per cent.
2 Union status of establishment is determined by whether or not unions were recognised at the workplace for purposes of bargaining.
3 The 'other' category includes answers such as 'union pressure, change in payment systems, retention/recruitment, change in working practices', inter alia. This information was kindly supplied by Neil Millward.
Source: 1984 Workplace Industrial Relations Survey.

Table 10.3 Factors influencing the level of pay in the most recent settlement

Source: Blanchflower and Oswald, Internal and External Influences on Pay Settlements, British Journal of Industrial Relations, Vol XXVI, No 3, 1988.

EXAMINATION QUESTIONS

1 What factors determine the elasticity of demand for labour? Explain how you would expect the degree of elasticity to affect
a) the wage level
b) the employment level of a group of workers who are all members of a trade union.
(JMB, 1987)

2 'Unless someone has repealed the law of supply and demand, I am afraid that the higher the price that is asked for labour the less labour will be employed.' (The Right Honourable Norman Tebbit, MP, Secretary of State for Employment, July 1982) Explain and critically assess this statement.
(AEB, June 1989)

3 To what extent can minimum wage legislation solve the problem of low pay?
(London, June 1987)

4 Explain why doctors earn more than nurses.
(London, June 1987)

A TUTOR'S ANSWER TO QUESTION 3

Low pay is regarded as an economic problem because it means that some people have a low standard of living. Many ideas have been put forward to deal with the problem of low pay. It is often suggested that a statutory minimum wage is one of the most effective means of dealing with this problem.

If we consider a single labour market we can analyse the consequences of establishing a legal minimum wage above the existing equilibrium wage in this labour market. In the diagram below demand for labour is represented by DD and supply of labour is represented by SS. The equilibrium wage is OW and OM workers are employed.

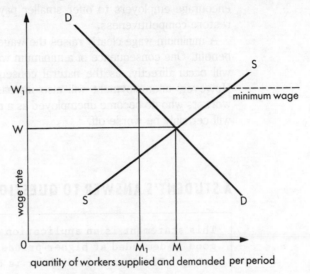

Fig. 10.8 Tutor's answer

If the minimum wage is set above OW, for example at OW_1, those workers who receive the higher wage clearly gain when a minimum wage is established. However, by raising the price of labour, the minimum wage leads to a reduction in the number of workers employed, which now falls to OM_1. In other words, fewer workers are employed at a higher wage. In terms of economic theory, they lose employment because their marginal revenue productivity is less than the statutory minimum wage. If we add together all the labour markets affected in this way, then this implies an increase in unemployment nationally should a legal mimimum wage be established. So setting a legal minimum wage may raise the earnings of the low paid workers still employed, but make those that become unemployed worse off.

The *extent* to which unemployment rises as a result of the minimum wage depends on the *elasticity of demand for labour*. In fact, the elasticity of demand for labour in each market will depend on: i) the elasticity of demand for the *product* which that labour produces; ii) the ease with which other factors of production can be substituted for labour; and iii) the proportion of total costs which are made up of labour costs.

Since low paid workers are often *unskilled* there is likely to be some substitutability between factors. In addition low paid workers are often employed in *labour intensive occupations* such as local authority ancillaries, cleaners and canteen staff. In these cases labour costs form a large proportion of total costs. Both of these factors will tend to make demand for low paid workers *relatively elastic*. The greater the elasticity of demand for labour, the greater will be the impact of a legal mimimum wage on the numbers employed.

Another factor to consider is the effect of school leavers on employment. If the minimum wage applies to all workers, this will reduce the incentive of firms to take on and train young workers since their higher wage will represent an effective increase in training costs. This has very serious implications and could lead to major skill shortages in the future and a consequently slower growth of productivity.

Another possible consequence of a statutory minimum wage is a reduction in the mobility of labour. The price mechanism functions in the labour market (as well as in product markets) and discharges its role of allocating workers to the highest bidders. By *reducing the differentials* available from changing jobs, a statutory minimum wage reduces the incentive of workers to seek better paid alternatives. Here again productivity might be adversely affected in the future, because expanding industries might not be able to offer a wide enough differential to persuade workers to leave their existing jobs.

The establishment of a statutory minimum wage might also lead to wage demands from trade unions in order to safeguard their established differentials. If pay awards are granted in excess of productivity, this will generate inflation and might well leave the *real wage* of the low paid unchanged, even after the establishment of a legal minimum wage. In fact the relative position of the low paid might be adversely affected as a result of such pay awards!

If inflation is generated it is also possible that a statutory minimum wage will adversely affect the position of the low paid workers in another way. Higher prices in the domestic market will make exports less competitive and imports more competitive. This will lead to unemployment in the domestic economy. To the extent that those workers who become unemployed were previously employed in low wage occupations, they will be adversely affected by the statutory minimum wage. Furthermore, any lack of competitiveness might encourage employers to offer smaller pay increases to their workers in an attempt to restore competitiveness.

A minimum wage clearly raises the wages of some workers. However, not all workers benefit. One consequence of a minimum wage will be an increase in unemployment. This will occur directly, as the natural consequence of an increase in the price of labour. However, unemployment will also increase for many other, indirect, reasons. Those workers who do become unemployed as a result of introducing a statutory minimum wage will certainly be worse off.

A STUDENT'S ANSWER TO QUESTION 2

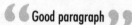
Good paragraph

Explain the importance of diminishing returns in determining the shape of the MRP curve

This statement is an application of the law of demand, that less of a good is demanded at higher prices than at lower prices, to the labour market. The demand for labour is derived from demand for the product labour produces. Therefore an increase in wages will lead to an increase in the price of the product labour produces, and, as the amount consumed falls, the demand for labour will fall.

The demand for labour can be explained in terms of the marginal productivity theory. When a firm operates in a perfectly competitive market AR = MR and the marginal revenue product of labour (MRP) can be expressed as MRP = MPP x AR, where MPP = marginal physical product. The diagram below shows the MRP and ARP (average revenue product) curves of a firm in perfect competition.

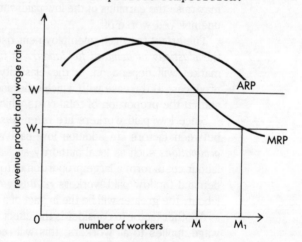

Fig. 10.9 Student's answer

At a wage rate of OW_1 the firm will employ OM_1 workers. However, at a wage rate of OW, the firm only employs OM workers. As the price of labour rises, the amount demanded falls.

The MRP curve therefore shows us demand for labour by the individual firm. However, if we assume this firm is 'typical' of other firms in the industry, then, if we multiply its MRP curve by the number of firms in the industry this will give us the industry's, or market, demand curve for labour. Because demand for labour by each individual firm is inversely related to the wage rate, the industry's demand for labour is also inversely related to the wage rate. Therefore, a rise in the wage rate will indeed lead to a reduction in the number of workers employed. Since we have proved this is true for all industries, it must be true for the economy as a whole.

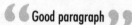
No – you have simply shown why higher wages lead to unemployment in the model you are using

However, the marginal productivity theory is based on several assumptions which are not always realistic. It assumes that firms aim to maximise profit and equate MC with MRP. In fact not all firms aim to maximise profit, and if they don't the theory has no relevance for employment in these industries. In addition firms might be prepared to pay higher wages to workers than profit maximisation dictates if it avoids costly strikes or the threat of some other industrial action. Yet another reason why firms might not be profit maximisers is that their function might not be to make a profit in the first place. Charities, cooperatives, and government departments are all major employers who do not aim at profit maximisation. In these cases the idea that wages are closely related to marginal revenue product is not correct. Therefore, in all of these cases Norman Tebbitt's statement does not apply.

Even firms which are not profit maximisers must often break even. Higher wages can still cause unemployment in these cases

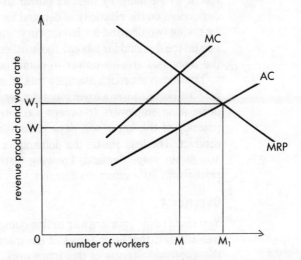

Fig. 10.10 Student's answer

Even when firms are aiming to maximise profit it does not necessarily follow that an increase in wages leads to a reduction in the number of workers employed. If the increase in wages is matched by an equivalent increase in productivity MRP will increase and therefore there is no reason why higher wages should lead to unemployment.

Give more explanation here

In addition higher wages will not necessarily lead to unemployment if the labour market is monopsonistic. A monopsonist is a sole buyer of labour and in these circumstances in order to attract additional workers it is necessary to increase the wage rate of all workers. Therefore the marginal cost of an additional worker is less than the average cost of all workers. The situation is shown diagrammatically above. At the initial wage rate OW, the firm is earning a surplus per worker at the profit maximising level of employment OM. A trade union could force an employer to raise the wage rate to OW₁, which results in an increase in the number of workers employed to OM.

Identify the surplus on your diagram

Even when there is no trade union and MPP does not increase, if firms are able to increase the price at which their product is sold, MRP will still increase. If wages are rising generally in the economy there is no reason why higher prices should lead to a reduction in sales because consumers will have higher incomes with which to pay higher prices.

Sales of exports might fall and cause unemployment

In conclusion it can be seen that there is only a limited amount of truth in Norman Tebbitt's statement. In some situations it probably has a great deal of truth, but when workers are members of a trade union they can protect themselves against unemployment as a result of higher pay awards. In addition it has been shown that when firms do not aim to maximise profit a rise in wages will not necessarily cause unemployment.

No. Relatively high pay awards cause unemployment whether there is a union or not

Remember to explain the determinants of elasticity of demand for labour and why this is important in determining the effect of higher wages on unemployment

OUTLINE ANSWERS TO QUESTIONS 1 AND 4

Question 1

Elasticity of demand for labour measures the extent to which a change in the price of labour causes a change in the demand for labour. Having explained this you must go on to discuss the determinants of elasticity. The main factors are the elasticity of demand for the product (because the demand for labour is a derived demand), the proportion of total costs which consist of labour costs and the ease with which other factors of production can be substituted for labour. Take care to explain why each of these affects the demand for labour and give some examples to illustrate your points.

To answer the second part of the question it is necessary to explain the derivation of the industry's demand for labour curve. If a trade union has complete control over the supply of labour to the industry then its power to obtain pay increases for its members is crucially dependent on the elasticity of demand for labour. You could illustrate the importance of this by taking two demand for labour curves and for any given pay increase, show that the less elastic the demand for labour, the smaller is the reduction in employment. Because of this, the union has greater power to obtain pay increases.

The above approach assumes that all other things remain equal. In fact unions might be able to persuade employers not to lay workers off by offering a productivity deal, by persuading employers to accept a cut in profits, or by threatening industrial action. The potency of the latter will depend to a large extent on the elasticity of demand for the product. The less elastic the demand for the product, the more readily will the employer accept any wage demand, knowing that these can be passed on to consumers in higher prices with little effect on demand.

Question 4

You could begin your answer to this question by discussing the determination of wages in a free market, that is, in terms of the marginal productivity theory. You could then answer the question in terms of this framework.

In the case of doctors, the absolute supply and the elasticity of supply are both much lower than for nurses. You must explain this in terms of entry qualifications, years of training, and so on. It is also likely that the value of 'MRP' for doctors is significantly higher than that for nurses, and again you must explain why this is so. Together, these supply and demand factors will lead to a 'prediction' of higher earnings for doctors than for nurses.

INTEREST, RENT AND PROFIT

GETTING STARTED

The previous chapter focussed on the return to labour. In this chapter we are concerned with rewards to other factors of production. In the classical sense interest is the return to capital, rent is the return to land and profit is the return to the entrepreneur.

INTEREST AND RATES OF INTEREST

ESSENTIAL PRINCIPLES

INTEREST AND ITS COMPONENTS

Interest is sometimes treated as the reward for postponing consumption but more often it is viewed as the price that has to be paid for the use of funds. In other words, interest is the amount the borrower pays over and above the original amount borrowed. For convenience it is usually expressed as an annual rate so that if one person borrows £5,000 for one year at 10 per cent, the total amount repayable in one year's time will be £5,500.

Strictly an interest payment has several components:

- A payment is necessary to persuade holders of funds to forego current consumption and so release funds for lending. After all, for most of us current consumption is preferable to future consumption. The payment of interest persuades individuals to overcome their time preference for current consumption.

- A payment is necessary to compensate for risk. There is a risk that the borrower will default on repayment of the loan when such repayment falls due. There is also the risk that inflation will reduce the real value of the amount lent so that it will buy less at the time repayment is made.

- A payment is necessary to cover the costs of administration associated with borrowing and lending.

THE RATE OF INTEREST

Economists use the term '*the* rate of interest' as if there was only one such rate. In fact, there are many different rates of interest such as those charged on mortgages, bank loans, hire purchase agreements and so on. This is to be expected, and in general, interest rates vary with the creditworthiness of the borrower and with the duration of the loan. Nevertheless, after allowance has been made for these two factors, there still remains a *minimum* (or net) rate of interest that must be paid by all borrowers.

Where interest rates in particular markets are *above* this minimum, even after due allowance has been made for the specific circumstances of the loan and the borrower, funds will tend to move to those markets. The increase in supply will *bid down* interest rates in those markets. Conversely, the shortage this creates in other markets will *bid up* interest rates in those markets. Thus, in the long run, the *net* interest rate in all markets tends to equality, and this provides some justification for the notion of a single rate of interest. Any reference to 'the' rate of interest therefore implies reference to a single, *representative*, rate of interest. When interest rates *in general* are rising or falling, this will be reflected in appropriate movements in *any* rate of interest which is monitored.

THE REAL RATE AND THE NOMINAL RATE

> **Real rates take account of inflation**

The *nominal* rate of interest is the annual amount that must be paid on borrowed funds. It is this rate of interest which is quoted in all financial markets. However, the *real* rate of interest takes account of inflation. In order to calculate the real rate of interest we simply deduct the rate of inflation from the nominal rate of interest. Thus, if the nominal rate of interest is 12 per cent and the rate of inflation is 8 per cent, the real rate of interest is 4 per cent. In this chapter we are mainly concerned with the nominal rate of interest.

BASE RATES

All banks have a *base rate* of interest. This is simply the underlying rate of interest to which all of the other rates of interest are related. For some borrowers the rate of interest charged might be 2 per cent above base rate; for others it might be 3 per cent above base rate, and so on. When a bank changes its base rate, all the other rates of interest operated by the bank will change.

Economists have long been interested in what determines the rate of interest and, over the years, several theories have evolved which seek to explain how interest rates are determined. Here we concentrate on only two theories: the *loanable funds theory* and the *liquidity preference theory*.

THE LOANABLE FUNDS THEORY

This is an early theory of how interest rates are determined. Although its significance decreased after the evolution of the liquidity preference theory, it is again gathering respectability as an explanation of how interest rates are determined. The *loanable funds theory* focusses attention on the demand for, and supply of, loanable funds and the interaction of these in determining the rate of interest.

DEMAND FOR LOANABLE FUNDS

This theory assumes that the *demand* for loanable funds is a derived demand that stems from the demand for capital investment by different sectors of the economy. If firms and individuals wish to invest more than they currently save, they must borrow the excess. However, if all other things are equal, the quantity of funds demanded will depend on the cost of those funds, i.e. on the rate of interest, because capital equipment will only be purchased if the expected *net* return from its operation is above some minimum acceptable level. The lower the rate of interest, the lower the cost of capital and, if all other things are equal, the greater the net return from any capital investment. Because of this the demand for loanable funds will be greater at lower rates of interest and vice versa, that is, the demand curve for loanable funds will be normal in shape.

In the real world of course, the demand for loanable funds is not simply determined by the demand for capital investment by firms. In particular households demand funds for the purchase of housing and many consumer durables. However, there is no doubt that demand for funds for these purposes is inversely related to changes in the rate of interest.

SUPPLY OF LOANABLE FUNDS

The loanable funds theory assumes that the supply of loanable funds is determined by the level of savings in the economy. For most individuals the level of savings depends on such factors as current income, holdings of wealth and the rate of interest. If all other things are equal, a rise in the rate of interest increases the *opportunity cost of current consumption* because a rise in the rate of interest makes an even higher level of consumption possible in the future. Because of this it is argued that the supply of loanable funds will vary *directly* with the rate of interest; i.e. savings rise when the rate of interest rises, and vice versa.

Determination of interest rates

Fig. 11.1 illustrates the determination of interest rates in terms of the loanable funds theory.

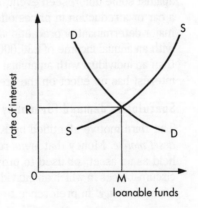

Fig. 11.1 Supply and demand for loanable funds

In Fig. 11.1, DD represents the demand for loanable funds and SS represents the supply of loanable funds. The equilibrium rate of interest is R because this is the only rate at which supply of, and demand for, funds are equal. At any rate of interest above R there is excess supply of funds, and therefore the rate of interest will fall. At any rate below R there is excess demand, and therefore the rate of interest will rise. Once established at R, the rate of interest will not change unless there is a change in the conditions of demand and/or the conditions of supply. For example, technological advances might cause an increase in the demand for loanable funds, while a rise in income might cause an increase in the supply of loanable funds. The former would tend to pull the rate of interest up, while the latter would tend to pull it down.

THE LIQUIDITY PREFERENCE THEORY

This theory is sometimes referred to as the '*monetary*' theory of interest rates or the '*Keynesian*' theory of interest rates, after its originator, John Maynard Keynes. In this theory the rate of interest is determined by the demand for money to hold and the supply of money, rather than the demand for and supply of loanable funds. An important feature of the liquidity preference theory is that it focusses attention on the reasons why people prefer to hold money than assets, that is, the reasons why the community has a preference for liquidity.

DEMAND FOR MONEY

Keynes identified three motives for holding money, in other words three reasons why individuals and organisations demand money. Each is considered in turn.

Transactions demand for money

Everyone needs to hold some money in order to carry out ordinary, everyday transactions such as paying for bus fares and other routine purchases. The sum of all the individual balances held by individuals and institutions for such purposes gives the community's demand for *transactions balances*. Since transactions balances are held with the intention of financing purchases they are unlikely to be affected by changes in the rate of interest.

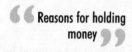
Reasons for holding money

One of the main determinants of the demand for transactions balances is the *level of income*. For most individuals (and certainly for the community as a whole) as income rises, expenditure increases. However, the *frequency with which income is received* is also an important factor in determining the transactions demand for money. For example, if an individual receives £140 per week and spends it at the rate of £20 per day, the average weekly holding of money (or the average weekly demand for transactions balances) is £70, and the annual level of expenditure is £7,280. On the other hand, if the same individual were paid on a four weekly cycle, the income received would be £560 every four weeks. Again if expenditures were spread evenly throughout the period, the average weekly holding of money would be £280 (4 times as high as before!) – but the annual level of expenditure would remain constant at £7,280. In this case what is true for the individual is true for the nation. Changing the frequency with which income is received will change the community's demand for transactions balances: the more frequently a given annual sum is paid, the higher the demand for transaction balances.

Precautionary balances

The demand for *precautionary* balances represents money balances held as a precaution against some unforeseen event, such as unanticipated repair work becoming necessary on a car or a reduction in prices offering the prospect of an unanticipated bargain. Again the major determinant of precautionary balances is likely to be the *level of income*. An individual with an annual income of £30,000 might be expected to hold larger precautionary balances than an individual with an annual income of £5,000! It is normally assumed that the rate of interest has no effect on the precautionary demand for money.

Speculative demand for money

The third motive identified by Keynes for holding money is the *speculative motive* or the *asset motive*. Money that is *not* required for transactions or precautionary purposes can be held as an asset, or used to provide funds for borrowers. The problem is to identify the circumstances in which an individual or institution will prefer to hold surplus balances in the form of *money*, in preference to *assets* that will earn interest.

SECURITIES

In the liquidity preference theory it is assumed that only one type of asset is available to individuals and institutions, namely *securities*. These are basically IOU's and we shall see in Chapter 12 that when a person makes a loan to the government they receive a government security. These IOU's will usually be redeemed at some stage in the future, but until then the holder of the security receives interest. We therefore have to decide under what circumstances a person or institution will prefer money to securities, and vice versa.

An example: consols

For simplicity let us consider the case of a security with no fixed redemption date, such as a consol which is a security, or bond, issued by the UK Government, therefore having no risk of default. The holder of these securities receives an annual interest payment and the rate of interest is fixed in terms of the face value of the security. Thus if the nominal price, that is face value, of a security is £100 and the rate of interest is 4 per cent, the holder of this security receives £4 annually. Although consols carry no fixed redemption date there is an active market in them which simply means that holders of consols can find ready buyers should they wish to sell them. However, as with all market prices, the price of consols will vary with supply and demand so that although the holder of the security receives the same fixed payment annually, the price of the security in the market is *not* fixed.

To see what happens to the market rate of interest, or *yield*, (R) when security prices change, let us consider two examples.

Example 1: it is assumed that when sold the price of the consol is £120.

Example 2: the sale price of the consol is £80.

$$\text{Example 1: } R = \frac{£4}{£120} \times 100 = 3.33\%$$

$$\text{Example 2: } R = \frac{£4}{£80} \times 100 = 5\%$$

> The market price of securities is inversely related to the rate of interest

Notice that as the *price of the security falls*, the *rate of interest rises*, and vice versa. This is because although the annual interest payment on the security is fixed at £4, in **example 1** the purchaser of the security gives up £120 to receive that annual payment of £4, but in **example 2** the security purchaser only parts with £80 to receive the same annual £4 interest.

This is a very important relationship, because, if an investor *expects* the price of securities to fall (i.e. the rate of interest to rise), he or she will prefer to hold money rather than securities. This is the case because, if security prices do fall, the investor makes a capital loss. On the other hand, if security prices are expected to rise (the rate of interest to fall), securities will be preferred to money, and an expected capital gain will be made.

Zero and infinite speculative demand

This is easy to understand in the case of an individual investor, but *not all investors have the same expectations* about security prices. At any moment in time some investors will expect there to be a rise in interest rates while others will expect a fall. However, the more interest rates rise, the more investors will come to expect the next change in interest rates to be downwards, i.e., the next change in security prices will be upwards. Because of this, as interest rates rise and rise, investors will *increasingly prefer* to hold securities rather than money because of the expectation of making a capital gain when interest rates fall. In fact there must be some rate of interest that is so high that *everyone* expects the next change in interest rates to be downwards; and here the *speculative demand for money will be zero*. The opposite is also true. As interest rates fall and fall the more investors will come to expect the next change in interest rates to be upwards, i.e., the next change in security prices to be downwards. Here money will increasingly be preferred to securities because of the expected capital loss from holding securities. Again there must be some low rate of interest when *everyone* expects the next change in interest rates to be upwards, i.e., the next change in security prices will be downwards. In this case the demand for speculative money balances will be *infinite*, because no-one will be willing to purchase securities.

THE LIQUIDITY PREFERENCE CURVE

Since transactions balances and precautionary balances are held with the intention of being used to make purchases as and when required, they are sometimes jointly referred to as the *demand for active balances*. The important point about the demand for active balances is that it is *not* responsive to changes in the rate of interest, i.e. it is interest rate inelastic. The demand for speculative balances on the other hand is sometimes referred to as the *demand for idle balances* since it represents money that is demanded because its face value is fixed and there is therefore no risk of capital loss.

Liquidity preference schedule

Fig. 11.2 shows that when the demand for active balances (La) and the demand for idle balances (Li) are *added together* we have the community's total demand for money or liquidity preference schedule (i.e. LP).

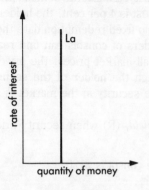

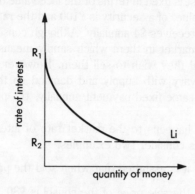

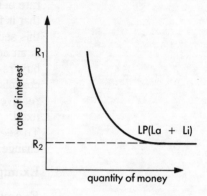

Fig. 11.2 Liquidity preference schedule

THE SUPPLY OF MONEY

In the liquidity preference theory this is assumed to be determined by the monetary authorities (the Treasury and the Bank of England). This implies that on a day-to-day basis the supply of money is *not* influenced by changes in the rate of interest. In the long term however changes in the rate of interest do exert considerable influence on the supply of money, but this can be ignored because the liquidity preference theory concentrates on the determination of the rate of interest at a particular point in time when the money supply is fixed.

What determines interest rates?

The interaction of supply and demand for money determines the rate of interest. In Fig. 11.3 the demand for money is given by LP and the supply of money is given by SM. This gives an equilibrium rate of interest of R.

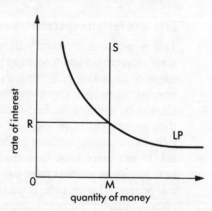

Fig. 11.3 The equilibrium rate of interest

At any rate of interest above R, the supply of money exceeds demand and this will pull down the rate of interest, while at any rate of interest below R the demand for money will exceed supply and this will bid up the rate of interest. Once the rate of interest is established at R, it will remain at this level until there is a change in the demand for money and/or the supply of money. This implies that the authorities have two choices:

- they can fix the supply of money and allow interest rates to be determined by the demand for money.
- they can fix the rate of interest and adjust the supply of money to whatever level is appropriate so as to maintain the rate of interest.

THE LIQUIDITY TRAP

We have seen that in the liquidity preference theory there is some low rate of interest at which everyone expects the next change in interest rates to be upwards. Here the demand

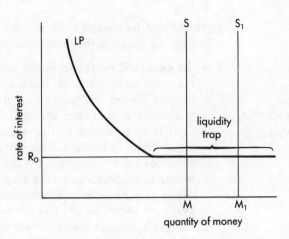

Fig. 11.4 The liquidity trap

for money is infinitely elastic since no-one will be prepared to purchase securities. In this case a change in the supply of money will not necessarily have any affect on the rate of interest. For example, in Fig. 11.4 if LP shows the demand for money and SM the supply of money then the equilibrium rate of interest is determined at R_o. Now if the authorities engineer an increase in the money supply to $S_1 M_1$, there is no change in the rate of interest. The increased money supply is simply absorbed into idle balances because no-one can be persuaded to purchase securities. This is referred to as the *liquidity trap* and the implication is that because changes in the money supply have no influence on the rate of interest, monetary policy cannot be used to influence other variables such as consumption and investment when the rate of interest is R_o.

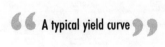

Importance of the liquidity trap

THE TERM STRUCTURE OF INTEREST RATES

In practice the authorities are not only interested in the *level* of interest rates, they are also interested in the *structure*. The *term structure of interest rates* refers to the *spread* of interest rates paid on the *same type of assets* with different times to maturity. It relates to securities which carry a fixed rate of interest and have a specified maturity date. In general, the longer the time to maturity, the greater the return on a security. Remember, although the amount received is fixed as a proportion of the nominal value of a security, the rate of interest, or yield will vary because the market price of the security varies.

THE YIELD CURVE

Fig. 11.5 shows the general relationship between the yield on a security and the length of time to maturity. This is usually referred to as the *yield curve*.

A typical yield curve

Fig. 11.5 Yield curve

The yield curve in Fig. 11.5 is referred to as a *normal* yield curve because the yield increases as the length of time to maturity increases. This is to be expected because if all other things are equal:

■ the risk of default increases over the time along with the risk that inflation will erode the real value of interest payments and the initial capital sum when it is repaid

■ lenders require compensation for loss of liquidity so the longer they forego current consumption, the greater the amount of compensation required.

Expectations and the yield curve

The normal yield curve is drawn on the assumption that all other things remain equal and in particular that no change is expected in the rate of interest. When such changes *are* expected, the shape of the yield curve will change.

- **An expected increase in the rate of interest**: In this case the yield curve will rise more steeply and will reach a higher level than the normal yield curve. This is because *lenders* will seek to avoid being locked into securities which will have a relatively low yield after interest rates increase. They will therefore prefer to hold short term securities so that when these mature they can re-lend their funds at higher rates of interest. This implies an increase in the demand for short term securities and a reduction in the demand for long term securities. On the other hand *borrowers* will prefer to borrow long term because after interest rates increase there will be no increase in their borrowing costs. This implies an increase in the supply of long term securities and a reduction in the supply of short term securities. These changes in demand and supply will tend to increase the price of short term securities (depress short term interest rates) and depress the price of long term securities (increase long term interest rates).

Fig. 11.6 shows the effect of an expected increase in interest rates on the yield curve with Y representing the normal yield curve and Y_1 the yield curve after the expected increase in interest rates.

<blockquote>Expectations will affect yield curves</blockquote>

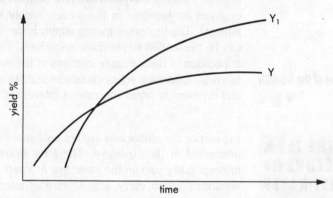

Fig. 11.6 Yield curve after an expected increase in the rate of interest

- **An unexpected reduction in the rate of interest**: As might be expected, the effect this has on the yield curve is exactly opposite to an expected increase in the rate of interest. Here *lenders* will prefer to hold long term securities, so locking in the higher rate of interest after interest rates fall. This implies an increase in demand for long term securities and a fall in demand for short term securities. On the other hand *borrowers* will prefer to borrow short term, so enabling them to reduce their interest payments on long term borrowing after interest rates fall. This implies an increase in the supply of short term securities and a reduction in the supply of long term securities. The result is a reduction in the price of short term securities (increase in short term interest rates) and an increase in the price of long term securities (fall in long term rates).

A shift in the yield curve from Y to Y_1 shows the effect on the yield curve of an expected reduction in the rate of interest, see Fig. 11.7.

In certain circumstances a strong expectation of a fall in interest rates can produce a descending yield curve (see Fig. 11.8 on p.156).

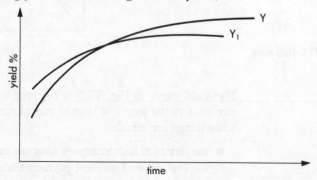

Fig. 11.7 Yield curve after an expected reduction in the rate of interest

RENT AND ECONOMIC RENT

In most cases a factor of production is assumed to have *transfer earnings*. Transfer earnings are defined as the minimum amount necessary to keep a factor of production in its present occupation. Any *excess earnings* above transfer earnings are referred to as *economic rent*. Much more is written about economic rent in the Tutor's Answer on p.157.

URBAN RENTS AND CITY CENTRE PRICES

It is sometimes alleged that retail prices in outlets occupying city centre locations are higher than they are for the same items sold in outlets located away from the city centre, because city centre rents are higher than elsewhere. It is certainly true that city centre rents are generally higher than elsewhere but it is not always true that retail prices are higher in the city centre. Even in cases where retail prices are higher this is not necessarily because retailers pay higher rents in the city centre.

Reasons for higher rents

Higher rents stem from the increasing demand for city centre sites which have an inelastic supply. The increasing demand for city centre sites in turn stems from the relatively high demand for the goods and services sold in city centre locations.

So any higher prices that are observed for goods sold in city centres are as likely to be the result of the greater *demand* existing in such locations as of the higher *cost* factors due to higher rents. Indeed, the *only* reason that costs (rents) are higher is due to the increased demand amongst retailers for the favourable city centre sites which are in short supply.

SHOULD ECONOMIC RENT BE TAXED?

It is often suggested that economic rent should be taxed. The reasoning behind this is that since economic rent is a *surplus* rather than a *cost of supply*, a tax on economic rent will be borne entirely by the factor of production receiving economic rent. This will leave the supply of that factor, and therefore the output it produces, unchanged. For example, when a monopolist is currently earning supernormal profit and producing at the profit maximising level of output, a tax on the supernormal profit will not lead the monopolist to change the output produced. The tax will certainly lower the amount of profit earned, but it will *not* change the profit maximising level of output.

A tax on economic rent would not affect supply because the tax has no effect on the costs of production. It is simply a tax on the excess earnings of a factor over and above the amount necessary for that factor to be supplied. For example, in the case of urban and development land, landowners frequently do little or nothing to improve the quality of the land and simply benefit from an increasing demand. Taxing the surplus that results from this will have no effect on supply.

Difficulties of implementation

The case for taxing economic rent is therefore a powerful one. However, there are major difficulties with implementing such a tax. In the first place it is extremely difficult to *identify* economic rent. If a tax *exceeds* the value of the surplus, then the supply of the factor of production will be reduced and its price, along with the price of whatever it produces, will be increased. Another problem is that not all economic rent that is earned is true economic rent. It might simply be *quasi rent*. Quasi rent refers to income that is entirely a surplus in the short run, but *part* of which is a *transfer earning* in the long run. Taxing this will reduce the long run supply of the factor of production. Here again the result might be rising prices.

INTEREST RATES

APPLIED MATERIALS

An article in the *Accountant's Record*, June 1987, entitled *Interest Rates – Understanding and Forecasting their Movements*, provides considerable insight into the causes of changes in interest rates in the UK. It is argued that a major factor is the *expected change in the foreign exchange value of sterling*. The principle of *covered interest parity* implies that when account is taken of the various expected exchange rate changes, interest rates around the world would tend to be equal. Remember, it is now very easy for investors to withdraw funds from one country and to invest them in another. So, for example, if sterling is expected to *depreciate* against the dollar, i.e., exchange for less dollars, sterling interest rates must exceed dollar interest rates by an amount which exactly compensates for the expected fall in the value of sterling against the dollar. This idea is explored in more detail in Chapter 15 but is mentioned here because of its importance in determining interest rates.

The article also emphasises the role of *inflation* in determining interest rates. Inflation causes a fall in the value of money and in order to compensate lenders for this fall they require interest payments. Here again there is an international dimension. We shall see in Chapter 15 that a higher rate of inflation in one country will cause a fall in that country's exchange rate and *covered interest parity* would predict a higher rate of interest to offset this.

Expected changes in the exchange rate are therefore important in determining interest rates, but another important factor is the *government's monetary policy*. When the government restricts the money supply there will be upward pressure on interest rates (see Fig. 11.3). Similarly if government borrowing increases (and all other things remain equal), the greater demand for loans will result in upward pressure on interest rates.

THE BANK OF ENGLAND

In its Quarterly Bulletin, the Bank of England publishes regular information on *yield curves*. Fig. 11.8 shows some recent yield curves. Can you explain their 'unusual' shape?

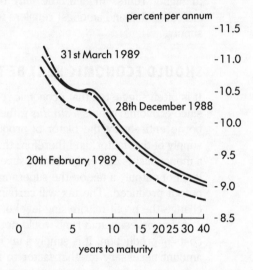

Fig. 11.8 Time/yield curves of British government stocks

An indication of the real rate of return on capital employed in different industrial groups is given in Table 11.1 and Table 11.2 illustrates the importance of profit as a source of internal finance.

	1984	1985	1986	1987
Capital Goods	15.6	15.9	16.4	18.9
Consumer Groups	17.1	17.7	18.0	19.9
Other Groups	16.7	17.0	17.3	20.4
All Industrial Groups	16.7	17.2	17.7	20.0

Source: Bank of England Quarterly Bulletin, Vol 28, No 4, November 1988.

Table 11.1 Real rates of return on capital employed

	1988
Internal	44.3
Bank Borrowing	34.8
UK Capital Issues	6.8
Other	14.1

Source: Financial Statistics, No 325, May 1989.

Table 11.2 Sources of funds for UK industrial and commercial companies: Percentage shares

EXAMINATION QUESTIONS

1   Are profits a reward for a useful service?

(Oxford, 1967)

2   Distinguish between economic rent and transfer earnings.   (*20*)
    With reference to examples, explain what determines the economic rent received by factors of production.

(*80*)

(*Total 100 marks*)

(London, June 1989)

3 'It is irrational for people to keep their wealth in the form of money because money earns no interest'. Discuss.

(AEB, Nov 1988)

4 How are interest rates determined?

(London, June 1987)

A TUTOR'S ANSWER TO QUESTION 2

Economic rent is defined as a surplus earned by any factor of production over and above the minimum price at which that factor would be supplied. The minimum price at which a factor will be supplied is referred to as its supply price, and hence economic rent is a surplus over supply price.

The supply price of a factor of production might also be referred to as a factor's transfer earnings. Any factor of production that is offered less than the amount it could receive in its next best paid alternative employment will transfer to that alternative. The diagram below is used to illustrate the concepts of economic rent and transfer earnings.

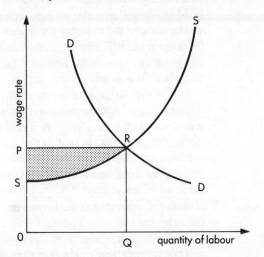

Fig. 11.9 Tutor's answer

In the diagram, S and D represent the relevant supply and demand curves for any factor of production. In this market the equilibrium price is P. However, all units except the last unit employed would have been prepared to accept a lower price than P. In fact, the very first unit would have been supplied at a price of approximately S. All units except the last unit supplied therefore receive an amount in excess of their supply price or transfer earnings. Because of this the area PRS is referred to as *economic rent* and the area OSRQ is referred to as *transfer earnings*.

For any factor of production, economic rent is determined by demand for that factor of production and its transfer earnings. However, in the case of labour a small number of individuals receive incomes which are sometimes hundreds of times greater than the average income. In these cases the transfer earnings of the individual concerned are often relatively low so that the bulk of their earnings consist of economic rent. The most often quoted examples are probably film stars and pop singers. These individuals possess unique qualities, the supply of which is inelastic in the sense that their abilities cannot be duplicated.

However, it is not sufficient to possess unique abilities to earn relatively high rewards. After all, everyone has some unique ability! Instead it is necessary to possess those unique abilities which are demanded by others and for which people are prepared to pay. It is, therefore, demand which accounts for the relatively large earnings of pop singers, film stars and some individuals from the sporting world such as some boxers and footballers. In this sense economic rent is demand determined. The diagram (Fig. 11.10) is used to illustrate this point.

Above some relatively low rate of pay, the supply of this individual's services become totally inelastic. The actual rate of pay is determined by the interaction of supply and demand at W, but, because of the inelastic supply, the bulk of this person's earnings consist of economic rent, equal to WRNS.

Sometimes factors of production earn economic rent in the short term which is eliminated in the long term. In this case economic rent is referred to as *quasi rent*. For

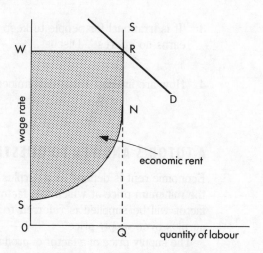

Fig. 11.10 Tutor's answer

example, during a housing boom the earnings of building site workers rise substantially, the increase consisting of economic rent. Here again the importance of demand in determining economic rent is apparent. However, for many of the jobs performed on building sites there are no long run barriers to the entry of new workers. So as new workers enter the industry the higher earnings in part disappear and are therefore seen to be quasi rent. It is important to note that although economic rent is demand determined, any *given* increase in demand for a factor of production will confer *more* economic rent the *less elastic* the supply of that factor.

Part of the earnings of capital might also consist of economic rent. Some types of capital equipment are highly specific and cannot be transferred to an alternative use. For example, it is doubtful that a dockyard or a coal mine have any alternative uses. Conventional theory of the firm teaches us that in the short run, firms will continue in production as long as earnings at least cover the variable costs of production. Because of this, the transfer earnings of fixed capital in the short run are the *variable costs of operating it*, and the entire earnings of fixed capital such as dockyards and coal mines *in excess of this* might be considered economic rent. However, earnings must ultimately cover depreciation, so it is only the excess over and above this *plus* the variable costs of operation which can be considered economic rent in the long run.

The entrepreneur might also earn economic rent in the form of supernormal profit. The minimum reward acceptable to the entrepreneur in the long run is *normal profit*. Any entrepreneur not earning at least normal profit will transfer to an alternative occupation. Normal profit is therefore the *transfer earnings* of the entrepreneur and anything in excess of this is supernormal profit or economic rent. For many entrepreneurs however, supernormal profit turns out to be nothing more than quasi rent. Unless an entrepreneur patents a particular process, ideas can often be copied by others and supernormal profits are consequently competed away in the long run. Where patents or other barriers to entry exist, however, an entrepreneur might have a monopoly position and economic rent can be earned for as long as barriers to entry prevent the emergence of competition. In the pharmaceutical industry, for example, patents prevent rival firms from producing identical drugs. The government has issued guidelines on target rates of return for drug companies to aim at so as to avoid the NHS paying an excessive amount for drugs and conferring economic rent on drug producers.

For some types of land, economic rent forms a large part of the income owners receive. In some cases such as remote hills and valleys, land is often used for sheep farming, but appears to have little alternative use. In other cases, land earns considerably more in one use than in another. In recent years large tracts of agricultural land have been turned over to building land; once planning permission is granted on a particular piece of land its value rises substantially over what it can earn as agricultural land. In such cases the rise in land values is clearly economic rent, since landowners do nothing to improve the quality of the land; they simply obtain permission for its use to be changed!

It is clear that any factor of production can earn economic rent and the main determinant of such rent is *demand* for the factor of production. However, *elasticity of supply* is also an important determinant of economic rent. When rising demand drives up factor earnings, the higher level of earnings will attract other units of the factor into the industry, unless there are barriers to entry which prevent this. If no barriers exist, supply of the factor will be relatively elastic and this will mitigate the effect of increasing demand on factor incomes and, therefore, on the level of economic rent earned.

A STUDENT'S ANSWER TO QUESTION 1

> The economist's definition is different. Remember normal profit is regarded as a cost of production

> But we can still discuss the advantages and disadvantages for society

> Profits are only necessary for production in capitalist societies

> No. People would still produce for their own consumption

> Good paragraph

> Depends why profits are rising. You should relate this to changes in demand and the operation of the price mechanism

> A weak conclusion

Profits are usually defined as the difference between total revenue and total cost. If total revenue exceeds total cost firms make a profit but if it does not they make a loss. This is the risk entrepreneurs take – their businesses might make losses and when this happens entrepreneurs lose the money they have invested in their businesses.

However, entrepreneurs aim to make profits. In fact it is usually assumed by economists that entrepreneurs aim to maximise profits and this simply means that they aim to make as much profit as possible from the resources they control. Profits are therefore the entrepreneur's reward and to decide whether profits are the reward for a useful service, we must ask if the entrepreneur provides a useful service. The answer is really a value judgement because we have no way of saying whether something is useful or not. It is a matter of opinion. All that we can do is to look at the functions of the entrepreneur.

The entrepreneur's first function is that of risk taker. If individuals or groups of individuals are unwilling to bear the risks of production nothing would be produced. Profit is therefore necessary to persuade the entrepreneur to undertake production and if profits are not earned in the long run entrepreneurs cease production and leave the industry. This implies that, without profit, society would be worse off because nothing would be produced.

Profit also encourages entrepreneurs to undertake investment in new technology. It encourages research and development along with the adoption of innovations. Entrepreneurs who fail to do this will experience falling sales and consequently falling profits. We must be careful to distinguish between inventions and innovations. Scientists are often responsible for inventions, but it is entrepreneurs who see the commercial uses for new inventions. For example, science was responsible for the creation of micro-electronics but it is entrepreneurs who are responsible for devising commercial uses for them. Without profits there would be no incentive for entrepreneurs to seek out commercial applications for inventions.

Another function of profit is that it guides entrepreneurs. When profits are rising in one industry and falling in another this indicates that society desires more of the commodity where profits from production are rising and less of the commodity where profits are falling. Without profits, more especially changes in profits, entrepreneurs would not know what society most desired from its available resources. This implies that in the absence of profits there would be an inferior allocation of resources.

Because of all of these factors my opinion is that profits are a reward for a very useful service and without them society would be worse off.

> Some good points here but in general the essay is superficial. You could have included a discussion of the entrepreneur as a factor of production and discussed the importance of normal profit.

OUTLINE ANSWERS TO QUESTIONS 3 AND 4

Question 3

One way to begin your answer to this question is to define interest and show that if money is lent it earns interest for the lender whereas money that is held earns nothing. You could then go on to explain that individuals have a time preference for current consumption and that to overcome this time preference it is necessary to offer interest. It seems that holding money is therefore irrational because it implies individuals forego current consumption without compensation.

However, it is not necessarily irrational to hold money. Money is needed by both individuals and organisations for transactions and precautionary purposes. You must explain these motives for holding money and their determinants in some detail, stressing the convenience of holding money in terms of immediate spending power. In the real world expenditures and receipts are often irregular and uncertain especially for businesses and in these circumstances holding money is the rational thing to do. You must also discuss the speculative demand for money stressing that it is a desirable store of wealth when its value is more certain than that of other assets, that is, when interest rates are low and the next expected change in bond prices is downwards. In these circumstances the opportunity cost of holding money is low and the risk associated with holding bonds is high.

In the modern world many financial institutions have accounts which offer liquidity and interest. These are discussed in the following chapter but when they are available it is clearly irrational to hold cash that is surplus to immediate requirements.

Question 4

You could begin your answer by defining the rate of interest and why economists look at a single representative rate. You could then discuss either the loanable funds theory or the liquidity preference theory to explain how interest rates are determined. These theories explain the general *level* of interest rates but the *structure* of interest rates depends on the expectations investors hold at any moment in time. You should briefly explain this in terms of the shape of the yield curve.

Further reading

Stanlake, *Introductory Economics* (5th edn), Longman 1989: Ch. 19. Interest; Ch. 20, Rent; Ch. 21, Profit.

MONEY AND BANKING

GETTING STARTED

Despite the fact that we are all familiar with money and use it almost every day of our lives, it is difficult to define exactly what money is. Over the years a variety of commodities have been accepted as money, ranging from precious metals to shells. In fact, the term *pecuniary* is derived from the word 'cattle' and *salary* from the word 'salt' indicating that in the past these commodities have functioned as money. It is because of this that economists say 'money is as money does'. In other words, anything which performs the functions of money, is money.

ESSENTIAL PRINCIPLES

One term frequently used in connection with money is *liquidity*. An asset is more liquid the more swiftly and less costly it can be converted into the means of payment. It follows that money is the most liquid asset of all. In modern economies money takes two forms: cash (i.e. notes and coin) and bank deposits. There are several kinds of bank deposit with varying degrees of liquidity. For instance, *sight deposits* are immediately spendable, but *time deposits* can only be withdrawn after a period of notice has been given to the institution holding the deposit. Because of this, there are several different official measures of the money supply, each reflecting a different measure of liquidity in the economy. It is important to be familiar with the different measures of the money supply.

In the UK bank, deposits are by far the most important component of the money supply, accounting for about 90 per cent of the total value of all transactions. However, care must be taken to distinguish between the role of the bank deposits and the role of the cheques. Cheques are simply the means of transferring a bank deposit from one person to another. It is the bank deposit which is accepted in settlement of a debt, not the cheque. A cheque that cannot be honoured against a bank deposit is worthless.

FUNCTIONS OF MONEY

There are four functions which money performs:

To act as a medium of exchange or means of payment

Money is unique in performing this function, since it is the only asset which is universally acceptable in exchange for goods and services. In the absence of a medium of exchange, trade could only take place if there was a double coincidence of wants; in other words, only if two people had mutually acceptable commodities to exchange. Trade of this type takes place on a basis of *barter*.

Clearly, barter would restrict the growth of trade. It would also severely limit the extent to which individuals were able to specialise. By acting as a medium of exchange money therefore promotes *specialisation*. A person can exchange his labour for money, and then use that money to purchase the output produced by others. We have seen in Chapter 4 that specialisation greatly increases the wealth of the community. By acting as a medium of exchange money is therefore fulfilling a crucial function, enhancing trade, specialisation and wealth creation.

The remaining functions of money stem from its use as a medium of exchange.

To act as a unit of account

By acting as a medium of exchange, money also provides a means of expressing value. The prices quoted for goods and services reflect their relative value and in this way money acts as a unit of account.

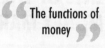
The functions of money

To act as a store of wealth

Because money can be exchanged immediately for goods and services it is a convenient way of holding wealth until goods and services are required. In this sense money acts as a store of wealth.

To act as a standard for deferred payment

In the modern world, goods are often purchased on credit, with the amount to be repaid being fixed in money terms. It would be impractical to agree repayment in terms of some other commodity; for example, it may not always be easy to predict the future availability or the future requirements for that commodity. It is therefore money which serves as a standard for deferred payments.

CHARACTERISTICS OF MONEY

For any commodity to function as money it must possess certain characteristics. The main characteristics are briefly summarised:

Acceptability

No asset can function as money unless people are willing to accept it in settlement of a debt.

Durability

To function as money an asset must be durable. After all during its working life any unit of currency changes hands many times and an asset which deteriorated quickly would not be acceptable in settlement of a debt.

Divisibility

To function as money an asset must be capable of division into smaller units to accommodate transactions of differing value.

Portability

Trade often takes place between individuals and organisations located miles from each other and sometimes at opposite sides of the world. To function as money an asset must therefore be portable.

THE CREATION OF BANK DEPOSITS

We have already mentioned the importance of bank deposits as a component of the money supply. But what are bank deposits and how are they created?

Bank deposits come into being in one of three ways:

- when a bank receives a deposit of cash
- when a bank buys a security
- when a bank makes a loan

We shall look at each of these in turn but it is important to realise that whichever way bank deposits are created, a bank must always ensure that its liabilities and assets are equal. Deposits are the liabilities of a bank, since they are bound to honour all demands for cash from individual depositors up to the full amount deposited in each individual's account. In other words, deposits are claims against a bank. The assets which banks hold, however, can take a variety of forms, but they always give the bank a claim against someone else. Notes and coin, for example, give commercial banks a claim against the central bank (the Bank of England in the UK) whereas securities and advances give the bank a claim against the borrower.

BANK DEPOSITS AND THE MONEY SUPPLY

One important aspect of bank deposit creation is its effect on the *money supply*. We can illustrate this by looking at each of the three ways in which bank deposits are created. The examples below record the initial impact of a £100 creation of bank deposits on the bank's assets and liabilities:

- **Cash deposits**: when a bank receives a deposit of £100 cash, the effect on its balance sheet is:

Liabilities	Assets
Deposits + £100	Notes and coin + £100

  It is clear that a deposit of cash has no initial impact on the money supply. The same amount of money exists, it is simply held in a different form. In this example an individual has simply exchanged £100 cash for a bank deposit of £100.

- **Buying a security**: when a bank buys a security for £100 the effect on its balance sheet is:

Liabilities	Assets
Deposits + £100	Securities + £100

  In this case the bank's purchase of a £100 security increases the money supply by £100. This is because securities, which are not acceptable in exchange for goods and services, have been exchanged for a bank deposit which is acceptable.

- **Making a loan**: when a bank grants a loan of £100 the effect on its balance sheet is:

Liabilities	Assets
Deposits + £100	Advances + £100

  Again, the granting of a £100 loan *increases* the money supply by £100. This must be so because deposits which are immediately acceptable in exchange for goods and services, have been exchanged for a debt (an advance which is repayable at some future date).

THE MULTIPLE EXPANSION OF BANK DEPOSITS

Although the purchase of securities and the granting of loans leads to an increase in the money supply, banks cannot purchase securities or grant loans indefinitely. They are obliged to pay out cash on demand to account holders up to the limit of whatever is held in each individual's account. They must therefore keep sufficient cash to meet all possible demands for it. Nevertheless, on any particular day only a relatively small portion of the funds held by banks will be withdrawn because of the widespread use of cheques and credit cards. There may well be a very substantial outflow of funds, but there is also likely to be a very substantial inflow. Because of this, the net change in a bank's holdings of cash on any particular day is likely to be relatively small. They are therefore able to lend a substantial part of the funds deposited with them. If all banks in the system do this, and we can expect them to do so since lending is their most profitable activity, the effect will be a multiple expansion of credit following an initial deposit of cash. The following hypothetical example is used to illustrate this process.

Example

Assume that on any particular day banks wish to maintain a ratio of 10 per cent cash to total deposits. Assume further that there is no absence of willing borrowers so that banks will lend 90 per cent of all cash deposited with them. So, if a bank receives a cash deposit of £1,000 it will lend £900 in the form of advances. The effect of these transactions on the bank's balance sheet is set out below.

Liabilities	Assets	
Deposits £1000	Cash	£1000
Deposits £900	Advances	£900

We can assume that having been granted loans, borrowers will spend them, with cash being withdrawn from the bank to meet these expenditures. The £900 used by borrowers to finance purchases will flow back into the banking system as someone else's deposits and will be indistinguishable from any other inflows. Thus, 90 per cent of these deposits (i.e. £810) will be re-lent. Again, this will flow back into the banking system with 90 per cent of these deposits (i.e. £729) being re-lent. It is apparent that the *initial* deposit of £1000 cash leads to an eventual increase in bank deposits many times greater than the initial cash deposit.

This process does not, however, go on indefinitely. In fact, the eventual increase in bank deposits is the sum of a geometric progression which reaches an upper limit as the number of terms in the progression rises. In general, the eventual increase in deposits following an initial deposit of cash is equal to:

$$\frac{1}{\text{cash ratio}} \times \text{cash reserves}$$

In this particular case we have:

$$\frac{1}{10/100} \times £1000$$

❝ A multiple expansion of bank deposits ❞

In other words, an initial cash deposit of £1000 leads to an eventual increase in bank deposits of £10,000. Since the cash ratio is 10 per cent, this is to be expected. We are simply saying that bank deposits expand until the initial deposit of cash is just sufficient to meet day-to-day demands for cash by depositors. The size of the cash ratio, therefore, sets the *upper limit* on the extent to which bank deposits can be expanded following an initial deposit of cash.

It is important to realise that *individual* banks do not create credit simply by expanding their deposits by some multiple of their cash reserves. If an individual bank did this it would quickly experience a *net outflow of cash* as it was forced to *honour cheques* drawn on these deposits. In other words, there will be payments into other banks. Clearly, such a situation could not continue for long. Instead, each individual bank simply re-lends a part of whatever is deposited with it. However, the effect of this is to create a situation where the combined total level of deposits held by all banks is a multiple of their combined cash reserves.

FINANCIAL INTERMEDIATION

Financial intermediation refers to the process whereby funds are channelled from those who wish to lend to those who wish to borrow. Financial intermediaries therefore include banks, building societies, insurance companies, pension funds and so on. Financial intermediation arises because lenders and borrowers have different requirements in terms of risk and time.

- *Maturity transformation* is an important function of financial intermediaries. They borrow short and lend long. They are able to do this by attracting short term deposits and then attracting other funds to repay the original borrowings when the need arises.

- *Risk reduction* is another important function of financial intermediaries. If one person lends directly to another the entire risk of default is borne by the lender. However, by depositing funds with a financial intermediary the original lender eliminates the risk of default almost completely. For its part, the financial intermediary is able to spread the risk over many transactions and, through interest charges to *all customers*, can ensure it is compensated for losses arising out of default. It is also in a better position to estimate the likelihood of default by a borrower than an individual lender.

In this chapter we will be considering *bank financial intermediaries*; other institutions that participate in the money markets are referred to as *non-bank financial intermediaries*. The distinction between these is a legal one and is not always clear cut. Some of the more important non-bank financial intermediaries include building societies, finance houses, the National Savings Bank, insurance companies and pension funds.

THE STRUCTURE OF BANKING

THE BANK OF ENGLAND

The Bank of England is the central bank in the United Kingdom. It has a wide range of functions, but the following are among the most important:

Monetary policy

The Bank has responsibility for implementing the government's monetary policy.

Banker to the government

The government maintains an account with the Bank of England (the Exchequer Account) through which all tax revenues and current government expenditure are passed. It also maintains another account (the National Loans Fund) through which all government borrowing and lending are passed.

Management of the foreign exchange reserves

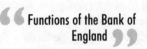
Functions of the Bank of England

As agent for the Treasury the Bank manages the Exchange Equalisation Account. This account holds the country's reserves of gold and foreign currency which are used to influence the external value of sterling in line with the government's foreign exchange rate policy.

Banker to the banking system

All banks above a certain size are obliged to hold deposits at the Bank of England. In addition, the London clearing banks hold operational deposits which gives them current account facilities at the Bank of England. It is by transferring these operational deposits that inter-bank settlements are made at the end of each working day as the final stage of the clearing process. They also provide the banks with facilities through which they can obtain additional supplies of notes and coin when necessary.

Lender of last resort

An important function of the Bank of England is that it acts as lender of last resort to the banking system. This simply means that if the banking system is short of liquidity, the Bank of England will always be prepared to lend to it. However, as we shall see, it reserves the right to specify what rate of interest it will charge when lending to the banking system. We shall also see that in making finance available to the banking system the Bank of England deals only with a group of institutions known as the discount market.

Note circulation

The Bank is the sole note issuing authority in England and Wales. In this context, its responsibilities are the printing, issue and withdrawal of bank notes.

THE DISCOUNT MARKET

The London discount market is primarily a market in short term funds and consists of nine discount houses. Together these comprise the London Discount Market Association (LDMA). The discount houses borrow at short term, mainly from the commercial banks and use these funds to carry out their primary function, *discounting* short term instruments of credit, that is, short term securities (see below). Much of the borrowing is at 'call', which means that the bank can ask for repayment at any time. These funds are used by the discount houses to purchase a variety of short term instruments such as Treasury bills, commercial bills and gilt-edged securities which are close to maturity. (The securities in which the discount market deals are discussed on pp.170–71. Indeed, the discount houses are the principal market makers in bills, and by borrowing from the commercial banks they provide them with a modest return on short term loans. Currently all eligible banks are obliged to maintain at least an average of 2½ per cent of their eligible liabilities in the form of secured money with the discount market.

Discounting and the discount rate

A security is discounted when it is purchased for less than its face value. The difference consists of interest which accrues from the date of purchase until the date on which the security matures, i.e., when its face value is paid by the drawee to the holder of the security. For example, if a security due to mature in ninety one days' time with a face value of £100,000 is discounted at 10 per cent, the discount is:

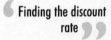
Finding the discount rate

$$£100,000 \times \frac{10}{100} \times \frac{91}{365} = £2,493.15$$

The seller of the bill therefore receives £97,506.85 and in this case the discount house charges a rate of interest of:

$$\frac{£2,493.15}{£97,506.85} \times \frac{365}{91} \times 100 = 10.26 \%$$

The difference between interest payments on borrowed funds and interest receipts from discounting, is profit (or loss) for the discount houses.

Functions of the discount market

The function of any discount house is to earn a profit from their activities. This is the reason they are in business. However, in carrying out its activities the discount market performs several important economic functions:

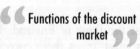
Functions of the discount market

- The discount houses are the *primary market makers* in short term securities. As market makers they are always prepared to buy and sell (make a market) in suitable securities. The securities in which they deal are discussed more fully on pp. 170–71 but are typically those with only a few months to maturity. In buying securities the discount houses provide a source of short term credit for those with securities to sell.

- As well as buying securities the discount houses also sell securities to investors. Such investors have differing requirements in terms of the desired maturity date of securities and the amount of funds they wish to invest. The discount houses are able to arrange portfolios (groups) of securities to match the requirements of investors thereby reducing 'search costs' for the latter. For example, they purchase Treasury bills at the 'weekly auction' and, if approached, will sell these and other securities when they are closer to maturity.

- The discount houses also perform an important role in financing the government's short term borrowing. Each week the Bank of England issues Treasury bills by tender, the so called weekly auction, and the discount houses collectively agree to 'cover the tender'. This simply means that they submit a bid for *all* the bills on offer, thus ensuring that the government is provided with the funds it requires. In practice the discount market only takes up a portion of the weekly issue, the remainder being allocated to those who submit the highest bids. To ensure that the discount market is always able to carry out this function, uniquely in the UK, it has direct access to the Bank of England as lender of last resort.

- The discount market performs a crucial role in the implementation of the government's monetary policy. It is, in effect, the fulcrum through which the Bank of England engineers changes in short term interest rates. The way in which the Bank does this is discussed on pp. 173–4.

- The discount houses borrow a large proportion of their funds from the commercial banks. Some of this money is at 'call' and repayment can be demanded almost immediately. Other funds are lent overnight. In this way the discount houses provide the commercial banks with highly liquid, yet profitable, assets.

THE CLEARING BANKS

The clearing banks are so called because they handle the exchange and settlement of cheques. One of their main functions is therefore the *provision of a payments mechanism*. A second important function of the clearing banks is in *accepting deposits*. However, we are mainly concerned with a third function, namely the *provision of finance*. The clearing banks are major providers of short term finance, and their activities in the money market have an important bearing on the money supply. The eligible liabilities (ELs) of the clearing banks consist mainly of deposits, but their assets are more varied.

The asset side of the balance sheet

- **Notes and coin**: these are the bank's most liquid but least profitable asset.

- **Balances at the Bank of England**: of the three assets maintained at the Bank of England only *operational deposits* are a liquid asset. *Cash ratio deposits* are not liquid, since all deposit takers with ELs in excess of £10 million are obliged to maintain such deposits at the Bank of England equal to ½ per cent of the ELs. Equally, *special deposits* are not liquid. More will be said about these later, but they are basically deposits 'frozen' at the Bank of England and repaid only at the Bank's discretion.

- **Bills**: the banks hold a variety of bills, but these are grouped in Table 12.1 as Treasury bills, eligible bank bills, eligible local authority bills and other bills. The precise nature of these bills is discussed on pp. 170–71 and we shall see below that they are of fundamental importance in the implementation of the government's monetary policy.

- **Investments**: these consist largely of the banks' holdings of gilt-edged securities, i.e. government bonds of various maturity dates. Company bonds (i.e. debentures) are also within this heading, as are holdings of equity (shares).

- **Advances**: these are the banks' most profitable asset and consist of loans and overdrafts made to private customers.

> Assets of the clearing bank

Liquidity and profitability

We have already seen that banks have the ability to create deposits by making loans. Indeed, this is their most profitable activity, and it appears on the asset side of the balance sheet as 'advances'. Unfortunately advances are not easily converted into cash should the need arise, i.e. they are illiquid. Once granted they cannot be called in unless a customer defaults in some way, such as failing to meet interest payments. Investments are another profitable asset representing as they do long term loans. However, they can also be risky. While they can easily be sold on the stock exchange, their prices cannot be guaranteed. A bank forced to sell investments might therefore be compelled to do so at unfavourable prices. In general, the least liquid and most risky assets carry the highest rates of return, but banks also require liquidity so as to meet sudden outflows of cash caused by withdrawals from customers. This is why banks make short term loans such as *money at call* to the discount market, or *overnight loans* to the other money market institutions as well as to the discount market. The problem for banks is to arrange their balance sheets so as to achieve the highest profit with acceptable degrees of risk and liquidity. The main assets of the commercial banks are discussed above.

MERCHANT BANKS

Merchant banks perform a variety of functions in both the capital and money markets.

Acceptance business

This was one of the earliest activities of merchant banks. For a fee they simply add their name to bills of exchange issued by traders. In this way they guarantee payment of bills on

LIABILITIES (£m)		ASSETS (£m)	
Sterling liabilities		*Sterling assets*	
Notes Outstanding	1330	Notes and Coin	2655
Deposits, of which:		Balances with the Bank of England, of which:	
Sight deposits	127311	Cash ratio deposits	1229
Time deposits	246209	Operational deposits	237
Certificates of deposit[2]	42124	Special deposits	–
Other sterling liabilities	61219	Market loans	
		LDMA, of which:	
Other currency liabilities		Secured	9348
		Unsecured	119
Deposits, of which:		Other UK monetary sector	83130
Sight and time deposits	573454	UK monetary sector CD's	13429
Certificates of deposit[2]	82154	Building society CD's and time deposits	1738
Other foreign currency liabilities	29957	UK local authorities	1092
		Overseas	26158
		Bills, of which:	
		Treasury bills	1331
		Eligible local authority bills	196
		Eligible bank bills	8892
		Other bills	752
		Advances	278364
		Investments	21381
		Other sterling assets	28386
		Other currency assets	
		Advances	157892
		Market loans	473212
		Bills	4262
		Investments	40795
		Other foreign currency assets	9160
Total liabilities	1163758	Total assets	1163758

Table 12.1 Banks in the UK: combined balance sheet of monthly reporting institutions[1] as at 30 June 1989

[1] Generally those with total balance sheet of £100m or more, or eligible liabilities of £10m or more, other than members of the LDMA

[2] and other short-term paper (short-term securities) issued.

maturity should the drawee default. Accepted bills of exchange are therefore highly marketable (liquid) securities.

Issuing business

Functions of the merchant bank

One of the earliest functions of merchant banks was to raise finance for overseas trading activities but during the present century they have become more active in raising finance in the home market. In particular they now undertake the *issuing* and *underwriting* of share issues by joint stock companies and charge a fee for this service. More recently still they have combined this with financial advice, e.g. advice on the desirability of a merger.

Wholesale banking

Wholesale banking is a term used to describe *large scale dealing in deposits* and is the most important activity of the London money markets. The sums involved are not less than £¾ million and are placed for terms ranging from overnight to several months and in some cases years. The merchant banks have become active participants in the market for wholesale deposits and this is by far their main deposit-taking activity. In this context they are active participants in the Euro-currency markets (p. 170). Like all banks they earn income on the difference paid to attract funds and the amount charged when lending funds.

Foreign banks

The number of foreign banks operating in London has grown rapidly in recent years, from 77 in 1960 to around 450 today. In the main, foreign banks are concerned with international banking activities and are active participants in the Euro-currency markets. Indeed the bulk of their business is concerned with wholesale banking activities and, as yet, retail banking activities account for a small proportion of their activities. However, since deregulation the retail side of their activities has grown rapidly and they now compete with commercial banks for private customers. Many also compete for wholesale deposits in the domestic money market.

<table>
<tr><td>

BANKING REGULATIONS

</td><td>

In August 1981 the Bank of England introduced important new measures concerned with the activities of the *monetary sector*. All of the institutions described in this chapter, both bank and non-bank financial intermediaries, are included in the definition of the monetary sector, which currently comprises:

</td></tr>
</table>

- all recognised banks and licensed deposit-takers
- the National Savings Bank
- the Trustee Savings Bank
- the Banking Department of the Bank of England
- those institutions in the Channel Islands and the Isle of Man which have opted to adhere to the new arrangements

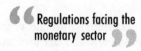

Institutions of the monetary sector

The regulations currently in force concerning the monetary sector are:-

- All banks and licensed deposit-takers with *eligible liabilities* (ELs) in excess of £10m are required to keep non-operational deposits with the Bank of England equal to ½ per cent of total ELs. The purpose of this is to provide the Bank of England with funds and resources rather than to enable it to control the growth of ELs within the monetary sector.

- Special deposits are extended and now apply to all institutions within the monetary sector having ELs greater than £10m.

Regulations facing the monetary sector

- All eligible banks, that is recognised banks whose acceptances (i.e. accepted bills) are eligible for rediscount at the Bank of England, are required to hold secured call money with the LDMA. This must equal at least 2½ per cent of their ELs. They are also required to hold an amount equal to a further 2½ per cent of their ELs, with other institutions in the money and gilt-edged markets, making 5 per cent in total. The purpose of this is to ensure an adequate supply of funds to enable the bill and gilt-edged markets to function efficiently. We shall see on p. 170 that this is necessary if the Bank's own open market operations are to be effective.

- The previous reserve assets ration, in which a minimum of 12½ per cent of selected liquid assets had to be kept against liabilities, was abolished in 1981. The Bank will, however, continue to monitor the liquidity ratios of the banks to ensure that they are adequate.

- In normal circumstances the Bank will no longer publicly announce its Minimum Lending Rate (MLR), that is the rate at which it rediscounts first class bills when acting as *lender of last resort*, but will maintain it within an unpublished band. This is to give market forces a more prominent role in determining short term rates, which will be allowed to fluctuate within the unpublished band without the authorities intervening. This does not mean that MLR can only fluctuate within the limits initially set by the unpublished band. The authorities might vary the position of the band from time to time, and in any case they have reserved the right to make public announcements about MLR in exceptional circumstances.

THE SECONDARY MONEY MARKET

Alongside the *primary* market described above there has grown a *secondary* or *parallel* money market. This has grown rapidly since the 1960s, mainly because the secondary money market has not been subjected to the same degree of regulation by the authorities as has the primary market. Put simply, willing borrowers who have been unable to obtain funds in the primary market have turned to other institutions. These institutions have therefore grown and now compete for deposits with the primary market. The more deposits they can attract, the more loans they can create and this increases their income.

The principal markets which together make up the secondary market are described below.

THE INTER-BANK MARKET

On any particular day certain banks will have a shortage of funds, while other banks will have a surplus. Shortages and surpluses are matched as far as possible by borrowing and lending in the inter-bank market. Dealings are normally in sums of £250,000 or more. Money may be lent at call, overnight, or for any period up to about five years. However, the bulk of lending in the inter-bank market is for three months.

THE MARKET FOR STERLING CERTIFICATES OF DEPOSIT

Components of the secondary money market

The nature of CDs is discussed on p.171 but it is important to note here that certificates of deposit are a *negotiable security*. In other words, they can be sold on the open market at prices determined by supply and demand. The banks have benefitted particularly from the growth of a market in CDs because, by issuing such certificates (i.e. creating claims against themselves), they are able to obtain additional funds which can then be on-lent at a higher interest rate.

THE EURO-CURRENCY MARKET

When an exporter receives payment for goods or services in foreign currency, these can be deposited with a bank or some other licensed deposit-taker. The exporter therefore has a foreign currency deposit which will be on-lent to willing borrowers by the institution holding the deposit. It is this on-lending of foreign currency by European institutions that has given rise to the term 'Euro-currency market'.

In terms of the value of deposits held, this is the largest of the parallel money markets. Companies, banks, and even governments, borrow in the Euro-currency market, and although funds can be borrowed for as long as five years, most borrowing is for six months or less.

INSTRUMENTS OF THE LONDON MONEY MARKET

The London money market deals mainly in instruments (i.e. securities) with one year or less to maturity. The main instruments traded are summarised below and any institution dealing in these instruments is therefore a participant in this market.

BILLS OF EXCHANGE

Bills of Exchange are IOUs given by one person, usually a buyer of goods, to another person, usually a seller of goods. The drawee promises to pay the drawer a fixed sum of money at a specified future time. The drawer of the bill therefore gives the drawee time to sell the goods before paying for them. In the absence of this credit, buyers might not have sufficient cash to place orders and this would leave manufacturers without markets for their goods. However, bills of exchange are negotiable securities and once *accepted* are eligible for discounting. This has important implications because if manufacturers granted trade credit the reduction in their cash flow might make it impossible to finance further production without borrowing funds and incurring interest charges. In other words by providing credit any institution discounting a bill of exchange enables production and distribution to continue uninterrupted.

TREASURY BILLS

Treasury bills are issued by the Bank of England on behalf of the government and normally mature ninety-one days after issue. Like bills of exchange these are a promise to pay a fixed sum of money. The rate of interest the government pays on its short-term borrowing is therefore determined by the price at which Treasury bills can be sold at the weekly tender. The higher the bid price, the lower the rate of interest the government pays on its short-term borrowing.

LOCAL AUTHORITY SECURITIES

> **The various instruments of the London money market**

Local authorities issue bonds which frequently mature within one year. They also issue bills which conventionally mature within ninety-one days. Like Treasury bills these are issued by tender and, as governments have issued fewer Treasury bills, so the discount houses have acquired more local authority bills.

CERTIFICATES OF DEPOSIT

A certificate of deposit (CD) is a document certifying that a deposit has been placed with a bank, and that the deposit is repayable with interest after a stated time. The minimum value of the deposit is usually £50, 000 and CDs normally mature in twelve months or less, although they have been issued with a five-year maturity.

SHORT-DATED BONDS

As well as the securities discussed so far, a host of other securities are traded on the money market. As time goes by any security issued for a fixed number of years will approach its maturity date. The discount market discounts securities with *five years or less* to maturity, but in general it is only when securities have one year or less to maturity that they are traded on the money market.

EURO-CURRENCY CERTIFICATES OF DEPOSIT

These are similar to sterling certificates of deposit, but are given as evidence of a *foreign currency deposit* with a UK bank. Dollar certificates of deposit are the most important instrument traded in the Euro-currency deposit market. The most important outlet for Euro-deposits is the interbank Euro-currency market. Although banks might borrow from one another for as long as five years, most borrowing is for six months or less. Indeed, a substantial amount is typically lent overnight. As they approach maturity, certificates of deposit become more attractive to money market institutions because of their higher degree of liquidity.

EURO-BONDS

The Euro-bond market specialises in the provision of medium term finance. In this market banks arrange, on behalf of borrowers in the UK, to issue and to underwrite bonds. These bonds are usually taken up (i.e. purchased) by private investors who supply the appropriate amount of foreign currency. Like other securities, as Euro-bonds approach maturity they become more liquid and so are traded on the London money markets in the same way that other short term instruments are traded. (See above – 'short-dated bonds'.)

MEASURES OF THE MONEY SUPPLY

> **Different measures of the money supply**

Until now we have discussed the general area of money and liquidity without specifically defining the money. Fig. 12.1 shows those most commonly used in the UK at the present time and the relationship between them. The fact that there are several measures of the money supply appears to make any reference to this concept ambiguous. However, the different measures of the money supply aim to reflect different levels of liquidity within the system. Some measures of the money supply, such as M0, M1 and M2, provide an estimate of the level of transactions balances or *immediate* spending potential in the economy. These are referred to as *narrow* money. The *broad* measures of money in the

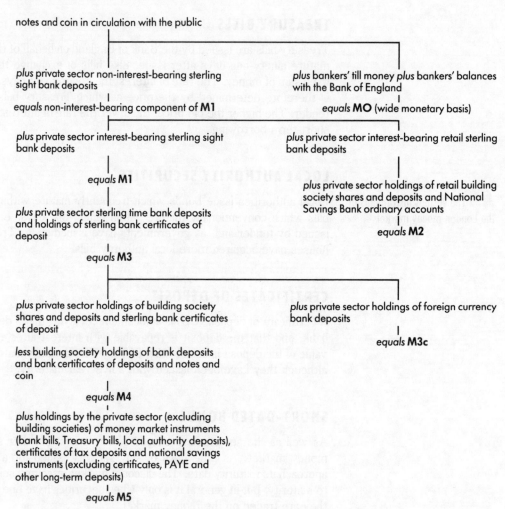

Fig. 12.1 Monetary aggregates and their components

UK are M4 and M5. These include assets which are 'near money', such as Treasury bills.

One problem for the authorities is that having several measures of the money supply sometimes makes it difficult to assess whether monetary policy is restricting the growth of the money supply or not because the different measures of the money supply sometimes move in different directions with some aggregates rising when others are falling.

Currently the authorities take the view that narrow money is an accurate indicator of monetary conditions and, as we shall see in Chapter 17, they set targets for its rate of growth. However, the wider aggregates are also important but they are much more difficult to measure and interpret – especially during periods of rapid change in financial markets. For example, the distinction between banks and building societies is becoming increasingly blurred with building societies now providing current accounts and cheque guarantee cards for customers along with cash point facilities and loans to meet a variety of requirements. Banks, on the other hand, have become active in the provision of mortgage finance. However, the deposits of building societies are not included in the narrower monetary aggregates.

THE MECHANICS OF MONETARY POLICY

The term monetary policy is usually taken to include all the measures which influence the supply of money and/or the price of money (i.e. the rate of interest). In the UK, the Bank of England has overall responsibility for the implementation of monetary policy. It uses a variety of techniques but it is important to be clear that the Bank cannot opt to control both the supply of money and the rate of interest *simultaneously*. A policy of controlling interest rates implies that the money supply must be allowed to vary so as to meet changes in the public's demand for money at the target rate of interest. If the authorities did not allow the money supply to vary in this way an increase in demand for money would pull up interest rates and vice versa.

More specifically the implication of an interest rate target is that the Bank must allow commercial banks to vary the level of their operational deposits by absorbing cash surpluses which emerge in the money market or by relieving any shortages through its role of lender of last resort so as to preserve the existing level of money market rates. A money supply target on the other hand implies that the Bank must not mop up any surpluses or relieve any shortages of money which develop, irrespective of how far short term rates rise or fall. The techniques available to the authorities to achieve the aims of monetary policy are now considered.

OPEN MARKET OPERATIONS

This technique involves the sale or purchase of government securities on the open market by the Bank of England. It can be used to reduce or to increase the stock of money (i.e. bank deposits) in circulation with the public.

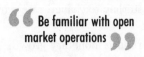

> Be familiar with open market operations

Suppose the Bank of England wishes to *reduce* the money supply by open market operations. The Bank of England *sells* securities to the non-bank private sector, that is, to households and firms other than those engaged in banking in the private sector. These securities will be paid for by cheques drawn against deposits with the commercial banks. The Bank of England will settle these claims against banks by deducting the appropriate amount from their operational deposits. If necessary, the banks will be able to replenish their operational deposits at the Bank of England by calling in their loans to the discount market. However, there will still be a reduction in their overall level of liquidity, since loans to the discount market are liquid assets and these have now fallen in total. This reduction in liquidity will compel banks to reduce their lending (i.e. bank deposits) otherwise they risk being unable to honour all the claims that bank lending creates against them.

If the Bank of England wishes to *increase* the money supply by open market operations, it will *purchase* securities from the non-bank private sector. In this case the banks operational deposits increase. Assuming that there are willing borrowers, then this extra liquidity can be used to increase their lending, that is, bank deposits increase.

INTEREST RATE POLICY

In practice open market operations have been used less frequently for controlling the money supply in recent years. Instead, the authorities have relied much more on money market intervention to influence interest rates, and in this way to control the growth of bank lending. A rise in interest rates might be expected to damp down the demand for bank credit, thus restricting growth of the money supply and vice versa.

The techniques of interest rate policy are complex, but under the present arrangements the clearing banks inform the Bank of England daily about the target they are aiming at for their assets. This information, together with the Bank's estimate of flows between the commercial banks and the public sector, as well as seasonal patterns, etc., enables the Bank to estimate the likely shortage or surplus of funds in the money market. This estimate is announced at about 9.45 a.m., and if necessary, a revised estimate is announced at noon. If the Bank estimates that the market will be *short* of funds, it informs the discount houses that it is prepared to *buy* bills from them. However, it does not stipulate a price, and the discount houses must offer bills to the bank at prices of their choosing. If the Bank of England considers that the rate of interest implied by these offers (remember the relationship between security prices and the rate of interest) is consistent with the conduct of monetary policy, it will accept the offers, and the shortage of funds will be relieved. However, if the Bank considers that the rate of interest implied by these offers is too low, then it will decline to buy the bills and the discount houses will be compelled to make further offers of bills at lower prices (implying higher rates of interest). When the Bank wishes to engineer a *fall* in short-term rates of interest it simply *increases* the price at which it is prepared to buy bills from the discount houses.

How does the Bank engineer a change in short term rates?

The question might be asked as to how the Bank will engineer a change in short-term rates when the market is *not* short of funds, and so does not need to deal with the Bank. In fact, this is an unlikely occurrence, because the Bank can create shortages by increasing the weekly Treasury bill issue. Since the LDMA agree to cover the tender, this will create a shortage of funds. Alternatively, the Bank can 'fund' the national debt (see below). To engineer a fall in short term rates the Bank simply buys securities thus creating a surplus of funds in the money markets.

Another way in which the Bank can affect short-term rates is provided by the 1981 regulations. Under these the Bank retains the option, in exceptional circumstances, to reveal in advance the rate at which it will operate in the market for a short period ahead. It has used this option on several occasions and it has proved very effective with all institutions acting quickly to fall into line with the Bank's wishes once it has made these known. The alternative of course would be for the Bank to implement measures which would force institutions to comply with its intentions!

Problems of controlling money supply by using interest rates

There are several problems associated with using interest rates to control the money supply:

- Changes in the rate of interest cause changes in the sterling exchange rate which might conflict with the aims of the authorities.

- Sometimes relatively high interest rates are needed to reduce monetary growth. As well as being unpopular with home-buyers, this causes the retail price index to rise. High interest rates also reduce the rate of investment in fixed capital and hence reduce future economic growth.

- Changes in interest rates usually work only after a considerable time lag has elapsed. (The relatively high rates of interest during 1988/89 took many months to damp down consumer spending)

SPECIAL DEPOSITS

When the Bank of England makes a call for special deposits, it requires banks and licensed deposit-takers with ELs in excess of £10m to place funds in a special account at the Bank. Although these funds earn interest, they are effectively 'frozen', since those making the deposits do not have the right to withdraw them. The Bank of England alone decides when special deposits will be repaid. The level of special deposits is fixed as a percentage of ELs and payment is again made by a reduction in operational deposits, that is, cash reserves at the Bank. A call for special deposits is the most direct means currently available to the Bank for reducing the liquidity position of banks and licensed deposit-takers and is therefore the most direct means of controlling their lending. As the stock of liquid assets falls, banks are again forced to cut their lending. Special deposits can be released when the Bank wishes to see an expansion of the money supply.

No call has been made for special deposits since the 1970s because, as with any selective control mechanism, the result of using them has often been rapid growth of business by those organisations *not* subject to these controls. The authorities take the view that such growth is undesirable because it represents growth of less efficient institutions, that is, institutions which only grow when other institutions are subjected to controls. This explains the emphasis on control through changes in the rate of interest, which affects all institutions indiscriminately and does not therefore encourage the growth of inefficient institutions.

FUNDING

This involves the sale of more long-term debt (e.g. bonds) and the issue of less short-term debt (e.g. Treasury bills). Since Treasury bills are short-dated securities they are highly liquid assets because they can be sold easily and quickly on the money market. By issuing fewer Treasury bills the authorities can reduce the degree of liquidity in the system, and thereby restrict the ability of the banks to make loans. If a bank's holdings of Treasury bills falls and its holdings of long- term securities increases, it is likely to cut its lending for two main reasons:

- Longer-term securities are not eligible for re-discount at the Bank of England and are therefore less liquid.

- Although longer-term securities can be sold on the capital market, their value is less certain.

These are important considerations, since they imply that if a bank needs to replenish its holdings of cash because of a sudden outflow of funds, it might be forced to sell its securities at unfavourable prices. Rather than risk this, banks would tend to cut their lending.

FISCAL POLICY

The authorities believe that there is a close association between the amount the public sector borrows (*the public sector borrowing requirement* or PSBR) and the growth of M3. This relationship is discussed in detail on pp. 250–53, but it is important to note here that at the present time the authorities believe that a reduction in the growth of M3 is impossible without a reduction in the size of the PSBR. Consequently they have made a reduction in the PSBR one of their main mechanisms for controlling the growth of M3.

MONETARY BASE CONTROL

This technique of monetary control has not so far been used in the UK but is still favoured by many economists, especially those economists referred to as *monetarists*. The technique is simple enough. Banks would maintain a minimum proportion of their deposits in base money (normally defined as notes and coin plus operational deposits at the Bank of England) either because this is mandatory or because it is prudent for them to do so. The authorities can then either:

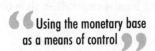
" Using the monetary base as a means of control "

- control the supply of base money and so control the growth of bank deposits; or
- use divergencies in the growth of base money above the desired trend to trigger interest rate increases; higher interest rates will in turn limit the growth of borrowing and hence correct the divergence.

So far there has been little official support for either technique though the former has received most criticism and the authorities have taken the view that any attempt to limit the growth of deposits by controlling the supply of base money would lead to a distortion in the money supply figures. In other words, it might well control the growth of bank deposits, but might lead to a significant change in the composition of the money supply, with assets not officially included in narrow measures of the money stock, such as commercial bills of exchange functioning as money.

SUMMARY

Despite the availability of a wide range of techniques for controlling the money supply, recently the authorities have relied most on:

- limiting the growth of the PSBR;
- limiting the extent to which the PSBR is financed through the banking sector; and
- interest rate policy

APPLIED MATERIALS

THE STERLING MONEY MARKET

An article in the National Westminster Bank Quarterly Bulletin entitled *The Sterling Money Market and the Determination of Interest Rates* provides an analysis of the Bank's operating procedures in the Money market.

The article emphasises that the Bank operates at the short end of the market, that is, seeks to influence short term interest rates and, in particular, the 7-day rate. It can do this by buying or selling bills on a sufficient scale so as to create a surplus or shortage of bankers' cash (operational deposits). However, in practice the authorities do not always seek to achieve this. The Bank buys or sells on a modest scale seeking only to make the market aware of its desire to achieve a particular rate of interest. Other money market operators, being aware of the power of the authorities to achieve their aim by coercion, are quick to ensure that interest rates fall into line with the intentions of the authorities once these intentions are known. The Bank's operations in the money market therefore function as a system of communication as well as a mechanism of control.

It is also explained that the Bank's declared current aim is to maintain short term (7-day) rates within an undisclosed band having an upper limit and a lower limit. The whole band will shift from time to time in keeping with the changing interest rate targets set by the authorities. The authorities also reserve the right to publish their target rate if circumstances demand it (as happened in 1986 when the authorities disclosed their minimum lending rate as an indication to the market of their intention to see no further reduction in the sterling exchange rate). In practice, however, only the upper end of the band has been relevant for control purposes because over-funding sales of government debt to the non-bank sector has meant a persistent shortage of bankers' cash which the Bank has then been able to relieve on *terms of its own choosing* by buying bills in the market.

Despite its declared intention it seems that the Bank has been dealing in all maturities up to 3 months. Indeed it reports its dealing rates twice daily in four maturity bands:

Band 1: up to 14 days
Band 2: 15 to 33 days
Band 3: 34 to 63 days
Band 4: 64 to 91 days

and these are taken as the Bank's estimate of the optimum course of the 7-day rate over the next 13 weeks. In other words they are taken by the market as an attempt by the authorities to give an indication of the expected future course of interest rates. The market has often been ready to accept this indication so that the 3-month rate has adjusted to the Bank's band 4 rate. On other occasions the market has taken a different view of the future course of interest rates and the Bank has preferred to alter its band 4 rate rather than be seen to publicly disagree with the market.

EXAMINATION QUESTIONS

1 Why do all advanced economies have a central bank (such as the Bank of England)?
(London, January 1989)

2 a) Explain how the pattern of lending of commercial banks reflects their conflicting aims of liquidity and profitability. *(13)*

b) In what ways are commercial banks important to the running of an economy? *(7)*

(Total 20 marks)
(Scottish, 1988)

3 Explain why it is
a) difficult to define and
b) to control the money supply

(AEB, Nov 1988)

4 Explain briefly with the aid of a numerical example, 'the money (or credit) multiplier'. Discuss the significance of the money multiplier for monetary policy.
(AEB, June 1988)

A TUTOR'S ANSWER TO QUESTION 1

The fact that all developed economies have a central bank indicates the existence of a general consensus that central banks perform indispensible functions. In the UK the central bank is the Bank of England and although it has certain specific functions, its major activities are the same as any other central bank.

One of the main functions of the Bank is that it acts as banker to the government. This embraces several activities. It handles receipts for example from the Inland Revenue Department or from privatisation of assets such as British Telecom. It also releases funds to meet the spending commitments of the different government departments. Moreover, when there is a shortfall of receipts over expenditure the Bank offers 'overdraft' facilities to the government via 'ways and means' advances. Such advances are for relatively short periods of time – often overnight – and more permanent government deficits are financed by issuing securities such as Treasury bills. This implies another important function performed by the Bank of England: that of handling the government's borrowing. Indeed in the UK the Bank has responsibility for administering the National Debt. This means it issues securities, pays interest to holders of existing securities and repays sums borrowed when securities mature. There is no doubt that such arrangements are more conveniently handled by a single agent such as the Bank of England because it is then easier to select the optimal timing for new issues and redemptions of securities.

Another major function of the Bank of England is to implement the government's monetary policy. Monetary policy aims to control the cost or availability of credit. To implement monetary policy the Bank has several options open to it. One option which has been used regularly in recent years is manipulating the rate of interest. The Bank does this by buying or selling securities in the money markets so as to achieve the desired rate of interest. For example, it can create a shortage of funds in the money markets by issuing sufficient Treasury bills to create the shortage, it can then relieve the shortage of funds by lending to the discount market at interest rates of its own choosing. Alternatively the bank can use open market purchases and sales of securities to change the liquidity position of the banks and so change their ability to make loans. For example, when securities are purchased by the Bank of England, cheques will be drawn against the central bank in favour of sellers of securities. Recipients of these will present them for payment at their own commercial banks. These banks in turn will present them to the central bank for payment which will be made by book entry at the central bank so that the operational deposits of the commercial bank increase. The increased liquidity will facilitate an increase in lending by the commercial banks if demand for loans exists.

The Bank can also issue 'requests' to the monetary sector including banks and building societies to cut back on their lending or to discriminate in favour of certain groups such as firms involved in exporting. On occasion the Bank has given force to its requests by issuing directives but it is usually sufficient for the Bank to let its views be known to ensure compliance with its wishes.

The Bank can also impose physical constraints on lending by certain financial institutions by calling for 'special deposits'. These are deposits which are 'frozen' at the Bank and to which those making them have no access. However, while there is no doubt that special deposits effectively restrict lending by institutions forced to lodge them, they tend to encourage lending by institutions not obliged to make them and consequently have not been used in recent years.

When implementing monetary policy the Bank sometimes functions as 'lender of last resort' to the banking system by making loans to the discount market when it is short of liquidity. However, it has also acted as lender of last resort in a different way so as to avoid the possibility of a banking collapse. For example, in 1974 support was given to some organisations, many calling themselves banks, who were in danger of collapse because they had invested heavily in property before the collapse of property prices. Similarly it made assistance available to Johnson Matthey Bankers when they collapsed in 1985.

By offering assistance the Bank is not simply acting as lender of last resort, but is also exercising a supervisory role aimed at ensuring stability of the financial system. In this capacity it draws up regulations to govern the conduct of financial institutions, particularly in respect of their liquidity reserves, and has strict guidelines according to which organisations can refer to themselves as banks.

The Bank also has responsibility for managing the Exchange Equalisation Account through which foreign exchange receipts are converted into sterling and sterling is converted into foreign exchange so as to honour overseas commitments such as payment for goods and services. More fundamentally the EEA intervenes in the foreign exchange market so as to ensure that the foreign exchange value of sterling is in line with the government's target rate of exchange. It does this by adding to the supply of sterling when demand is rising, and reducing supply of sterling when demand is falling.

In England and Wales the Bank is the sole note issuing authority. This is an important function because the note issue is now fiduciary and is therefore backed by securities rather than gold. The Bank responds passively to changes in the demand for cash by the public but a persistent over issue of notes would quickly result in a loss of confidence in the acceptability of Bank of England notes in settlement of a debt.

The Bank of England is also banker to the monetary system. All banks and licensed deposit takers are required to hold operation deposits at the Bank and these are used as current accounts. Any institution requiring cash withdraws it from operational deposits.

These deposits are also used to settle any interbank indebtedness that arises out of the clearing process.

The role of the central bank is therefore important and diverse. In the case of the UK the role of the Bank of England is evolving as the role of the government in the economy evolves and, more recently, as the financial environment evolves. The active involvement of the government in the economy increased the importance of monetary policy in particular and in the absence of a central bank the implementation of this policy would be considerably more difficult.

A STUDENT'S ANSWER TO QUESTION 3

It is difficult to define the money supply because 'money is as money does'. This simply means any commodity can serve as money if it performs the functions of money. To understand why this is so we must first outline the functions which money performs.

The main function of money is to act as a medium of exchange. Without money for trade to take place there would need to be a 'double coincidence of wants'. This means that two people must each possess a commodity that the other requires. Not only this they must also agree what rate these commodities will exchange at. For example, if one person has food to trade and another person has clothing they must also agree how much food is worth one item of clothing. We can immediately see a problem because while food is fairly easy to divide into smaller units it is not so easy to subdivide an item of clothing into smaller units.

Mention barter

It is not divisible without destroying its value!

Money removes all of these difficulties. It is acceptable in exchange for goods and services. One person can exchange clothing for money and then spend as much of this money on food as desired. Money can therefore be used to assign values to goods and services which are traded and there is no need for a double coincidence of wants to exist. It is also clear that because not all of the money received from clothing has to be spent at once, money serves as a store of value. In addition because we can agree prices today for the delivery of goods in the future, money functions as a standard for deferred payment.

It is easy to see the functions money must perform but not so easy to see which assets will perform these functions. In modern economies like that of the UK money consists of notes and coin and bank deposits. Cheques are also used as money because these are often given in settlement of debts when purchases are made. The number of cheques which are received daily shows that they are clearly acceptable to most traders.

No. Bank deposits are money. Cheques are simply the means of transferring ownership of bank deposits

The main problem with defining the money supply is that some assets are more liquid than others. Something is liquid when it can easily be converted into cash. Notes and coin are liquid and so are cheques. However, bank deposits are less liquid. Some can be converted into cash immediately and are known as demand deposits. However, others require notice of withdrawal, sometimes as long as 90 days. These bank deposits are not very liquid and are therefore not counted as money.

Sight deposits are highly liquid

Because it is difficult to define the money supply it will always be difficult to control it. However, the authorities have different definitions of the money supply which consist of different aggregates and this is what they seek to control.

You should specify these

How does this affect the money supply?

The major technique the authorities have relied on in recent years is interest rate policy. In particular they have increased interest rates in an attempt to damp down consumer spending. This has not proved very effective and consumer spending does not therefore seem very responsive to changes in the rate of interest. The other

It is more responsive in the long run

problem is that changes in the rate of interest often bring about changes in the sterling exchange rate. For example, when the rate of interest in the UK increases this tends to increase the value of sterling on the foreign exchange market and this makes it difficult for firms to export their products.

Another problem is that the demand for money might change and in this case the money supply might have to adjust to avoid the rate of interest rising too far above the level desired by the authorities or falling too far below the desired level. Such changes in the money supply might not always be in keeping with other economic policies pursued by the government. The problem therefore depends on whether the demand for money is stable or not. A stable demand for money is better for the authorities because they will be aware of what will happen to the money supply if they bring about a given change in the rate of interest.

In conclusion it can be seen that it is very difficult to define money because any asset which is acceptable in exchange for goods and services can function as money. However, there are certain money aggregates which the authorities seek to control but they have not always been successful as recent experience demonstrates.

> This essay makes some valid points but it is confused in places and lacks depth in others

OUTLINE ANSWERS TO QUESTIONS 2 AND 4

Question 2

a) You could begin your answer to this question by defining liquidity. Basically it concerns the ease with which an asset can be turned into cash without capital loss. You could then go on to discuss the reasons why banks require liquidity. The main reasons are:-

1 To meet withdrawals by customers
2 To meet any overnight indebtedness
3 To meet statutory obligations concerning cash ration and operational deposits
4 To reduce risk. The more liquid an asset the less risk it carries. The latter links liquidity with profitability, but other factors, especially the length of time over which loans are granted, are important. It is important to refer to the items in the banks' balance sheet when discussing these points.

b) This part of the question requires an analysis of the functions performed by commercial banks. The main points to discuss are that banks are financial intermediaries and their main functions are maturity transformation and risk reduction. Firms and the government are able to ensure their financing requirements are met. In the absence of commercial banks this would be more difficult and therefore you must analyse the different types of finance that banks provide to government and industry. They also provide advice to firms and manage investment funds which provide pensions. Another important activity is to provide foreign exchange arrangements which facilitates international trade.

Question 4

The money supply multiplier is explained elsewhere but this question asks only for a *brief* example. It is sufficient to explain that banks need to maintain liquid assets to meet withdrawals by customers but will lend anything in excess of what is required for this purpose. Since all banks will do the same there will be a money multiplier equal in value to the inverse of the fraction of total deposits retained as liquid assets. Remember to give a numerical example to illustrate the process!

Clearly the money supply multiplier has considerable significance for monetary policy. Any change in the availability of liquid assets to the banks will have a multiplied impact on the money supply (assuming there is unsatisfied demand for loans) and therefore on aggregate money demand. You could discuss this in terms of the Keynesian framework discussed in Chapter 9. You could then contrast this with the monetarist view that a change in the money supply simply leads to inflation. In this case the size of the money supply multiplier is important in bringing about changes in the rate of inflation following any change in the availability of base money. The distinction between real and nominal effects of the money supply multiplier could then be examined.

In practice it is a matter of doubt that the value of the money supply multiplier is stable. It is likely to change over time as the public's demand for cash changes. If it changes unpredictably then monetary policy is made considerably more difficult to plan and implement.

Further reading

Griffiths and Wall, *Applied Economics: An Introductory Course* (3rd edn) Longman 1989: Ch. 15, The UK Financial System; Ch. 16, Money.

Herbert, *Money and the Financial System* (2nd edn) Longman, 1989

Sedgewick, *The Changing Structure of the UK Financial System*, Longman 1989

Stanlake, *Macroeconomics: An Introduction* (4th edn), Longman 1989: Ch.11, Money; Ch. 12, The Structure of Banking; Ch. 14, The Control of the Money Supply.

THE VALUE OF MONEY

GETTING STARTED

In itself, money has no intrinsic value. It derives value because it is acceptable in exchange for goods and services. The value of money is therefore determined by the prices of goods and services purchased with money. Clearly, if all prices in the economy rise, then a given amount of money will exchange for (or buy) fewer goods and services. In this case the value of money has fallen. Conversely, if all prices in the economy fall, the value of money has risen.

This seems simple enough, but the problem is that over any given period of time not all prices in the economy move in the same direction or by the same amount. Some prices rise and others fall. Some rise by more than others, and so on. In practice, therefore, it is difficult to measure changes in the value of money, and economists use a technique known as *index numbers* to estimate changes in an average of prices. Not all price changes are considered, merely those of most significance to the average person.

The cause of changes in the value of money, that is, the cause of price changes, is a subject which has long been discussed by economists. The earliest attempt to explain the cause of changes in the value of money is the *quantity theory of money*. The earliest version of this theory proposed a direct relationship between changes in the money supply and changes in the price level; but it is the more refined version, associated with Irving Fisher, that is usually considered most significant.

ESSENTIAL PRINCIPLES

QUANTITY THEORY OF MONEY

Fisher's quantity theory of money is based on the *equation exchange*. This is usually expressed in the following way:

$$MV_t = PT$$

where　M = the total money stock

　　　V_t = the transactions velocity of money, i.e. the number of times each unit of currency is spent over a given period of time.

　　　P = the average price level

　　　T = the total number of transactions which take place over a given period of time

However, T is difficult to measure since it includes second-hand and intermediate transactions. For policy purposes therefore, a more useful formulation of the equation of exchange is:

$$MV_y = PY$$

where　M = the total money stock

　　　V_y = income velocity of circulation or the number of times each unit of currency is used to purchase final output in any given period of time

　　　P = average price of final output

　　　Y = the total volume of real output produced in a given period of time

Since P is the average price of final output and Y is the total volume of final output, PY is simply another way of expressing GNP.

Whichever formulation we consider, the equation of exchange is nothing more than an identity or a truism. Both sides of the equation must, by definition, always be identical equal. MV_t is total spending in the economy and PT is total receipts in the economy. By definition, total spending in one period must equal total receipts in the same period. Similarly, GNP in any particular period is equal both to total final expenditure, MV_y, and to the value of receipts, PY, from the sale of final output.

Despite this, the equation of exchange forms the basis of the quantity theory. Fisher and other classical economists assumed that the economy had an in-built tendency to establish equilibrium at full employment. They therefore believed that the total volume of transactions was fixed in the short run by the amount that can be produced at full employment. Additionally, they also assumed that the velocity of circulation was determined independently of changes in the money supply and changed so slowly over time that it could be treated as a constant. Accepting both these propositions leads to the conclusion that M varies directly with P.

> **" The quantity theory relates money supply directly to prices "**

However, this still does not provide an adequate explanation of how the price level is determined. A further assumption frequently made by monetarist adherents to the quantity theory is that the authorities can control the money supply. Thus the basic prediction of the quantity theory becomes one in which changes in M cause changes in P, and that there can be no change in P independently of a prior change in M. Although, as we shall later see, the quantity theory has been reformulated, most notably by Friedman, Fisher's version remains the basis of all monetarist thinking.

INDEX NUMBERS

We have seen that changes in the value of money imply a change in the average price level. Changes in the average price level are *measured by* index numbers and in the UK the most publicised index is the index of retail prices.

INDEX OF RETAIL PRICES

This purports to measure changes in the cost of living experienced by an average household over a particular period of time. The technique is simple enough. A representative sample of the population provides a detailed record of their expenditure over a given period, usually a month, and this is used to estimate the expenditure pattern of the 'average household'. This estimate of expenditure is used to derive the *items* to be included in the index and the *weights* assigned to them; the weight being based on their relative importance. Those items which account for a large proportion of total expenditure

	YEAR 1				YEAR 2			
Item	Price	Weight	Index No.	Weighted Index No.	Price	Weight	Index No.	Weighted Index No.
A	£1.00	4	100	400	£1.50	4	150	600
B	£2.00	2	100	200	£2.50	2	125	250
C	£5.00	3	100	300	£6.00	3	120	360
D	£4.00	1	100	100	£6.00	1	150	150
Index of prices	= 1000/10				Index of prices	= 1360/10		
	= 100					= 136		

Table 13.1

over the period are assigned a higher weight than items which account for a smaller proportion of total expenditure. Table 13.1 illustrates the basic principles involved in computing the index of retail prices.

In the base year (Year 1): each commodity is assigned an index number of 100. The weighted index number of each commodity is then obtained by multiplying the index number by the weight. Adding up all the weighted index numbers and dividing by the sum of the weights, gives the value of the price index. In the example provided the value of the price index in the base year is 100. In fact this will always be the value of the index in the base year, because *each* commodity is assigned a value of 100. In calculating a *weighted price index* in the base year we are therefore effectively multiplying 100 by the sum of the weights and then dividing the answer by the sum of the weights.

Finding the Retail Price Index

In the next period, (Year 2): the index number of each commodity is simply the price of the commodity in Year 2 expressed as a percentage of its price in Year 1. So we see that the price of commodity A in Year 2 is 150 per cent of its price in Year 1, and so on. Again, this is multiplied by the relevant weight for each commodity, and the total of all the weighted index numbers which results is divided by the sum of the weights to give the price index (that is, the average weighted value of all price changes) in Year 2. In this case the price index in Year 2 is 136 indicating that the average family has experienced a rise in the cost of living of 36 per cent between Year 1 and Year 2.

Problems of interpreting changes in the RPI

Changes in the RPI are the most widely used measure of changes in the rate of inflation in the UK. However, for several reasons changes in the RPI might not accurately measure changes in the rate of inflation. The following are some of the major reasons for this:

- A retail price index such as that illustrated in Table 13.1 measures changes in retail prices experienced by the *average family*. However, different families will have *different patterns of consumption* which might deviate substantially from that used to construct a price index. For example, families with children consume different goods and services than families with no children. Similarly changes in the prices of goods and services affect people differently. For example, non-smokers are unaffected by changes in the price of tobacco, and changes in the mortgage rate only affect home-buyers.

The need for caution in interpreting changes in the RPI

- Over time patterns of consumption change. For example, more fish is now consumed and less red meat than a decade ago. Consumption of alcohol has increased in the last decade and so on. If an index is to be accurate, the weights must be altered to reflect these changes.

- Care must also be taken to monitor changes in the types of institution used by consumers. Here again patterns have changed, with small independent retailers declining in importance and supermarkets increasing in importance. Data on prices charged in different retail outlets must reflect expenditure by consumers in them if an index is to be accurate.

- Over time the quality of goods changes. For example, pocket calculators are now more reliable and have a greater range of functions than models available only a few years ago. Simply monitoring price changes ignores such quality improvements.

■ New goods become available and again the index must be altered to take account of these if it is to be accurate. For example, few houses had a home computer or a video in the 1970s and yet they are now quite common.

In practice weights in the RPI and the range of goods monitored *are* altered to allow for the changes mentioned above. This undoubtedly improves the accuracy of the RPI in the short term, though it makes comparisons over long term periods less precise.

THE TAX AND PRICE INDEX

66 **An alternative index** 99

The index of retail prices measures changes in the cost of living. But what people can buy with their earnings depends on the deductions from their pay, in particular those made in respect of *income tax* and *national insurance contributions*, as well as on the average level of prices when take home pay is spent. The tax and price index shows how the purchasing power of income is affected by changes in both *direct taxes* and *prices*.

Changes in prices, as measured by the retail price index, have a weight of about 75 per cent in the tax and price index, while changes in income tax and national insurance contributions account for the remainder. Like the retail price index, the tax and price index is a composite index reflecting the weighted experience of groups of households with different tax liabilities. The tax and price index is therefore an attempt to reflect what has happened to the purchasing power of the average household's take home pay.

DEMAND-PULL INFLATION

This occurs when there is excess demand for real output at the existing price level. In other words, aggregate demand exceeds aggregate supply. We have analysed this situation in terms of the inflationary gap on pp. 123–4 but the assumption there was that prices remain constant. The 45° line used to explain the Keynesian model of income determination on pp. 117–18 is effectively the aggregate supply curve of the economy. In practice, an excess of aggregate demand over aggregate supply at the existing price level, which *cannot* be fully accommodated by an expansion of output, will result in the price level being pulled upwards until aggregate demand and aggregate supply are brought into equality.

The process is sometimes likened to an auction. In the early stages of bidding for an item, demand usually exceeds supply, and price is pulled upwards until demand *equals* supply. Similarly, in the real world, if demand exceeds the limited amount of output available at the current price level, then the price level rises. However, when the economy is producing at less than full capacity, and there are substantial amounts of unemployed resources, it is likely that a rise in demand will be accommodated by an expansion of *output*, with little or no effect on the average price level. But as the economy approaches full employment it becomes increasingly difficult for output to respond, and in these circumstances excess aggregate demand is at least partly manifested in higher prices. Once full employment is reached, however, any increase in aggregate demand is entirely reflected in higher prices. Because of this, *demand-pull inflation* is particularly associated with economies which are at or near full employment. The effect of increases in aggregate demand on output and the price level is illustrated in Fig. 13.1.

Aggregate supply and aggregate demand are initially in equilibrium at OY with an

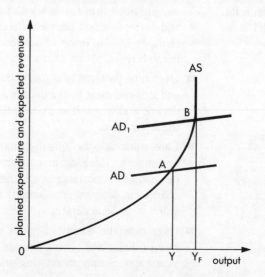

Fig. 13.1 The effect of an increase in aggregate demand on real output and the price level

average price level of AY/OY; that is, price equals average expenditure on output, i.e. total expenditure (total receipts of firms) divided by total output. A rise in aggregate demand to AD_1, results in an increase in output to the full employment level OY_F, but also an increase in the price level of BY_F/OY_F. Any further increase in aggregate demand will simply result in higher prices, because no further expansion of output is possible.

Despite this apparently simple analysis, care must be taken to avoid confusion. As the economy approaches full employment resources become increasingly scarce and growing competition for these will bid up their price. Firms will therefore experience rising costs. However, these cost increases are not exogenous. They are the direct result of a higher demand for final output. We shall see in the following section that an *exogenous* rise in costs will result in an upward shift of the entire aggregate supply curve, rather than a movement along it.

COST-PUSH INFLATION

This occurs when pressure on prices results from an *exogenous* rise in costs. Since the share of national income paid to labour is about 70 per cent of the total of all incomes paid, wage increases in excess of productivity increases have been an important source of rising costs. Any depreciation of sterling will also have an important impact on costs in the UK (see pp. 217–19), since the UK depends heavily on imported raw materials.

An exogenous increase in costs, whatever its source, raises firms' costs at all levels of output. After an increase in costs, any given level of output will therefore only be supplied at a higher price. Although individual firms might be willing to absorb an increase in costs by cutting profits, it will be impossible for all firms to do this. Therefore the aggregate supply curve shifts upwards. With an unchanged level of aggregate demand the effect of an exogenous increase in costs on output and the price level is shown in Fig. 13.2.

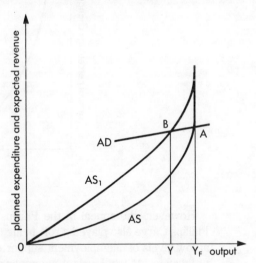

Fig. 13.2 The effect of an exogenous increase in costs on aggregate supply, real output and the price level

Aggregate supply and aggregate demand are initially in equilibrium at output OY_F with the price level at AY_F/OY_F. Subsequently, an exogenous rise in costs shifts aggregate supply to AS_1 and, if all other things remain equal, equilibrium will be restored when output has fallen to OY and the price level has risen to BY/OY.

Because of the importance of wages in firms' costs, economists have coined the term *wage-push inflation* to indicate a situation when the main source of cost increases is wage increases in excess of productivity increases. Again, this is more likely to occur at higher levels of employment; as shortages of skilled labour develop, unions are usually more able to negotiate higher pay awards.

THE INFLATIONARY SPIRAL

In practice it is not always easy to distinguish between cost-push and demand-pull inflation. For example, a rise in costs which pushes up prices will also result in higher factor incomes. At least part of these will be spent domestically and the extra demand, especially if there is a shortage of capacity, is likely to pull prices up still further. These price increases imply a fall in the real income of wage earners. It is likely that trade unions will demand compensatory pay rises, giving a still further push to inflation.

In practice, the inflationary spiral will not go on indefinitely. There are several reasons for this. The tax and benefit system acts to automatically stabilise the economy; increased expenditure on imports and a reduction in exports will raise leakages and cut injections etc... Nevertheless, because of the potentially adverse effects of inflation, especially on the balance of payments, governments have pursued policies to actively reduce the rate of inflation rather than merely to allow the process to peter out in the fullness of time. These policies are discussed in Chapter 16.

THE PHILLIPS CURVE

Relating unemployment to inflation

The relationship between unemployment and inflation is generalised in the Phillips Curve. In its original form this curve indicated a negative correlation between the rate of change of wages and the level of unemployment. The impressive feature of the Phillips Curve was that the relationship it identified had been remarkably stable for a continuous period of almost a hundred years. Soon after the original Phillips Curve was identified it was quickly discovered that there was also a significant, and stable, negative correlation between the rate of change of prices and the level of unemployment. Moreover, it was widely believed by policy makers that because the relationship had been stable for almost a hundred years, it would remain stable in the future. It therefore appeared to offer policy makers a range of policy choices. A *particular level of unemployment* could be traded off against a *particular rate of inflation*. For example, a lower level of unemployment implied a higher rate of inflation, and vice versa. This inverse relationship between unemployment and the rate of inflation is shown in Fig. 13.3.

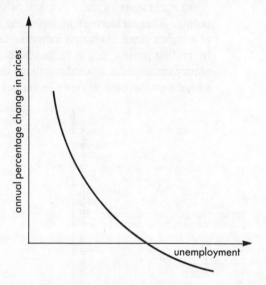

Fig. 13.3 The Phillips Curve

However, the appeal of the Phillips Curve was not just in its apparent stability. The Phillips Curve also played a role in identifying the *causes* of inflation. High rates of inflation at low levels of unemployment supported *both* the demand-pull and cost-push explanations of inflation. At low levels of unemployment, buoyant demand would pull up prices, while trade unions would be in a strong bargaining position from which they could negotiate relatively high pay awards. Buoyant demand in the economy would lower employers' resistance to pay demands since rising costs could more easily be passed on as higher prices. In contrast, at high levels of unemployment, demand in the economy would be less buoyant and the bargaining position of unions weaker.

THE BREAKDOWN OF THE PHILLIPS CURVE

For over a decade economic policy in the UK was implicitly based on the Phillips Curve. However, it became apparent in the late 1960s that the relationship identified by Phillips was not as stable as at first believed. Fig. 13.4 shows the course of inflation and unemployment in the UK since 1969.

It is clear that a higher rate of inflation than previously is now consistent with any given level of unemployment. Various reasons have been advanced to account for this. Some economists claim that the Phillips Curve has simply moved outwards from the origin; some possible reasons for this are examined below. However, an alternative explanation is provided by the monetarists who claim that the Phillips Curve was never more than a short-run phenomenon that had no long-run validity. This view is examined in the following section.

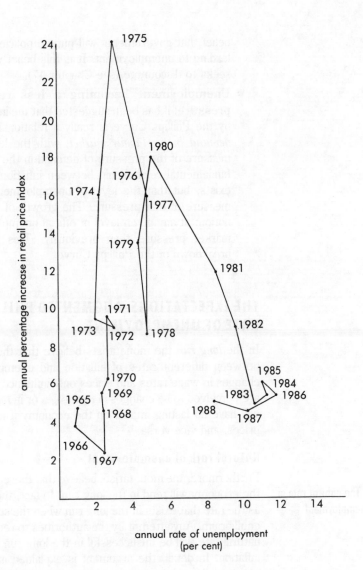

Fig. 13.4 Breakdown of the Phillips Curve

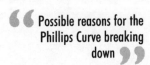

Causes of the breakdown of the Phillips Curve

- **Increased unemployment and welfare benefits:** one possible explanation for the breakdown of the Phillips Curve is the increasing availability of unemployment and welfare benefits. These reduce the financial pressure on the unemployed to obtain work. In this sense there is a greater willingness to accept unemployment. Taking longer to find alternative employment would cause an increase in the unemployment figures. The statistics may then show that any *given* level of aggregate demand, and therefore rate of inflation, is associated with a *greater* level of unemployment than previously. This would shift the Phillips Curve rightwards and outwards, changing the inflation-unemployment relationship in the way observed in Fig. 13.4. This is arguably not so much a cause for concern, as an indication that social policies designed to alleviate the financial hardships of unemployment are actually working.

- **Demographic changes:** it is likely that the demographic changes which have taken place during the post-war period have had a significant impact on the labour market, affecting the relationship between inflation and unemployment. For example, in the post-war period the female activity rate rose almost annually until about 1977, and although it has declined slightly since then, there are still currently some 10.5 million women in the labour force. Labour turnover among women is considerably higher than among men. As a result, any *given* level of aggregate demand, and therefore rate of inflation, may again be associated with a *greater* level of unemployment than previously. This also would lead to a rightward and outward shift in the Phillips Curve.

- **Union militancy:** another possible factor is that trade union militancy has increased, so that unions have felt less constrained in their wage demands by the threat of unemployment than previously; wage and price inflation would then be higher at any given level of unemployment. Union militancy may have been encouraged by the

belief that governments will pursue policies which prevent rising labour costs from
leading to unemployment. It is this belief which the medium term financial strategy
seeks to discourage (see Chapter 17).

■ **Unemployment becoming a less reliable indicator of labour market
pressure**: it has been suggested that the inflation-unemployment relationship implied
by the Phillips Curve is really a relationship between inflation and the *pressure of
demand in the labour market*; with the level of unemployment providing a proxy
measure of the pressure of demand in the labour market. The argument is that the
fundamental relationship between inflation and pressure in the labour market still
exists, but that the level of unemployment no longer provides an accurate proxy
measure of that pressure. The growth of the black economy tends to support this
notion; at any given level of official unemployment there may now be *greater* labour
market pressure than previously. This might partly account for the apparent
breakdown of the Phillips Curve.

THE EXPECTATIONS-AUGMENTED PHILLIPS CURVE AND THE NATURAL RATE OF UNEMPLOYMENT

In the *long run* the monetarists believe that there is no stable relationship, or *trade-off*,
between different rates of inflation and unemployment. The monetarists suggest that
changes in wage rates and prices only influence workers and employers in so far as they
are perceived to be changes in *real wages* or in *real prices*. Thus a rise in money wage rates
will have no lasting impact on the economy if it is accompanied by an equivalent rise in
prices, and vice versa.

Natural rate of unemployment

Furthermore, the monetarists believe that there is a *natural rate of unemployment* to which
the economy will tend in the long run. In fact, the natural rate of unemployment is defined
as the rate that exists in the long run when the supply of, and the demand for, labour are in
equilibrium. Any attempt by the authorities to reduce the level of unemployment below the
natural rate will be unsuccessful in the long run, and will simply result in a higher rate of
inflation. In detail, the argument is explained in terms of Fig. 13.5. For simplicity it is
assumed that unemployment is initially at the natural rate U_n, that actual and expected
inflation is zero (i.e. the real wage is expected to remain constant) and that there is no
change in productivity so that prices and wages change by the same proportion

P^e = 0% is the short run Phillips Curve that exists when the actual and expected rate
of inflation are zero.
P^e = 4% is the short run Phillips Curve that exists when the actual and expected rate
of inflation are 4% and so on.

> **The natural rate of unemployment**

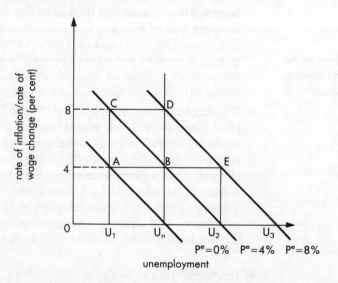

Fig. 13.5 The
expectations-augmented Phillips
Curve

If the government attempts to reduce the level of unemployment to U_1 by an expansion
of the money supply by 4 per cent, the initial result will be an increase in aggregate
demand. Eventually this will pull prices up (by 4 per cent if the quantity theory holds), and

this implies a rise in the real profits of producers. They will therefore expand output, and in order to attract more workers they will raise the wage rate; to retain higher profits per unit of output, employers will raise wages *by less than* the increase in prices. Workers will not immediately *perceive* this fall in their real income, because the expected rate of inflation is zero; they will therefore interpret the higher money wage awards as an increase in real wages. The economy will therefore move to point A.

However, this does not represent a long run equilibrium situation, since it is based on *money illusion*. Once workers realise that, far from rising, their real wage has actually fallen, they will demand pay rises at least sufficient to restore their real wage. But when wages and prices have *both* risen by 4 per cent, the real profits of producers will revert to their original level and they will no longer have any incentive to produce the higher level of output. They will therefore cut back production to their equilibrium level and unemployment will increase.

However, while the economy moves up the short run Phillips Curve $P^e=0\%$ it does not move back down it simply because unemployment rises. The expansion of the money supply ensures that the price level remains at the higher level. In terms of the equation of exchange, since V_y and Y are constant, an increase in M must lead to an increase in P. Thus equilibrium is restored when the economy moves to point B.

The expected and actual rate of inflation is now 4 per cent and the appropriate Phillips Curve is therefore $P^e=4\%$. Any further expansion of the money supply, for example, by another 4 percentage points, will initially take the economy to point C. However, the reduction in unemployment only occurs because the actual rate of inflation is different from the *expected* rate. Once workers realise that their expectations were incorrect, the advantage to producers from the higher rate of price inflation will disappear and equilibrium will be restored when the economy moves to D. Because of this, it is suggested that in the *long run* the Phillips Curve is *vertical* at the natural rate of unemployment. Any attempt to reduce unemployment permanently below the natural rate will simply result, in the long run, in an accelerating rate of inflation. It is for this reason that the monetarist approach is sometimes referred to as the *'accelerationist' theory of inflation*.

> The vertical Phillips curve

The conclusion of the monetarist interpretation of the Phillips Curve is that inflation is entirely a monetary phenomena caused by an excess supply of money, in other words, by an increase in the money supply which is greater than the average rise in productivity. Hence the belief that control of the money supply is all that is required to reduce inflation. For example, in terms of Fig 13.5, if the economy is at point D and the government wishes to restore average prices to the level that existed *before* there was any expansion of the money supply, it must reduce the money supply by 8 percentage points. If it did this all at once the economy would initially move to U_3, as the fall in prices that results from the lower money supply reduces real profits and leads firms to cut back output and to lay off workers. Once expectations of inflation are adjusted to the lower level (here 0%) there would be lower wage settlements and real profits would be restored to their former levels. In response to this, output would rise and unemployment would fall as more workers were taken on. Equilibrium would be restored when unemployment was re-established at the natural rate, i.e. at point U_n.

It is of course possible to achieve the same reduction in inflation, that is from 8 per cent to zero, without such heavy unemployment. All that is required is for the government to reduce the money supply in *stages* until the total reduction is 8 percentage points. For example, if the government reduces the money supply by 4 percentage points the economy will move from D through point E to point B. If the money supply is then reduced by a further 4 percentage points the economy will eventually establish equilibrium at U_n. Again, the total reduction in the rate of inflation is 8 percentage points, but in this case it is achieved with a temporary increase in unemployment of only $U_2 - U_n$ compared with an increase of $U_3 - U_n$ when the money supply is reduced in one action by 8 percentage points.

Despite this, accepting the natural rate hypothesis does not imply that governments are powerless to influence the level of unemployment in the long run, that is, reduce the natural rate. It simply implies that unemployment cannot be *permanently* reduced by expanding aggregate demand. In order to reduce unemployment below the current natural rate, governments must act on those factors which determine the natural rate of unemployment, i.e. factors affecting the long term supply of, and demand for, labour at any given real wage rate. These factors include the mobility of labour, the techniques of production, the extent of welfare benefits restrictions in competition and so on. These are usually referred to as *supply-side factors* and they are discussed on pp. 253–4.

THE RATIONAL EXPECTATIONS HYPOTHESIS

The monetarist analysis presented above is based on the assumption that changes in the *actual* rate of inflation precede changes in the *expected* rate. It is, however, possible that if governments publicly announce that the rate of growth of the money supply is to be reduced to a certain level, this will then influence *expectations* of inflation. In other words, to the extent that the government's target rates of growth for the money supply are publicised and are believed, then *rational* expectations about the future rate of inflation may be formed. If this leads to lower pay awards, inflation can be reduced without significantly affecting unemployment. Indeed, if the economy is initially at point D (the natural rate of unemployment with 8 per cent inflation) in Fig. 13.5, a reduction in the money supply of 8 percentage points will, provided rational expectations lead to pay awards falling by exactly the same proportion, lead to a movement *straight down* the vertical Phillips Curve to point U_n.

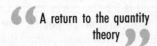

WHAT IS MONETARISM?

At its simplest level, monetarism is a set of beliefs about the way in which changes in the money supply affect other macroeconomic variables such as the rate of inflation and nominal national income. These beliefs are based on an impressive volume of statistical information which shows a highly significant correlation between changes in the money supply and changes in the rate of inflation. However, the statistics only show an *association* between these two variables. They do not show that one is *caused* by the other. Nevertheless, the monetarists are unshakeable in their belief that changes in the money supply are the only cause of changes in the rate of inflation. While there are many varieties of monetarism, this belief is common to them all. The following discussion is an outline of the basic principles of monetarism which provide the theoretical underpinnings for this belief.

> 66 Association is not necessarily cause! 99

THE DEMAND FOR MONEY

All monetarists accept the early quantity theory of money which focuses on the importance of changes in the money supply. However, the revival of monetarism as an economic doctrine stems largely from Friedman's re-statement of the quantity theory. This differs from the early quantity theory in that it focuses attention on the importance of the *demand for money* to hold.

Friedman's re-statement of the quantity theory

In his re-statement, Friedman suggested that the demand for money is determined by the same general factors which influence the demand for other goods and services. However, of all the factors Friedman considered, only the *level of income*, the *price level* and the *expected rate of inflation*, had any significant effect on the demand for money. Furthermore, Friedman claimed that the relationship between the demand for money and its determinants was highly *stable* over time. This is extremely important since such stability could not exist unless the *velocity of circulation* was also relatively stable. An increase in the demand for money to hold will reduce its velocity of circulation and vice versa. Therefore if it can be shown that the demand for money is stable, velocity is also stable.

> 66 A return to the quantity theory 99

It is important to understand that in arguing that velocity is stable, the monetarists are not arguing that it is constant. Instead they have always claimed that velocity changes only slowly over time and in a predictable way. In this sense it is stable from one period to the next. We shall later see that this has important implications for policy purposes.

For simplicity it is sometimes suggested that Friedman's view implies that the demand for money is a stable function of nominal national income. While not strictly correct this does not seriously misrepresent Friedman's view. In the long run the *actual* rate of inflation and the *expected* rate of inflation coincide and hence the main determinants of changes in the demand for money are changes in the actual rate of inflation (i.e. changes in the price level) and changes in real income (i.e. changes in nominal GNP). Monetarists therefore argue that when there are changes in the *supply of money*, this will lead to changes in nominal GNP which will bring the demand for money into equilibrium with the supply.

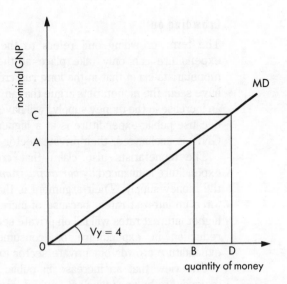

Fig. 13.6 The demand for nominal money

Explanation of theory

Fig. 13.6 is used as a basis for explanation. If the demand for money is constant at 25 per cent of GNP then V_y must equal 4. If the initial level of GNP is £200m then, assuming supply and demand for money are in equilibrium, the quantity of money demanded (and supplied) will be equal to £50m. If the money supply now increases, nominal GNP will increase and hence demand for money will also increase. For example, if the *money supply* increases by £10m, equilibrium can only be restored when the *demand for money* increases by £10m. If V_y is unchanged, this implies an increase in nominal GNP of £40m. This must happen because if the money supply increases and all other things are unchanged, people will be holding excess money balances relative to the amount they demand. The excess will be spent and will cause nominal GNP to increase until demand for money is brought into equilibrium with the increased supply of money.

However, this simple approach is ambiguous because an increase in *nominal* GNP can consist entirely of an increase in real income, prices unchanged, or entirely of an increase in prices, real income unchanged, or a combination of both. The monetarists claim that in the *short run* nominal GNP will consist of an increase in *both*. However, in the *long run* they argue that the level of real income is determined by institutional factors such as the capital stock, the mobility of labour, the rate of technological progress, and so on. Such factors are *not* influenced by changes in the money supply. While it is possible that changes in the money supply will bring about changes in real income in the short run, such changes will only be transitory and in the long run real income will return to the level that would have existed *before* the increase in the money supply. Hence, an increase in the money supply above the rate of growth of real income will, in the long run, simply lead to higher prices.

This, of course, explains why, in the short run, unemployment falls below the natural rate as the money supply increases. As demand and prices rise, firms expand output and unemployment falls. Hence the economy moves up the appropriate short-run Phillips Curve. However, as expectations of inflation adjust to the higher rate, output reverts to that level which would have existed if there had been no increase in the money supply, and unemployment reverts to the natural rate.

The transmission mechanism

The route through which the effect of a change in the money supply is transmitted to the economy is referred to as the *transmission mechanism*. The monetarists argue that an increase in the money supply will leave people holding excess money balances at the existing level of GNP. Consequently, spending will increase as people divest themselves of unwanted holdings of money. The important point is that the monetarists claim that this increased spending will be on a whole range of goods and services. (This contrasts with liquidity preference theory which implies that it will be spent on securities.) As demand increases, output and prices will rise until people are *persuaded* to hold the increased money supply in order to finance the increased value of their transactions. In other words, nominal GNP goes on rising until the increase in the supply of money is matched by an increase in the transactions demand for money, so that supply and demand for money are brought back into equilibrium.

Crowding out

The term 'crowding out' refers to the extent to which an increase in public sector expenditure can only take place at the expense of private sector expenditure. The monetarists claim that in the long run crowding out occurs on a one-for-one basis. As we have seen, the monetarists argue that any increase in public expenditure that is financed by an increase in the money supply, will have *no* effect on *real* GNP in the *long run*. However, because public expenditure is at a higher level and because aggregate expenditure (real GNP) is unchanged, then private sector expenditure must have been crowded out.

The monetarists also claim that crowding out occurs even when public sector expenditure is financed by *borrowing from the non-bank public* so that there is no change in the money supply. Their argument is that increasing borrowing by the public sector will force up interest rates, because of increased competition for funds. The main impact of higher interest rates will fall on private sector investment, although there will also be some reduction in expenditure on consumer durables. Again, increased public sector expenditure crowds out private sector expenditure.

The view that an increase in public sector expenditure crowds out private sector expenditure by an equivalent amount, even when money supply is constant, can easily be explained in terms of the identity $MV_y = PY$. Since the monetarists argue that V_y is constant, and since there has been no change in M, then PY, that is GNP, must also be constant. However, public sector expenditure has *increased*, so that private sector expenditure must have fallen by an equivalent amount within the constant GNP. In other words, an increase in public sector expenditure, even when financed by borrowing from the non-bank private sector, does not change the level of GNP, it simply changes its structure because public expenditure increases and private expenditure falls.

The monetary rule

The monetarists therefore believe that increasing the money supply has no long-run effect on the level of real GNP, it simply leads to higher prices. They also believe that attempts to manage the economy by using demand management techniques, increase *uncertainty*. This in turn makes it difficult for business to plan, and leads to less investment in research and development, in capacity, and so on. Because of this the monetarists suggest that governments should abandon attempts to manage the level of aggregate demand, and should instead aim for a *steady* rate of growth of the money supply in order to achieve a particular rate of inflation. Again, their basic argument can be explained in terms of the identity $MV_y = PY$. If Y grows at an average 5 per cent per annum and V_y by 1 per cent per annum, then a government aiming to achieve an annual inflation rate of 2 per cent must achieve a growth of the money supply of approximately, but no more than, 10 per cent. (You can check this by substituting in $M = PY/V_y$.)

> 66 Linking money supply to inflation 99

MONETARISM AND KEYNESIANISM COMPARED

There is in fact a great deal of agreement between monetarists and Keynesians. They *both* accept the equation of exchange, and broadly agree on the determinants of the demand for money. However, they disagree on which factors are *most* significant in affecting the demand for money. This is clear in the following differences between the two schools.

THE TRANSMISSION MECHANISM

Monetarists' view

The monetarists believe that an increase in the money supply leads to an increase in demand for *all* goods and services, with financial assets (securities, etc.), being just one in range of items on which expenditure will increase. In other words, financial assets are not regarded as unique, in the sense of being close substitutes for money. An increase in the money supply will therefore lead to a direct increase in spending on goods and services, rather than just on financial assets. Nevertheless, any part of the extra money supply that is spent on securities will raise security prices, i.e. reduce interest rates. However, money demand is assumed by monetarists to vary with the level of national income and not with the rate of interest, so that little or none of the extra money supply is absorbed into idle balances as interest rates fall (i.e. demand for money is interest rate inelastic). Consequently all that the fall in interest rates will do is to encourage *further* consumer spending on goods and services, and of course investment expenditure.

In **summary**, the monetarists argue that an increase in the money supply leads to an increase in aggregate expenditure because:

- increased holdings of money will mainly be spent on goods and services.
- an increase in the money supply will lead to lower interest rates which encourages further consumer (and investment) spending.

In the long run, because of its effect on aggregate expenditure, an increase in the money supply has a relatively large effect on GNP.

Keynesians' view

66 **Comparing Keynes and the monetarists** 99

Keynesians, on the other hand, maintain that the demand for money is, in general, responsive to changes in the interest rate. They argue that financial assets *are* a close substitute for money and that an increase in the money supply will lead to increased expenditure on these. This will raise security prices, and the fall in interest rates that this implies will lead to a *more than proportional* increase in the demand for money, as people are persuaded to hold larger idle balances. The rate of interest continues to fall until supply and demand for money are brought into equilibrium. However, because demand for money is interest rate elastic, an increase in the money supply leads to a less than proportional fall in the rate of interest.

Furthermore, the Keynesians argue that aggregate expenditure is interest rate inelastic, any given change in interest rates therefore leads to a less than proportional change in expenditure. For example, an increase in the money supply is, via a fall in the rate of interest, mainly absorbed into idle balances and consequently has little impact on aggregate expenditure. This implies that an increase in the money supply has relatively little effect on GNP. The opposite is true when the money supply is reduced. Because of this the Keynesians argue that monetary policy is not a very powerful tool of economic management.

In **summary**, the Keynesians believe that the effects of changes in the money supply are transmitted to the economy via changes in the rate of interest, but that overall there is little impact on GNP.

THE VELOCITY OF CIRCULATION

Implicit in the **monetarist** transmission mechanism is the belief that the velocity of circulation is *unaffected* by changes in the money supply. Hence a change in M leads to a *proportional* change in GNP.

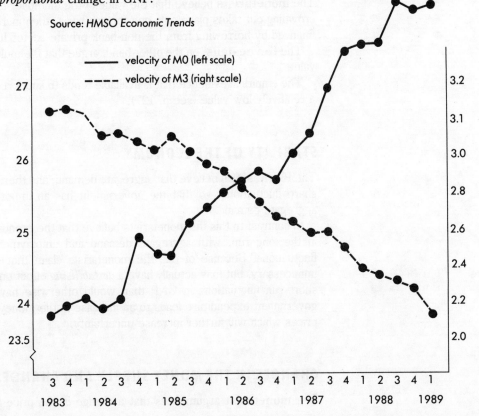

Fig. 13.7

However, the **Keynesians** do not accept that the velocity of circulation is unaffected by changes in the money supply. For example, they argue that because an increase in the money supply has relatively little effect on GNP then, because of the identity of $MV_Y =$ GNP, V_Y must fall when the money supply increases, and vice versa. For the Keynesians the extreme case occurs when the rate of interest is *so low* that the demand for money is infinitely elastic. This is the so-called *liquidity trap* (see pp. 152–3) and in these circumstances an increase in the money supply has no effect on the rate of interest at all and consequently *no effect* on the level of GNP. This can only occur when, for each change in the money supply, there is an exactly off-setting change in the velocity of circulation; i.e. when an increase in the money supply is completely absorbed into idle balances.

It is worth noting that because the **monetarists** deny that the velocity of circulation can change in response to changes in the money supply, they also deny the existence of any liquidity trap.

The available empirical evidence is inconclusive. In the short run velocity fluctuates and appears quite unstable. In the longer run it appears to follow a clearly identifiable trend. However, even here the evidence is ambiguous. Prior to about 1982, broad money velocity followed an identifiable upward trend. Since then it has followed a downward trend! (See Fig. 13.7.)

CROWDING OUT

We have seen that the **monetarists** believe that crowding out takes place on a one-for-one basis.

However, the Keynesians argue that this will only be true when the government increases its expenditure at a time when the economy is at full employment. At levels below this, an increase in government expenditure will draw more resources into employment, raising real GNP and real expenditure, so that private investment expenditure need not fall. One important reason why this happens, according to the Keynesians, is that the government borrows and spends funds that would otherwise have been saved. In other words, borrowing to finance government expenditure transfers funds from lower velocity users to higher velocity users. The resulting increase in aggregate demand then results in an increase in aggregate supply.

THE MULTIPLIER

The **monetarists** believe that the value of the multiplier is relatively low. For example, if crowding out takes place on a one-for-one basis, then increased government expenditure financed by borrowing from the non-bank private sector has a zero multiplier effect.

The **Keynesians**, on the other hand, argue that the multiplier will have a relatively high value.

The empirical evidence that is available tends to support the view that the multiplier has a relatively low value (see p. 127).

STABILITY OF THE ECONOMY

The **Keynesians** believe that aggregate demand, and therefore employment, is subject to sharp fluctuations, so that the government has an important role to play in stabilising aggregate demand.

In contrast to this the monetarists believe that the economy is inherently stable, at least in the long run, with aggregate demand and employment not being subject to sharp fluctuations. Because of this the monetarists claim that stabilisation policy is not only unnecessary, but may actually have a *destabilising* effect on the economy, causing greater short run fluctuations in GNP than would otherwise have occurred. Where increased government expenditure leads to an increase in the money supply, it will result in higher prices which will further increase uncertainty.

CHANGES IN THE MONEY SUPPLY AND CHANGES IN THE PRICE LEVEL

The **monetarist** argument is that a change in the price level can only be caused by a change in *money supply*, and that a change in the money supply is all that is required to cause a change in the price level.

The **Keynesian** position is that a change in the *velocity of circulation* can cause changes in the price level which are independent of changes in the money supply. Nevertheless, the Keynesians agree that changes in the money supply are *correlated* significantly with changes in the price level. However, they do not accept that this implies *causation*. They argue that the money supply is determined endogenously and simply responds passively to changes in the demand for money and therefore to changes in the price level.

APPLIED MATERIALS

THE DEMAND FOR MONEY

An article in *The Economic Review* Vol 6, No 4, March 1989, entitled *The Demand for Money*, examines the different theories of the demand for money which have already been discussed in this chapter; it also assesses the empirical evidence. One point made early is that any empirical investigations are hampered because financial innovation makes changes necessary in the different definitions of money. For example, in recent years many building societies have begun offering chequing accounts and even cash point facilities. Such definitional problems are ignored in this article which concentrates on M1 as the basic definition of narrow money and therefore provides a measure of transactions demand for money. The article shows that the M1 velocity of circulation tended to rise along an identifiable trend until about 1982. It is claimed that until about 1982 the long run transactions elasticity of demand for money was approximately unity, i.e., an increase in the volume of transactions of 1 per cent led to an increase in real transactions balances (nominal transactons balances divided by the average price level) by 1 per cent. The empirical evidence also suggests that transactions balances had an interest elasticity of about −5, i.e., an increase in the rate of interest on alternative assets from 10 per cent to 11 per cent, and tended to reduce holdings of M1 balances by about 5 per cent. More recently other factors have influenced demand for transactions balances. Probably the most important factor has been the rapid growth of interest bearing chequing accounts. Interest was not paid on such accounts in earlier years and therefore demand for M1 was more responsive to changes in interest rates. In particular, an increase in interest rates increased the opportunity cost of holding non-interest bearing sight deposits (included in M1) and encouraged deposit holders to transfer these to interest bearing deposits (not included in M1). Another factor has been the increase in the number of people holding bank accounts which might have increased aggregate demand for M1.

MORTGAGE COSTS AND THE RPI

The Lloyds Bank Economic Bulletin, No 103, July 1987 examines the arguments for removing mortgage costs from the RPI. As it stands both changes in house prices and changes in mortgage costs caused by changes in the rate of interest are included in calculating the RPI.

One of the main points to consider is that housing represents a form of investment and should not be included in the RPI any more than changes in the price of other investments such as stocks and shares should be included.

In addition changes in housing costs, especially interest payments, are very volatile and tend to make changes in the RPI a misleading indicator of changes in the underlying rate of inflation. For example between 1985 and 1986, changes in the RPI fluctuated between 2.4 and 7 per cent whereas the range was only 3.2 and 5.6 per cent when housing costs are excluded. It is argued that the higher rate of change of the RPI encourages higher pay demands, but the lower rate does not serve to reduce them to the same extent. In other words it is suggested that changes in the RPI have a psychological effect on wage demands.

Table 13.2 shows the contribution made by changes in the costs of different inputs to the final price of manufacturing output. Labour costs consistently make the greatest contribution but this does not necessarily indicate that the cost push hypothesis is correct. For example, an increase in the money supply could lead to an increase in demand for final output and encourage employers to increase wages.

	UNIT LABOUR COSTS	INPUT COSTS	BOUGHT-IN SERVICES	MARGINS (RESIDUAL)	PERCENTAGE CHANGE
1980	9.9	3.7	5.2	−3.4	15.4
1981	4.2	2.9	2.7	−2.4	7.4
1982	1.3	2.3	1.1	2.2	6.9
1983	−0.1	2.6	0.9	2.0	5.4
1984	0.6	3.0	0.9	0.6	3.1
1985	2.1	1.0	1.3	1.3	5.7
1986	1.6	−3.4	1.0	4.9	4.1
1987	0.2	1.7	0.9	1.6	4.4
1988	0.9	1.6	1.7	0.6	4.8

Table 13.2 Contributions to output* prices in manufacturing** from changes in cost components

* Percentage Points
** Excluding Food, Drink and Tobacco

Source: Bank of England Quarterly Bulletin, August 1989, Vol 29, No 3

EXAMINATION QUESTIONS

1 Explain the meaning of the term 'demand for money'. Compare the Keynesian and Monetarist views of the demand for money and indicate their respective policy implications.

(JMB, 1989)

2 a) Outline the main functions of money. (6)

b) Explain some of the problems which arise when constructing a price index to show changes in the value of money over time. (7)

c) Discuss how inflation affects the efficiency with which money fulfils its functions.

(7)
(*Total 20 marks*)
(Northern Ireland, 1988)

3 Is it meaningful to identify different causes of inflation?

(London, Jan 1989)

4 What are the costs and benefits of inflation? Do the benefits of inflation ever justify a government allowing inflation to continue in an economy?

(AEB, June 1989)

A TUTOR'S ANSWER TO QUESTION 3

Most economists would agree that inflation is entirely a monetary phenomenon in the sense that no inflation is permanently sustainable in the absence of an increase in the money supply. However, one group of economists, usually referred to as monetarists, not only accept this basic proposition but argue that inflation can only be caused by an increase in the money supply.

The monetarist view is based on the belief that in the long run the demand for money is a stable function of a few key variables and is determined independently of changes in the money supply. Because of this, the monetarists argue that the velocity of circulation will also be stable. If this is correct it follows that an increase in the supply of money will, in the long run, simply result in a fall in its value, that is, a rise in the price level. Their view is summarised in the equation of exchange which states that $MV_Y = PY$, where M is the money stock, V_Y the income velocity of money, P the average price of final output and Y the volume of real output.

One of the major controversies surrounding the monetarist argument is their inability to give any concrete definition of the long run, so that it is not possible to test their theory. They accept that in the short run an increase in the money supply might, in fact, lead to an increase in real output. However, in the long run they argue that real output will revert to its trend rate of growth, i.e., to the rate of growth that would have been achieved if there had been no increase in the money supply. This, they argue, will be achieved because in the long run there is a natural rate of unemployment to which the economy will tend and, by implication, a natural rate of growth of output. Hence their belief that any increase in the money supply above the underlying rate of growth of productivity will, in the long run, manifest itself in higher prices rather than higher output. The mechanism is simple. An increase in money growth will cause excess demand for output at the current price level. In other words, prices are pulled upwards until aggregate demand and aggregate supply are brought into equality.

Other economists argue that changes in money growth are one possible cause of inflation, but not necessarily the only cause. This view is generalised in the demand-pull theory of inflation which stresses that inflation is especially likely to occur when the economy is at, or near, full employment. At lower levels of output it is probable that supply will respond to any increase in demand. However, as the economy approaches full employment, shortages of skilled labour and other supply bottlenecks will mean that increases in aggregate demand will lead to higher prices. Two points need to be stressed here. There is no implication that the natural rate of unemployment is the minimum long run rate attainable or that any increase in aggregate supply will only be temporary.

Increased money growth might cause inflation but there are other possible causes. An increase in demand for exports or a reduction in aggregate savings, for example, will both lead to an increase in aggregate demand. If this theory of inflation is correct, then the monetarists are incorrect to assert first, that an increase in the money supply will cause inflation at levels of output substantially below full employment, and second, that inflation can only be caused by an increase in the money supply.

Despite this, proponents of the demand-pull theory accept that inflation cannot continue indefinitely unless there is a continuous increase in the money supply. This is because higher prices will require higher expenditures by consumers, and this is only possible if the money supply increases. Proponents of this theory therefore accept that changes in the velocity of circulation are not necessarily a cause of rising demand, but do not accept that the *cause* of inflation is necessarily an increase in the money supply. Instead the money supply might simply be increased to *accommodate* an increase in demand.

There is another basic theory of inflation which relates rising prices to rising costs of production which are not initially caused by rising demand. It is usually argued that the main sources of rising costs are rising labour costs, because of wages increases outstripping productivity growth, and rising imported raw material costs caused by a fall in the value of sterling on the foreign exchange market. Whatever the source of cost increases, the cost-push theory implies that they are passed on to consumers in the form of higher prices. Again, the process cannot continue indefinitely, unless the money supply is increased to accommodate the higher price level.

At the present time it is possible to argue that rising demand associated with the consumer boom is the cause of inflation. However, it is also true that the growth of average earnings exceeds the growth of productivity, and this might be taken as support for the cost-push hypothesis. It therefore seems possible to distinguish between different causes of inflation but in practice it is no simple matter. A different interpretation of events can be used to dismiss the cost-push theory. It is possible to argue that rising demand for final output pulls up prices and results in increased competition for labour thus driving up earnings above any increase in productivity. It is also true that the money supply has been rising faster than productivity and it is possible that this might be responsible for generating the higher level of demand that ultimately gives rise to higher earnings.

Despite the inability to distinguish conclusively between the different causes of inflation an understanding of the inflationary process is essential for the formation of policy. If the causes of inflation are incorrectly understood, policies to tackle inflation are unlikely to succeed. However, it is not always easy to subject the various theories of inflation to unambiguous statistical evaluation. This is particularly true with the monetarist approach, since it is claimed that changes in the money supply only affect prices after an unpredictable and variable time lag. Nevertheless, if the monetarists are correct, then there is a stable long term relationship between changes in the money supply and changes in its value, all that is necessary to reduce the rate of inflation is to reduce the rate of growth of the money supply.

A STUDENT'S ANSWER TO QUESTION 4

> **Definitions well used at the start of the essay**

> **You might also mention other groups e.g. pensioners**

> **By which group?**

> **What are the consequences of this in terms of living standards!**

Inflation is usually defined as a continuous fall in the value of money and exists when there is a continuous rise in the price level. This can have several advantages and disadvantages for the economy as a whole and for certain individuals compared with others.

At the outset it is important to distinguish between anticipated and unanticipated inflation. When inflation is fully anticipated, it is often possible for individuals and organisations to protect themselves against any adverse effects of inflation or to ensure that they reap maximum benefit. When inflation is unanticipated it is impossible to do either of these. When considering the costs and benefits of inflation it is important to remember this distinction.

It is often suggested that borrowers gain and lenders lose during periods of inflation because the real value of a debt falls. This implies that, when repaid, funds have a lower purchasing power than at the time they are loaned. This is certainly true, but whether borrowers gain and lenders lose depends on what happens to the real rate of interest, that is the difference between the nominal rate of interest and the rate of inflation. If the real rate of interest is positive, then lenders are not penalised and there is no gain to borrowers because of inflation.

Another group that might be penalised by inflation are those on incomes that are not linked to changes in the rate of inflation. Those who belong to powerful trade unions might be able to negotiate increases in wages that keep pace with rising prices but those in weaker unions such as cleaners or canteen workers are likely to experience a fall in real income. Similarly union representation in retailing is not strong and many shop workers will probably experience a fall in real income as a result of inflation.

For the economy as a whole, however, it is not easy to predict the effect of inflation. For example, if the cause of inflation is rising demand it is likely that profits will increase. This will result in a redistribution of income away from consumers in favour of producers. Rising profits might also encourage investment in additional productive capacity and this might be considered an advantage of inflation because it will make higher levels of output possible in the future. However, there will only be an increase in profits if inflation is *not anticipated*.

During periods of rapid inflation it is possible that inflation will result in an increase in purchases of assets that provide a *hedge* against the effects of inflation. For most people, property is a more desirable asset during periods of inflation than money savings. However, if resources are used to increase the availability of housing, the opportunity cost of this is investment in productive assets. In other words, inflation might encourage an increase in the ownership of non-productive assets as people attempt to preserve the real value of their wealth.

Another way in which the economy might be adversely affected by inflation is that if the rate of inflation in the UK is above the rate in other countries, the sterling exchange rate will depreciate. This will reduce the price of exports abroad and in this way might be considered a benefit to firms involved in exporting. However, if the economy is at full employment, the increased demand might result in an even higher rate of inflation. However, the lower rate of exchange will also raise the price of imports and here again the effect might be to generate an even higher rate of inflation.

In deciding if the benefits of inflation ever outweigh the costs, one of the most important issues to consider is the possibility of a *trade off* between inflation and employment. The Phillips Curve originally suggested that a stable relationship existed between the rate of inflation and the level of unemployment and governments could therefore choose which combination of employment and inflation they thought most desirable. Lower unemployment implied more inflation and vice versa. In these circumstances the costs of inflation might be considered a reasonable price to pay for lower unemployment. However, it is now known that any benefits of lower unemployment caused by inflation are only temporary because the economy has a natural rate of unemployment and inflation does not lead to a permanent reduction in unemployment below this natural rate. Any attempt by the government to reduce unemployment below this natural rate by monetary and fiscal policies simply causes more inflation without any long run benefits.

It seems therefore that there are few benefits of inflation but many costs. Because of this it is difficult to argue that there are circumstances when governments would be justified in allowing inflation to continue. However, we must remember that the costs and benefits of inflation depend partly on what the rate of inflation is. A lower rate of inflation might have benefits that disappear at higher rates of inflation.

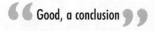 Good, a conclusion

Quite a good essay but it would have been better if you had considered the implications of the distinction between anticipated and unanticipated inflation

OUTLINE ANSWERS TO QUESTIONS 1 AND 2

Question 1

The demand for money refers to the amount of money individuals and organisations wish to hold. In defining demand for more it is important to distinguish between demand for nominal money balances and demand for real money balances (nominal money balances divided by the price level). You could then go on to explain that it is important to understand what determines the demand for money because changes in the demand for money can cause changes in other aggregates such as the rate of inflation and unemployment.

The Keynesians argue that money is demanded for three reasons and these are explained on p. 150. The Monetarists, on the other hand, argue that demand for money depends on a smaller number of variables, and in particular the level of income, see pp. 190–91. You must explain both approaches in detail.

You could then argue that demand for money can be analysed in terms of the equation of exchange which both Keynesians and Monetarists accept. One of the main points of difference between them is whether V_Y is stable. This is important because if V_Y is stable this implies that the demand for money is stable, because changes in M will cause proportional changes in nominal GNP. The Keynesians believe that V_Y is unstable and that the demand for money is therefore unpredictable (see pp. 192–3). Monetarists take the opposite view.

For policy purposes Keynesians argue that monetary policy has relatively little impact on GNP and only exerts an influence if changes in the rate of interest cause changes in the level of investment. Any change in GNP might be a change in nominal GNP, real GNP, or a combination of both. For the Monetarists an increase in money growth which exceeds the increase in productivity leads to a change in nominal GNP and, in the long run, no change in real GNP. In other words it leads directly to inflation! You must explain these views highlighting crowding out and the concept of the natural rate.

Question 2

a) The functions of money are explained on pp. 162–3.

b) The problems of interpreting a price index are explained on pp. 183–4.

c) Inflation implies a fall in the value of money and you must analyse the implications of this for the functions money performs. An important point to stress is that if inflation is at relatively low rates, such as 2 per cent, it is unlikely to have any impact on the efficiency with which money performs its functions. The same is not true at relatively high rates of inflation.

The most important function of money is that it acts as a medium of exchange. However, to perform this function money must be acceptable in settlement of a debt. If money loses its value quickly it will cease to act as a medium of exchange. Similarly it will cease to act as a store of value, a standard for deferred payments, or a unit of account. If money is losing its value it clearly cannot act as a store of value! Additionally, people will be more reluctant to agree to contracts, the value of which are expressed in money terms because there will be greater uncertainty. This uncertainty might make short term contracts preferable to long term contracts and might divert resources into property rather than productive assets. Contracts could be indexed to take account of inflation but this would impair the functioning of the price mechanism because shortages of some goods would develop if indexation prevented an increase in their relative prices.

Further reading

Begg, Fischer and Dornbusch, *Economics* (2nd edn), McGraw-Hill 1987: Ch. 27, Inflation.

Glaister, *The Causes and Control of Inflation* (2nd edn), Longman 1989.

Glaister, *The Meaning, Measurement and Consequences of Inflation*, (2nd edn) Longman 1989.

Griffiths and Wall, *Applied Economics: An Introductory Course*, (3rd edn) Longman 1989: Ch. 17, Inflation.

Stanlake, *Macro-economics: An Introduction*, (4th edn) Longman 1989: Ch. 15, The quantity of money and the price level; Ch. 16, Output, demand and the price level; Ch. 17, Inflation.

CHAPTER 14

INTERNATIONAL TRADE AND PROTECTION

ABSOLUTE ADVANTAGE

COMPARATIVE ADVANTAGE

THE TERMS OF TRADE

PROTECTION

APPLIED MATERIALS

GETTING STARTED

International trade arises for many reasons, but the most obvious one is that different countries have different factor endowments, and the international mobility of these factors is severely limited. International trade therefore makes available to consumers in one country, products which are only produced in other countries.

However, the fact is that the vast majority of goods and services which countries buy from abroad they could produce domestically for themselves. The main reason they are imported is that they can be produced with *greater relative efficiency* by foreign firms than by domestic firms. This is the crux of the matter: countries might be capable of producing the same goods, but they are unlikely to produce them with equal efficiency. The *law of comparative advantage* implies that countries gain when they specialise in the production of those goods and services in which they have the greatest relative efficiency. These can be traded for the other goods and services they require.

One of the main advantages of *international specialisation* is that by concentrating on the production of those goods and services in which it does have the greatest *relative* efficiency, a country may even increase its *absolute* level of efficiency. For instance, larger outputs will make possible economies of large-scale production. If these cost reductions are passed on to the consumers, then the gains from specialisation will be reflected in lower prices. It is also argued that if there are no restrictions on investment, funds will flow to those activities which offer the greatest return. Because of this, it is sometimes suggested that international specialisation will, in the long run, bring about a more efficient utilisation of world resources.

Although the potential gains from international trade are vast, countries invariably impose *restrictions on trade*. There are various reasons for this, but not all are supported by economic analysis. Great care must be taken in assessing the validity of *economic* arguments advanced in support of protection since they are sometimes based on subjective factors, or on a misunderstanding of the *long run* effects of restricting trade.

ESSENTIAL PRINCIPLES

For simplicity our analysis of international trade is limited to the simple case: two countries producing the same two goods. However, the conclusions can be generalised and applied to a world consisting of many countries producing many commodities.

ABSOLUTE ADVANTAGE

A country is said to have an absolute advantage in the production of a commodity when it is more efficient than other countries at producing that commodity. In other words, when it can produce more of a commodity than other countries using the same amount of resources. When two countries each have an absolute advantage in different commodities, total world output can be increased (and both countries can gain) when each country specialises in the production of those commodities in which it has an absolute advantage.

COMPARATIVE ADVANTAGE

Even where a country has an absolute advantage in the production of *both* commodities, trade can still be mutually beneficial so long as each country has a *comparative* advantage. Table 14.1 is used as a basis for explanation.

	TONNES OF WHEAT THAT CAN BE PRODUCED FROM X RESOURCES	NUMBER OF CARS THAT CAN BE PRODUCED FROM X RESOURCES
Country A	40	10
Country B	20	8

Table 14.1

Country A has an absolute advantage in the production of both wheat and cars since, with a given amount of resources, it can produce more of *both* goods than Country B.

However, if we examine the domestic opportunity cost ratios it is clear that each country has a relative, or comparative, advantage in the production of one commodity.

In **Country A** the domestic opportunity cost ratio is such that 4 tonnes of wheat must be given up for each car produced.

In **Country B** the domestic opportunity cost ratio is such that only 2.5 tonnes of wheat must be given up for each car produced. A country has a comparative advantage in that product for which it has a *lower domestic opportunity cost ratio* than its competitor. Country B, therefore, has a *comparative* advantage in the production of cars since, for each car that is produced, less wheat is sacrificed in B than in A.

Country A by the same reasoning has a comparative advantage in the production of wheat. For each tonne of wheat produced Country A must sacrifice 0.25 cars, whereas in **Country B** each tonne of wheat produced 'costs' more, i.e. 0.4 cars.

It is easy to show that if both countries specialise in the production of the good in which they have a comparative advantage, the combined output of both goods will be greater than when each country produces both goods. We can show this by taking a *marginal* change. If A produces 1 tonne *extra* wheat (comparative advantage in wheat), it *gives up* 0.25 cars. If B produces 1 tonne *less* of wheat (comparative advantage in cars) it *gains* 0.4 cars. So with wheat production unchanged, there has been a net 'gain' of 0.15 cars by specialising according to comparative advantages.

However, specialisation and trade can only be mutually beneficial if the terms of trade, that is, the rate at which one good exchanges for another, lie somewhere between the respective domestic opportunity cost ratios. This is easily demonstrated. For example, if the terms of trade are that one car exchanges for 3 tonnes of wheat, this reduces the cost of cars in terms of wheat for Country A, and reduces the cost of wheat in terms of cars for Country B. Hence any given amount of one good foregone gives both countries more of the other good after trade than is possible from domestic production.

ASSUMPTIONS

In discussing the possibility of trade in terms of absolute and comparative advantage several assumptions have been made. Some have been explicitly mentioned, but others have not. These are important because the absence of such conditions in the real world will considerably reduce the possible gains from trade. The main assumptions on which our discussion of absolute and comparative advantage is based are set out below.

Perfect factor mobility

We have assumed that countries can shift resources from the production of one good to the production of another good. In practice there is likely to be a certain amount of factor immobility which will prevent this, especially in the short run.

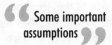

> Some important
> assumptions

Constant costs

In assuming constant costs we are discounting the possibility of lower unit costs as output expands, for instance because of higher economies of scale or unit costs as output expands, because of diseconomies of scale. In practice, this is unlikely to be the case and it is much more realistic to suppose that a country may only have a comparative advantage in the production of a particular commodity up to a certain level of output. If production expands *beyond* this point, then rising costs will reduce or even remove altogether the country's comparative advantage.

Technical change

Changes in technology bring about changes in productive efficiency. Because of this, a country might have a comparative advantage in the production of a particular commodity at one point in time; but this might be lost to another more technologically advanced country at a different point in time.

Barriers to trade

Countries do not always trade freely with each other. The existence of restrictions on trade clearly limits the scope for specialisation between countries.

Divergence between real values and money values

It has been assumed that the money prices of goods accurately reflect their domestic opportunity costs. For example, where the domestic opportunity cost ratio was four tonnes of wheat for one car, we have implicitly assumed that the price the consumer pays for a car is four times the price paid for a tonne of wheat. In a world of perfect competition where price is equated with marginal cost, this will be the case; but in the real world, where prices are distorted by imperfect competition in factor and product markets, as well as by taxes and subsidies, it is unlikely to be the case. Since consumption and production decisions are based on money values rather than real values, if money prices are out of line with real costs, it may no longer be possible for countries to gain from trade by specialising in the production of those commodities in which they have a real (comparative cost) advantage.

THE TERMS OF TRADE

The terms of trade are the rate at which one nation's output exchanges against another nation's output. In the previous examples we assumed only two countries, each trading a single product. However in the real world, where many countries trade many different commodities, it is not so easy to estimate the terms of trade. In practice, the prices of commodities traded are measured by an index of prices. The *terms of trade index* is the ratio of an index of export prices to an index of import prices. Thus, the terms of trade index can be calculated as:

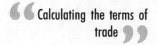

> Calculating the terms of
> trade

$$\frac{\text{Index of export prices}}{\text{Index of import prices}} \times 100$$

In the base year the value of the terms of trade index will be 10, i.e. $100/100 \times 100$. Changes in the terms of trade are measured by changes in the value of this index.

FAVOURABLE AND UNFAVOURABLE MOVEMENTS IN THE TERMS OF TRADE

A movement in the terms of trade is said to be *favourable* whenever export prices rise relative to import prices; in other words, whenever the terms of trade index rises. Care must be taken here because this does not *necessarily* imply that the terms of trade index has a value of greater than 100! If the terms of trade index in one year is greater than its value the previous year, then there has been a favourable movement in the terms of trade. Conversely, a movement in the terms of trade is said to be *unfavourable* whenever the terms of trade index falls.

Favourable movements in the terms of trade are so called because they imply a 'favourable' change in the opportunity cost of imports in terms of exports. For example, if export prices rise while import prices remain constant, a *given volume* of exports will exchange for a *greater volume* of imports. In other words, a favourable movement in the terms of trade makes *possible* an increase in real income. Because of this the *price effects* of an increase in the terms of trade are said to be favourable when export prices rise faster than import prices (or when export prices fall more slowly than import prices). Unfavourable movements in the terms of trade occur when the opposite is true.

Interpretation

Great care must be taken over interpreting a favourable or unfavourable movement in the terms of trade. It is the *price* changes which are favourable or unfavourable. The overall effect on revenue from exports or expenditure on imports of a favourable movement in the terms of trade might actually be disadvantageous, and vice versa. This is because changes in revenue and expenditure consist of price *and* volume changes. A favourable movement in prices might have an adverse effect on the volume of exports sold, or on the volume of imports bought. For example, where demand for exports is elastic, a rise in the price of than proportionate reduction in the volume of exports sold. In this case, the so-called favourable movement in the terms of trade might actually cause a balance of payments problem!

TYPES OF RESTRICTION ON TRADE

PROTECTION

Despite the potential gains from trade, countries sometimes adopt measures to restrict international trade. There are various types of restriction including the following.

Tariffs

These are simply taxes placed on import commodities. Where a tariff is levied on a commodity its price is increased in the domestic economy. Tariffs may be *specific*, i.e. lump sum, in nature, or *ad valorem*, i.e. proportional to the value of the article. They can be applied individually to particular products or across the board.

Quotas

These are a volume restriction on imports. Specific limits are placed on the quantity of particular products that can be imported. Again they can be applied selectively or across the board.

Subsidies

66 Types of protection 99

By subsidising exported commodities their competitiveness can be increased in foreign markets. Subsidising domestic products lowers their price and so reduces competition from imports.

Exchange controls

By restricting the supply of foreign currency to particular purchases, governments are able to exercise a great deal of control over which commodities are imported, and in what quantities.

The new protectionism

The new protectionism encompasses a variety of restrictions some of which are difficult to identify as a restriction on trade. Some common *non-tariff* barriers used as protective measures in recent years include:

- **Voluntary export restraints (VERs)**: these are agreements between two countries such that one country agrees to limit exports of particular goods to another country for a specific period of time. One example of this is the Japanese agreement to limit the export of cars to the UK.
- **Government contracts**: it is possible that governments deliberately place contracts with domestic producers as a means of restricting imports.

- **Customs procedures**: in some countries customs procedures are deliberately excessive. The most often quoted example is that of France who insisted that imports on video equipment must pass through an office in Poitiers, many miles from the ports of entry. With a staff of only eight this undoubtedly resulted in a delay of several weeks in the import of video recorders.

- **Health and safety standards**: strict standards can be imposed on imports such as restrictions on the ingredients of foods or the exhaust emission levels from cars to protect domestic industry.

MOTIVES FOR PROTECTION

There are several arguments for protection but at the present time most economists consider these arguments to be quite weak.

To aid economic recovery

It has been argued that if domestic industry is protected, demand will switch from imports to domestic goods and services and this will raise output and employment in the domestic economy. This, in particular, is the view of the *Cambridge Economic Policy Group*. However, protection imposes a welfare loss on consumers (see pp. 205–6), might encourage inefficiency in protected firms and could lead other countries to retaliate which would damage exports thus offsetting any gains in terms of output and employment. Exports might also fall if protection in the UK leads to a reduction in incomes abroad (because imports into the UK have fallen) leaving foreigners with less ability to purchase British output.

To remove a balance of payments deficit

❝ Reasons for protection ❞

Here again it is suggested that widespread protection can remove a balance of payments deficit. The argument is similar to that outlined above but the point is that protection does not remove the cause of the deficit which is lack of competitiveness. Often this might be lack of non-price competitiveness in areas such as quality, reliability, delivery, design, inefficient marketing and so on!

To reduce structural unemployment

In this case protection is directed to a single industry. It has the same possible effects as that previously outlined with respect to protecting industries to aid economic recovery. However, in this case it is less likely to reduce incomes abroad because protection is only granted to a single industry, but more likely to encourage inefficiency in that industry.

To protect an infant industry

It is sometimes suggested that in the early stages of growth, infant industries require protection from foreign competition. However, it is almost impossible to identify potentially successful infant industries and bearing the risks of financing infant industries is the function of the entrepreneur. Entrepreneurs will finance infant industries when they believe they will be successful in the long run. If they are not prepared to do this the prospects of success must be thought poor.

Strategic reasons

Another possible motive for protection is that it is considered desirable to produce certain essential goods, such as food and energy, domestically rather than become dependent on another country for their supply. In these circumstances supply might be withheld to exert political pressure. Strategic factors are one reason for the CAP operated by the EC.

PROTECTION AND CONSUMER WELFARE

The effect of a tariff on consumer welfare can be considered in terms of Fig. 14.1.

Domestic supply and demand are represented by S and D respectively. The *world* price of this commodity is OP and supply of this commodity in the domestic economy is perfectly elastic at the ruling world price, assuming there is no restriction on imports. Sales in the domestic economy are therefore OQ_1 with OQ being supplied by domestic producers. If the government now imposes a tariff of PP_1, the price of this commodity in the *domestic*

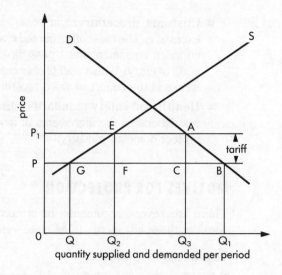

Fig. 14.1 The effect on consumer
welfare of a tariff

market rises to OP_1, total consumption falls to OQ_3 and domestic output increases to OQ_2. The welfare effects of the tariff are a loss to consumers, that is, a loss of consumer surplus, equal to PP_1AB. However, this is not the total welfare loss to society since PP_1EG of the surplus is transferred from consumers to producers and $ACFE$ is transferred from consumers to the Exchequer as tax revenue. However, the areas ABC and EFG represent pure welfare loss because there is no offsetting gain to any other group in the economy.

APPLIED MATERIALS

WINNERS AND LOSERS: 1992

The Lloyds Bank Economic Bulletin No 121, January 1989, is entitled *1992 Winners and Losers*, and outlines some possible effects from creating a single European market. It stresses that the main effect will be to increase competition and the main gainers will therefore be consumers. (By implication, consumers bear the main costs of protection.) The article lists the importance of different barriers to competition as revealed by a survey of UK firms. Table 14.2 lists these barriers.

The article also lists the areas where the UK has a comparative advantage in relation to Europe as in some sectors of electrical engineering, pharmaceuticals, food and drink, precision and medical equipment, insurance and airlines. These are the industries most likely to gain by the creation of a single European market.

1 Technical standards and regulations	5 Transport market regulations	The first two barriers were
2 Administrative barriers	6 Implementation of EC law	ranked closely together and
3 Frontier delays and costs	7 Capital market restrictions	were thought to be important
4 Public procurement restrictions	8 Differences in VAT, excise taxes	by much larger proportions than any of the remainder.

Table 14.2 Importance of barriers
ranking in a survey of UK firms   *Source:* Lloyds Bank Economic Bulletin, No 121, January 1989

EXAMINATION QUESTIONS

1 Explain carefully the theory of comparative advantage. Is the theory of any use in explaining the pattern of world trade?

(London, January 1989)

2 Analyse and evaluate the possible *causes* and *consequences* of a deterioration in a country's terms of trade.

(Cambridge, 1989)

OUTLINE ANSWERS TO QUESTIONS 1 AND 2

Question 1

It is useful to begin your answer to this question by distinguishing between absolute and comparative advantage. You could then go on to explain, using a numerical example, how countries gain from specialisation and trade. The pattern of world trade at least partly confirms the theory of comparative advantage with some countries specialising in certain goods and services. Coffee from Brazil, electronic equipment from Japan, nitrates from Chile; Switzerland specialises in banking, Zambia in copper, and so on. However, countries produce a variety of goods and services which seems to conflict with the law of comparative costs. One reason for this is that the law is based on certain assumptions which might not hold in the real world. These must be discussed. Another reason why the law might fail to predict the pattern of world trade is that countries might not wish to trade with some countries for political reasons or they might not wish to fully specialise for strategic reasons.

Question 2

You could begin your answer to this question with a definition of the terms of trade followed by a numerical example to distinguish between *favourable* and *unfavourable* movements in the terms of trade.

A change in the terms of trade implies a change in export prices and/or import prices. Several factors might bring this about including:

- A relatively high (or low) rate of inflation in the exporting country compared with importing countries will cause changes in the terms of trade. For example, an excess of aggregate demand over aggregate supply, or costs rising faster than productivity will raise the value of the terms of trade index because it will cause a rise in domestic, i.e., export prices.

- Exchange rate changes will also affect the value of the terms of trade index. For example, when a country's currency depreciates, the domestic price of its exports will be unchanged, but the domestic price of its imports will increase. Depreciation will therefore reduce the value of the terms of trade index; appreciation reduces the domestic price of imports, and therefore raises the terms of trade.

- Changes in commodity prices can also have a powerful effect on the terms of trade. When their price is bid up on world markets, or when producing countries restrict supply and force up price, the terms of trade index of the exporting countries will rise; for importing countries the terms of trade index will fall. A slump in commodity prices has the opposite effect.

- Changes in the terms of trade might be caused by 'bottlenecks' in the supply of exports or imports. For example, a bottleneck may occur when demand for exports increases, perhaps because of an increase in the national income of a major buying country, but exports cannot respond to increased demand because of a shortage of skilled labour or some other input. In these circumstances export prices will rise relative to import prices, and the terms of trade will rise. The opposite occurs when demand for imports increases and supply is inelastic.

Further reading

Begg, Fischer and Dornbusch, *Economics* (2nd edn), McGraw-Hill 1987: Ch. 31, International Trade and Commercial Policy.

Greenaway, *New Ways of Restricting Imports*, The Economic Review, Vol 3, No 2 November 1985.

Griffiths and Wall, *Applied Economics: An Introductory Course* (3rd edn), Longman, Ch. 24, Protectionism.

Harrison, *International Trade and Finance*, Longman 1987: Ch. 1, The Gains from International Trade; Ch. 2, Restrictions on Trade.

Stanlake, *Introductory Economics* (5th edn), Longman 1989: Ch. 27, International Trade.

GETTING STARTED

In Chapter 14 we looked at the gains from international trade. Over any given period of time the total financial dealings of one country with the rest of the world are recorded in its balance of payments account. However, just as individuals can sometimes spend more than they currently earn and finance this by borrowing, so countries can sometimes spend more than they currently earn. When this happens and a country imports a greater value of goods and services than it exports, we say it has a *balance of payments deficit*. When the value of exports exceeds the value of imports a country is said to have a *balance of payments surplus*. Although a balance of payments deficit is often taken as cause for concern and a surplus a sign of economic strength, one advantage of a deficit is that it allows residents of one country to consume more than they currently produce, thereby raising current living standards.

In the real world, international trade and payments are only possible if there is an international *means* of payment. Although most currencies can be converted into other currencies via the foreign exchange market, most international trade is financed through the use of *vehicle (or reserve) currencies*. These are simply currencies that are acceptable as a means of settling international indebtedness. The US Dollar is the main vehicle currency, though Sterling and the Deutschmark are also used as vehicle currencies.

THE BALANCE OF PAYMENTS

ESSENTIAL PRINCIPLES

A country's balance of payments is simply an annual record of its financial dealings with the rest of the world. In practice, all transactions which make up the balance of payments are either *autonomous transactions* or *accommodating transactions*. Autonomous transactions are those which take place for their own sake. They reflect voluntary decisions to buy, sell, lend or borrow. Accommodating transactions, on the other hand, are those which are necessary because the net value of all autonomous transactions yields either a deficit in the balance of payments (outflows > inflows) or a surplus (inflows > outflows).

In the UK all international transactions are recorded in the current account of the balance of payments and/or the capital account (now referred to as *Transactions in UK assets and liabilities*) of the balance of payments. The accounts are constructed on the principle of *double entry bookkeeping* thus ensuring that the accounts always balance in *accounting terms*. One entry shows the *original transaction*, the other shows the *way in which it was financed*. For example, the purchase of cars from Japan would be recorded as a visible import in the current account. It would also be recorded in the capital account as perhaps a loan from an overseas bank if this is how the deal was financed.

THE CURRENT ACCOUNT

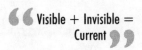

Visible + Invisible = Current

This account records dealings in *visible trade*, that is, exports and imports of goods, and *invisible trade* which consists mainly of trade in services. As Table 15.1 on p. 210 shows, the visible balance (−£20,557m) when added to the invisible balance (£5,621m) gives the current balance (−£14,936m).

Trade balance

The state of the *visible balance*, or trade balance, is of great importance because it indicates the extent to which the UK depends on the rest of the world for the *goods* it consumes. We shall see on pp. 221–2 that a lack of international competitiveness has been a major factor in the decline of the manufacturing sector (usually referred to as *deindustrialisation*) in the UK in recent years. When visible imports exceed visible exports, it is still of course possible for this deficit to be offset by a surplus on invisibles since it is the sum of the visible balance and the invisible balance which gives the current balance.

State of the current account

The state of the current account is of great importance because it indicates a nation's *net* surplus or deficit in its trading with the rest of the world. As Table 15.2 shows, the UK has often had a deficit on the trade balance which has been more than offset by a surplus on the invisible account giving an overall surplus on the current account. However, the extent of the current account deficit in recent years has been a particular cause for concern. More is said about this below.

THE CAPITAL ACCOUNT (CHANGES IN UK EXTERNAL ASSETS AND LIABILITIES)

This section of the balance of payments account records capital movements between the UK and the rest of the world. Such *capital* movements are undertaken by governments, firms and private individuals, and may be short term or long term. Capital outflows are given a negative sign in the accounts, and capital inflows a positive sign.

Long-term capital flows
These consist of

- *direct investment*
- *portfolio investment*
- *other external assets (liabilities) of central government*

Visible trade			Capital Account (Transactions in UK assets and liabilities)		
Exports	80157		**Transactions in assets**		
Imports	−100714		Direct investment overseas	−15110	
Visible Balance		−20557	Portfolio investment overseas	−10308	
			Loans to overseas residents by UK banks	−19261	
Invisible trade			Other private lending and deposits overseas	−2328	
			Changes in official reserves	−2761	
Sea transport	3544		Other external assets of central government	−894	
	−4501		**Transactions in liabilities**		
		−957			
Civil aviation			Direct investment in UK	7804	
	3192		Portfolio investment in UK	3597	
	−4125		Loans to UK residents from overseas banks	33856	
		−933			
Travel					
	6085		Other private lending and deposits from overseas	5561	
	−8127		Other external liabilities of central government	902	
		−2042			51720
Financial and other services					
	14156		Net transactions		1058
	−4960				
		9196	Balancing item		13878
General government					
	518				
	−2354				
		−1836			
Interest profits and dividends					
	55564				
	−49793				
		5572			
Transfers					
	2117				
	−5383				
		−3576			
Invisible balance		5621			
Current balance		−14936			

Table 15.1 UK balance of payments (£m):1988

	NON-OIL EXPORTS	NON-OIL IMPORTS	NON-OIL BALANCE	OIL BALANCE	INVISIBLES	CURRENT ACCOUNT
1980	41.0	40.0	1.0	0.3	1.8	3.1
1981	41.6	41.3	0.3	3.0	3.6	6.9
1982	44.7	47.1	− 2.4	4.6	2.5	4.7
1983	48.2	56.7	− 8.0	7.0	4.9	3.8
1984	55.4	66.9	−11.5	6.9	6.6	2.0
1985	61.9	72.3	−10.5	8.1	5.7	3.3
1986	64.5	77.2	−12.8	4.1	8.9	0.2
1987	71.0	85.3	−14.4	4.2	7.3	− 2.9
1988	74.6	97.5	−22.9	2.3	5.6	−14.9
			Projections			
1989	85.0	108.0	−23.0	1.5	6.2	−15.3
1990	94.7	116.8	−22.1	3.2	6.8	−12.1
1991	104.4	125.7	−21.3	2.7	7.5	−11.1

Source: Lloyds Bank Economic Bulletin, No 127, July 1989.

Table 15.2 Balance of payments

Direct investment

This refers to the creation of real physical assets such as factory buildings whereas portfolio investment refers to purely financial transactions such as the purchase or sale of equity in joint stock companies. Other external assets (liabilities) of UK government includes such items as subscriptions to international organisations, for example, contributions to the EC budget or overseas aid.

Short-term capital flows

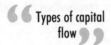
Types of capital flow

These consist of lending by, or borrowing from, banks as well as private lending and deposits overseas. Entries into these sections of the capital account arise mainly because of transactions in the current account. For example, the import of goods might be paid for by running down a bank deposit held in a bank abroad. However, it might also represent the purchase and sale of short term instruments by foreign nationals with surplus funds to invest. For example, overseas residents might purchase Treasury bills, commercial bills of exchange, or local authority bills and these purchases would lead to an inflow of foreign currency. They might also deposit funds in bank accounts in London for convenience. These short-term capital flows are purely monetary flows, since they do not involve the creation of physical assets. Because of this they are highly liquid and are sometimes referred to as *hot money* since they can be moved from one country to another very rapidly in response to expected changes in interest rates and/or exchange rates. The volatile nature of hot money can be a source of pressure on a country's exchange rate and, as we shall see, can be a problem for the authorities.

CHANGES IN THE OFFICIAL RESERVES

These arise because any deficit or surplus on the current account is not completely offset by other transactions in the capital account. A negative entry indicates that the authorities have used part of the reserves to bring the balance of payments into balance and vice versa. It is important to note, however, that the change in the reserves is not necessarily identical to the balance of payments deficit or surplus, because the authorities sometimes borrow from abroad to finance a deficit.

THE BALANCING ITEM

The balance of payments account records the effect on foreign currency earnings and expenditure of millions of transactions. In calculations of this magnitude there are bound to be errors and omissions; the balancing item records the collective value of these. Its value is known because the Bank of England's records show the net result of all foreign currency transactions. A positive value, as in Table 15.1 indicates that there have been unrecorded net exports and a negative figure that there have been unrecorded net imports.

BALANCE IN THE BALANCE OF PAYMENTS

Because the balance of payments always balances, this does not imply that it never gives cause for concern. When discussing deficits or surpluses in the balance of payments, attention focuses on the current account because it is this account which records *autonomous transactions*. *Autonomous transactions* in the capital account simply ensure that the deficit is financed or the surplus disposed of. Balance in the accounts is achieved by *accommodating transactions* and, in the case of deficit countries at least, there is a limit on the ability of the authorities to sustain these. For instance, a deficit leads to an outflow of foreign currency reserves which are limited in value, or borrowings from abroad which are also limited by foreign perceptions of credit-worthiness, etc. Clearly, balance of payments deficits cannot be sustained indefinitely.

Distinguish accommodating from autonomous transactions

THE RATE OF EXCHANGE

Exchange rates are the rate at which one country's currency can be exchanged for other currencies in the foreign exchange market. There are various kinds of exchange rate system, but for simplicity economists identify two broad types: *floating exchange rates* and *fixed exchange rates*. The determination of exchange rates in each of these is considered in turn, but first we must clarify what is often a source of confusion over the use of terminology.

- In markets where exchange rates *float*, an increase in the external value of a currency is referred to as *appreciation* and a decrease in the external value of a currency is referred to as *depreciation*.
- In markets where exchange rates are fixed, when the authorities raise the external value of the currency to a higher fixed parity we refer to *revaluation*. A change to a lower fixed parity is referred to as *devaluation*.

FLOATING EXCHANGE RATES

Where exchange rates are allowed to float freely, the value of one currency in terms of others is determined by the operation of market forces. In other words, the interaction of demand for, and supply of, that currency in the market for foreign exchange.

DEMAND

Demand for foreign currency arises out of the desire to purchase another country's exports or to invest abroad. For example, the demand for sterling in the foreign exchange market arises partly from the desire of foreigners to purchase UK goods and services, or to invest in the UK. Like all normal demand curves the demand for sterling varies inversely with its price. The reason for this is simple. Consider the external value of sterling in relation to American dollars; at a rate of exchange of £1 = $2, it is clear that £100 export from the UK costs an American importer $200. If the rate of exchange *falls* to £1 = $1.80, the *same* £100 export now costs an American importer only $180. At the lower price more British exports will be demanded. Consequently, as the rate of exchange falls, there will be a rise in the quantity of sterling demanded on the foreign exchange market to pay for these exports.

SUPPLY

Similarly, the supply of sterling on the foreign exchange market arises from the demand of UK importers for goods and services produced abroad, or from the desire to invest abroad. For example, in order to buy American exports UK importers will require dollars. These can be obtained through the foreign exchange market where sterling is exchanged for dollars. So the supply of sterling on the foreign exchange market is derived from the demand for imports into the UK, and from the need to purchase foreign currencies to finance UK investment overseas.

The supply curve

The supply curve for sterling (or any other currency) on the foreign exchange market will also be normal-shaped, with the supply of sterling varying directly with its international price. For example, if the current rate of exchange is £1 = $1.50, a $300 American export will cost an importer in the UK £200. However, if the rate of exchange *increased* to £1 = $1.60, the same good costing $300 in America would now have a price in the UK of £187.50. In other words, as the rate of exchange rises, the price of imports falls. At the lower domestic price we can assume that more imports will be demanded. It follows that as the rate of exchange increases there will be a rise in the quantity of sterling supplied to the foreign exchange market.

The equilibrium rate

In a free market, exchange rates will be determined by the interaction of demand for, and supply of, the currency. The rate established will be the equilibrium rate and there can be no deviation from this unless the *conditions* of demand or supply change. Fig. 15.1 illustrates how the exchange rate for sterling against dollars is determined.

Fig. 15.1 shows that with demand and supply conditions given by DD and SS the equilibrium exchange rate is £1 = $2. At any rate of exchange below this there will be a shortage of sterling and its exchange value will rise. At any rate above this there will be a surplus of sterling and its exchange value will fall.

Factors influencing floating exchange rates

The factors which cause changes in floating rates are many and varied. Changes in a

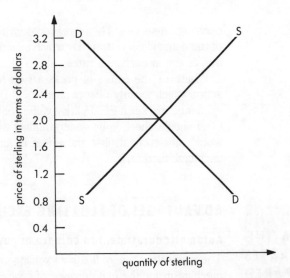

Fig. 15.1 The equilibrium rate of exchange

country's current balance are clearly important, since sales of exports and purchases of imports are major factors affecting the demand for, and supply of, different currencies on the foreign exchange market. Changes in interest rates are also important, as these are likely to cause changes in short-term capital flows and therefore in the demand/supply schedules. Rumours of expected changes in exchange rates are also likely to influence short-term capital flows. For instance, capital gains can be made by moving funds into a currency *before* it appreciates against other currencies, and then back into the original currency after appreciation. Capital losses can be avoided by moving funds out of currency *before* it depreciates, and then back into it after depreciation. (See the *Tutor's Answer* to Question 1).

FIXED EXCHANGE RATES

It is possible for governments to fix the external value of their currency in relation to other currencies. A fixed exchange rate is maintained by intervention through central banks in the foreign exchange market. Such intervention is designed to offset changes in the conditions of supply or demand in the foreign exchange market which would otherwise cause fluctuations in exchange rates. The way in which *exchange rate stability* is maintained by *intervention* is explained using Fig. 15.2.

Assume that the rate of exchange between sterling and dollar is fixed at £1 = 2 and that supply and demand conditions for sterling are initially represented by SS and DD respectively. If the UK demand for imports now increases, there will be an *increase in the supply of sterling* on the foreign exchange market shown by the shift in the supply to S_1S_1. This will cause downward pressure on the sterling exchange rate and in a free market its value would fall to around £1 = 1.60. However, because the authorities are committed to maintaining the exchange rate for sterling at £1 = \$2, they will be forced to buy the excess supply of sterling (AB) that exists at this exchange rate, using dollars from the foreign

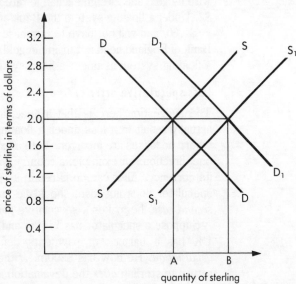

Fig. 15.2 Maintaining a fixed exchange rate

exchange reserves. The increased demand for sterling is shown by an outward movement of the demand curve to D_1D_1 which exactly offsets the increase in supply and prevents any movement in exchange rates.

Whatever the cause of pressure on fixed exchange rates, the authorities must take action which exactly offsets changes in the conditions of supply or demand in the foreign exchange market if fixed parity values between different currencies are to be maintained. (You should check your understanding of this by considering what action the authorities would take to neutralise the effect of an increase in demand for sterling on the foreign exchange market.)

ADVANTAGES OF FLOATING EXCHANGE RATES

Automatic adjustment to balance of payments disequilibrium

The main advantage of floating exchange rates is undoubtedly that it provides an *automatic* mechanism for the maintenance of balance of payments equilibrium. Thus, if demand for imports by the UK is rising relative to the rest of the world's demand for UK exports, there will be an excess supply of sterling on the foreign exchange market. This will cause the sterling exchange rate to *depreciate*, reducing the price of exports in foreign markets and raising the price of imports in the domestic market. As exports become cheaper foreigners will buy more of them, and as imports become more expensive fewer will be bought by domestic residents. It is therefore argued that currency depreciation will prevent the emergence of deficits on the balance of payments; equally, that currency appreciation will eliminate any emerging surplus.

In practice, movements in exchange rates do not always eliminate deficits and surpluses as simply as implied here, and this aspect of exchange rates is examined more fully on pp. 217–21.

Greater freedom to pursue domestic goals

Because floating exchange rates make the balance of payments self-correcting, it is sometimes argued that governments are free to pursue whatever policies they wish in the domestic economy. Specifically, governments are more free to pursue policies designed to achieve full employment and economic growth. Under fixed exchange rates, a 'dash for growth' may result in an increase in imports – a balance of payments crisis – and therefore a deflation of domestic demand to curb imports. This is the familiar 'stop-go' cycle. The argument here is that the exchange rate will *automatically* fall to eliminate any emerging deficit and to reduce the need for any deflation of domestic demand. Again, this is something of an over-simplification, but there is general agreement that floating exchange rates give governments greater freedom of action in the domestic economy.

Economies in the use of foreign exchange reserves

Suppose there is pressure on the pound under a fixed exchange rate system, as was the case in Fig.14.2. In this case, the Bank of England would have to intervene to buy sterling with its gold and foreign exchange rate reserves in order to maintain the par value at £1 = $2. Under a floating system the Bank of England can simply let the pound depreciate to £1 = $1.60, and will not have to purchase the excess supply of sterling A-B. As a result the Bank of England need not maintain gold and foreign exchange rates to as high a value under a floating system as under a fixed system.

Less speculative activity

The suggestion here is that a speculative movement of funds out of a currency could actually result in a loss under a floating system; unlike the fixed exchange rate system where no losses are incurred. With a fixed exchange rate system the pressure builds up in one direction; for example, a country with a balance of payments deficit can hardly revalue its currency. All it can do is retain its present par value or devalue. In the *first case* the speculator does not lose, should he have moved his money out of the currency; in the *second case*, he makes a speculative gain.

Suppose a speculator has £100m and that the initial rate of exchange is £1 = $2. If the UK has a balance of payments deficit he may move out of sterling as he fears *devaluation*. He now has $200m. *If* the UK *does devalue* to, say, £1 = $1, then he can return to sterling *after* the devaluation and receive £200m, i.e. a capital *gain* of £100m. If

Advantages of a floating rate

he is wrong and sterling resists devaluation, he can return to sterling and receive £100m, i.e. no loss, except for transactions costs (brokerage fees, etc.).

The situation is different under a floating rate system because the possibility of a capital gain exists. It is argued that this encourages speculative activity and might destabilise exchange rates. If speculative pressure builds up in one direction it might bring about the changes speculators expect (self-fulfilling expectations). With a floating rate system the pound can therefore depreciate, or appreciate because of speculative activity.

These arguments constitute a powerful case for floating exchange rates. However, there are disadvantages and these are discussed below.

DISADVANTAGES OF FLOATING EXCHANGE RATES

Increased uncertainty

It is sometimes suggested that floating rates increase *uncertainty* in international trade. The possibility of changes in the external value of different currencies might deter long-term international investment or might make firms reluctant to negotiate long-run trade contracts with different countries. There is much greater certainty when foreign exchange rates are fixed.

Increased speculative activity

There are also disadvantages!

We have seen that an argument in favour of a floating system is that it allegedly deters speculative activity as there are now possibilities of *losses*. But there are also greater opportunities for *gains*, given the greater number of changes taking place in exchange rates. This might encourage speculative activity under floating exchange rates.

Increased volatility of exchange rates

Frequent short-run changes in exchange rates can have serious repercussions in the domestic economy. Where exchange rates float, flows of capital into a currency, attracted by higher short-term interest rates, can cause some currencies to appreciate; while flows of capital out of a currency can cause it to depreciate. When a country's currency appreciates, its exports become less competitive in world markets, and industries which produce import substitutes find it more difficult to compete in the domestic economy because imports become relatively cheaper. Conversely, when a country's currency depreciates, export and import competing industries boom. Where appreciation or depreciation is caused by a fundamental change in the pattern of world consumption or changes in a country's comparative advantage, these changes in exchange rates might be necessary and desirable. However, where exchange rates float, fluctuations can be caused by speculative flows in response to changes in short term interest rates. Because of factor immobility such currency changes can lead to a serious misallocation of resources and cause unemployment. Where rates of exchange are fixed, intervention by the authorities in the foreign exchange market will avoid short run fluctuations. Fundamental changes in supply or demand conditions for particular currencies can be accommodated by a change from one fixed parity to a lower or higher fixed parity as appropriate.

IS SPECULATION DESTABILISING?

It was implied in the previous section that speculation can destabilise floating exchange rates. However, it can be argued that far from destabilising exchange rates, speculation acts as a stabilising influence! Remember that speculators buy when prices are low and sell when prices are high in order to realise speculative gains. They therefore add to demand when price is falling, thereby limiting the extent of any price reduction, and add to supply when price is rising, thereby limiting the extent of any price rise. The effect of speculation is therefore to limit the extent of movements in exchange rates.

Another way in which speculation might have beneficial effects is when speculators correctly anticipate the effect on exchange rates of any change in policy by the authorities. For example, a reduction in the rate of interest would normally lead to a depreciation of the exchange rate. However, when a reduction in the rate of interest is anticipated by speculators they will sell currency and thus move the exchange rate in the direction that it would have moved anyway. But since speculators sell currency at different times, the argument is the exchange rate will adjust more smoothly than the abrupt change that will follow an unanticipated reduction in interest rates.

Notwithstanding these arguments, capital flows are now so vast, and so easily converted from one currency into another, that it is possible for exchange rates to *overshoot* their underlying equilibrium rate because of speculation. Overshooting has serious implications for domestic industry such as a reduction in demand for exports because of an overpriced exchange rate. Because of this, to the extent that speculation causes overshooting, it should be considered harmful.

DIRTY FLOATING OR MANAGED FLEXIBILITY

Although fixed exchange rates were maintained between most of the world's major currencies for over 25 years after the Second World War, for most of the period since 1972 rates of exchange have been allowed to float. However, this does not necessarily imply that floating rates of exchange are superior to fixed rates, since there has been no commitment to allow exchange rates to float freely. The system that now exists is effectively a compromise between fixed and floating rates. The authorities often intervene to neutralise short run pressure on exchange rates, but market forces now play a more important role in the determination of exchange rates. This exchange rate system is usually referred to as *managed flexibility*, although because the authorities do not always make it clear that they are using the reserves to support a currency's external value, the system is sometimes referred to as *dirty floating*.

THE EUROPEAN MONETARY SYSTEM (EMS)

There are two main strands to the EMS: the ERM and the ECU. The ERM is the *exchange rate mechanism* whereby participating countries agree to maintain exchange rates vis a vis other participating countries within 2 per cent (6 per cent in the case of Italy) of the agreed rate. The ECU is the *European Currency Unit*. The value of the ECU is determined by a weighted average basket of EC embmer currencies. As well as there being an agreed rate between all participating currencies in relation to each other, each currency has an agreed value against the ECU with the same 2 per cent margin of fluctuation. The purpose of this is to generate a *divergence indicator* equal to 75 per cent of the agreed value of any currency against the ECU. There is a presumption that the authorities of any country whose currency deviates by *more than 75 per cent* of its *agreed value against the ECU*, and therefore approaches the 2 per cent limit, will *intervene* to halt the divergence.

(Whether Britain should become a full member of the EMS is discussed on p. 222.)

REAL AND EFFECTIVE EXCHANGE RATES

Throughout this chapter we have ignored any ambiguity over our definition of exchange rate changes. Indeed, there is no ambiguity when exchange rates are fixed, because when one country changes the external value of its currency it does so by an equivalent amount against the currencies of all its trading partners. For example, when sterling was devalued by 14.3 per cent in November 1967, this was the rate of devaluation against *all* currencies. However, when exchange rates float it is possible for a currency to be appreciating against some currencies and depreciating against others. Alternatively, it might depreciate against some currencies by a greater amount than against other currencies, and so on. A more sophisticated measure of the exchange rate is then necessary in order to assess whether a particular currency is appreciating or depreciating.

One way would be able to take a straightforward average of the way one currency has moved against all other currencies. However, this would be unsatisfactory because some exchange rate changes are more important for a country than others. A second possibility would be to construct a '*trade weighted index*'. Such an index for the UK, for example, would show the value of sterling measured against an average of all other currencies weighted according to their importance as a trading partner. Here again, this is not entirely satisfactory because it takes no account of the fact that the UK does not only trade bilaterally with its partners, but also competes against them in world markets. It is necessary to take this fact into account when measuring the importance of exchange rate movements for a country's balance of payments.

There is no universally accepted measure of the *effective exchange rate* for a currency, but the method used at the moment takes both factors mentioned above into consideration.

So, in the case of the effective exchange rate for sterling, the weight attached to the US dollar and to the Japanese yen are both greater than the share of UK exports to, or imports from, these countries. This is because both of these countries are important competitors for the UK in many world markets.

In summary, we can say that at present effective exchange rates are designed to answer the following question: 'What uniform percentage change in the sterling exchange rate against every other currency would have had the same effect on the UK's trade balances as the set of changes that have actually taken place?'

The real exchange rate

The real exchange rate is an index which takes account of differences in international rates of inflation on the competitiveness of exports and imports. For example if sterling appreciates against the US dollar by 5 per cent, this does not necessarily imply that UK goods will be 5 per cent more expensive relative to USA goods. This will only be the case if there is no inflation in the UK or the USA. In this case a 5 per cent appreciation in the *nominal sterling exchange rate* also implies a 5 per cent appreciation in the *real sterling exchange rate*. However, if there is inflation in one or both countries, changes in the nominal exchange rate will be different from changes in the real exchange rate. The real exchange rate is usually expressed as:

> **Expressing the real exchange rate**

$$e^r = eP^*/P$$

Where e^r is the real exchange rate, e is the effective exchange rate, P^* is an index of foreign prices and P is an index of the domestic price level. We can now see what happens to the real exchange rate if there is inflation in the UK of 10 per cent, inflation in other countries of 4 per cent and a 2 per cent depreciation of sterling. If we assume the effective exchange rate depreciates from 100 to 90, the result of these changes is $(90 \times 110/104 = 95.19)$ a depreciation in the real effective exchange rate of about 4.81 per cent.

When the value of the real exchange rate falls (either because of a relatively much lower domestic rate of inflation, a relatively higher rate of inflation abroad or because of a rise in the effective exchange rate), British goods become more competitive and vice versa.

INTERNATIONAL LIQUIDITY

International liquidity refers to the supply of internationally acceptable assets, that is, those assets acceptable in settlement of an international debt. The main component of international liquidity is, of course, vehicle or reserve currencies such as the American dollar but gold and SDRs are also acceptable in settlement of a debt. SDRs are an asset created by the International Monetary Fund (IMF) specifically to be used as international liquidity and, subject to certain restrictions, they are acceptable by all IMF member countries.

The growth of international liquidity is an important issue. If international liquidity does not grow at the same rate as the value of international trade this will restrict the growth of trade. We have already noted the importance of specialisation and trade for the growth of output and therefore the growth of world living standards. An adequate supply of world liquidity is essential if trade is to continue to grow. More is written about international liquidity on pp. 226–7.

EXCHANGE RATE CHANGES AND BALANCE OF PAYMENTS ADJUSTMENT

Whether changes in the exchange rate succeed in removing a balance of payments deficit or surplus depends on many factors. We concentrate here on those factors which determine whether a downward movement in the exchange rate, that is devaluation or depreciation, will succeed in removing a balance of payments deficit. For simplicity, the use of the term depreciation in this appendix will refer to either. Whether revaluation or appreciation will succeed in removing a balance of payments surplus depends on the opposite set of factors.

Depreciation exerts its most powerful impact on the current account of the balance of payments. Before we formally consider the circumstances in which it will remove a balance of payments deficit, therefore, it is important to be clear about the way in which depreciation affects the prices of exports and imports. When a currency depreciates it reduces the *foreign price of exports*. For example, if sterling depreciates against the dollar from £1 = $1.20 to £1 = $1.10, then the price of a car exported to America which costs £10,000 in the UK falls from $12,000 before depreciation to $11,000 after depreciation.

The sterling price of the car is unchanged: depreciation *reduced the foreign price*.

The situation is exactly the opposite for imports. Depreciation raises the *domestic price of imports*. Again, if sterling depreciates from £1 = $1.20 to £1 = $1.10, the price of a good imported by the UK which costs $2,400 in America rises from £2,000 to £2,181.8. The dollar price of the good is unchanged: depreciation *raises the domestic* price.

There are two broad approaches to the balance of payments adjustment: the *elasticities approach* and the *absorption approach*. Each is considered in turn.

THE ELASTICITIES APPROACH

This approach stresses the effect of *relative* price changes on the balance of payments. It implies that whether depreciation will remove a balance of payments deficit or not depends primarily on the price elasticity of demand for exports and for imports, since it is this above all else that determines the *net change* in the flow of funds to the current account following depreciation. If demand for *exports* is elastic (i.e. greater than one), depreciation will lead to a rise in *foreign currency earnings* because the proportionate increase in quantity sold will be greater than the proportionate reduction in price. However, the *foreign price of imports* is unchanged so that any reduction in the quantity bought will lead to a reduction in *foreign currency expenditure*. In other words, if elasticity of demand for imports is greater than zero, foreign currency expenditure on imports will fall following depreciation.

The Marshall-Lerner condition

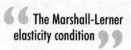
The Marshall-Lerner elasticity condition

The importance of these elasticities of demand are generalised in the *Marshall-Lerner* condition. This implies that depreciation will lead to an improvement in the balance of payments if the sum of the price elasticities of demand for exports and imports exceeds unity. The following example clarifies this.

Example: For simplicity the balance of payments is presented in foreign currency values. Assume sterling depreciates against the dollar by 10 per cent from £1 = $1.20 to £1 = $1.08. Thus export prices (which are denominated in foreign currency) fall in the ratio 0.12/1.20, that is, a fall of 10 per cent. Import prices, on the other hand, (which are denominated in sterling), rise in the ratio 0.12/1.08, that is, a rise of 11.1 per cent*. If the elasticity of demand for exports is 1.6 and the elasticity of demand for imports is 1.5, the effect on the balance of payments of this depreciation is easily demonstrated.

Initial balance of payments position

Exports ($M)	Imports ($M)
2000	2100

Sterling depreciates by 10 per cent

Elasticity of demand =   Elasticity of demand =

$$1.6 = \frac{\% \triangle QX}{\% \triangle PX} \qquad 1.5 = \frac{\% \triangle Qm}{\% \triangle Pm}$$

therefore % △QX = 16%   therefore %△Qm = 16.5%

After depreciation

Exports ($M)	Imports** ($M)
2145.6	1750.35

* This is easily verified. A good costing $1.20 in America costs a UK importer £1 before depreciation and £1.11 after depreciation, an increase of 11.1 per cent.

** The relationship between total revenue (expenditure) and elasticity of demand was discussed in Chapter 4. Care must be taken when measuring the change in import expenditure, however, because the foreign price of imports is unchanged. This implies that a 16.65 per cent reduction in quantity demanded will lead to a 16.65 per cent reduction in foreign currency expenditure on imports. It is a good idea to work out several examples of your own to satisfy yourself of the importance of the Marshall-Lerner condition.

'J' curve effect

However, over time, demand for exports and imports is much more elastic. Patterns of consumption and investment flows change in response to the price changes brought about by depreciation. Because of this, depreciation only leads to an improvement in the balance of payments in the long run. The initial deterioration and subsequent improvement in the balance of payments is usually referred to as the *'J' curve effect*. The adverse initial impact on the balance of payments is often thought to average around 18 months or so. The general effect is illustrated in Fig. 15.3.

It seems that, so long as the elasticity conditions are favourable, depreciation will lead to an improvement in the balance of payments position. However, elasticity conditions are unlikely to be favourable in the short run. It takes time for people to adjust their patterns of consumption and change their investment plans. The result is that depreciation *initially* leads to an increased balance of payments deficit. Foreign currency spending on imports is largely unchanged, because much the same quantity of imports are consumed at an unchanged foreign price. On the other hand, foreign currency earnings fall because much the same volume of exports are sold at a lower foreign price. Hence, the balance of payments *initially* deteriorates after depreciation.

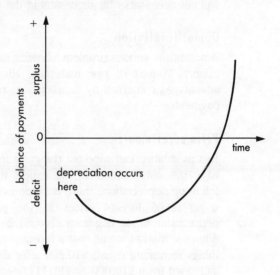

Fig. 15.3 The 'J' curve effect

THE ABSORPTION APPROACH

This analysis of balance of payments adjustment is based on the income accounting identity.

$$Y = C + I + G + X - M \text{ which can be rewritten as}$$
$$Y - (C + I + G) = X - M$$

i.e. $Y - A = X - M$ where A = Domestic absorption

This implies that the balance of payments of a country is equal to domestic income minus domestic expenditure (or absorption). A deficit on the balance of payments will exist when the country absorbs more goods and services than it produces, that is when $(C + I + G) > Y$.

It follows from this that depreciation or devaluation can only succeed if it increases domestic output (income) relative to absorption, or reduces absorption relative to domestic output (income). The absorption approach therefore places much more emphasis on the level of domestic demand as the main determinant of the balance of payments position rather than on relative price levels.

The absorption approach shows that when there is full employment in the economy it is impossible to raise domestic output (income) and therefore it is necessary to deflate the domestic economy in order to reduce absorption and to release resources for export production. However, elasticities are still important. Simply depressing domestic demand does not guarantee that the resources released will be transferred into export production, though it is usually effective in reducing demand for imports.

GENERAL PROBLEMS OF ADJUSTMENT

Despite the general predictions of these two approaches to the balance of payments adjustment, there are other factors which have an important influence on the effect of depreciation. Essentially both approaches are *static*. In the real world there are other dynamic factors to consider. These include the following.

Income effects

If depreciation succeeds in reducing the flow of imports, it will bring about a reduction in the national income of those countries whose exports, which are the counterpart of these imports, have fallen. As income in these countries falls, their own ability to import from the depreciating country will fall. This will have a particularly significant effect where demand for imports in these countries is *income elastic*. Additionally, it is possible that falling national income will tend to reduce the pressure on prices and make exports from these countries more competitive. This will be particularly important where demand for their exports is *price elastic*. Because of these income (and price) effects in the foreign country even if export revenues rise for the domestic country after depreciation, they might subsequently fall. Similarly, any reduction in domestic imports might be subsequently reversed. To the extent that income (and price) effects operate in this way, depreciation will not necessarily be successful in the long run.

Domestic inflation

A potentially serious problem following depreciation is domestic inflation, especially where imports consist of raw materials. Rising import costs can quickly erode any price advantages conferred by depreciation, resulting in a continuing deficit on the balance of payments.

Price adjustments

Just as inflation can wipe out the gains from depreciation, administered price changes can have the same effect. In the export market, instead of offering lower foreign prices following depreciation, there is some evidence that firms raise domestic prices and in so doing retain foreign prices at the pre-depreciation level. For example, following depreciation of sterling from £1 = $1.20 to £1 = $1.08, a product costing £10,000 in the domestic market would cost a foreign importer $12,000 before depreciation and (all other things remaining equal) $10,800 after depreciation. However, if the domestic price was increased from £10,000 to £11,111, depreciation would have an imperceptible impact on the foreign price.

Exporters

Exporters might have many reasons for wishing to maintain price stability. It avoids the threat of retaliation by foreign firms and the possibility of a damaging price war. Where a multi-national corporation has subsidiaries in many countries it might wish to avoid competition between these by administering price changes to offset those brought about by depreciation. Probably most important of all, however, is that by raising domestic prices (and keeping the foreign price constant) firms are able to increase profits. The same volume of goods and services are sold but at a higher price. For whatever reason, to the extent that prices are adjusted in the way described above, the effect will be to mitigate the gains from depreciation.

POLICIES TO DEAL WITH A BALANCE OF PAYMENTS DEFICIT

Broadly, there are three courses open to *deficit* countries: *depreciation* of the currency, *deflation* of the domestic economy, or some form of *direct restriction on imports*. In practice, countries are unlikely to adopt only one of these to the exclusion of the others and might even adopt a combination of all three.

- **Depreciation:** This involves lowering the exchange rate with the aim of increasing receipts from abroad and reducing expenditures on imports. The success of this policy in removing a deficit therefore depends on the elasticities of demand for exports and imports. However, it also depends on whether rising import prices leads to a higher domestic rate of inflation. If this happens, the relative advantage conferred by depreciation will quickly be eroded.

66 *Dealing with a balance of payments deficit* 99

- **Deflation:** Deflating the level of aggregate demand works in two ways.
  - As demand and output fall, the ability to buy imports falls.
  - In the longer term, deflation reduces the domestic rate of inflation, and so increases the competitiveness of exports.

  The attraction of this policy is that if it is severe enough, deflation will always remove a balance of payments deficit. The disadvantage is that it works by depressing domestic income, which lowers living standards and increases unemployment. Moreover, deflation does not offer a permanent means of removing a balance of payments deficit – unless the level of demand is permanently depressed. As soon as demand is expanded the deficit will reappear.

■ **Restricting imports**: Restrictions on imports can take several forms: *tariffs, quotas, subsidies on domestic products* and so on – although none of these is an option available to the UK because of its membership of the EEC. Such measures will probably be successful in the short run but have considerable disadvantages. They might provoke retaliation, lead to higher prices and encourage inefficiency overall, resulting in a less efficient allocation of resources. (See pp. 204–6).

RECENT CHANGES IN THE UK BALANCE OF PAYMENTS

APPLIED MATERIALS

The Lloyds Bank Economic Bulletin No 127, July 1989, analyses the recent changes in the UK balance of payments. Table 15.2 shows the changes that have occurred in recent years and the projected changes.

The recorded deficit in 1988 was second in absolute size only to that of the USA and at 3.8 per cent of GDP was superceded only by Australia among the larger industrialised countries. However, it is argued that the figures are subject to a wide margin of error. The balancing item for 1988 (see Table 15.1 on p. 210) of £13.9bn probably implies unrecorded invisibles perhaps of £5bn but the remainder most likely consists of unrecorded capital inflows.

Despite this the deterioration of the current account over since 1980 is obvious. The surplus up till the middle of the decade was due to surpluses on oil and invisibles. However, the fall in the price of oil in 1986 reduced the size of the oil surplus. The surplus on invisibles also peaked in 1986 and the decline since then has been due to an increase in the deficit on travel and civil aviation. Although not shown in Table 15.2, there has been an increase in interest and profit earned abroad relative to interest and profit paid abroad because, since the abolition of capital controls in 1979, there has been a considerable increase in investment abroad.

The fundamental problem of the UK balance of payments is a weak non-oil trading sector. Fig. 15.4 shows the changes that have occurred between 1980 and 1988 in the different product groups. Chemicals is the only product within the manufacturing sector where the UK has a surplus but even here the ratio of exports to imports is falling. Since earnings from manufacturing account for about 40 per cent of current earnings, see Table 15.1 on p. 210, the performance of the manufacturing sector is crucial.

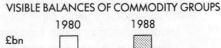

VISIBLE BALANCES OF COMMODITY GROUPS

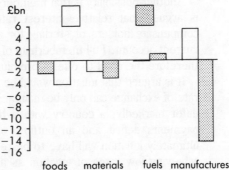

Fig. 15.4 *Source*: Lloyds Bank Economic Bulletin No. 127, July 1989

The deficit might not be a problem if it was caused by imports of capital goods which might be expected to raise productivity in the future. However, the deficit on capital goods in 1988 was only £1.2bn and imports in this category account for only 14 per cent of imports.

Another argument is that the deficit has acted as a safety valve during a period of rapid expansion of the domestic economy and prevented the excess of domestic demand over domestic output from generating inflation. However, despite the deficit, the effective exchange rate for sterling appreciated because of substantial capital inflows, and this kept down any increases in import prices at a time when domestic prices were rising.

Over the longer term the deficit will handicap the conduct of macroeconomic policy. Its effects will be to increase instability of exchange rates and/or interest rates. Higher interest rates are likely to cause a reduction in real investment and therefore in economic growth. As Fig. 15.5 shows this is more likely to happen because of the way the deficit has been financed, that is, mainly through bank lending. These inflows of hot money make the exchange rate vulnerable to changes in confidence and will make relatively high interest rates more likely.

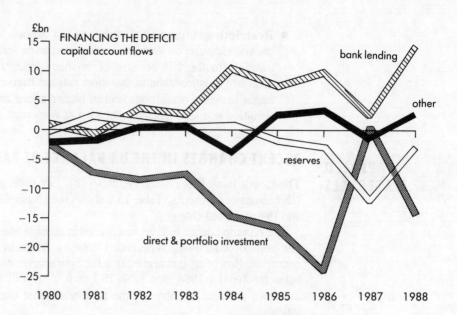

Fig. 15.5 *Source*: Lloyds Bank
Economic Bulletin No. 127, July
1989

One way of improving the balance of payments is by *expenditure switching* from foreign to domestic output by allowing sterling to depreciate. Statistical evidence suggests that a 1 per cent decline in competitiveness reduces exports by 0.25 per cent. However, with some sectors of the economy operating at near full capacity it might also be necessary to adopt some *expenditure reducing* policies.

UK MEMBERSHIP OF THE EMS

An article in the British Economy Survey Vol 19, No 1, Autumn 1989 briefly examines the case for UK membership of the EMS. One advantage is that joining the EMS would provide a means of achieving a more stable exchange rate. This would remove an element of uncertainty from international trade and would prevent sterling rising or falling rapidly in response to changes in the price of oil, for example. A rapid appreciation of sterling can handicap exporters and a rapid fall might be inflationary.

Another possibility is that membership of the EMS would permit lower interest rates. It is argued that relative interest rates in the UK are higher because of the need to compensate holders of sterling for accepting the risk of depreciation due to the weak current account. Full memberhsip of the EMS would remove the risk of depreciation and therefore the need to offer a premium would disappear.

It is argued that inflation would be lower if Britain participated fully in the EMS. A fixed rate of exchange can only be maintained if countries have similar rates of inflation. If these differ markedly, a country with a higher rate of inflation will experience a balance of payments deficit and an outflow of reserves. This cannot continue indefinitely and ultimately inflation will have to be reduced. Given the commitment of EMS members to achieving low rates of inflation as a full member Britain would be compelled to adopt policies which also achieve a low rate of inflation.

One reason Britain has not so far joined the EMS is that the government would not be able to vary interest rates or the money supply if these measures put pressure on the exchange rate. It would also be impossible for the government to use the exchange rate as an instrument of economic policy (see pp. 249–50). There is also the problem of ensuring that the sterling exchange rate was not overvalued in relation to other currencies in the system because this would handicap exporters.

EXAMINATION QUESTIONS

1 What factors determine the foreign exchange value of the pound sterling? Explain how, if at all, the level of domestic interest rates can lead to changes in the rate of exchange.

(JMB, 1989)

2 a) Distinguish with examples between current and capital transactions in the UK balance of payments account. (10)

   b) Outline and explain the major changes in the UK balance of payments current account in recent years. (15)

   (*Total 25 marks*)
   (Scottish, 1989)

3 'If unit costs rise faster at home than abroad the exchange rate will have to fall.'
   'A sudden outflow of capital will trigger depreciation.'
   'A large rise in the domestic money supply raises prices by inducing depreciation of the exchange rate.'
   Discuss these statements

   (Oxford, 1988)

4 'An efficient financial system, based upon either fixed or floating exchange rates, requires an adequate supply of liquidity and a mechanism for ensuring orderly balance of payments adjustments.' Discuss.

   (AEB, Nov 1986)

A TUTOR'S ANSWER TO QUESTION 1

The foreign exchange value of the pound sterling is the rate at which one unit of sterling exchanges for other currencies. In effect, it is the price of sterling in terms of another currency. For example, the exchange rate for sterling against the US dollar is the quantity of dollars than can be bought with one pound sterling. Despite the fact that the value of sterling can be expressed in terms of many currencies, the practice on the foreign exchange market is to quote the rate of exchange between sterling and the US dollar. The same convention is used throughout this essay.

In a free market, that is, one without government intervention, the rate of exchange for sterling will be determined by the supply of, and demand for, sterling. Demand for sterling is derived from foreign demand for UK goods and services, or because overseas residents intend investing in the UK. They supply foreign currency in exchange for sterling. The supply of sterling, on the other hand, is derived from demand by UK residents for imports of goods and services or to undertake investment overseas. UK residents supply sterling in exchange for foreign currency. With given supply and demand conditions the rate of exchange will gradually settle at its equilibrium level. The diagram below is a simplified illustration of the process.

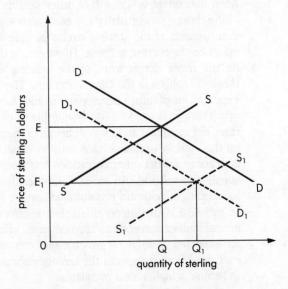

Fig. 15.6 Tutor's answer

Demand for sterling is represented by DD and supply of sterling is represented by SS. For simplicity it is assumed that demand for and supply of sterling are both elastic so that as the sterling exchange rate rises, there is an increase in the quantity of sterling supplied and a reduction in the quantity of sterling demanded. Given the supply and demand conditions illustrated, the rate of exchange will settle at E; no other exchange rate can exist in the long run.

To answer the question of what factors determine the foreign exchange value of the pound sterling it is therefore necessary to explain what determines the supply of, and demand for, sterling on the foreign exchange market. In fact the state of the current account is usually seen as a major determinant of the exchange rate in the long run. If all other things are equal, a current account surplus implies excess demand and appreciation for a country's currency and vice versa. However, the current account is important in another way. In particular, it indicates a country's ability to finance its overseas expenditures with overseas earnings. A current account surplus is therefore taken as a sign of economic strength and will attract investment from overseas residents seeking to place their funds in a strong currency. Countries with a strong current account therefore tend to have strong exchange rates, that is, their currency is likely to appreciate against (some) other currencies.

Whether a country's current account is in surplus or deficit depends on several factors. One of the most important is undoubtedly relative inflation rates. When the rate of inflation in one country is high relative to its trading competitors, other things equal, its exports will become less competitive on world markets and imports will become more competitive in the domestic economy. In terms of the diagram (Fig. 15.6) this implies a reduction in demand for sterling from DD to D_1D_1 (as overseas residents demand fewer exports) and an increase in supply of sterling from SS to S_1S_1 (as UK residents demand more imports). In other words the current account deteriorates and sterling depreciates on the foreign exchange market. The notion that relative inflation rates exert a powerful influence on the rate of exchange is embodied in the *purchasing power parity theory* which states that exchange rates will adjust until a unit of one currency exchanges for an amount of foreign currency which buys exactly the same basket of goods abroad that can be purchased in the domestic economy with a unit of currency. This can be expressed as $e = P/P^f$ where e is the exchange rate, P is the domestic price level and P^f is the foreign price level. However, strict purchasing power parity is unlikely to be observed because many goods are purchased domestically but are not traded internationally. Only the latter will affect the exchange rate. Nevertheless, there is little doubt that in the long run relative inflation rates are an extremely important determinant of exchange rates.

Another factor that influences the current account is comparative advantage. When technological change leads to the creation of different goods and services or changes the efficiency with which these can be produced by different countries, this can bring about changes in the state of the current account and result in some countries moving from surplus to deficit or deficit to surplus in certain key areas. The strength of Japan in producing motor cars and electronic equipment is a major reason for the strong current account surplus. For the UK, however, several sectors which were formerly strong in comparison with other countries have now declined in importance and this decline has not been fully offset by growth of other sectors.

Purchasing power parity and comparative advantage are undoubtedly the major long run determinants of the sterling exchange rate and they exert this influence because of their effect on the current account. However, in the short run the influence of other factors will be the major determinant of the sterling exchange rate and will exert their influence through changes in the capital account. The foreign exchange market responds quickly to expectations of future developments and short term funds, or 'hot money', can be invested or withdrawn in response to favourable or unfavourable expected changes in the exchange rate. For example, an *expected* change in the price of oil is likely to have an *immediate* effect on the sterling exchange rate with an expected reduction in oil prices causing sterling to depreciate against other currencies and vice versa. Again this can be explained in terms of supply and demand. An *expected* depreciation of sterling will cause a reduction in demand for sterling as potential investors will prefer to invest in other currencies. It will also cause an increase in the supply of sterling as investors withdraw their funds from the UK and invest in other currencies. The combined effect will cause sterling to depreciate. Similarly, an expected change of government can cause depreciation of sterling if the foreign exchange market expects the new government to adopt monetary and fiscal policies that will cause a higher rate of inflation.

However, the major factor causing short run changes in the sterling exchange rate is the *rate of interest* available on funds invested in the UK relative to rates available in other countries. An unanticipated *increase* in the rate of interest in the UK relative to that available in other countries will, if all other things are equal, cause an *appreciation* of sterling and vice versa. This is simply because, if all other things are equal, the increased return from investing in sterling will cause an inflow of funds (an increase in demand for sterling) and a reduced outflow of funds (a reduction in supply of sterling) as UK residents cut investment abroad.

The effect of an unanticipated *reduction* in the rate of interest on sterling can be illustrated in terms of the diagram above. Supply of, and demand for, sterling are initially represented by SS and DD respectively and the rate of exchange is E. If all other things remain equal, an unanticipated reduction in UK rates of exchange shifts the demand curve for sterling to D_1D_1 and the supply curve of sterling to S_1S_1 and as a result the sterling exchange rate *depreciates* to E_1.

However, as previously explained, the foreign exchange market responds rapidly to changes in *expectations*. Because of this, changes in the rate of interest might not have an *identifiable effect* on the rate of exchange. For example, if all other things are equal and the current account is expected to show a relatively large deficit, sterling would tend to depreciate in anticipation of the adverse figure being published. Because depreciation is *expected*, investors will attempt to withdraw their funds *before* depreciation thus avoiding the capital loss implied by depreciation. However, the government might not wish to see sterling depreciate and to avoid this might raise the rate of interest. In fact (to avoid any change in the exchange rate) interest rates will have to increase until the higher return from investing in the UK just exactly matches the expected capital loss from depreciation.

In the long run the main influence on the sterling exchange rate is the current account and this is determined mainly by the *rate of inflation* in the UK relative to inflation rates in competitors' countries. Changes in comparative advantage also have an effect in the long run. However, in the short run changes in the rate of interest are the main influence on the sterling exchange rate.

A STUDENT'S ANSWER TO QUESTION 2

Question 2

> a) Current account transactions deal with expenditures by domestic residents on goods and services (visible and invisible imports) and earnings from overseas expenditure on goods and services (visible and invisible exports). Visible trade for the UK consists mainly of manufactured goods and semi-manufactured goods though for some countries exports of primary goods are the main component of visible exports. Indeed, the UK is a large importer of raw materials. Invisible trade consists entirely of trade in services. Invisible exports from the UK include such items as transport services provided by the UK merchant fleet and commercial airlines as well as tourism. When foreigners come to the UK they acquire sterling to finance purchases while they are here. To obtain sterling they supply foreign currency and their expenditures in this country, therefore, represent the export of a service.
>
> The capital account deals with international investment and capital transactions that have taken place between the UK and overseas residents. This includes direct investment, which represents investment in factory buildings and equipment; and portfolio investment which represents investment in securities and consists mainly of purchases of equity.
>
> b) After a strong surplus on the current account in the 1980s the UK current account has now slipped back into very heavy deficit. One significant development has been a huge increase in the import of manufactured goods. One reason for this has

It is important to distinguish between autonomous and accommodating transactions

Why do consumers prefer imports, e.g. design, reliability after sale service, ... etc.? They are also often cheaper

> **Again, non-price competitiveness is a major factor**

> **The rest of the world do not require so many UK products – a fall in demand not in supply is the causal factor**

been that the government has significantly reduced income taxes and this has led to an increase in disposable income. As this has increased, expenditure on goods and services has increased. This has been referred to as the 'consumer boom' and the main effect of this has been that demand for domestic goods and services has outstripped supply of domestically produced goods and services. The difference has been made up by imports.

However, lower taxes and icreased consumer spending do not fully account for the deterioration in the current account. It is important to ask why the rest of the world have not increased their purchases of UK exports to the same extent as the UK has increased its purchases of imports. One very important reason for this is that inflation in the UK is rising again and is currently greater than that experienced by most of our competitors. A relatively high rate of inflation in the UK tends to make imports very competitive in the home market and exports less competitive in the world market.

An important reason for the reduction in UK exports is the process of deindustrialisation. The manufacturing sector of the UK economy is declining and therefore the economy is unable to produce the goods the rest of the world require. In addition, if the UK manufacturing sector was still strong, demand for imports of manufacturing output would be lower as UK residents purchased from domestic suppliers.

OUTLINE ANSWERS TO QUESTIONS 3 AND 4

Question 3

Each of these statements must be explained in detail. The first asks for a discussion of purchasing power parity (see p. 224) though you should also explain why purchasing power parity is unlikely to provide a complete explanation of short run exchange rates.

The second statement is also discussed on p. 224 in the 'Tutor's answer'.

The third statement requires a more wide-ranging discussion. An increase in the money supply might lead to an expected increase in the domestic rate of inflation and this might cause depreciation of the exchange rate. In other words the *chain of causation* is the opposite of that suggested in the statement. However, it is also true that in a country like the UK which depends on imports of basic materials and semi-finished manufactures, depreciation will lead to an increase in input prices and consequently an increase in final prices, that is, inflation.

Question 4

One way to begin your answer to this question is by briefly setting out the criteria for an efficient financial system. Basically the efficiency of any system depends on it providing:-

- a sufficient amount of world liquidity so as to facilitate the growth and expansion of world trade.
- a mechanism for dealing with balance of payments surpluses and deficits.
- confidence in the stability of the system.

You could then go on to describe the operation of a fixed exchange rate system stressing the importance of reserves to the authorities for intervention purposes. You should also outline the assets which make up a country's reserves (gold, reserve currencies and SDRs). When a country's reserves are relatively small, its scope for intervening in the foreign exchange market to maintain the external value of its currency is limited. In these circumstances even a short run balance of payments deficit will require swift and decisive action in the domestic economy (see pp. 220–21) which might have been averted if a greater stock of reserves had been held.

However, there is another problem. Under a fixed exchange rate system there is not necessarily a mechanism for ensuring orderly balance of payments adjustment. For those countries whose currency functions as a reserve currency, confidence in the system will only be maintained so long as its current account is not seen as foreshadowing devaluation. If this is not the case, speculators have a one-way option and might precipitate devaluation.

You could then go on to consider the determination of freely floating exchange rates stressing that, in theory at least, there is automatic adjustment through exchange rate changes, to balance of payments deficits and surpluses. However, in recent years exchange rates have shown some tendency to 'overshoot', that is, go on appreciating or depreciating in response to some external shock such as a change in oil prices, beyond the 'true' equilibrium rate. Once an exchange rate starts appreciating or depreciating it is possible to make speculative gains. Consequently large capital outflows or inflows will be encouraged and this can cause overshooting.

However, while the greater degree of flexibility in exchange rates implied by floating undoubtedly contributes to balance of payments adjustment it could be argued that the increased likelihood of exchange rate changes reduces confidence. This is clearly a relevant point, but care must be taken not to exaggerate its importance. After all, traders can insure themselves against the risks of exchange rate changes through the forward market.

Further reading

Begg, Fischer and Dornbush, *Economics* (2nd edn), McGraw-Hill 1987: Ch. 32, The International Monetary System and International Finance.
Griffiths and Wall, *Applied Economics: An Introductory Course* (3rd edn), Longman 1989: Ch. 22, Exchange Rates; Ch. 23, The United Kingdom Trade Performance.
Harrison, *International Trade and Finance*, Longman 1987: Ch. 4, The Foreign Exchange Market and Exchange Rate Systems; Ch. 5, The International Monetary System.
Stanlake, *Macroeconomics: An Introduction* (4th edn), Longman, 1989: Ch. 20, The Balance of Payments and the Rate of Exchange.

PUBLIC
FINANCE

GETTING STARTED

In the UK the main instrument of fiscal policy is the government's annual budget. Traditionally the budget contains a record of government revenue and expenditure for the year gone by, as well as the government's plans for raising revenue to meet planned expenditure during the coming year. The main reasons for public expenditure are discussed on pp. 241–2.

When planned expenditure exceeds planned revenue a budget deficit exists. This is important because it implies a net increase in injections into the circular flow of income. However, a budget is financed by borrowing, and, in recent year, more attention has been paid to the effect of increased government borrowing on the money supply. The National Debt is the total accumulated sum of all outstanding government debt.

Government revenue is raised mainly from taxation, and it is customary to distinguish between direct and indirect taxation. One distinction is that direct taxation is collected by the Department of Inland Revenue and indirect taxation is collected by the Customs and Excise Department.

One point to bear in mind when reading this chapter is that there is quite a lot of statistical information on government revenue and expenditure. This is deliberate. Familiarity with this type of information will often prove invaluable in coping with examination questions on this topic!

ESSENTIAL PRINCIPLES

THE BUDGET

The Budget is an occasion when the Chancellor presents an account of government expenditure and revenue for the ending financial year and presents his estimates of revenue for the coming financial year to Parliament. The estimates of expenditure for the coming financial year are presented to Parliament earlier in the year, usually in January.

Public money 1989–90			
			Pence in every £1
Where it comes from		Where it goes	
Income tax	23	Social security	26
National insurance contributions	16	Health	12
Value added tax	14	Defence	10
Local authority rates	10	Education and science	10
Road fuel, alcohol and tobacco duties	9	Home Office and legal departments	4
Corporation tax	11	Transport	3
Capital taxes	2	Scotland, Wales and Northern Ireland	9
Interest, dividends	3	Other departments	13
Petroleum revenue tax and oil royalties	1	Debt interest	9
Other expenditure taxes	6	Other	4
Other	5		
Total	100		100
	(£185bn)		(156.8bn)

Fig. 16.1 *Source*: Economic Progress Report 14 March 1989

Fig. 16.1 provides a summary of the proportion of revenue raised from the different sources and the proportion spent on different categories. Further information on expenditure is given in Figs. 16.6 and 16.7 on p. 241 and in Table 16.4 on p. 242.

However, the Budget is not simply a financial statement. It is the main instrument of economic policy and considerable significance is attached to whether the government has a budget surplus or deficit and the size of that surplus or deficit. When the government achieves a budget surplus its estimated revenue exceeds its estimated expenditure and this surplus can be used to redeem part of the National Debt. However, when the government has a budget deficit, its planned expenditure is greater than its estimated revenue and the difference must be made good by borrowing. Such borrowing becomes part of the Public Sector Borrowing Requirement (PSBR) and adds to the National Debt.

It used to be argued that the Chancellor should deliberately aim for a budget surplus or deficit as a means of varying injections and leakages into the circular flow of income so as to achieve certain economic objectives. In particular it was argued that if aggregate demand was insufficient to generate the full employment level of national income, the government should aim at a budget deficit so as to increase injections so raising income and employment. However, the effect of the budget on injections and leakages is no longer considered as important as its effect of the money supply. In particular when the government has a budget deficit, the way in which this is financed can have a profound impact on the growth of the money supply. This issue is considered fully on pp. 230–32.

THE REGULATOR

Although rates of direct taxation can only be changed in the annual budget with Parliamentary approval, the Chancellor has much more flexibility in varying the rates of certain indirect taxes. Specifically, export and import duties can be changed by up to 10 per cent of the *current* rate and VAT by up to 25 per cent of the current rate. The Chancellor can therefore change the *current rate* of VAT (15%) to a lower limit of 11.25 per cent, or to an upper limit of 18.75 per cent without parliamentary approval.

BORROWING REQUIREMENTS

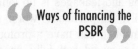

" The CGBR is different from the PSBR "

THE CENTRAL GOVERNMENT BORROWING REQUIREMENT

The main component of the CGBR is the overall *budget deficit*. However, the CGBR is not exactly equal to the government's budget deficit because it includes certain items of expenditure such as the National Insurance Fund which are not part of the budget. We shall later see that the size of the CGBR has an important bearing on the growth of the money supply because it is the largest component of the PSBR. This explains why the size of the budget deficit has acquired great significance in recent years.

THE PUBLIC SECTOR BORROWING REQUIREMENT

The PSBR is the total amount the public sector needs to borrow from the private sector and from overseas for the year ahead. It therefore consists of borrowing by the central government, by the local authorities and by the public corporations. However, care must be taken here because part of central government borrowing is on-lent to other institutions *within* the public sector. To the extent that the CGBR is on-lent in this way it reduces the amount the rest of the public sector needs to borrow from the private sector and from overseas. In other words, it has already been included in total public sector borrowing. Only that part of borrowing by local authorities and public corporations that has *not* been on-lent by the central government adds to the PSBR. The structure and financing of the PSBR for 1989–90 are summarised in Table 16.1.

Structure	(£ million)	Financing	(£ million)
Central government borrowing requirement*	−12848	Net borrowing from	−8332
less Central government lending to local authorities	4968	Financial institutions other than banks	1975
less Central government lending to public corporations	984	Industrial and financial companies	−1554
		Personal sector	−3348
Central government borrowing requrement (own account)	−6896	Sterling borrowing from banks	−3211
plus Local authority borrowing from other sources	4506	Sterling deposits with banks	299
plus Public corporations from other sources	2968	Foreign currency borrowing from banks	−62
		Foreign currency deposits with banks	−136
Public sector borrowing requirement	14370	Direct external finance	14370

* This mainly consists of the Budget deficit

Source: Financial Statistics HMSO

Table 16.1 The structure and financing of the PSBR

THE PSBR AND THE MONEY SUPPLY

" Ways of financing the PSBR "

The most publicised aspect of the PSBR is its effect on the money supply, and in particular its relationship with M3. In practice, the effect of an increase in the PSBR on the money supply is uncertain since its impact on M3 may be offset in whole or in part by a change in any of the other components which make up M3. Nevertheless, the authorities remain convinced that there is a central link, and it is possible to identify some of the ways in which the PSBR might lead to an increase in M3.

The extent to which the PSBR leads to an increase in M3 depends on the way in which the PSBR is financed. In fact, there are several methods of financing the PSBR:

- by borrowing from the non-bank private sector
- by borrowing from the banking system
- by borrowing from overseas or in foreign currency
- by issuing more cash (notes and coin) to the public

The effect of these different methods of financing the PSBR on M3 is considered in turn.

BORROWING FROM THE NON-BANK PRIVATE SECTOR

When the PSBR is financed by borrowing from the *non-bank private sector* there will be no direct effect on M3. The sale of debt to the non-bank private sector simply transfers bank deposits from the private sector to the public sector. When the government spends this money, deposits move back to the private sector and the money supply is unchanged.

BORROWING FROM THE BANKING SYSTEM

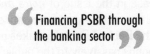
Financing PSBR through the banking sector

However, the same is not true when the PSBR is financed through the *banking sector*. When the banking sector buys public sector debt, their purchase will be paid for by a reduction in operational deposits at the Bank of England. At this stage there has been no change in the money supply. One asset has simply been substituted for another and the liabilities of the banking sector are unchanged. However, the government has *additional deposits* and when these are spent the funds will flow back into the banking sector. This will increase the assets and liabilities of the banking sector; and extra bank deposits are included in M3. Each additional deposit in government hands as a result of selling public sector debt to the banking sector represents an increase in the money supply. The direct effect of sales of public sector debt to the banking sector is therefore an equivalent increase in bank deposits and hence in M3.

The *direct* effect on M3 of the banking sector purchasing public sector debt is the same whether short-term debt or long-term debt is purchased. However, the *indirect* effects are likely to be very different.

Short-term debt

When the banking sector buys *short-term debt* such as Treasury Bills, their operational deposits at the Bank of England decrease, but there is no overall change in their liquidity position. They have simply substituted one liquid asset for another liquid asset. When the government spends its additional deposits and they flow back into the banking system, the money supply will increase in the way described above. However, the overall liquidity of the banking sector will have increased with the receipt of extra bank deposits, and the banks will increase their lending to the discount market (so as to meet legal requirements) and to private customers. The increased liquidity of the banking sector might therefore lead to a multiple expansion of bank lending. The extent to which this happens depends partly on the availability of willing borrowers and partly on acquiescence by the authorities. In other words, we are assuming that the authorities take no off-setting action to 'mop up' the excess liquidity. The ways in which this might be done are discussed in Chapter 12. If there is a multiple expansion of bank deposits, financing the PSBR by the sale of short-term debt to the banking sector might ultimately lead to a more than proportional increase in the money supply.

Long-term debt

The situation is different when the banking sector buys *long-term debt*. In this case, their operational deposits at the Bank of England decrease and their investments increase. In other words, they have exchanged a liquid asset (operational deposits) for an illiquid asset (investments). When the government spends the deposits it has borrowed and they flow back into the banking system the money supply will increase. However, to the extent that these deposits are lent to the discount market as money at call, there will simply be a restoration of the banking sector's original liquidity position. In other words, although the money supply increases via extra bank deposits, there will be no significant change in the overall liquidity position of the banking sector and no multiple expansion of the money supply.

Clearly, if the authorities aim to control the growth of the money supply, the issue of long-term securities is preferable to an increase of short-term securities. However, it is not always possible or desirable to sell long-term debt and in these circumstances the authorities are compelled to sell short-term debt. The reasons for this are discussed in Chapter 17.

BORROWING FROM OVERSEAS OR IN FOREIGN CURRENCY

When the government borrows from *overseas or in foreign currency* the receipts must be paid into the Exchange Equalisation Account at the Bank of England in exchange for an equal value of sterling. The sterling balance is then paid into the government's account at the Bank of England. When the government spends these deposits, cheques will be drawn against them, and when they are cleared operational deposits at the Bank of England will increase and M3 will have increased. However, if there is unsatisfied demand for loans and the government does not sell securities to the non-bank private sector so as to reduce operational deposits, there will also be a multiple increase in the money supply as bank lending increases.

BORROWING BY ISSUING MORE CASH TO THE PUBLIC

Finally, to the extent that the PSBR is financed by an increase in the issue of *notes and coin*, the money supply will increase. This is rather obvious since one of the components of M3 is notes and coin in circulation with the public. However, the Bank of England makes no attempt to control the issue of notes and coin and simply responds passively to the public's demand for cash. This has never been an important means of financing the PSBR, at least in recent years, so that issuing more notes and coin has had little impact on the growth of M3.

THE NATIONAL DEBT

The *national debt* is the total accumulated sum of all outstanding central government debt. Table 16.2 shows that in 1988, its value stood at £192,605m. It also shows the relative importance of different securities which make up the national debt.

31 March 1988	
Distribution	(£ million)
Market holdings	
Public corporations and local authorities	1152
Monetary sectory	9126
Other financial institutions	77900
Overseas holders	
International organisations	4514
Central banks	7343
Other	10240
Other holders	62926
Total market holdings	173201
Official holdings	19404
Total	192605
Composition	
Treasury bills	3691
Government stocks	144103
Non-marketable debt	44811
Total	192605

Table 16.2 The distribution and composition of the national debt

Source: Bank of England Quarterly Bulletin, November 1988, Vol 28, No 4.

In the UK most of the national debt is held by domestic residents. This is referred to as *internal debt*. That part of the national debt held by non-UK residents is referred to as *external debt*. Table 16.2 shows that at the end of March 1988 about 11 ½ per cent of total national debt was held externally.

THE BURDEN OF THE NATIONAL DEBT

It is sometimes alleged that the existence of the national debt imposes a burden on the community. This argument takes many forms, but the one most often quoted is that a burden is imposed via the community being taxed to meet interest payments on the debt. When any part of the debt is redeemed, this too must be met out of current tax receipts. The implication is that the overall level of taxation would be lower if the national debt did not exist.

In fact, the suggestion that a burden is transferred to the present generation from previous generations is largely groundless and does not stand up to close examination. The main issues are summarised below.

❝ Why the national debt may be less of a burden ❞

- When the government borrows it does so to increase its own expenditure above current tax yields. To borrow from its own residents implies that the rest of society is cutting back on consumption (i.e. saving) with the resources released being transferred to the public sector. In fact, as Table 16.2 shows, approximately 90 per cent of internal debt is in private hands (market holdings) so that increases in the national debt have largely implied a cut in private consumption. To the extent that society cuts its consumption, the burden of government borrowing falls on the generation alive at the time the borrowing takes place. It is then that consumption is cut in order to release resources for the public sector.

- Although interest payments on the national debt are met out of tax revenue this does not necessarily imply the existence of a burden. The generation which receives interest payments from holding the national debt is also the generation which pays taxes to meet those interest payments. To the extent that the national debt is held internally, there is simply a redistribution of income within the community. Taken as a *whole*, the community is neither better off nor worse off. The same argument applies when any part of internal debt is redeemed.

Nevertheless, there are three ways in which the national debt can impose some cost on the present generation:

Debt held externally

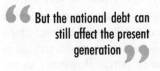

To the extent that national debt is held *externally*, it does impose a burden on present and future generations. When the government borrows abroad, the nation as a whole is able at that time to import more than it exports. In other words, borrowing from abroad makes it possible for domestic consumption to exceed domestic output. However, subsequent interest payments on the debt, together with its final redemption, give foreigners claims on domestic output which can only be met from exports. In this case domestic consumption will be less than domestic output. A burden has therefore been transferred to future generations who must cut their consumption because of debts incurred in the past. In this sense, external debt imposes a very real burden on future generations.

But the national debt can still affect the present generation

Administration costs

There are costs of *administering* the national debt which are paid out of current tax receipts. If the national debt did not exist these costs would not be incurred and instead of administering the debt resources could be put to other uses. However, the cost of administering the national debt amounts to less than £200m which is a small proportion of GNP (see Table 8.1, p. 103). Nevertheless this is the opportunity cost society bears.

Effects on initiative

The higher levels of taxation necessary to meet interest payments on the debt might have a disincentive effect on effort and initiative. If this is the case, it will reduce GDP below the level that would otherwise be attained. It will also adversely affect the rate of economic growth. The ways in which higher taxation might have a disincentive effect are discussed on pp. 237–8 but the empirical evidence on the existence of disincentive effects is controversial.

All that can be said with certainty is that external debt does impose a burden on the community. Nevertheless, it is important to keep the extent of this burden in perspective. Table 16.2 shows that only about 11½ per cent of the national debt is held externally. Furthermore, the real value of this, like the real value of all debt, is eroded by inflation. Because of inflation a smaller volume of output is given up when the debt is redeemed than is gained when it is incurred. Currently the sterling national debt has fallen to just over 30 per cent of GDP compared with a figure in excess of 100 per cent 30 years ago.

Finally, in assessing the extent of any burden it is necessary to consider the use to which borrowed funds have been put. If they have been put to some productive use, such as improving the infrastructure, then far from passing on a burden to future generations, the capacity for greater future output is created.

THE CANONS OF TAXATION

TAXATION

In 1776 Adam Smith set down four *canons* of taxation. These are still important today and provide a set of conditions against which any tax can be judged. The canons of taxation are:

- **Certainty** : the type and timing of taxes should be known with certainty to those paying them
- **Convenient** : a tax should be as convenient as possible for the tax payer
- **Economy** : a tax should be as cheap to collect as possible. In more modern jargon we might say a tax should be as *cost effective* as possible
- **Equity** : taxation should be as equitable as possible in the sense that there is equality of sacrifice

The canons of taxation

More recently another principle of taxation has been added. It is that a tax system should be consistent with the overall aims of economic policy. If it was not, the implementation of a tax could be counter-productive. An example of consistency between taxation and economic policy is the way the tax system acts as an *automatic stabiliser*. Specifically when demand in the economy is buoyant and taxes and income are rising, tax revenues rise *more than proportionately* as people are drawn into the tax net or the higher tax bracket and more goods on which VAT is levied are purchased. This *automatically* limits the effect of rising demand on inflation. When demand is falling the opposite occurs limiting the effect on unemployment. The benefit system also automatically stabilises the economy. When incomes are rising, the payment of social security benefits falls and vice versa.

THE STRUCTURE OF TAXATION

Taxation in the UK is usually classified as *direct* or *indirect*. Direct taxes are collected by the Department of Inland Revenue, and in the main are levied on incomes and transfers of capital. Indirect taxes, on the other hand, are collected by the Customs and Excise department. They are sometimes referred to as expenditure taxes since they are levied mainly on spending. However, the traditional distinction between direct and indirect taxes is that the incidence, or burden of a direct tax is borne by the person on whom the tax is levied. This burden cannot be transferred to another person or party. However, as we shall see, the burden of an indirect tax can often be passed on to a third party.

DIRECT TAXES

The main direct taxes levied in the UK are summarised below.

Personal income tax

For tax purposes in the UK both earned and unearned income are treated together. Tax is levied on gross income minus various allowances, such as the single person's allowance. After all deductions have been made, taxable income was subject to the following rates in 1989-90.

Rate %	Taxable income (£)
25	0 – 20,700
40	Over 20,700

One feature of income tax in the UK is that it is *progressive*. In other words, the *marginal rate of taxation is greater than the average rate*. However, care must be taken here because the higher rates of tax only apply to *increments* above the upper limit of each tax band. Therefore, for example, someone with a taxable income of £25,000 pays income tax at the rate of 25 per cent on the first £20,700 and 40 per cent on the remainder.

" Types of direct tax "

Corporation tax

This tax is levied on company profits, whether earned at home or abroad, after deducting allowances such as interest on loans. However, dividends to shareholders are *not* tax deductible, and corporation tax is levied on profits *before* any part is distributed to shareholders. The rates of corporation tax in 1989/90 stood at 25 per cent for firms with taxable profits under £150,000 and at 35 per cent for firms with taxable profits over £750,000. Intermediate rates operate between these two levels.

Petroleum revenue tax

This is levied at different rates on the net incomes from each field in the North Sea after deducting royalties and operating costs. In fact, there are three elements of North Sea oil and gas taxation. A *royalty* of 12½ per cent is levied on the value of the well-head deposits of oil and gas. *PRT* is then levied on company incomes, and finally, *corporation tax* is levied on company profits.

Capital gains tax

This tax is levied on the increase in the value of capital assets between the time of purchase and the time of sale. There are exemptions such as a person's main dwelling residence, life assurance policies, and so on. In addition, there is a non-taxable allowance, which stood at £5,000 in 1989–90. Only capital gains in any year above this basic allowance are subject to taxation though capital losses can be offset against any gains. The rate of capital gains tax depends on the rate at which income tax is paid. For those who pay income tax at the basic rate capital gains tax is levied at 25 per cent and for higher rate tax payers it is levied at 40 per cent.

Inheritance tax

This is a tax levied on transfers at time of death and is levied at the constant rate of 40 per cent on the excess of any transfers above £110,000. Inheritance tax is therefore a *proportional tax*.

INDIRECT TAXES

Indirect taxes can either be *specific* or *ad valorem*. Specific taxes have a fixed money value per unit, whereas *ad valorem* taxes are levied as a percentage of value. In this case, the amount paid in tax varies directly with the value of purchases subject to taxation.

The main indirect taxes levied in the UK are VAT and the excise duties on tobacco, oil and alcohol. These are summarised below.

Value added tax

"" Types of indirect tax ""

In terms of revenue raised, this is undoubtedly the most important of all indirect taxes in the UK and accounted for 14 per cent of the total tax yield in 1989/90. It is a proportional or *ad valorem* tax and is currently levied at the rate of 15 per cent. The mechanics of VAT are set out in Table 16.3.

VALUE ADDED (£)		PURCHASE PRICE TO SELLER EXCLUDING VAT (£)	PURCHASE PRICE INCLUDING VAT (£)	SELLING PRICE EXCLUDING VAT (£)	VAT LIABILITY (£)	VAT CREDIT (£)	VAT DUE (£)
100	Manufacturer imports raw materials	0	0	100	15	0	15
100	Manufacturer sells to wholesaler	100	115	200	30	15	15
50	Wholesaler sells to retailer	200	230	250	37.5	30	7.5
150	Retailer sells to customer	250	287.5	400	60	37.5	22.5

Cost to customer = £460 of which VAT = £60

Table 16.3

Basically, firms supplying products on which VAT is levied add VAT to the total value of their output, but deduct VAT already paid on inputs. In other words, tax is levied only on the *value added* at each stage of production.

Not all commodities are subject to VAT. Certain stages in the production of particular commodities are exempt from VAT, while others are zero-rated. Where an exemption applies, traders do not charge VAT on their own output, but are unable to claim back any VAT charged on their inputs as in the case of postage, rent, and insurance. Where commodities are zero-rated no VAT is levied and traders can claim back from the customs and excise department any VAT already paid on their inputs as in the case of exports, children's clothing and food (except meals eaten out).

Excise duties

These are levied on domestic and imported goods with the *aim* of *raising revenue*. As Table 16.5 on p. 242 shows, of all the excise duties, most revenue is raised from tobacco, oil and alcohol. In all three cases, excise duty is a large proportion of purchase price and the large sums raised from sales of these products is therefore an indication that demand for them is relatively inelastic. It is certainly true that in recent years increases in price caused by higher excise duty have had little *lasting* impact on consumption!

THE INCIDENCE OF TAXATION

Economists refer to the question of who actually bears the burden of taxation as the *tax incidence*. Despite this, it is not always easy to identify the person or organisation on whom the tax incidence usually falls. In some cases it is possible for those who make tax payments to the authorities to pass the burden of taxation onto others. This is especially true in the case of indirect taxation as Fig. 16.2 shows.

The imposition of a tax on sales equal to ac per unit shifts the supply curve for this commodity vertically upwards by the amount of tax, i.e. from SS to S_1S_1. Price rises from OP to OP_1. However, the price increase is less than the full amount of the tax, showing

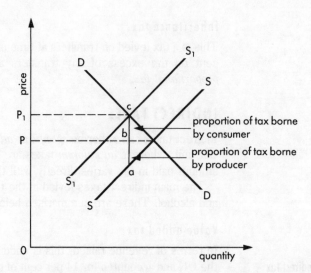

Fig. 16.2 The incidence of an indirect tax

that producers pass on only part of the burden of the tax. In this case consumers bear bc of the tax incidence, and producers bear ab.

For any given product, there is a distribution of the tax burden after the imposition of an indirect tax, i.e.

$$\frac{\text{consumers' share of tax burden}}{\text{producers' share of tax burden}} = \frac{\text{elasticity of supply}}{\text{elasticity of demand}}$$

So, if supply is more elastic than demand, the consumers' share of the tax burden will exceed the producers' share, and vice versa.

TAXATION POLICY

We can broadly identify three main reasons why governments levy taxes:

- to finance the provision of public goods and services
- to provide a powerful tool of economic management policy
- to redistribute income and wealth

The first of these has already been considered and the second and third are examined in Chapter 17. There is no doubt that taxation policy in the UK achieves all three aims. However, there is a great deal of controversy about whether present policy is the most *efficient* means of achieving these aims. The remainder of this section is devoted to a discussion of these areas of controversy.

For taxation to be economically efficient it should not lead individuals or companies to change their behaviour, except where such changes are the intended result of taxation. Since the majority of taxes are raised to provide the government with revenue, this implies that in general, taxes should extract money from the economy in as '*neutral*' a way as possible. In fact, there are several reasons why such neutrality might not be achieved.

TAXATION AND INCENTIVES

The way in which taxation affects incentives is probably the most controversial of all the issues surrounding the operation of tax policy. This is mainly because it is difficult to test any of the hypotheses in such a way that the results clearly indicate how taxation affects incentives. Nevertheless, several possibilities can be identified.

THE LAFFER CURVE

The Laffer Curve is illustrated in Fig. 16.3 and shows how tax revenue and tax rate are related.

If there is no taxation, that is, the tax rate is zero, tax revenue must also be zero. At the other extreme if the tax rate is 100 per cent, tax revenue will again be zero because all production except that required for subsistence will cease. The tax rate of 100 per cent totally removes the incentive to work. Between these two extremes, different rates of taxation have a different effect on production. The problem for the authorities is to set the tax rate at that level which maximises tax revenue and therefore minimises the

" A case for limiting tax rates "

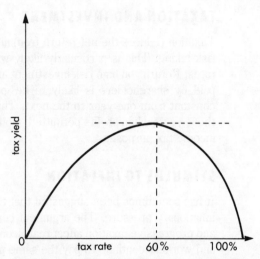

Fig. 16.3 The Laffer curve

disincentive effect. Some studies for the UK suggest that a *composite* tax rate, that is, including direct and indirect taxes as well as social security payments, of 60 per cent will maximise tax revenue. The composite tax rate in the UK is currently estimated at about 40 per cent, implying that *higher* taxes would have no disincentive effect. This is completely at odds with the government's belief, and that of most *supply side economists*, that lower taxes are necessary to increase incentives!

THE POVERTY TRAP

A potentially serious disincentive effect arises when individuals are caught in the *poverty trap*. The poverty trap does not, as it is often thought, denote the existence of poverty. Indeed, it is the result of efforts to relieve poverty by providing benefits. Basically, the poverty trap arises because benefits are withdrawn the higher up the income scale a family moves. With higher income, therefore, a family faces both a rising tax bill *and* the reduction or withdrawal of its social security benefits. In cases where people pay income tax at the rate of 25 per cent and national insurance contributions at the rate of 9 per cent, the marginal rate of tax is 34 per cent. However, when the rate at which benefits are withdrawn is added to this, the *effective* marginal rate of tax is much higher and in certain income ranges it can exceed 100 per cent!

THE UNEMPLOYMENT TRAP

The *unemployment trap* is similar to the poverty trap in that its existence is due to the availability of benefits. However, whereas the poverty trap affects those in employment, the unemployment trap affects those who are unemployed. In some cases the benefits available while unemployed are equal to or greater than the after-tax income that would be earned by accepting employment. When an unemployed person's disposable income falls by accepting employment, the effective marginal rate of tax on earnings is over 100 per cent. The effect of this is to create a serious disincentive for those who are currently unemployed to seek employment. Furthermore, the implication is that any attempt to price the unemployed into jobs by cutting wages actually worsens the unemployment trap. Indeed, one reason put forward for taxing unemployment benefit is to reduce the extent of the unemployment trap by lowering the *effective* rate of benefit.

> 66 **Know about unemployment and poverty traps** 99

TAXATION AND THE INCENTIVE TO WORK

It has been suggested that relatively high rates of income tax reduce the incentive to increase earnings through working overtime, accepting promotion, and so on. There is also a view that high rates of taxation encourage a certain amount of absenteeism by reducing the loss of earnings which results from being absent. However, the available evidence on these matters is inconclusive and it is just as possible that relatively high rates of taxation will provide an incentive to work. This would be the case where individuals aim at a *given level* of after-tax income, and need to work overtime, accept more responsibility, and so on, in order to achieve it.

TAXATION AND INVESTMENT

Taxation reduces the net return from investment and so might discourage enterprise and risk-taking. This is particularly likely when shareholders pay income tax at progressive rates. Returns on high risk investment are variable, and over any given period the total tax paid by shareholders is likely to be greater in this case than when returns are fairly constant from one year to the next. This would happen because higher dividends paid in those years when profits permitted, would push shareholders into higher taxable bands for income tax purposes.

STIMULUS TO INFLATION

It has sometimes been suggested that the nature of income tax in the UK might increase inflationary pressure. The argument centres on the way relatively high rates of inflation and progressive taxation affect real income. Where pay awards rise in line with retail prices and workers continue to pay the same proportion of their income in taxation, real income will be constant. However, if wage awards push earnings into higher taxable bands, the *proportion* of income paid in tax will rise and real income will fall. The higher average rate of tax which results from incomes rising in a progressive tax system is referred to as fiscal drag. If workers demand further pay rises in response to falling real incomes the process will repeat itself; prices will rise still further and real income will fall as earnings are pushed into still higher taxable bands. In other words, prices will rise faster than after-tax income.

Example

The following example illustrates the problem. Assume that the first £2,000 of earnings is untaxed. Thereafter the following rates of taxation apply.

TAXABLE EARNINGS (£)	TAX RATE
1–1000	30 per cent
1001–2000	40 per cent
2001–3000	50 per cent
Over 3000	60 per cent

If gross income rises from £5,000 in Year 1 to £7,000 in Year 2, we can see in Fig. 16.4, how the amount paid in taxes rises.

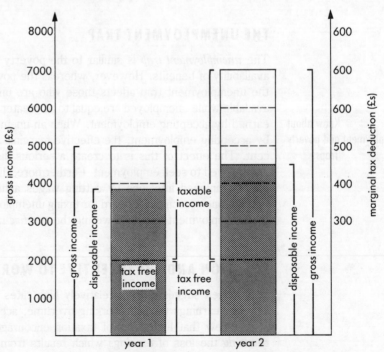

Fig. 16.4 Rise in taxes paid

Gross income increases by 40 percent (2,000/5,000), but disposable income, or net income, increases by only 21 percent (800/3,800). Suppose now that prices increase over the same period by 25 per cent. Disposable income at *constant prices* will fall from £3,800 in

Year 1 to £3,680 (i.e. £4,600 × 100/125) in Year 2. In other words, *real income* will fall by over 3 per cent despite a rise in *gross income* of 40 per cent. (Non-taxable allowances and taxable bands are usually increased in the budget partly to avoid this effect, but where they are not adjusted in line with inflation some groups will experience a fall in real income.)

Fiscal drag

This process whereby individuals are forced into higher tax bands because of rising income is referred to as *fiscal drag*. Governments have sometimes been accused of using fiscal drag as a means of financing their expenditures. If higher expenditures generate inflation they can be financed without increasing the rates of taxation because inflation will draw people into higher tax brackets and therefore increase government revenue from taxation.

REFORM OF THE TAX SYSTEM

A NEGATIVE INCOME TAX

This proposal is sometimes referred to as a reverse income tax and aims to reduce the effect of the poverty and unemployment traps on the financial incentive to work.

Ways of reforming the tax system

Minimum income guarantee

There are many variations of the basic idea. One involves the establishment of a minimum income guarantee (the poverty line) which is fixed in cash terms according to the circumstances (number of dependents, etc.) of each particular family. The cash benefit, that is the minimum income guarantee, would be paid in full to those without any other form of income. It would therefore replace the present social security system. Thereafter tax would be levied on the whole of a person's earned income.

Example

The *operation of this system* is explained using Fig. 16.5. We assume that the minimum income guarantee is £4,000 and that earned income is taxed (via loss of cash benefit) at the constant rate of 50 per cent.

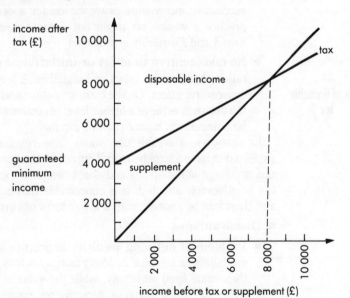

Fig. 16.5 Minimum income guarantee

When the family has no other income, it receives the full minimum income guarantee of £4,000. For each additional £1,000 earned, the rate of cash benefit falls by £500. This is equivalent to a marginal rate of tax of 50 per cent. The break-even point is £8,000. When family income reaches this level no cash benefit is received and no income tax is paid. For incomes above this level a positive rate of tax applies.

Tax credits

A slightly different proposal involving the establishment of tax credits has received most official support in the UK. Under this system tax credits would replace non-taxable allowances and all tax payers would be given a tax credit irrespective of income. All income would then be assessed for tax without exempting any initial amount. If the tax credit exceeds the tax payable, the difference will be paid out of cash support; if the tax liability exceeds the tax credit, the difference is due in tax payment.

Example

This system of taxation is easy to operate and therefore cheap to administer. For example, if the tax rate is 25 per cent, then an individual with a *tax credit* of £40 per week and no other source of income would receive £40 per week in state benefit. If this person now accepted employment at a *wage* of £40 per week, their tax liability would be (0.25) £40 = £10 per week. This person would therefore receive £30 per week in state benefit (i.e. the tax credit minus the tax liability) giving a total weekly income of £70. At a wage of £160 per week this person would receive no state benefit nor pay any tax since their tax credit exactly equals their tax liability. Positive income tax would only be paid when wages exceed £160 per week.

CHANGING THE TAX BASE

There are three tax bases: wealth, income and expenditure. However, there are practical problems associated with the taxation of wealth and in recent years emphasis on tax reform has concentrated on shifting the tax base away from income and on to expenditure. In other words, it has been suggested that less revenue should be raised from taxing incomes and more from taxing expenditures.

The advantages and disadvantages of direct and indirect taxes are considered in the outline answer to question 1. The advantages and disadvantages of a wealth tax are summarised below.

Wealth tax

- **Advantages**

  - **Equity considerations**: there is no doubt that the possession of wealth adds to a person's standard of living. For example, income in the form of rent or interest, is often earned on accumulations of wealth. An egalitarian principle is that those who have more should pay more. On equity grounds economic theory supports the imposition of a wealth tax because the law of diminishing marginal utility implies that successive increments of wealth confer a declining amount of utility. However, in practice a wealth tax might not operate equitably (see below *Problem of defining wealth* and *Possibility of evasion.*)

  - **No disincentive to effort or initiative**: it is argued that wealth depends on *past*, rather than *present*, effort and initiative. A wealth tax is therefore unlikely to have a disincentive effect. On the contrary, effort and initiative might even be encouraged by the desire to achieve a higher level of consumption, which, if wealth is taxed, can only be obtained via higher current income.

> **"Impacts of a wealth tax"**

In *summary*, a wealth tax would raise revenue for the government but might be expected to have a largely neutral impact on the economy as regards incentives. However, this argument is not strong and doubt has been expressed that effort and initiative would not be adversely affected. It is conceivable that individuals might accumulate less wealth and therefore be content with a lower level of current income if wealth were taxed.

- **Disadvantages**

  - **Problem of defining wealth** : in practice it is difficult to define wealth and even more difficult to value it. Many assets such as jewellery and works of art would have their value fixed arbitrarily, while the value of other forms of wealth such as pension rights or future earnings depends on assumptions about future inflation, interest rates, survival prospects, and so on.

  - **Possibility of evasion** : there is also likely to be widespread evasion since wealth owners would have a powerful incentive to conceal their holdings of taxable assets. It would therefore not only be difficult to define wealth, it would be virtually impossible to measure it accurately. This would make the tax inequitable in its operation since the wealth of some individuals is more readily identified and assessed than that of others. For example, it is difficult to value shares in joint stock companies and, as recent experience has shown, even the value of property can fluctuate. Other forms of wealth such as the possession of antiques and art treasures are difficult to identify and, in the absence of selling them, impossible to value.

  - **Problem of payment** : other problems would arise in paying the tax. If wealth owners were forced to sell off part of their assets to meet their tax liability this might depress asset prices. There would then be problems of reassessment, with assets failing to realise the value ascribed to them for tax purposes. There might also be a general reluctance from people to purchase assets whose price is likely to fall because of market sales and on which future tax would be levied.

- **Cost** : a final argument against a wealth tax is that it would be difficult to administer and expensive to collect.

LOCAL TAXATION

Formerly local taxation was through a system of rates which were a tax on property values. This system is soon to be replaced by a *community charge* or *poll tax*. The reasons for the change and assessment of the change is given in the outline answer to Question 2.

Poll tax

The poll tax will only be levied on the occupants of a household who are eighteen or over although there are some exceptions. The poll tax is clearly going to operate regressively but the government has taken the view that progressive taxation would be an inappropriate way to levy local taxation because it would give individuals an incentive to move to areas levying the lowest rate of tax which might add to the housing shortage in certain areas.

APPLIED MATERIALS

GOVERNMENT EXPENDITURE PLAN

Every year, usually in January, the government publishes its expenditure plan for the coming years. Fig. 16.6 shows the latest estimates of central government expenditure in cash terms and real terms and provides some interesting historical information. Fig. 16.7 shows central government expenditure as a percentage of GDP for the same period. Table 16.4 shows how public expenditure on different economic activities has changed in recent years.

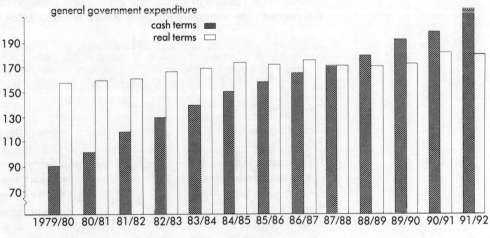

Fig. 16.6 Planned central government expenditure in real and money terms

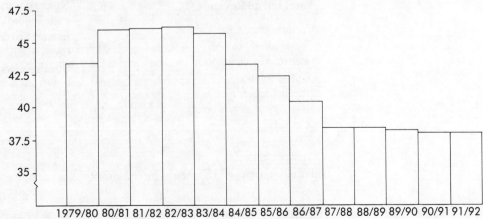

Fig. 16.7 Central government expenditure as a percentage of GDP

Despite the fact that central government expenditure is expected to rise in real terms, it is expected to fall still further as a percentage of GDP from its peak of 46.5 per cent in 1982/83. The government has failed to achieve its objective in the earlier part of the decade

£ million	1979–80	1984–85	1989–90	1991–92
Defence	9,226	17,201	19,200	22,100
Overseas aid	802	1,091	1,355	1,540
Other overseas services	1,305	1,684	1,815	2,580
Agriculture, fisheries, food and forestry	1,038	2,412	2,337	2,810
Trade, industry, energy and employment	2,892	8,976	6,852	6,690
Education and science	9,350	16,981	22,483	25,270
Arts and libraries		818	1,136	1,240
Transport	2,972	5,547	5,931	6,970
Housing	4,699	4,396	3,236	3,500
Other environmental services	2,873	4,950	5,690	6,080
Law, order and protective services	2,586	6,090	8,606	10,190
Health and personal social services	8,899	19,615	26,940	30,230
Social security	19,400	39,299	49,141	60,500
Miscellaneous	1,982	2,971	4,343	5,100

Table 16.4   *Source:* Economic Progress Report, No 143, March 1982, Public Expenditure Plans 1989–90 to 1991–1992, HMSO

of holding its own expenditure constant in real terms, but it has certainly achieved a reduction in the claim of central government on resources!

Every year, usually in March, the government publishes its estimates of tax revenue in the Budget. The estimates for 1989–90 are given in Table 16.5.

£ billion			
1989–90 BUDGET FORECAST			1989–90 FORECAST
RECEIPTS			
Inland Revenue:		Vehicle excise duties	2.9
Income tax	46.9	Oil royalties	0.6
Corporation tax[3]	22.4	Gas levy	0.4
Petroleum revenue tax	1.4	Local authority rates[4]	20.6
Capital gains tax	2.1	Other taxes and royalties	3.3
Inheritance tax	1.1	**Total taxes and royalties**	**156.9**
Stamp duties	2.4		
Total Inland Revenue	**76.3**	National insurance and other contributions	34.0
Customs and Excise		Interest and dividends	7.0
Value added tax	30.0	Gross trading surpluses and rent	3.3
Petrol, derv duties etc.	8.8	Other receipts	5.2
Tobacco duties	5.1		
Alcohol duties	4.7		
Betting and gaming duties	1.0		
Car tax	1.4		
Customs duties	1.8		
Agricultural levies	0.1		
Total Customs and Excise	**52.9**		
General government receipts			**206.4**

Table 16.5   *Source:* Financial Statement and Budget Report, HMSO 1989–90

THE BURDEN OF TAXATION

Another aim of the government has been to reduce the burden of taxation. The Lloyds Bank Economic Bulletin of April 1989, No 124, is entitled *The Burden of Taxation*. Table 16.6 provides some comparative information on tax burdens in different countries and Table 16.7 shows how the burden of taxation in the UK has changed in the decade to 1988/89. Not only is the burden of taxation relatively high, it has also increased since 1979/80.

| | Changes, 1978/79–1988/89, per cent | | | | | | | | |
| | Tax as % of tax base | | | Tax base as % of gdp | | | Tax as % of gdp | | |
	1978/79	1988/89	% change	1978/79	1988/89	% change	1978/79	1988/89	% change
Income taxes	16.5	14.3	−13	65.5	64.8	−1	10.8	9.3	−14
NIC + surcharge	10.5	11.2	+7	67.3	61.9	−8	7.0	6.9	−1
Corporation taxes	13.3	17.9	+34	16.9	21.8	+28	2.3	3.9	+71
VAT	4.6	9.3	+100	59.7	62.5	+5	2.8	5.8	+110
Excise duties, etc.	52.2	57.0	+9	11.6	11.2	−1	3.3	4.0	+21
Total taxes	33.1	37.6	+14	100.0	100.0	0	33.1	37.6	+14

Table 16.6 Selected taxes: rise in burden

Notes: (Tax as % of tax base) × (Tax base as % of gdp) = (Tax as % of gdp).
For definition of tax bases, see chart B. Taxes omitted: capital taxes, oil and gas taxes.

Source: Lloyds Bank Economic Bulletin No 124 April 1989

	(At market prices)	Excluding[2] North Sea		(At market prices)	Excluding[2] North Sea	
1978/79	33.1	34¼	Treasury projections			1 Including national insurance contributions.
1979/80	33.8	35	1989/90	37.5	37½	
1980/81	35.7	36¼	1990/91	36.9	36¾[3]	2 North Sea oil income is excluded from gdp, and North Sea taxes from tax revenue. Thus if the average North Sea tax rate is equal to the total UK tax burden, the figures in the two columns are the same.
1981/82	38.5	38¾	1991/92	36.6	36[3]	
1982/83	38.5	38¼	1992/93	36.1	35¼[3]	
1983/84	38.0	37¾				
1984/85	38.8	37¾				
1985/86	38.0	37¼				3 After 'fiscal adjustment'
1986/87	37.7	37¾				*Source:* Financial Statistics, Financial Statements and Budget Report, 1989/90.
1987/88	37.7	37¾				
1988/89	37.6	37½				

Table 16.7 UK tax burden[1] as % of GDP

Source: Lloyds Bank Economic Bulletin No 124, April 1989

ANALYSIS OF TAX REVENUE, %

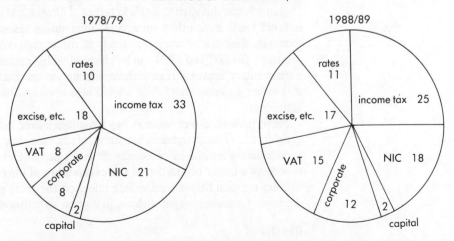

Fig. 16.8 *Source:* Lloyds Bank Economic Bulletin No. 124, April 1989

Alternative analysis of 1988/89: Personal 38%, corporate 19%, expenditure 43%
Note: North Sea included in corporate taxes. Miscellaneous taxes included in excise etc.
Source: *Financial Statistics, Financial Statement and Budget Report* 1989/90

Fig. 16.8 shows how the burden of certain taxes has changed. The largest reduction is in the burden of income tax and the largest increase is in the burden of VAT. This is quite significant in terms of the government's aim of reducing the burden of income tax relative to VAT. Note also that national insurance contributions are levied on earned income and might therefore add to any disincentive effect from income tax.

EXAMINATION QUESTIONS

1 Using economic analysis and relevant examples, discuss the relative merits and demerits of direct and indirect taxes.

(London, June 1988)

2 Assess the case for the introduction of an annual community charge or poll tax upon adult residents as a means of financing local authority expenditure.

(AEB, Nov 1987)

OUTLINE ANSWERS TO QUESTIONS 1 AND 2

Question 1

You could begin your answer to this question by defining *direct* and *indirect taxes*. In general, direct taxes are levied on the incomes of individuals and firms and on transfers of wealth. Indirect taxes, on the other hand, are levied on specific goods and services and must be paid by the consumer or producer of these goods or services.

You could then go on to discuss the relative merits and demerits of direct and indirect taxation. It is frequently alleged that the relatively high rates of personal income tax in the UK have a powerful disincentive effect on effort and initiative. You could discuss the poverty and unemployment traps, lower mobility of labour, the possibility that risk-taking and investment will be discouraged, and so on. Using income and substitution effects you can demonstrate that sometimes when an individual is offered higher wages they will work fewer hours! Taxing profits through corporation tax might reduce the finance available to firms for investment in R&D as well as additional capacity both of which can affect the future growth of output as well as the quality and competitiveness of UK products. These are major reasons for the government's reduction in corporation tax (in stages) from 52 per cent when it first took office to 32 per cent (25 per cent for smaller companies).

It is usually argued that an increase in indirect taxes such as VAT would have fewer disincentive effects than an increase in direct taxation (this is one of the main arguments for shifting the burden of taxation away from direct taxes in favour of indirect taxes). However, this is by no means certain. For example, the higher prices implied by higher indirect taxes will reduce income and make leisure cheaper in terms of goods foregone. (Again you can demonstrate this in terms of income and substitution effects.) Despite this, indirect taxes have other advantages over direct taxes which should be discussed. For example, they can be used selectively to discourage consumption of demerit goods; they are more flexible, and rates can be changed within certain limits by the Chancellor without parliamentary approval (i.e. without waiting for the Budget); they are cheaper to collect and easier to understand. You should also mention that they *both* function as automatic stabilisers.

Nevertheless, direct taxation has advantages over indirect taxation which must also be considered. The progressive nature of income tax makes it particularly useful in redistributing income more equally (indirect taxes tend to act regressively because they represent a larger proportion of the expenditure of lower income groups); higher rates of indirect taxation have an immediate effect on the retail price index, and this might lead to demands for higher wages and set in motion an inflationary spiral.

Question 2

The annual community charge is a tax to be levied on persons over the age of 18. There are some exceptions, for example, members of a religious order such as monks, but the majority of people 18 and over will be liable for the tax.

One reason for the introduction of the poll tax was dissatisfaction with the rating system. *Rates* were basically a tax which was related to the value of the property. Because they were not related to current income they were criticised as acting regressively. (The type of property people occupy frequently reflects their *past* income rather than *current* income especially for many retired people.) They also varied widely between different rating authorities.

The poll tax widens the tax base and is more equitable in the sense that those who benefit from local expenditure now pay for it. Rates tended to be paid by house-owners rather than all adult occupants of a dwelling. It was estimated that only one third of the electorate paid rates in full! Moreover the business community will henceforth pay a single uniform tax set nationally. This implies that high spending municipal authorities will have to levy from its electors a higher rate of poll tax and in this way local authorities might become more accountable to local electors.

However, the poll tax is not related to income and is probably even more regressive than the local rates which it replaced. The cost of collecting the poll tax is relatively high and there is likely to be widespread evasion. (The rates were cheap to collect and difficult to evade!) In addition by levying taxes per person rather than per dwelling, the poll tax is likely to encourage low density occupation and discourage the sharing of large homes with other people. This could add to the shortage of accommodation in some areas, particularly the south-east, and reduce mobility of labour. Removing a tax on property and replacing the rates with a poll tax is likely to contribute to raising house prices and again this could reduce mobility of labour.

Further reading

Begg, Dornbusch and Fischer, *Economics*, (2nd edn) McGraw-Hill 1987: Ch.15, Taxes and public spending: the government and resource allocation.
Griffiths and Wall (eds), *Applied Economics: An Introductory Course* (3rd edn), Longman 1989: Ch. 13, Public expenditure, Ch. 14, Taxation.
Stanlake, *Introductory Economics*, (5th edn) Longman 1989: Ch. 30 Income and expenditure of public authorities.

CHAPTER

17

MANAGING THE ECONOMY

THE AIMS OF ECONOMIC POLICY

INTERDEPENDENCE OF AIMS

INSTRUMENTS OF POLICY

THE MEDIUM—TERM FINANCIAL STRATEGY (MTFS)

CURRENT MACROECONOMIC POLICY

PRIVATISATION

DEREGULATION

APPLIED MATERIALS

GETTING STARTED

In 1944 the government published a White Paper on Employment Policy which stated that: 'The Government believe that, once the war has been won, we can make a fresh approach, with better chances of success than ever before, to the task of maintaining a high and stable level of employment without sacrificing the essential liberties of a free society.' Since then there has been a change in the approach to achieving this objective, but there is no doubt that it remains an important *long-term* goal of all political parties. However, governments have other objectives which at times have taken precedence over employment levels as the main *short-term* goal. In recent years considerable importance has been attached to reducing the annual rate of inflation. At other times the balance of payments deficit has been the most pressing problem, and so on.

The overall aims of economic policy have not changed, but the means of achieving these aims has. For most of the post-war period, governments pursued their aims by managing the level of aggregate monetary demand. Such an approach is essentially Keynesian, since it implies manipulating the level of aggregate demand (that is, C + I + G + X − M) so as to influence nominal income (Y). This approach is usually referred to as *demand management*.

More recently, and certainly since the late 1970s, the emphasis has changed from managing aggregate demand to what has come to be termed '*supply-side economics*'. At its simplest, supply-side economics is the use of microeconomic incentives to achieve macroeconomic goals. Supply-side economics thus reflects the view that the macroeconomic system can only operate efficiently if each microeconomic market (the labour market, the capital market and so on) operates efficiently. The emphasis of macroeconomic policy has therefore shifted away from simply managing the overall level of aggregate demand, to the pursuit of policies which enable each microeconomic market to operate efficiently.

ESSENTIAL PRINCIPLES

THE AIMS OF
ECONOMIC
POLICY

The economic aims of the government can be briefly stated as the maintenance of full employment, a relatively low and stable rate of inflation, equilibrium in the balance of payments and economic growth. Each is considered in turn.

FULL EMPLOYMENT

We have already seen that all governments are concerned with employment levels, but the 1944 White Paper was careful to make no specific mention of how full employment was to be defined. Similarly, governments express their concern to bring unemployment levels down, but have chosen not to define full employment. In fact, the concept of full employment is difficult to define because the minimum level of unemployment that can be achieved at any particular time is constantly subject to change and cannot be zero because as the demand for various goods and services changes, so does the demand for the labour which produces them (see Chapter 10). The level of employment that can then be achieved will depend on the distribution of that demand between different goods and services and on the mobility of labour. The more that demand is concentrated on labour intensive goods and services and the more mobile the population, the lower the level of unemployment that can be achieved. The government's aim in this area is therefore to achieve some level of employment which is considers acceptable. We shall later see that because its aims are not independent of one another, what is considered to be an acceptable level of unemployment is to a certain extent dictated by the priority governments give to achieving their other economic aims.

Natural rate unemployment

A different definition of full employment is the level which exists when unemployment is at the natural rate. However, the natural rate of unemployment is extremely difficult to estimate and any estimates that are produced would be subject to a wide margin of error. A further complication is that the natural rate is not constant from one period to the next but will change as those factors which determine it change. (See Chapter 13).

> **Governments try to achieve several objectives at the same time**

PRICE STABILITY

This is another important objective of governments, although price stability does not imply a commitment to zero inflation. Changing supply and demand conditions for various products will lead to price changes in the various product markets; this is, of course, an inevitable feature of any economy where the price mechanism operates. Additionally, although academic opinion is divided, there is considerable support for maintaining a moderate rate of inflation rather than aiming to eliminate it altogether. A moderate rate of inflation, it is argued, will provide a spur to investment because it will give producers 'windfall' profits. However, while there is majority support for maintaining a moderate rate of inflation there is certainly no agreement about what constitutes such a rate, although 1.5–2 per cent has been suggested. Again, all that can be said is that it is for the government to decide what rate is acceptable, given the constraints imposed by its other aims. We should note that when the government is aiming to reduce the rate of inflation, its choice of policy will at least be partly determined by whether inflation is due to excess demand (demand-pull inflation) or to rising costs (cost-push inflation).

EQUILIBRIUM IN THE BALANCE OF PAYMENTS

This is not a concept that can be easily defined. However, since all imports must ultimately be paid for by exports, one definition is that the flow of *autonomous debits be equalled by the flow of autonomous credits*. At any moment in time, a country might have a surplus or deficit in its balance of payments so that autonomous debits and credits will not necessarily be equal. The concept of equilibrium must therefore be related to some time period over which a balance should be achieved.

There is a further problem, in that a balance between debits and credits will also depend on the exchange rate system which operates. When exchange rates *float*, balance between autonomous transactions is guaranteed; at least it is under certain circumstances such as a 'pure' float. But when exchange rates are *fixed*, autonomous transactions must either be encouraged or discouraged if balance is to be achieved. We have seen that attempts to manage the exchange rate have serious implications for policy in the domestic economy. Balance of payments equilibrium might therefore be said to exist when, over a given period of time, autonomous transactions cancel out in such a way that does *not impede* the government's efforts to achieve its other policy aims.

ECONOMIC GROWTH

Another important aim of governments is to manage the economy in such a way that economic growth will be fostered. There are many definitions of economic growth. It is sometimes taken to mean the growth of capacity of productive potential for the economy as a whole because in the long run this is the only way of increasing the size of real GDP. This definition implies an outward movement of the economy's production possibility curve. However, the usual definition of economic growth is an increase in real GNP.

Policy objective

Economic growth has been given high priority as a policy objective, because if the growth of output exceeds the growth of population, per capita income will rise; i.e. the standard of living will rise. In the longer term, the compound effect on output of a constant rate of growth is impressive. For example, if output grows every year by 2 per cent, GDP will double in approximately 36 years; but if the growth of output can be increased to 3 per cent each year, output will double in approximately 24 years!

INTERDEPENDENCE OF AIMS

" Conflicts can occur "

The use of demand management to achieve these economic aims led to a major policy dilemma for successive governments. The problem was that it proved impossible to achieve all aims simultaneously, so that governments faced a conflict of policy objectives. We have already seen in Chapter 13 that the use of high levels of aggregate demand to achieve full employment often conflicted with price stability. However, it also conflicted with the balance of payments objective. As demand in the economy increased and incomes rose, so the demand for imports also rose. This was partly to be expected because of the high marginal propensity to import in the UK. However, the adverse impact of increased demand on the balance of payments was reinforced by higher domestic prices which made imports more competitive in the domestic market and exports less competitive in foreign markets. There is no doubt that increased home demand also resulted in goods initially produced for export being diverted to the domestic economy, where demand and prices were rising and where transport costs to market were lower. As a result, the level of unemployment a government could achieve was determined in part by the rate of inflation it was prepared to accept, and in part by its need to achieve balance of payments equilibrium. At times full employment was the major aim, while at others it was sacrificed to the more pressing problems of containing inflation and restoring equilibrium to the balance of payments.

The stop-go guide

This switch of policy objectives became known as the *stop-go cycle*. The stop phase of the cycle occurred when aggregate demand was reduced to combat inflation and/or the balance of payments deficit. As the economy slowed down and unemployment developed, these particular problems seemed to disappear; the government would then embark on the go phase of the cycle, expanding aggregate demand to bring unemployment down. As unemployment fell, the problems of inflation and the balance of payments deficit would re-emerge, and the cycle would be repeated. It has been argued that the stop-go cycle can be explained as the consequence of governments trying to reduce the level of unemployment below the natural rate. Each injection of demand temporarily reduced unemployment, but ultimately resulted in a higher rate of inflation and no permanent reduction in unemployment as the economy returned to the natural rate.

During the 1960s and 1970s, in an attempt to break out of this cycle, governments ceased to rely solely on managing the level of aggregate demand to achieve their aims, and began to make greater use of incomes policy and exchange rate adjustment as policy instruments. It was not until 1979, with the election of Mrs Thatcher as Prime Minister, that there was any radical change in the conduct of policy. These changes and the conduct of current macroeconomic policy are discussed further below.

Demand management also led to another problem. Successive governments believed that economic growth could be encouraged by greater investment and that this was more likely to be forthcoming when aggregate demand was rising. The reason for this was simple: rising demand would create a growing market in which the additional output that resulted from increased investment could be sold. However, the management of demand to encourage growth was rarely, if ever, the major policy objective of the authorities; more often price stability and balance of payments equilibrium took precedence over other aims. It is possible that the variable and unpredictable nature of aggregate demand discouraged the private sector from investing because it increased uncertainty.

<table>
<tr><td>

INSTRUMENTS OF POLICY

</td></tr>
</table>

FISCAL POLICY

This consists of variations in government income and expenditure. The main fiscal stance of the authorities is implied in the annual budget when the government outlines its income and expenditure plans for the coming financial year. However, in recent years it has become standard practice for chancellors to present an 'autumn statement' which might include changes in the rates of indirect taxation.

For most of the post-war period fiscal policy was the instrument used to bring about major changes in aggregate demand. Until the mid/late 1970s comparatively little attention was paid to the size of the PSBR. Indeed, the size of the PSBR was regarded as a *consequence* of fiscal policy and not a *target* in itself. In other words, the government set its expenditure and taxation levels to achieve that particular level of GDP which it considered consistent with its various economic objectives. It therefore regarded its own budget deficit as simply a residual which had to be financed in order to achieve that level of GDP.

MONETARY POLICY

> Governments can use various policy instruments

This consists of policies designed to influence the supply of money and/or its 'price', i.e. *the rate of interest*. As an instrument of demand management, monetary policy was regarded as subordinate to fiscal policy (until the mid/late 1970s). Whereas fiscal policy could bring about major changes in aggregate demand, the potency of monetary policy was questioned and it was relegated to the role of 'fine-tuning' the economy. In other words, its role was to bring about minor changes in aggregate demand which could not be achieved with fiscal policy. For example, the view was taken that when the economy approached the target level of output it might be necessary to adjust aggregate demand slightly upwards to achieve the employment target, or downwards to avoid any excess pressure which might generate inflation. Fiscal policy was considered unsuitable for such fine-tuning, because it produced major changes in aggregate demand and it also takes longer to exert its full effect; on the other hand, monetary policy was considered capable of achieving the minor adjustments required.

Since the mid-1970s, and especially during the 1980s, the role of monetary policy has been elevated and it now plays a major part in the conduct of economic policy. This is discussed in more detail later in this chapter.

EXCHANGE RATE POLICY

Sterling has been floating since 1972. As a result, exchange rate changes have been more frequent than when sterling had a fixed parity. Market forces were allowed greater freedom in determining exchange rates in the hope of freeing domestic policy from having to achieve a particular balance of payments position. To the extent that exchange rate changes offset a relatively high rate of inflation in one country compared to others, the balance of payments will prove less of a constraint thus freeing economic policy to be directed to achieving other economic objectives.

In practice exchange rates are influenced by many factors, not all of which are related to the underlying trends in the economy. For example, towards the end of the 1970s and for part of the 1980s, sterling had a tendency to appreciate partly because of the inflow of North Sea oil revenues. It has been argued that the strength of sterling seriously hampered the competitiveness of exports and consequently led to higher domestic unemployment. However, towards the end of 1984 and the early part of 1985 high interest rates in the US contributed towards sterling depreciating sharply on the foreign exchanges; it reached an all time low against the dollar in February 1985 of less than £1 +£ $1.04.

Because of the variety of factors that can cause changes in external currency values when exchange rates float freely, the authorities are likely to stick to 'dirty' or *managed' floating*. As a result they might still be compelled to pursue policies in the domestic economy which prevent severe short run fluctuations or which smooth the process of adjustment upwards or downwards. Moreover, because of the effect of changes in the exchange rate on the domestic economy, the government have sometimes opted to set an exchange rate target and have directed economic policy to achieving that target rate. This was most obviously the case during 1987 and part of 1988 when sterling 'shadowed' the Deutschemark. Since the spring of 1988 when the experiment ended, sterling has fluctuated more widely though the government is not prepared to allow sterling to float freely. For example, the relatively high interest rates in the UK partly reflect the government's desire to avoid a sharp depreciation of sterling as the current account moves deeper into deficit.

INCOMES POLICY

The final instrument the authorities have at their disposal is a *statutory* incomes policy, although they have sometimes preferred to negotiate a *voluntary policy*. In the UK, the term incomes policy has often been synonomous with wages policy, since it has mainly applied to wage increases. Although incomes policy can be used to redistribute income it has mainly been applied as an anti-inflationary measure in the UK. By establishing a norm for wage increases, incomes policy has sought to ensure that wage awards accord more closely with the growth of output, that is, productivity. If wages and productivity grow at the same rate, wage increases will have no effect on costs of production. Consequently they will have little, if any, effect on inflation.

Incomes policies

In the UK incomes policies have not been particularly successful as a long run anti-inflationary measure, although there is no doubt that they have sometimes been successful in the short run. One reason for their lack of success is that the norm has tended to be regarded as a minimum wage award on which more powerful unions have built further claims. Even when policy has been applied with the force of law so that wage increases have been limited, as soon as controls have been relaxed there has tended to be a 'catching up' phase with wage awards well above the growth of output.

Objections to incomes policies

Nevertheless, perhaps the main objections to incomes policy are that by establishing a norm they have reduced the incentive for workers to increase productivity, and that by removing flexibility in wage differentials they have led to lower mobility of labour. The price mechanism works in the labour market as well as in product markets, and by limiting the growth of wages in those occupations which are expanding and which require more workers, incomes policy reduces the incentive for workers to move. Again, this could limit the growth of productivity.

Because of these factors the present government believes that, in the long run, incomes policy has no particular advantages but that it does have serious disadvantages. However, this view is not shared by all and it is probable that incomes policy will again be used as a policy instrument at some stage in the future.

THE MEDIUM-TERM FINANCIAL STRATEGY (MTFS)

The conduct of economic policy changed decisively in 1980 when MTFS was introduced. The aims of the MTFS were to reduce the rate of inflation and to reduce the proportion of resources taken by the public sector. Inflation was to be reduced primarily by a reduction in the rate of growth of the money supply and the reduction in the proportion of resources taken by the public sector was to be achieved by a reduction in the absolute size of the PSBR, as well as by reducing it as a percentage of GDP. It was thought that reducing the PSBR would not only reduce the extent of crowding out, it was also anticipated that it would lead to lower interest rates because of the implied reduction in the demand for funds.

DECISIVE POLICY CHANGE

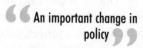

66 **An important change in policy** 99

This was a decisive change in policy in two ways. First it implied that the government accepted that the rate of growth of the money supply *determined* the rate of inflation and that *control of inflation could only be achieved by controlling the money supply*. It also implied an acceptance that the private sector used resources more efficiently than the public sector and therefore that economic growth was more likely to be encouraged by reducing the size of the public sector.

CONSERVATIVE GOVERNMENT POLICY

It is because of the increased emphasis on controlling the rate of money growth that the Conservative government has been referred to as 'monetarist'. In policy terms it has meant that monetary policy now occupies the dominant role in the government's economic strategy and that fiscal policy is no longer used as an instrument of short term demand management. Instead, considerably more importance is now attached to the effects of fiscal policy on the money supply and, as we shall see, on incentives.

Operation of MTFS

The MTFS involved setting declining targets for the growth of M3 and for the PSBR. These targets were not, of course, independent of each other and as we have seen, changes in the PSBR can bring about changes in M3. However, as the MTFS has evolved, targets are no longer set for M3. The targeted monetary aggregate is now M0 as Table 17.1 shows.

	1984	1985	1986	1986	1987	1988	1989	outturns
M0 (%pa)								
1984/85	4–8							5.5
1985/86	3–7	3–7						3.5
1986/87	2–6	2–6	2–6					4.0
1987/88	1–5	1–5	2–6	2–6				5.0
1988/89	0–4	0–4	1–5	1–5	1–5			7.5
1989/90			1–5	1–5	1–5	1–5		
1990/91					0–4	0–4		
1991/92					0–4	0–4		
1992/93						0–4		
PSBR (% of GDP)								
1984/85	2.25							3.25
1985/86	2.00	2.00						2.00
1986/87	2.00	2.00	1.75					1.00
1987/88	1.75	1.75	1.75	1.00				−0.75
1988/89	1.75	1.75	1.50	1.00	−0.75			−3.00
1989/90			1.50	1.00	0.00	−2.75		
1990/91				1.00	0.00	−1.75		
1991/92					0.00	−1.00		
1992/93						−0.50		

Table 17.1 The MTFS – recent targets and outturns

The government has been criticised for targeting M0 because it does not provide a measure of spending potential in the economy. However, less emphasis is now placed on achieving target rates of growth for the money supply and this aspect of the government's policy has been referred to as 'pragmatic monetarism'. This simply means that although control of the money supply remains an important part of economic policy, the government is prepared to accept variations in money growth to achieve its economic objectives. However, the government remains committed to a reduction in the PSBR and indeed a budget surplus was achieved in 1988/89 and further surpluses are forecast for the next few years.

PROBLEMS OF MTFS AS A POLICY STRATEGY

There are several problems with the MTFS as a policy strategy. One obvious criticism is that there is still no conclusive proof that controlling money growth will *guarantee* control of inflation. Any policy based on this approach is an act of faith rather than a proven policy option. There is also some doubt that controlling the PSBR will give sufficient control over the rate of money growth. For example, if the government is committed to maintaining a particular rate of exchange, a balance of payments surplus can cause an increase in money growth. (Net receipts from abroad imply an increase in foreign currency receipts which the authorities are committed to converting into sterling at the existing exchange rate through the Exchange Equalisation Account.) Similarly the link between the PSBR and the rate of interest is not clear. For example, if increased borrowing by the authorities is matched by an *autonomous* increase in savings, that is, an increase in savings motivated by an increased desire on the part of the community to save, there is no reason why interest rates should *necessarily* rise. Moreover, if government spending financed by a higher PSBR increases the receipts of firms in the private sector and as a result these firms cut down their own borrowing, a higher PSBR does not *necessarily* imply a higher *total* demand for loans. Because of this it is again uncertain how an increase in the PSBR will affect the rate of interest.

ADVANTAGE OF MTFS

Despite these problems one advantage of the MTFS is that it gives a clear indication of the government's intent. This provides firms in particular with the information they require to plan effectively. It also provides useful information for those involved in negotiating wages.

CURRENT MACROECONOMIC POLICY

One reason for distinguishing between macroeconomic policy and economic policy in general is because of the increased emphasis on microeconomic or supply side policies to achieve macroeconomic goals. In brief, the main instrument for the implementation of macro policy is monetary policy which is currently directed towards reducing inflation. Supply-side policies on the other hand are directed to achieving increased efficiency and a reduction in unemployment by improving incentives and removing restrictions which inhibit efficiency. Supply-side policies are discussed on pp. 253–4, but it is clear that the authorities aim to improve macroeconomic performance by increasing aggregate supply, rather than to adjust aggregate demand.

THE ROLE OF MONETARY POLICY

The conduct of macroeconomic policy has partly been dealt with in Chapters 15 and 16. Here we focus on the role of monetary policy. The methods used to implement monetary policy have changed since the MTFS was first unveiled. Rather than controlling the rate of money growth, greater emphasis is now placed on the use of interest rates not only to control the growth of spending, but also to influence the exchange rate which has become the chief instrument for controlling inflation.

IMPLEMENTATION OF THE MONETARY POLICY

The way in which the rate of interest and the exchange rate can be used to control inflation is simple. A relatively high rate of interest raises the exchange rate and therefore reduces the domestic price of imports. In an economy like the UK with its dependence on imported raw materials and its relatively high marginal propensity to import generally, this helps reduce inflation. However, this policy is also likely to have a favourable effect on inflation in another way. The relatively high rate of inflation implies that exporters must either reduce the sterling price of their goods, or accept a reduction in sales because of the higher price. If the sterling price is reduced, this leads directly to a reduction in the rate of inflation. If sales are reduced this will probably encourage moderation in wage settlements and therefore indirectly contribute to a lower rate of inflation. This is precisely what happened in the early 1980s when sterling appreciated. However, at that time appreciation of sterling was also accompanied by rising unemployment. The same is unlikely to happen now. On the one hand the appreciation of sterling has been less dramatic and on the other, company profitability is much higher.

However, as we have seen, high interest rates have an immediate adverse effect on the retail price index because of their impact on mortgage costs. As the RPI rises it could lead to increased demands for higher wages which, if achieved, will further increase inflation. Table 17.1 shows the extent to which the government has succeeded in achieving the changes it has sought in the various economic aggregates.

SUPPLY-SIDE ECONOMICS

The *aim* of supply-side policy is to remove obstacles which prevent or discourage people and firms from adapting quickly to changing conditions of market demand and changing techniques of production. It is argued that the implied increase in efficiency will encourage economic growth. Two aspects of supply-side policies, privatisation and deregulation are considered under separate headings.

❝ Supply-side policies ❞

The *emphasis* on supply-side policies stems from a belief that if markets can be made to operate more efficiently, this will encourage economic growth and employment without adding to the risk of inflation. We can see the effect of an increase in efficiency on aggregate supply in Fig. 17.1.

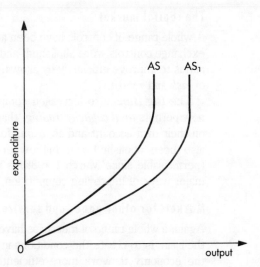

Fig. 17.1

If all other things remain equal, an increase in efficiency at all levels of output will shift the aggregate supply curve from AS to AS_1. Any given level of output now has a lower supply price, and a greater amount of output can be produced at full employment than previously. In the absence of any improvement in efficiency, attempts to achieve economic growth and full employment by increasing aggregate demand will not be sustainable, because they will generate inflation and a balance of payments deficit.

The various methods by which the government has attempted to improve the supply side of the economy can be discussed under the following headings.

Taxation

Measures have been introduced to ensure that, in general, people are better off in work than out of work. In particular, the basic rate of income tax has been reduced from 33 per cent in 1978 to a current level of 25 per cent. Further reductions are planned in the future. The threshold above which people start paying tax has also been increased by more than the rate of inflation. Additionally, unemployment benefit is now taxed. It is hoped that, among other effects, this will have a positive effect on the unemployment trap.

Corporation tax has also been reduced from 52 per cent to a lower rate of 25 per cent for smaller firms and a rate of 35 per cent for larger firms. The aim here is to encourage firms to invest in more productive capital by reducing the taxation of profits.

The labour market

Alongside these changes the government has introduced training schemes, the most important of which is the YTS which provides one year and two year training placements for sixteen and seventeen year olds respectively who leave school or college (or who cannot find employment). On completion of their YTS scheme, an estimated 60 per cent of trainees find employment or go into further education.

Other labour market measures

Other important labour market measures are the Employment Acts of 1980 and 1982 and the Trade Union Act of 1984 which have attempted to safeguard the interests of individual employees and to encourage more effective democracy within trade unions. Some of the main measures introduced are:

- Removal of legal immunities both for picketing, other than by employees at their place of work, and for secondary industrial action.
- Introduction and strengthening of the rights of employees dismissed for refusing to join closed shops.
- Removal of legal immunities from civil actions so as to make trade unions subject to injunctions and damages when they are responsible for unlawful industrial action.
- Removal of legal immunities from civil action in any industrial action which has not been agreed in advance by a secret ballot of the membership.

The aim of this legislation is to create a more flexible labour market, since it is believed that lack of flexibility is one of the major reasons why real wages have risen to levels which reduce employment.

The capital market

A whole range of controls have been abolished in the capital market. For example, in 1979 exchange controls were abolished; and in 1982 hire-purchase controls were abolished. The aim is to improve efficiency by allowing savings to go where there is the best combination of *risk* and *return*.

The *Big Bang* also increased competition in the capital market. The Stock Exchange now permits *dual capacity trading*, that is, it allows firms to simultaneously act as *principle* on their own account and as *agents* for their clients. Fixed commissions by brokers have also been abolished and full ownership of Stock Exchange firms by non-members (permissable since March 1 1986) is now permissable. All of these changes are seen as major ways of improving competition, and through this, efficiency.

Markets for other goods and services

Again, a whole range of measures have been introduced, and while they vary in significance their aim is to create the conditions in which the freer play of market forces can stimulate the economy to work more efficiently. Two measures are particularly important: *The Competition Act* (1980) and the programme of *privatisation and deregulation*. The former gives the Monopolies and Mergers Commission power to investigate individual firms suspected of operating 'anti-competitive practices'; they are referred to it by the Director-General of Fair Trading. The latter reflects the government's view that economic performance can be improved by subjecting firms and whole industries to the full rigours of the market – although the proceeds of privatisation have also helped to reduce the PSBR. The implicit assumption is that organisations in the public sector are sheltered from competition and that this leads to inefficiency. Whether this is true or not is debatable, but it certainly is true that on average the rate of return on capital employed in nationalised industries has for many years been lower than the rate of return in the private sector, while price increases have in general been higher.

In the financial sector the *1986 Building Societies Act* has enabled them to compete more effectively with the retail banks. In particular they are now able to offer cheque books and cheque guarantee cards. Several now also offer cash point facilities. Other provisions of the Act allowed the building societies to abandon their status as Friendly Societies and form themselves into public limited companies as the Abbey National has recently done. Building Societies are now also able to make unsecured loans up to certain limits for purposes other than house purchase and to compete for funds on the wholesale markets. In 1986 a limit of 20 per cent of total borrowed funds was originally set on the amount that could be borrowed from the wholesale markets. However, in 1988 this was raised to 40 per cent further increasing their ability to compete with retail banks.

PRIVATISATION

The term *privatisation* is usually taken to imply the transfer of assets from the public sector to the private sector. In this sense privatisation refers to a change in the *ownership* of assets. However privatisation can cover other activities, for example, ceasing to provide such activites as refuse collection through the public sector and putting them out to private contract. Despite this, it is the transfer of assets from the public sector to the private sector which has attracted most attention and on which we focus in this section. Furthermore, although this might include activities such as the sale of council houses, it is the sale of nationalised industries as well as industries in which the state has a major shareholding with which we will be concerned.

One point to be aware of at the outset is that privatisation is not simply a British phenomenon, it is happening in many countries throughout the world. The USA, France, Germany, Spain, Singapore, Jamaica, Chile, Turkey, and many other countries all have privatisation programs.

REASONS FOR PRIVATISATION

The reasons for privatisation in the UK are typical:

> " Some reasons for privatisation "

- A major aim of privatisation is to increase efficiency in the allocation and utilisation of resources.
- Another aim is to increase the extent of share ownership, partly for political reasons in the UK at least, but also because it is thought to affect the allocation and utilisation of resources.
- In the case of the UK, privatisation has been a major factor in cutting down borrowing by the government. Lower borrowing by the government has been a major part of the government's macroeconomic strategy.

Let us consider each of these in turn:-

Efficiency in privatised firms

Privatisation might encourage efficiency in privatised firms for several reasons. One is that there will be less government interference in pricing and investment decisions by these firms. Another reason is that there will be increased competition following privatisation.

It is certainly true that governments have often deliberately prevented nationalised industries from increasing their prices as a means of tackling inflation, and have altered investment in different industries as a means of varying aggregate demand. As privatised organisations, firms will be able to plan more effectively. However, efficiency in the allocation of resources might also be improved. We have already seen that when prices are prevented from rising, too much is consumed in relation to the optimum. Furthermore, it has been argued that increased investment in the nationalised industries has crowded out private sector investment, and the higher rate of return achieved in the private sector is taken as evidence that investment is more efficient when undertaken by the private sector.

However, there seems little evidence of increased competition following some privatisations. Indeed, some organisations such as British Gas have been sold as monopolies to increase their attractiveness to shareholders. It might be claimed that the government had little alternative since some industries are quite clearly natural monopolies, and that in any case, as private sector organisations, they must compete for funds on the capital market with other private sector organisations. Nevertheless, critics have argued that monopolies do not have to be efficient to be profitable, and that profitability is the main determinant of a firm's ability to raise funds on the capital market. Furthermore, it would have been possible to sell these industries as regional units which would be allowed to compete for business in each other's regions as seems likely to happen when electricity and water are privatised.

Increase in number of shareholders

Turning to the second aim of privatisation, the government has clearly had success in increasing the number of shareholders with over nine million private individuals in the UK owning shares in 1988. It has been argued that this will encourage efficiency because management are now accountable to shareholders with a vested interest in the efficiency and profitability of the companies in which they hold shares. However, few shareholders attend the AGM when the Board of Directors is elected and when they must account for the policies of the previous 12 months.

Raising revenue

As for the third aim of privatisation, there is no doubt that the government has achieved success in raising revenue through privatisation as Table 17.2 shows.

COMPANY	DATE	£m
British Aerospace	1981/82, 1984/85	389
Cable and Wireless	1981/82, 1984/85	1020
Britoil	1982/83, 1983/84, 1985/86	1053
Enterprise Oil	1984/85	382
British Telecom	1984/85, 1985/86, 1986/87	3682
British Gas	1986/87	5600
British Petroleum	1979/80, 1981/82, 1983/84, 1987/88	8054
British Airports Authority	1987/88	1275
Rolls Royce Aero Engines	1987/88	1080
Other		2256
Total		24791

Table 17.2 Major UK privatisations

Nevertheless it has been suggested that the government might have met with even more success if it had not underpriced some of the shares it has issued. For example, shares in British Telecom were issued at a price of £1.30, but by the end of the first day's trading they were quoted at £1.73, thus depriving the government of potentially an extra £1.295m revenue.

However, deciding on the price at which to issue shares so as to ensure that a sufficient quantity is sold is a notoriously difficult problem. Some have criticised the government for not issuing shares by tender. This was certainly a possibility open to the government, but was rejected probably because it was felt that this would not attract small investors with little or no experience of buying shares, to anything like the extent required to significantly increase the number of share-owning individuals.

DEREGULATION

Deregulation is the term used to describe the process of dismantling state regulations on the activities of the business sector. Like privatisation, deregulation is a world-wide phenomenon, though in this chapter we are only concerned with deregulation in the UK. It is useful to note, however, that while privatisation and deregulation sometimes overlap, as when an industry is denationalised and is also opened up to competition, this is not always the case. Before we consider the issue of deregulation, the reasons for regulating industry in the first place are considered.

THE REASONS FOR REGULATION

It is usually suggested that the main reason for regulation is to safeguard the *public interest*, although what constitutes the public interest differs from case to case. For example, the banks have been subject to regulation mainly because of the possibility of default, if there was a sudden large withdrawal of deposits by customers. A bank that was unable to honour withdrawals might well precipitate a run on other banks as well as itself. Air transport, as well as buses and coaches, have been subject to regulation for safety reasons. Television and radio broadcasting have been regulated, partly because it was felt that competition would reduce the quality of reception by causing interference. The regulation of agriculture has been partly to ensure that harmful chemicals are not used to increase yields, and partly to ensure that as an industry, agriculture survives so that food supplies cannot be cut off by a foreign supplier.

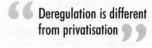 Deregulation is different from privatisation

Despite these cases the most complete regulations are those governing the nationalised industries which are given sole rights of supply. One of the most important arguments for nationalisation was that in some cases such as gas, water and electricity, a *natural monopoly* existed, and that nationalisation was necessary to ensure the public were not exploited by a private monopolist.

THE REASONS FOR DEREGULATION

The major reason for deregulation is that it is now thought that the public interest is better served by *competition* and that regulations not only restrict competition, but also impose higher costs on the firms subject to regulation. However, another factor is *technological advances* which have sometimes made deregulation essential if an industry is to survive the growth of foreign competition. For example, technological advances made automated dealing possible on the world's stock exchanges which substantially reduced the cost of transacting business. Technological progress also made it possible for a dealer in one financial centre, such as London, to transact business with another dealer in a different financial centre somewhere else in the world, with the latest dealing rates available on screen. When minimum dealing rates were abolished in New York, this precipitated reform of the London Stock Exchange (the Big Bang), because almost overnight it became cheaper to buy and sell securities in New York than in London! Without reform the London Stock Exchange would have ceased to be one of the world's leading financial centres.

If you refer back to the reasons for imposing regulations on industry it is hardly surprising that it has been suggested that efficiency in the allocation of resources is now given priority over safety standards. In fact there is no evidence that this is true and safety is still an important issue. What is different is the view that efficiency in the allocation of resources is better promoted by competition than by government controls on the behaviour of industry!

APPLIED MATERIALS

UNEMPLOYMENT IN THE UK

Fig. 17.2 shows that unemployment in the UK increased steeply in the early part of the 1980s but has now fallen from its peak of 3.5 million in 1986. One reason for the increase in unemployment was that the working population increased more rapidly than job opportunities. Fig. 17.2 provides some information on the changes in the working population, the numbers unemployed and the increase in self-employment that have occurred in recent years.

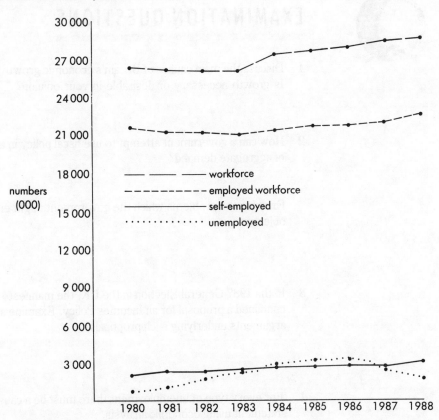

Fig. 17.2 *Source*: Monthly digest of statistics, HMSO

INDUSTRIAL TRAINING IN THE UK

An article in the British Economy Survey Vol. 18, No. 2, Spring 1989 examines *Industrial Training in the UK*. This is an important issue, not least because there is growing concern that a serious skill shortage might emerge in the future and restrict the rate of economic growth. Britain spends less than competing countries on industrial training, typically 0.15 per cent of turnover compared with 1–3 per cent in other countries such as Germany. Some reasons for lack of training by UK firms are:

- Firms typically overestimate the real costs of training partly because the trainees' contribution to output during training is often neglected.

- The number of trainees taken on annually by firms in the UK is often based on rule of thumb conventions rather than on serious attempts at forecasting.

- Trade union regulations have often restricted the number of apprentices taken on annually.

- Firms often 'poach' trainees on completion of their training so reducing the incentive of other firms to offer training.

EMPLOYMENT IN THE 1990S

The government's main response was outlined in the White Paper 'Employment in the 1990s' which was published in December 1988. The main thrust of policy is to establish a network of Training and Enterprise Councils (TECS) whose functions will be:

- to identify future skill shortages in local labour markets

- to draw up plans with the aim of encouraging quality training in each local labour market where potential skill shortages are identified

- to administer the training programs for young people including those on YTS programs

- to promote small business growth by providing counselling facilities for small firms and by administering the Enterprise Allowance Scheme

EXAMINATION QUESTIONS

1 Discuss the main causes of Britain's economic growth performance in recent years. Is growth necessary or desirable in your opinion?

(JMB, 1989)

2 How can a government attempt to use fiscal policy in an attempt to change the level of aggregate demand?

(60)

Examine the problems which the government might encounter in pursuing this objective.

(40)
(*Total 100 marks*)
(London, Jan 1989)

3 In the 1987 General Election in the UK, the manifesto of the SDP/Liberal Alliance contained a proposal for an Incomes Policy. Examine and discuss the economic arguments underlying such proposals.

(25)
(*Total 25 marks*)
(Welsh, 1989)

4 'For every type of unemployment there must be a cause and cure'. Discuss this statement using economic analysis.

(London, June 1988)

A TUTOR'S ANSWER TO QUESTION 1

Economic growth is usually defined to be an increase in a country's GDP. Governments usually try to encourage economic growth because if GDP per head can be increased the standard of living will rise. However, this does not mean that growth is always desirable. Recently, economists and politicians have argued that economic growth leads to harmful externalities such as 'global warming' due partly to the destruction of the Amazon rain forest.

There are many factors which cause economic growth. One of the most important factors is the quantity of capital per worker. The greater the capital : labour ratio, the higher the productivity of labour. This is important because if there is no change in the number of workers employed, an increase in productivity implies a higher level of GDP, that is, economic growth.

However, it is not only the quantity of capital employed that affects economic growth, it is also the quality of capital. This depends on technological progress. The productivity of capital can be increased if machinery is updated so that firms use the latest technologies available. This might mean scrapping existing machinery but the higher productivity will make it profitable for firms to do this. Since technological advances are encouraged when there is investment in research and development greater expenditure on this will encourage economic growth.

The quantity and quality of labour is another factor which is important in determining economic growth. The quantity of labour is determined by the population but countries with the highest populations do not have the highest economic growth. The important point is for countries to aim at the 'optimum population'. This is simply that level of population which maximises average product. When countries are not maximising average product they are either under-populated or over-populated and economic growth could be increased by moving to the optimum level.

The quality of labour depends on education and training. An educated labour force is easier to train and is likely to be more adaptable and enterprising. In addition a highly trained labour force is likely to be more mobile and this can have an important bearing on the growth of productivity.

These are the main causes of growth in the UK. There are great benefits to be gained from economic growth and there is no doubt that because of this economic growth is necessary. The main benefit is that it makes possible a higher standard of living. This is especially important in the UK because, at the present time, the UK has an ageing population, that is, the average age of the population is rising and there is a rising proportion of retired people in the population. When someone retires they continue to be a consumer but cease to be a producer. This means they consume what others produce. It is therefore important to achieve economic growth if living standards are not to fall.

Another reason why economic growth is necessary is that it makes investment in scientific research possible. This is particularly important in medicine where new vaccines prevent the spread of disease and new treatments make it possible to cure people of certain illnesses which only a few years ago claimed many lives; smallpox and TB are two examples.

Despite this there are costs of economic growth – especially environmental costs. There is no doubt that in the past the drive for greater economic growth has resulted in an increase in pollution. This pollution has many different consequences. It might simply be annoying because dumping toxic waste into a river makes it impossible to swim in that river. However, there are more serious consequences. There is overwhelming evidence that using lead in petrol has caused brain damage in certain young children! Acid rain, caused mainly by power stations that burn fossil fuels in the UK, is blamed for creating over ten thousand dead lakes in Scandinavia and many dead forests. Power is of course necessary for economic growth, but these externalities are clearly undesirable.

When considering the costs and desirability of economic growth, an important point to consider is that greater economic growth provides the means of dealing with the externalities it creates. It is a question of how society wishes to utilise its available resources. It might choose to use the benefits of increased productivity to increase consumption per head. On the other hand society might allocate its resources into cleaning up the environment and to producing the technology that imposes fewer externalities on society.

A STUDENT'S ANSWER TO QUESTION 3

An incomes policy is an attempt to control inflationary pressures by limiting the growth of incomes and, in particular, the growth of wages. Sometimes a wage freeze has been imposed which implies no wage increases. At other times a limited pay increase has been allowable up to an agreed norm.

On the whole incomes policies in the UK often appear to have been successful in the short run but less successful in the long run. One reason for this is that when the policy is ended there seems to be a move on the part of workers to make up for lost ground. When this happens the gains from an incomes policy are quickly lost.

However, there are other problems with an incomes policy. In the UK they have tended to operate unfairly in that those workers who have gained a pay award prior to the introduction of an incomes policy gain a relative advantage over those workers whose wage increases are restricted by the policy.

Another problem is that of providing an incentive to increase productivity. If there is no scope to offer higher rewards in return for higher productivity economic growth might be adversely affected. In the UK an attempt has been made to offer productivity bonuses in excess of any norm with the aim of encouraging productivity. Here again the policy can operate unfairly because increases in productivity are usually the result of using more efficient capital or substituting capital for labour. When firms invest in the latest technologies, productivity will increase and workers will be able to negotiate increased wages. However, workers employed in firms unwilling or unable to invest in new machinery will not be able to negotiate such increases.

Another objection to incomes policies is that they freeze an existing pattern of wage differentials and therefore prevent the market from functioning efficiently. For example, if there is an increased demand for a particular product it will be necessary to compete resources away from alternatives by offering higher rewards so that output can be increased. However, if an incomes policy is in operation this will prevent firms from offering higher wages in order to attract additional workers. In other words, an incomes policy might lead to a sub-optimal allocation of resources.

 There are some good points in this essay, but no attempt is made to relate the analysis to Britain's economic growth. For example poor industrial relations are sometimes suggested as affecting economic growth in Britain

OUTLINE ANSWERS TO QUESTIONS 2 AND 4

Question 2

a) You could begin your answer to this question by defining fiscal policy. It is the deliberate manipulation of the central government's budget, i.e., government expenditure and taxation, so as to increase net injections or reduce net leakages.

b) Discretionary fiscal policy is thought to be destabilising and, when used to stimulate aggregate demand, its effect is inflationary. It is destabilising because variation in aggregate demand makes it difficult for firms to plan their investment. It also causes changes in the rate of inflation. A budget deficit adds to the PSBR and depending on the way in which this is financed, it might lead to an increase in money growth. A budget surplus on the other hand leads to a lower PSBR and hence reduces money growth. However, you should also explain why changes in money growth lead to changes in inflation.

You could go on to consider the way in which changes in taxation and government expenditure affect national income and therefore employment in terms of the Keynesian model outlined in Chapter 9. Government expenditure on goods and services has a direct effect on aggregate demand and a secondary effect through the multiplier. However, its effect on national income and employment depend on several factors including whether expenditure is on capital intensive or labour intensive production, whether it is current or capital expenditure, the extent to which expenditure on goods requires imports of raw materials and so on. Each should be discussed as well as their implications for the multiplier.

The effect of changes in taxation, however, depends partly on the size of the MPC and the nature of any tax changes. For example, a reduction in the higher rates of income tax will have less impact on aggregate demand than a change in the personal allowance. Remember the effect on aggregate demand of a given change in taxation will be less than an equivalent change in government expenditure because a tax change will be partly offset by a change in the amount saved. In other words, a tax change does not bring about an equivalent change in spending.

One point to remember is that the effect of a change in government expenditure or a change in taxation on employment depends partly on the existing level of employment. When the economy is close to full employment a budget deficit (that is $G > T$) is likely to raise prices rather than employment. Indeed, the higher prices might adversely affect employment because consumers will turn to cheaper imports and exports will fall.

Question 4

Traditionally several types of unemployment have been identified and each could be discussed, along with the means of dealing with the type of unemployment identified.

Seasonal unemployment is, as its name suggests, caused by the changing seasons. For example, fewer building and agricultural workers are required in the winter than in the summer. Probably the only 'cure' for this type of unemployment is to encourage mobility of labour so that as workers become unemployed, their chances of obtaining re-employment are increased.

Frictional unemployment is sometimes referred to as *search* unemployment because it stems from a mismatch between the workers who become unemployed and the jobs that are available in the economy. Every month some 3–4 hundred thousand workers join the unemployment register and a similar number leave the register because they have found employment. Because of this frictional unemployment is not regarded as a problem.

Structural unemployment is caused by a reduction in the demand for a product, that is, it is caused by a change in the structure of demand. For example, the increased use of plastic instead of steel has caused a long term reduction in demand for steel and a reduction in the number of steel workers employed; increased competition from abroad has caused a reduction in demand for ship-building in the UK. Structural unemployment is often localised because of the decline of an industry which is localised. This is true of steel, ship-building, cotton, coalmining, and so on. One way of dealing with this type of unemployment is to encourage mobility of capital (so that industry moves to those areas with the severest unemployment problems) and mobility of labour (so that workers move to where vacancies exist or are retrained in the skills that are required in the area where they live).

Cyclical unemployment is due to a downswing in the trade cycle. In any economy there are regular recurring changes in the pattern of aggregate demand, sometimes rising, sometimes falling. This is referred to as the trade cycle. When demand falls there is a general reduction in demand for labour and unemployment. It used to be argued that governments could cure this type of unemployment by demand management. However, the belief now is that any reduction in unemployment as a result of demand management will only be temporary and will ultimately lead to higher inflation.

Voluntary unemployment is said to exist when people are unwilling to accept employment at existing real wage rates. It is argued that at any moment in time there is a *natural rate of unemployment* to which the economy will tend. At the natural rate many workers could find employment but only at a lower wage than they require. It has been suggested that governments could deal with this type of unemployment by cutting benefits paid to the unemployed. However, in general, the suggestion is that the natural rate can be reduced by supply-side policies, such as the training initiatives. If the natural rate can be reduced by retraining workers this implies that not everyone who is unemployed at the natural rate is voluntarily unemployed!

Further reading

Wall and Griffiths (eds), *Applied Economics: An Introductory Course* (3rd edn) Longman 1989, Ch. 25, Managing the economy.
Stanlake, *Macroeconomics* (4th edn) Longman 1989, Ch. 20, Managing the economy, Appendix, Incomes policy

INDEX